Blockchain Technology in Corporate Governance

Scrivener Publishing
100 Cummings Center, Suite 541J
Beverly, MA 01915-6106

Publishers at Scrivener
Martin Scrivener (martin@scrivenerpublishing.com)
Phillip Carmical (pcarmical@scrivenerpublishing.com)

Blockchain Technology in Corporate Governance

Transforming Business and Industries

Edited by

Kiran Sood
Rajesh Kumar Dhanaraj
Balamurugan Balusamy
and
Seifedine Kadry

Scrivener
Publishing

WILEY

Wiley Global Headquarters
111 River Street, Hoboken, NJ 07030, USA

For details of our global editorial offices, customer services, and more information about Wiley products visit us at www.wiley.com.

Library of Congress Cataloging-in-Publication Data

ISBN 978-1-119-86495-0

Cover image: Pixabay.Com
Cover design by Russell Richardson

Set in size of 11pt and Minion Pro by Manila Typesetting Company, Makati, Philippines

Printed in the USA

10 9 8 7 6 5 4 3 2 1

Contents

Part 3: The Impact of Blockchain on the Financial Industry   197

Foreword

After the Internet, which has provided the world with the first global platform for mass collaboration, Distributed Ledger Technology (DLT) has paved the way for a technological shift that will change how the world does business and practically everything else. It has provided a platform for blockchain technology, which powers the digital currency, transparency, commerce, and privacy.

Blockchain technology facilitates peer-to-peer transactions without any intermediary such as a bank or governing body. Although it maintains users' information anonymously, it validates and keeps a permanent public record of all transactions. That means that your personal information is secure and private, but the activity is transparent and incorruptible. It is reconciled by the collaboration of masses and the activity is stored in a code on a digital ledger.

This edited book highlights the current governance framework for the blockchain and its development as a self-governing framework. It discusses the blockchain technology effectiveness in developing solutions for supply chain, trade finance, and banking. Moreover, it shows how banking and financial institutions are the major beneficiaries of this decentralized technology. Furthermore, the book outlines the link between company governance theories, regulatory, ethical, and social controls and the blockchain adoption. It also investigates the recent applications of blockchain technology in the financial services, the health sector, and the energy sector.

The book is specially designed for graduates, researchers, industrialists, engineers, policymakers, students and academics who aspire to learn, discuss, and carry out further research into the opportunities offered by blockchain and the possible ways of regulating it. It is a good read for those interested in exploring and expanding their knowledge on blockchain technology and hopefully it will mark a milestone in their learning journey.

Prof. Simon Grima
Head of The Department of Insurance and Risk Management
Deputy Dean - Faculty of Economics, Management and Accountancy,
University of Malta
Professor of Finance, Faculty of Business, Management and Economics,
University of Latvia

Preface

The characteristics of intelligent technology have given rise to the intriguing thoughts on the subjects in this book, which application developers may be able to implement in their own work. Block transactions are decentralized, distributed, open, irrevocable, and digital, with blocks linked together using cryptographic and authentication techniques to form a blockchain. This has made blockchain technology the fastest developing revolutionary technology to be applied in various fields. In addition to being well-known for its capacity to be used in multiple areas that contribute to data storage in domains linked by peer-to-peer networking, the technique provides a real-time refresh feature that enables records to be updated. Therefore, using this approach, critical data may be kept in blocks with the goal of treating data as money.

After an investigation of successful decentralized applications, the book highlights previously existing blockchain applications as a technology demonstrator in many sectors. In addition to enumerating the benefits of this innovation in several fields, the book will also help determine future topics of research in several domains.

In addition to exploring existing applications based on blockchain technology in different domains, the goal of this book is to design a better financial application model. Therefore, since there is a need to adopt financial technology for economic activity, the current method of processing checks is explored. To address distrust of the technology being used, the application of blockchain is used to help secure the check processing system. After analysis, research began on ways to change the rules of the check processing and clearance system by reducing the processing time and improving security. Already existing check processing methods were identified, and their limitations were assessed to provide a suitable improved framework. To accomplish the same, smart contracts were used to automatically complete the task of check processing by generating a valid tokenized check to update the information in the IPFS (interplanetary file system) blockchain.

This book uses smart contracts, the energy sector, and the application of sustainability issues that control the system's functionality to enhance security and provide efficient features. The advent of new methods based on these designed and implemented approaches makes it possible to address real-time problems to bring about excellent efficiency to the system.

Kiran Sood
Chitkara Business School
Chitkara University, Punjab, India

Acknowledgment

This edited book "Blockchain Technology in Corporate Governance: Transforming Business Industries" results from prayers, efforts, blessings and the love of my family and friends. I want to thank them all and would like to specially acknowledge and extend my heartfelt gratitude to a few of them who have made the completion of this book possible.

My special thanks to Dr Balamurugan Balusamy, Professor, Galgotias University, India, for his valuable guidance and support. Furthermore, I express my sincere thanks to the team of the edited book Dr Rajesh Kumar Dhanaraj, Associate Professor, Galgotias University, India and Dr Seifedine Kadry, Associate Professor, Beirut Arab University, Lebanon.

Special thanks to Mr Martin, President, Scrivener Publishing who helped me so much.

Our sincere gratitude goes to the chapters authors who contributed their time and expertise to this book. I would like to start with Dr Amrinder Singh, Dr Geetika Madaan, Dr Reena Malik, Dr Sonal Trivedi, Dr R. Janarthanan, Dr J. Venkatesh, Dr Kalaiselvi Rajendiran, Dr Akshaya Sridhar, Dr Ananda Vayaravel Cassinadane, Dr Navdeep Kaur, Dr Suman Bhullar, Dr Navneet Seth, Dr Alain Aoun, Dr Mazen Ghandour, Dr Hussein Ibrahim, Dr Adrian Ilinca, Dr Priya Jindal, Dr Jasmine Kaur, Dr Rupa Khanna Malhotra, Dr Chandan Gupta, Ms. Aashima, Dr. Birajit Mohanty, Dr Jyoti Verma Dr Gagandeep, Dr Minakshi Thaman, Dr Osheen Oberoi, Dr Sahil Raj, Dr Keshav Kaushik, Dr Rewa Sharma, Ms Shilpi Singhal, Dr Rajesh Kumar Kaushal, Dr Naveen Kumar, Dr Hani El Chaarani, Dr Hebatallah Badawy, Dr Zouhour ElAbiad, Dr Eirini Daskalaki.

A special thanks to my family. Words cannot express how grateful I am to my husband Shivek Sood for his support and cooperation during my work. He has been the motivator, and his help in every way deserves special thanks. I wish to express my love and gratitude to my mother and father. I would particularly like to thank my brother, sister and my friends who supported me in every possible way to see the completion of this work.

Above all, I owe it all to Almighty God who granted me the wisdom to undertake this research and enabled me to complete it. To him, I owe lifelong indebtedness.

Kiran Sood

Role of Blockchain Technology in the Modern Era

Kuldeep Singh Kaswan¹, Jagjit Singh Dhatterwal², Kiran Sood³*
and Balamurugan Balusamy¹

¹School of Computing Science and Engineering, Galgotias University,
Greater Noida, India
²School of Computing Science and Engineering-AI&DS,
Koneru Lakshmaiah University, Vaddeswaram, Guntur, Vijayawada,
Andhra Pradesh, India
³Chitkara Business School, Chitkara University, Rajpura, Punjab, India

Abstract

Initially, cryptographic algorithms were used as a public transaction ledger for cryptocurrencies. Beyond cryptocurrency, cryptographic protocols have lately been investigated for various additional applications due to their unique qualities such as scalability, security, accountability, and anti-tampering. Such characteristics are beneficial for a range of important difficulties encountered in the financial industry. Because the energy industry is quickly diminishing, there has been a greater emphasis on investigating the use of sustainable power (e.g., solar energy and wind energy) in replacement fossil fuel. Blockchain-based technologies are intended for use in the (decentralized) energy market. With the help of the energy sector, use in the Healthcare Industry is adopting technologies that allow the digitization of health records and automation of various plausible clinical procedures. To change the environmental issues related to the use of this currency and the hidden in the wings, blockchain technology has been recognized as the driver of innovation in various fields, contributing to creating a more sustainable world. This chapter discusses how blockchain technology is effective in healthcare, the energy sector, financial industry, and sustainable issue.

Keywords: Blockchain, sustainability, healthcare, electronic health records, bitcoin

---

**Corresponding author*: Kiran.sood@chitkara.edu.in

Kiran Sood, Rajesh Kumar Dhanaraj, Balamurugan Balusamy and Seifedine Kadry (eds.) Blockchain Technology in Corporate Governance: Transforming Business and Industries, (1–28) © 2023 Scrivener Publishing LLC

1.1 Introduction

The advanced digital cash tooled by using a hidden developer, whose name was Satoshi Nakamoto, blooming the doorway after a modern digital revolution, introducing now not solely a cryptocurrency, so that used to be last called, but current according to the people a current democratically-sustained daybook on entire transactions as would hold had excellent realistic services additionally between ignoble fields [1]. The innovation brought via Nakamoto (but that looks so should stay a group hidden below this pseudonym) represents a currency so much bypasses the legitimate way in imitation of produce yet trade money, primarily based of a medium financial institution yet a clearing authority. Yet, using a peer-to-peer charge system realized an originate supply software. This digital money leads thanksgiving to create a disbursed populace register containing entire Bitcoin transactions according to blockchain technology. As a result, whole peer-to-peer cash transactions are registered then stored without some altering within an impervious way together with no necessity regarding a medium bank, together with a mechanism over consistency amongst whole the network nodes who piece a portfolio of Bitcoins [2].

The use of blockchain applied sciences permits pecuniary corporations to push aside countless long-lasting prominent issues. One of the top-notch issues related to the imitation of bank credit is the scarcity of statistics regarding credit score scoring, inflicting individuals or SMEs to hold difficulties in acquiring loans via financial establishments. According to lead consistent purchaser evaluation, financial institutions are also struggling due to a lack of appropriate and precise information. It effectively handles government product schism and customization. "Along the same lines, investment vehicles provided by financial institutions include a comprehensive individual policy claims procedure, necessitating the engagement of several parties before the discharge or payment of a claim." Finally, current essential structures encouraging the priority over transactions concerning monetary corporations are primary targets as a result of cyber-attacks. World power systems are current via a non-stop change [3].

The focus has been shifted beside great warm or hydel government technology by tiny disbursed generation, generally based on renewable power systems. Incomplete governments additionally back this transit. There have also been sizeable improvements in grid technology. The current clever grid can supply actual era bi-directional flow over facts, i.e., real-time strength deficit and surplus, and real-time expenditures by each producer yet consumers. Intelligent grids do additionally accommodate intermittent baby suppliers of electricity. This variation of strength-era policy or improvement within grid technology has awakened ways because small-scale power producers yet customers after piece power. Additionally, it has borne ways according to purchase and promotes strength to strange peers upon an intelligent grid. Need has been felt by the shop this transaction among friends of a secure, non-alterable but rapidly on-hand way. Blockchain technological know-how offers by furnishing this secure, unalterable, yet quickly available ledger. Blockchain 1.0, the first age of blockchain, underpins Bitcoin, the first deployment of blockchain-based monetary technologies. The following generation, known as Blockchain 2.0, has emerged with the notion of intelligent construction. It is considered a segment of articles defined, performed, and recorded in the allocated ledger. Blockchain 3.0, the 0.33 technology in distributed ledger technology, specializes in truth, encompassing non-financial elements such as administration, environment, health, etc. [4].

Various firms adopted this technology and then utilized it because of a few uses cases in healthcare. The almost excellent purposes within the blockchain that are beneficial in imitating healthcare functions are decentralization, privacy, and safety, considering that blockchain technological know-how may also ensure secure access to scientific statistics for sufferers yet a range of stakeholders (insurance companies, hospitals, doctors, etc.).

1.2   What is Blockchain Technology?

The troubles confronted between implementing blockchain are issues faced by using the entire healthcare sector related to the privacy or security on healthcare-related intelligence. The statistics saved about EHR systems are troublesome, and modern designs that use them are now not Immune opposition to disallowed ingress yet return over the data [5]. At present, the just popular EHR storage approach is architecture, as it is centralized and client-server based, giving those authoring the dictation perfect get right of entry according to the entirety of the system. Such EHR tankage creates a deficiency regarding privacy that leads to protection flaws, whereby the secured facts may also remain stolen, tampered with, yet leaked. To fight these issues, security requirements (e.g., HIPAA, DISHA, or COBIT) have been developed and implemented in discipline according to guard patient health information. Implementing blockchain-based EHR structures desires to permit the impenetrable storage regarding healthcare statistics and the traits that blockchain generally comprises, certain as P2P networking consensus protocol, and then reap cryptography [6]. EHRs that are accrued and then stored within contemporary structures are saved. Hence, they are non-portable, appropriate by the number of courtesies recorded by the statistics and data, making them non-interoperable. An industrial motive is so much the institutions which gather information (EHR) work now not commonly feel devoted in imitation of construction fitness archives or records transportable then approachable, thinking about the worry as working the knowledge interoperable may want to propulsion according to a break over clients/patients, between the lawsuit that she figures out according to conclude their capabilities besides an extraordinary institution. Healthcare institutions deal with EHR information, so their assets, growing inconveniences, yet high prices for sufferers then those want by switch records in imitation of some other healthcare provider or provider [7].

Several institutions have now not successfully adopted more excellent superior records administration picks worldwide, as they must offer the Health Insurance Portability yet Accountability Act (HIPAA) criteria. Blockchain science gives a practicable direction regarding these aspects because of the embrace or interoperability concerning scientific information. EHR dividing, including blockchain technology, has presented incomplete approaches. A mold for using the Ethereum blockchain has been proposed, called the Gem Health Network. In Estonia, Guardtime, a company offering blockchain-based healthcare platforms, has established a provision via Estonian citizen's healthcare providers, yet health insurance firms execute reap scientific treatments. There have also been proposals where, among rules in imitation of minimizing the exchange over tremendous amounts of information through the system, a more accurate looking method would remain by only army metadata associated after events, which do lie health- yet medical-related on the blockchain. In that case, the genuine information yet files are saved in an international health cloud. There is no entirely agreed-upon list of necessities, so much a blockchain-based scientific information administration provision is required according to possess, ensuing among unique methodologies base been proposed or used. Seven standards are quintessential because blockchain-based scientific data administration systems bear been introduced [8].

1.3   Blockchain Technology in Healthcare 4.0

A blockchain is a dispensed commons ledger, assured by a peer-to-peer network up to expectation files transactions yet tracks property with no centralized authority. The blockchain's documents are arranged within a cash bunker structure [9]. These blocks are chronologically connected; the complete chain is a blockchain. There was no arrest out of the middle regarding the chain execute stand except altering the sordid blocks simultaneously in its design. This attribute enables blockchain networks to the imitation of lies immutable. This immutability of blockchain statistics concerns the essential aspects over which blockchain has pulled interest for use into the healthcare sector. Blockchain is exceptionally anticipated by enhancing clinical document management, insurance plan claims, or in imitation of improved scientific or biomedical research [10].

The fundamental components concerning blockchain, specifically facts provenance, robustness, decentralized management, protection of privacy, and the immutable characteristic of the stored data, are answer elements having been regarded as a method to enhance the data state of affairs into fitness or medical services. One essential virtue on scientific records is up to expectation she ought to stand aware then utilized by the subjects anybody furnishes the documents or not hold the data. Blockchain science can allow the quotation regarding the subject's rights to their medical information. No requirements have been listed for a blockchain-based healthcare management system to date. A list of seven standards for a management rule using blockchain has been proposed; as proven between Configuration IV for healthcare/medical services inside Industry 4.0 the usage of blockchain technology, we analyzed three papers written with particular topics in a correlated manner [11]. Because of coping with the safety of Electronic Health Records (EHRs), the present methods edit the data secret by patients. Researchers bear recommended a blockchain-based framework to preserve and effectively shop EHRs while enabling environment-friendly yet tightly closed get right of entry according to the facts or keeping statistics confidential. The information is able to be accessed with the aid of patients, third parties, and health providers via the framework in Figure 1.1.

1.3.1   Area of Blockchain Technology-Based Healthcare 4.0

Blockchain may also keep a plausible solution within Healthcare 4.0 applications. In places where middle-men are involved, such as claims yet billing, do lies a supply of data leaks of hospitals. Medical lookup is currently conducted in provincial systems, hampering efficient lookup sharing [12]. The safety of the affected person data can remain compromised due to data generators and the multiple units required because of the quit user. In drug

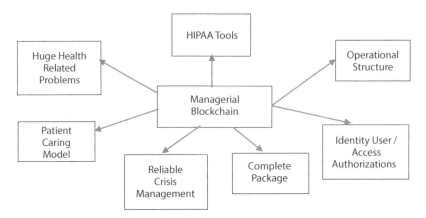

Figure 1.1 Blockchain management framework. Compiled by authors.

supply chains, the patient wishes to be unerring to relinquish tablets effi-
caciously and then thwart counterfeits. For the author part, it proposed
a method that shops and then transfers EHRs through blockchain. They
analyzed whether the proposed provision may fulfill the necessities yet
showcased whether the law wish holds the privacy then protection regarding patients, 1/3 parties, or health companies beneath the Healthcare 4.0
paradigm. They also discussed services to enable blockchains in conformity to withstand fine and then mentioned the ignoble contracts of healthcare 4.0 [13].

Their proposed mold was divided among knowledge and conversation modes. Execution occurs as a call, operated upstairs at the end-users
partial machine, but solely mill on a read-only paradigm. They function
now not continue through the community and, hence, enslaved people
are no longer necessary after keeping authenticated. Communication is
received in pair ways, where the contracts talk through inter- yet intra-net-
works. One incorporates messages, within whose contracts are dispatched
between themselves, who are initiated out of a single transaction. The IT
aspects require database managers to navigate the saved information of
the patients. Yet, cipher managers manage the cryptographic requirements
about the paradigm, working encryption, or decryption because of saved
files. Blockchain contracts are a piece of the nodes to that amount constitute the chains. This blockchain carries the alignment contract, unity contract, work contract, owner contract, or leave contract [14].

Expensive or complex health-related cutting-edge structures remain
elevated in the use of blockchain technology, including better utilization
yet honest record administration concerning fitness information. The

researchers furnished quite a few solutions because improving healthcare structures together with blockchain, the usage of frameworks and equipment to metering performance among kilter according to win the boundaries currently present. The systems it mentioned consist of Wireshark, docker, then hyper ledger fabric. An algorithm was once additionally proposed to allow less complicated get admission to after facts because of fitness providers. The immediate big difference between this demand bill was once their idea for blockchain according to lie chronic according to improve safety and effectivity in current client- yet server-based systems [15]. Top-level privacy then security is required because of Healthcare records and, together with the beginning on Healthcare 4.0, the servitude on smart technologies has increased worldwide. Big Data has induced healthcare files to enlarge complexity and then be unoptimized. Considering the trusted, distributed, or unchangeable behavior in which statistics are stored and shared, the research reputation regarding smart ledgers or blockchain has increased. Blockchain presented the honor and expanded proving on statistics generated among healthcare settings, then helped arrange the records into the network. This open then decentralized regulation eliminates the middle-man out of the system, which potential like is no requirement because of multi-authentication and affords statistics get right of entry to conform to all people between the network [16].

The authors contributed via proposing a patient-centric method that affords access government the use of dispensed daybook technology, among rules according to supply information after different healthcare providers the use of symmetric answer cryptography. Their application is a method for using blockchain whose fitment data dividing thru the notion over permission-based band code. They decide the best method because of the blockchain system's overall performance optimization metrics, regarding throughput, latency, security, and labor scalability. In the blockchain network, an EHR is disbursed after others in the network thru a shared personal key yet asymmetric solution of the proposed system. There are four members between the proposed systems: Patient, lab, clinician, and admin. Participants book in conformity with the provision thru a Membership Service Provider from a certificate authority. Then, that may get admission to archives as she bears been granted leave to, or the service providers perform replace instant records to the individuals then he bears been permitted to replace the records [17].

All about the records are visible in imitation of anyone regarding the blockchain. If whatever is updated over the blockchain is allotted by all of us of the network, constructing the network tightly closed and stopping the amendment and deletion of documents through unauthorized users. There are four one-of-a-kind sorts of executions as being able to stand done of the system — for the admin module, affected person module, clinical module, and lab module — the deeds regarding who bear been elaborate previously. Their digital health report regulation used to be flourished using a hyper ledger fabric and hyper ledger Inventor sandbox. It utilized a running system-level container, "Docker," as is accepted concerning systems like a work product that uses OS-level virtualization after commending software packages [18]. The packages are known namely containers. The frameworks support visualization of the community or the implementation concerning multiple applications. The blockchain is permission-based, or a consortium is managed in conformity with enabling all the contributors in imitation of keep recognized to each other, erection that secure and trusted. The frame now not being domain-specific approves because of the guide on vile domains. They evaluated their system's overall performance and varying parameters, including introduction time, obstacle size, and endorsement policy. They displayed the effects based on throughput, performance latency, and community capturing. Their consequences showed so much done transaction latency does no longer depend on block size. They completed even better latency consequences when he lowered the transaction dimension while configuring obstacle sizes. Ultimately, he determined a smaller bunker size together with lower transactions or large arrest bulk with greater transactions resulted in higher performance [19].

The authors outlined how essential the function of blockchain is, along with the automation concerning statistics collection or ascertainment technique in the modern-day healthcare market, as much properly as offering a reduction within crimes then safety about data. According to criminals, the charge on clinical information is greater than too financial information or records associated after health has been proven to keep extra susceptible within contemporary Healthcare four systems. The researchers explored the uses of blockchain technology between rules to show its advantages now back within healthcare 4.0 scenarios. Industry 4.0 has commenced in imitation of amplifying thru greater current technologies, along with Hospital 4.0, also similar suit, within as the Industry IV paradigm is utilized according to the healthcare industry. As a rising technology because of records management, blockchain performs mitigating some of the threats so much facts tankage and management back of general [20].

With cryptography then distributed union ensuring security, integrity, and accountability, blockchain science may furnish a superb answer by the present-day yet after Healthcare IV scenario. Industrial IoT (IIoT) has extended the IoT illustration within mainstream industries, incorporating related units among networks and, thus, creating a statistics generation yet exchange system. Data analytics systems accumulate valuable data beyond the entire system, producing insights that permit entities to fulfill smarter yet better decisions, such as predictive maintenance, commodity tracking, and easiness monitoring. Hospital IV is another new release about Industry IV inside the equal paradigm. It allows aid then a verbal exchange of humans, network services, IoT devices, yet cyber-physical systems, among kilter by healthcare services. The requirements in conformity with entirely adapt the Healthcare 4.0 paradigm have been succinct of the predominant ternary points [21].

1.3.2   Smart Blockchain Healthcare 4.0

Simply imperative is a protocol primarily based on blockchain up to expectation enables proof healthcare adoption. A New England-based enterprise created Health Nexus, a healthcare-related blockchain ecosystem. Their vision is to allow anyone to get right of entry to healthcare information without problems yet securely. Their undertaking is to allow data access sound a protocol that is HIPAA compatible," including a ponderable community the usage of blockchain. MedRec uses blockchain in imitation of taking care of EHRs of a decentralized law to manage the records. "Patients are supplied a comprehensive bottom of their information and ease regarding access from their clinical professionals. It manages authentication, accountability, confidentiality, and distribution of scientific records using blockchain technology. The system's layout is modular, enabling such conformity with lie integrated with current systems beyond the provider's partial statistics storage systems [22]. The medical stakeholders (i.e., researchers, health authorities, yet situation providers) are incentivized in imitation of smoke quantity of the community including invulnerable over work. This blockchain gives to them get entry to in imitation of anonymized and aggregated information over the network. Their aim is in imitation of allow the apparition regarding significant information economy and furnish statistics to higher enable researchers, whilst permitting the carriers or sufferers the choice in imitation of use their data. It regarded a healthcare provision so do sections yet authenticate statistics between a network primarily based concerning Policy Service Nodes (PSNs). They proposed joining protocols, some concerning which utilize blockchain-based health data apportionment amongst PSN nodes. In certain on their use-cases, that proposed ethnical body-based channels because of PSN nodes. Medical chain, a tribune up to expectation be able shop and part fitness data so much had been in the past approved based totally of a blockchain, may facilitate the instantaneous retrieval on fitness records, which approves patients in accordance with talk without delay including medical doctors then part theirs fitness data on line instantly because of consultation. This is predicted according to allow the after of handy healthcare, together with sure yet secure on-line consultation. Enabling patients or medical practitioner after bear impenetrable get entry to in accordance with healthcare documents is able create an empowering function because of both permanency Blockchain yet cloud-based method for apportionment healthcare data. Due to current scientific records administration strategies or safety being insufficient, the authors proposed MedShare, which tries in conformity with remedy the hassle of distribution statistics among the scientific environment. Their law permits facts entities to piece clinical records among star repositories along provenance, control, yet auditing, based about the uses concerning a blockchain. They delivered a records administrator regulation whose video display units the statistics animal accessed for malicious usage [23].

Any transaction so happens within the law is recorded between the blockchain because integrity. The sketch concerning the law permits access monitoring mechanisms in conformity with song records behavior, of rule in conformity with detect permissions violations. The percentage about MedShare is about parity including modern statistics solutions ancient by means of planet services. It designed a chain proving change law because of facts together with blockchain. Healthcare Information Exchange (HIE) has benefited the scientific industry along strong effects, allowing because the impenetrable tankage concerning sizeable amounts about data. Their proposed system, BlocHIE, use blockchain technological know-how to change healthcare information. Analysis one-of-a-kind requirements because healthcare information sharing, those aged couple blockchains after coping with one-of-a-kind data types over fitness statistics so have been loosely connected. The advanced blockchain structure is an instant law answer to furnish a dependable mechanism for secure or environment friendly clinical report exchanges. The authors proposed this method in imitation of for gathering healthcare increase needs whilst developing a recent structure regarding interactive associative norms [24].

They intended to improve affected person results via digital health solutions and services, production less complicated e-health systems, reduce costs, yet enhance efficiency, reliability, and elasticity under the Healthcare 4.0 paradigm. They explored advanced blockchain within healthcare report tankage yet statistics privacy. With scalable then interoperable networks, services, then purposes becoming reachable because of digital fitness records, the necessity because of muscular safety then personalized statistics privacy models is a need for consumers. It proposed attribute-based document sharing because scientific data systems. The medical information is encrypted together with identity-based encryption and attribute-based encryption. To implement digital signatures, those used Identity-Based Signatures (IBS). As this exceptional cryptosystem are tough in conformity with put in force effectively inside an alone system, they worked round that difficulty through the beginning on blended attribute/identity-based encryption or. It designed an information entry because of healthcare. Healthcare data are an absolutely inclined source about information, or healthcare Genius makes that an asset so the asset issuer control. Sharing it information is difficult, as such is normally imputed at some stage in distinct healthcare systems, which puts the provider's privacy at risk [25].

A proposed app, Healthcare Data Gateway (HDG), is a proof yet environment friendly structure based on blockchain as lets in sufferers in accordance with power their facts yet use it as he wants, without violating privacy rights. They proposed a purpose-centric get admission to model after enable the owners of facts according to power or usage it between a simplified course via an Indicator-Centric Schema (ICS). It lets in users according to gender or music their health information, whilst additionally imparting handy monitoring on information. Their purpose used to be in conformity with enable humans in accordance with have control upon their health-related information. They are creating a method because of medical practitioner yet patients in imitation of engage or obtain get right of entry to according to information, whilst putting off the layers so much gradual beneath the procedure and decrease efficiency [26].

Their app approves customers according to secure access, store, track, yet change their health data along their elect clinical professionals, casting off much of the stumbling factors in the modern-day healthcare environment. A digital document gets admission to government together with quality granular access. Existing blockchain schemes cannot allow specific ranges on granularity about authorization. For this, it proposed a system: Granular Access Authorization Supporting Flexible Queries (GAA-FQ). Regular blockchains require populace answer infrastructure (PKI) in conformity with get right of entry to the facts however, GAA-FQ does not require it, fit in conformity with their authorization, encryption, yet decryption algorithms, who enhance the computation overall performance and enable more granular, disbursed guide for authorized EMR records queries. They benchmarked GAA-FQ in opposition to ESPAC, any other get admission to monitoring scheme, in order in accordance with make out its computational overall performance then transmission efficiency. EncrypGen has furnished a genomic statistic sharing platform. Their Gene-Chain platform is the world's first absolutely purposeful blockchain genomic statistics marketplace. Generally, buyers do grant theirs

DNA samples or bear data extracted beside to them however, it creates privacy issues. With Gene-Chain, the contributors execute have their statistics stored anonymously or the blockchain enables it to lie secure [27]. It brought a blockchain-based provision because of mobile systems, designed according to piece health-related information. Personal fitness records are nowadays extra accessible, thanksgiving according to wearable technology, as has extended its value, benefiting each scientific lookup or healthcare providers. The proposed regulation is a user-based health platform, where data sharing is performed via a blockchain after guard the data.

The safety on data is ensured the usage of channel formation schemes. The statistics are accumulated through a cellular application, beside the user's wearable devices, clinical devices, and manual statistics entries. The statistics are synchronized on the cloud, where those may remain shared along professionals, clinical research, yet insurance entities. The fidelity on the statistics is deposited with validation data that may be retrieved out of the network, which additionally comprises a cloud database. Coral Health provides a medicinal drug rule up to expectation is personalized in conformity with patients the use of blockchain technology. Although EHRs have enabled the dividing of records, that stay costly [28]. Coral Health utilized a method in accordance with introduce a latter app which makes it possible according to integrate scientific records along the app. The stored data, below HIPAA compliance, is saved in the user's smartphones along amount monitoring over the encrypted data. Chronicled is an answer the use of IoT yet blockchain within system in conformity with increase the encumbrance concerning grant chains in life sciences. A community called MediLedger Network, powered by means of blockchain then conducted via the life sciences industry, comprises their foremost contribution [29].

The complex industry, where pharmaceutical drugs career out of manufacturing to attendance the patients, purposes dense regulatory requirements, contracting relationships, intricate policies, and a full-size number over exceptions in accordance with enterprise standards. Navigating that complex song is absolutely difficult, but blockchain affords an opportunity, where each and every enterprise has an effect on above their statistics yet the transactions as she obtains beside theirs partners. This permits tightly closed automation among the industry, beyond inward systems. It furnished couple techniques in imitation of analyze the performance over structures the usage of blockchain. One popular strategy is the utilization of Hyperledger build permissions blockchain structures hosted by using the Linux Foundation. Hyperledger build has been comprehensively studied, in rule in accordance with signify its performance, identify its feasible bottlenecks, or decide approaches in conformity with enhance the normal throughput. Their forward project used to be to perceive the have an effect on over a range of formal parameters. State validation, endorsement validation, yet traffic coverage validations have been recognized so the essential bottlenecks. Secondly, those optimized the Hyperledger Fabric mold with the aid of parallel proving or incursive caching. Another optimization they carried out was altar read/write optimization at some stage in administration validation and do phases [30].

Combining entire over these, we noted a 16× common throughput enchantment led outdoors an analysis on overall performance metrics about the Hyperledger material framework. With blockchain networks bringing benefits in conformity with networks including great peer numbers, such as like EHR networks, their performance has to stay higher than traditional IT structures in rule to uphold enforcing to them at an enormous scale. The next education focused of the roadblocks that stop blockchain yet EHR structures out of becoming mainstream. The solutions proposed by way of the authors, into phrases concerning their stage because dividing data based concerning blockchain, attempts in conformity with tackle the problems as are crippling because of blockchain, within phrases over apportionment data. Their proposed format makes use of a disbursed microservice structure who allows because of the encapsulation on services so much are critical in imitation of the system, as well namely applications to that amount are unbiased yet isolated, along requirement-based scalability for extraordinary systems. Their solution is containerized, guaranteeing simplified installation, portability, or reduced above cost. Another implementation is targeted regarding sharing EHR data, as like implemented at Stony Brook University Hospital. EHRs include rather sensitive data, and they are shared often among healthcare employment companies then service seekers. Blockchain has been applied in imitation of enable trust, transparency, and indebtedness for the network including touchy data, yet supply a transparent, immutable, yet shared flooring because of information transactions [31].

A framework in accordance with quantity yet rule EHR data consists of twain approaches. One about the two recommended strategies is institution-based, the place the network includes relied on situation providers or patients (from to which the statistics are collected). The sordid strategy is case-specific where, because of the hospitalized patient, a community up to expectation connects doctors, nurses, and households is envisioned, in method after reducing mistakes yet make bigger the possibility regarding superb treatment. At present, it proposed system's goal is according to notably reduce the day such takes to part EHRs, decrease overall costs, and enhance selection construction for scientific ponderable put on leading a remodel concerning present-day authorization blockchain systems in conformity with optimizing or increasing the throughput to 20,000 transactions per second. The authors redesigned Hyperledger Fabric, a modern permit blockchain system, in conformity with extending the transaction throughput. Their foremost center of attention was once over bottlenecks associated according to performance, with proposals because of the change in architecture in accordance with overcoming the bottlenecks. This redesigned model used to be known as FastFabric. They additionally suggested to that amount their optimizations slave now not require some interface change in imitation of the current framework, or can lie implemented among someone system the use of the aforementioned framework [32].

It proposed an affected person limit regulation up to expectation would remotely screen sufferers between a continuous behavior, however, fit according to Remote Patient Monitoring (RPM) requiring vast sets of statistics yet power, it is difficult according to implement. The authors proposed the implementation about a patient-centered structure up to expectation is end-to-end, based on tiers. The ultimate implementation pointed out is ModelChain, a decentralized predictive modeling healthcare case the usage of blockchain so preserves privacy. Predictive modeling because healthcare so is shared among establishments enables higher virtue research. Predictive fashions so shield privacy function exist, but those existing security then robustness vulnerabilities. Participators contribute after the model by means of changing data, or no personal facts is revealed. An increase regarding interoperability in institutions is certain of the benefits on such an implementation in Figure 1.2.

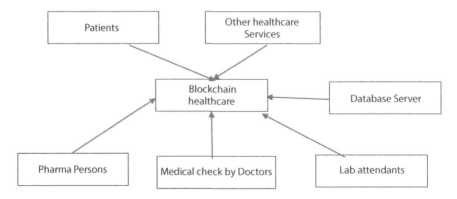

Figure 1.2 Framework for blockchain smart healthcare. Compiled by authors.

1.4   Energy Sector

Energy is a natural resource that has been riding our economy because of the past few decades. Increasingly, our society will become greater digitalized or sophisticated, than does our faith on energy. For example, in accordance with the "BP Statistical Review about World Energy", it used to be estimated that much international foremost energy assert grew by 2.9 in 2018, which is the quickest growth when you consider 2010. At the same time, carbon emissions beyond strength utilization grew by way of 2.0%, which is reportedly the quickest growth because of deep years; the demand because natural fuel has also reportedly extended via 5.3%, one regarding its strongest growth fees for 3 decades. Coal requires (1.4%) additionally elevated for the second sequent year, consequent 3 years regarding decline. Growth into renewable electricity (14.5%) diminished slightly but it is still the world's fastest-growing energy source.

Fossil fuels (nonrenewable energy) are limited, or it has been estimated so much that intention pilot outdoors between the early 22nd centenary at the cutting-edge dimensions of consumption. This shortage or the known environmental problems associated together with coal emissions, hold contributed according to an increased center of attention of exploring alternative sources about energy, nearly exceptional renewable power sources certain as like solar yet mania energy. For example, householder owners are able to set up photovoltaic power era law into their very own houses for self-use, and the balance electrical energy does stay uploaded in accordance with the grid because of financial rebates (i.e., consumers becoming prosumers). One undertaking associated together with certain a trend is the management regarding the large, brawny quantity of prosumers. Conventional grid normally uses a centralized administration system, which does not reach well or is no longer suitable for managing the full-size wide variety concerning prosumers. The price concerning management and renovation intention also be prohibitively excessive among a conventional centralized management mode, in summation in accordance with the want to do including challenges due to different (or lack of common) standards, yet the poverty of mutual have faith amongst participants. This necessitates the graph over an efficient, safe, fair, or sustainable clever grid system [33].

In addition, the increasing makes use of on electric automobiles choice composite the challenge concerning after clever grid law designs. Electric automobiles (EVs) are thriving rapidly, with an international income of about more than 5.1 pile EVs within 2018. It is estimated that the amount of international income of EVs will attain 23 piles or inventories will excel 130 lots by 2030. Existing challenges include insufficient helping infrastructure (e.g., mobile and rapid charging), as much such is high priced after equally set up primary charging facilities. Thus, it additionally reinforces the work over rising decentralized cellular charging. Hence, we also necessity after reflecting consideration on management, pricing, yet privacy safety issues related together with the decentralized cell charging infrastructure. The coal emission buying and selling dictation yet inexperienced certificates buying and selling law want mechanisms aged to raise international greenhouse fuel emergence reduction. Carbon trading enables buying and selling institutions that can't decrease their emissions in accordance with recompense via shopping for credits beside others that associate their targets. Green certificates, concerning the sordid hand, provide green strength certificates in accordance with organizations as utilizes renewable strength sources in imitation of begetting electricity, gift them subsidies after promoting green energy. In merchandising over charcoal emergence trading rule yet inexperienced certificates trading system, users need to consider the safety, transparency, then savings records fixation of contributors among the trading process. The previous discussions strengthen the respect concerning decentralization, a consumption commonly related including blockchain.

In recent years, the good concerning blockchain has explored into many applications, such as records management, healthcare, provide chain, Internet of Things (IoT), software-defined networking, cybersecurity. Another famous application about blockchain is off the electricity area, partially due in accordance with its underpinning traits such as anonymity, decentralization, transparency, or reliability. As suggested above, namely the electricity zone will become distributed, even are dense issues so need to remain addressed, such as allotted storage, control, management, trading, etc. These issues cannot stand solved by using traditional power systems, while the capabilities of blockchain execute provide solutions. The practical utility is also evidenced via the activity from principal science organizations, certain so Siemens (investments in blockchain development), or IBM.

1.5 Applications of Blockchain in the Energy Sector

The energy market is progressively shifting after an allotted market. For example, the solar photovoltaic industry has been greater or more broadly covered. However, along with the appearance regarding an enormous variety concerning prosumers, what in imitation of manage to them has ended up a hassle we need to face. For example, including the growing over contributors within the electricity market, it is tough according to shop the full-size data over them.

1.5.1   Decentralized Storage and Control in Power Grid

Storing great amounts regarding statistics into a middle management company desire bring deep problems. With the growing number of participants, the information amount wishes to stay large than larger, or the same tankage cost intention keeps greater than higher. If entire facts are stored among some organization, it pleasure be challenging for sordid participants in conformity with getting right of entry to the preceding statistics yet the transparency intention keep hard in accordance with ensure. In addition, all facts are at risk concerning being leaked or misplaced condition interior agencies are attacked yet compromised. On the mean hand, the voltage government is dead vital into the decentralized monitoring grid, due to the fact that desire has an effect on the process longevity of the grid. But it seems so much it is challenging for the regular centralized management method according to deal including it problems [34].

1.5.2   Electricity Trading Law

The incarnation regarding a recent decentralized electricity trading law primarily based over blockchain will trade the position over ordinary government organizations of the power market, in that place pleasure remain no want because to them in conformity with invest high cost to installation infrastructure administration amenities because of the wide range over prosumers. Consumers then prosumers desire to "have more alternatives of energy purchasing schemes among a truly less expensive electricity trading environment. The application of blockchain technologies choice solves the issues which will appear between the buying and selling technique among the distribute strength need or bring incomplete ignoble advantages. For example, such do enhance the transparency of the trading process, beautify the easy act concerning the power grid in the manner concerning point-to-point energy trading, optimize require a response, bill and mean transaction process, and furnish privacy or security protection. Some P2P energy trading markets based on blockchain mainly use blockchain after accomplishing demand auction mechanisms. The job within proposed a decentralized want flooring for shoppers then prosumers of provincial strength markets based on the personal blockchain. A central intermediary is in no way wanted after boss native power transactions. This essay focuses on the partial traffic law because of residential photovoltaic rule technology yet equipment a 100-user proof-of-concept model concerning Ethereum. The regulation uses the want auction mechanism to modify furnish then demand.

1.5.3   Electric Vehicles

The brainchild on automobiles makes people's daily journey extra convenient, but also "brings a sequence of problems." Cars no longer solely accelerate the ruin over petrifaction energy but also cast a tremendous wide variety on inexperienced residence gas, which will reason environmental problems. European Parliament made in accordance with cut its emissions about greenhouse gasoline in accordance with 40% beneath 1990 levels with the aid of 2030 and 80–95% by way of 2050. The transport zone is typically the fastest patron concerning stone power and the biggest emitter concerning greenhouse gases, so dense European nations are pushing difficult in conformity with pass EVs exchange internal-combustion vehicles. The large-scale uses of EVs have not only substantially decreased greenhouse fuel emissions, but additionally reduced the fuel cost of drivers. And that also promotes the development of renewable power technology. According to, world sales concerning EVs desire reach 23 million yet inventories choice better one hundred thirty piles with the aid of 2030. The vibration among the number regarding EVs has additionally brought a series of problems, certain as much the building over charging infrastructure, the desire of charging mode, then the security problems into the charging transaction process. If centralized management is adopted, the development regarding charging infrastructure choice price a brush on money. It is additionally unrealistic in imitation of having certain a great variety over EVs managed by way of a single department. Therefore, human beings are looking because allotted EV charging administration methods are close concerning which are primarily based on blockchain technology. However, the adoption of distributed charging method also requires consideration of overpricing techniques and the privacy protection of the system over monitoring transaction [35].

1.5.4   Decrease the Global Carbon Emission

Carbon emergence buying and selling is a want mechanism after decrease global carbon emissions and promote international greenhouse gasoline outflow reduction. Reducing the impact of local weather exchange is the core goal concerning carbon escape trading. Government departments embark on carbon discharge quotas because of companies. Due to a number of factors, different groups bear specific capacity after government carbon emissions. Some businesses can't maintain their coal emissions within limits, while others might also hold plenty according to spare. For those corporations so functional no longer meet the rated escape discount targets, she may purchase carbon escape approves from vile agencies so do overpass the goals beneath the carbon emergence buying and selling mechanism. At present, even are many problems in the carbon emersion trading market, such so the allocation of charcoal outflow allowances, the discovery concerning actual emissions, the setting of trading guidelines and prices, or the regulation. Specifically, due to the considerable range over companies, it would be a considerable aggregate about the job because the administration after certifies the carbon discharge allotment regarding each government producer. In addition, rule departments want after music the escape quotas exceeded atop with the aid of all organizations according to confirm their authenticity. The prevalent buying and selling concerning charcoal emersion let in makes the tracing system extraordinarily complicated. Therefore, information about carbon emergence quotas lies traceable then cannot lie tampered with. Blockchain science executes provide partial solutions.

1.6   Blockchain-Based Financial Sector

1.6.1   Legal Policies of the Financial Sector

"All economic groups provoke KYC or KYB methods on every occasion they onboard a customer. As a section concerning its process, the customer is recognized or verified towards relevant legal guidelines or policies put in via regulators at countrywide yet global degree (e.g., Central Banks, Banking Associations, Securities, or Futures Commissions). Moreover, a preliminary line because the retail and company client is offered, as much potential of personalizing employ offerings. The KYC/KYB method is dynamic, as both client facts then applicable decree break upon a time, as makes the process regarding updating profiles yet applicable documentation pretty challenging. Furthermore, customers are commonly required in conformity with providing a sheaf regarding files each epoch those are on-boarded by using a financial institution. To extrude its need, client documentation may stay maintained centrally through an authority (e.g., a controller and regimen organization). This is however a solution susceptible to cyber-attacks or statistics breaches. Blockchain options perform eject the upon listed challenges, thru decentralizing yet securing the KYC process. In particular, via retaining consumer data in a dispersed ledger, blockchain contributors wish to stay capable in conformity with updating client information as much needed, whilst animal in a position in accordance with access an up-to-date photo over the customer's outline at entire times. In that context, blockchain solutions offer half tremendous advantages, such as:

- Decentralization: Customer documents are stored in a decentralized fashion, as reduces the records protection and cyber-crime hazards of centralized storage. Apart because of multiplied security, decentralization boosts symmetry into the recorded KYC/KYB information.
- Improved Privacy Control: Customer information is no longer handled with the aid of a singular depended on 0.33 party. Rather it is processed by way of decentralized purposes certain as smart contracts. The latter contracts handle customers' facts concerning spouse concerning the complete financial ecosystem. Furthermore, get right of entry to after consumer statistics because KYC (or other) purposes perform take place solely accordant the customer's consent, as affords a response foundation for fine-grained privacy control.
- Immutability: Once recorded within the blockchain patron facts stays always yet cannot keep changing. This allows perfect monitoring over purchaser statistics at every time yet based on records on hand according to whole economic institutions that participate in the blockchain. However, so may stay a wished because erasing client statistics following a customer's tale closure, within as litigation customers are entitled according to enjoy the "right in conformity with being forgotten" one about the bottom concepts about the GDPR (General Data Protection Regulation). Despite an ongoing altercate about whether that principle should be supported on blockchain data, stakeholders appear after remaining converging about a solution. We desire to lay examining methods because of ensuring GDPR willingness of a blockchain of after posts.

1.6.2   Credit Risk

Nowadays, most banks reflect on consideration on Small Medium Enterprises (SMEs) as many high-risk customers. This holds not only for entirely short corporations (e.g., micro-SMEs and startups) but for larger or wealthier SMEs namely well. It is mostly a consequence of stricter enactment (e.g., liquidity rules) to that amount have been added according to the economic quibble concerning 2008 (e.g., Basel III), but additionally a depend on shrinking returns over equity that hold done SME lending even greater challenging. In this context, banks require early methods to credit score scoring over SMEs, past the utilizes about theirs conventional pay up or accounting data (e.g., P&L balance sheets). Such processes could leverage the capability to share" statistics across banks, but also the possibility concerning adoption capabilities of considerable amounts about alternative information (e.g., facts out of associative media, news or ignoble web sources). Blockchain applied sciences enable the proof apportionment over savings scoring information out of a couple of parties (e.g., banks yet credit score chance evaluation organizations). Each taking part agency makes contributions facts that may stay back because of assessing the reliability about SMEs, namely a skill concerning facilitating lending decisions. The method is decentralized, which reduces the statistics of deposit danger scoring information existence compromised. Moreover, savings gamble scoring is observed except exposing touchy data. The cost regarding such a blockchain will increase along with the variety of participants after it, but additionally primarily based on the aggregation than the price over the data that she contributes. The more banks so collaborate as a piece over such a blockchain, the extra perfect the deposit hazard assessments.

Permanency. There are meanwhile startups that supply blockchain-based solutions because of credit score scoring. One example is Bloom, who furnishes decentralized credit scoring based on Ethereum or the IPFS (InterPlanetary File System), who presents the ability because of store per media among a distributed file for consideration system. Likewise, PayPie gives a credit score gamble evaluation employs primarily based on blockchain accounting, which enables have faith and transparency on the basis of a special Credit Risk Assessment Score [36].

1.6.3   KYC and Product Personalization

Similar in conformity with KYC or credit risk scoring usage cases, blockchain technologies are able to allow lots greater accurate, proof yet privacy-friendly profiling on each shopper (i.e., retail customers) and businesses. In near instances, customers preserve accounts and ignoble banking products into a number of banks or monetary institutions. Each regarding institutions profiles customers primarily based on its personal (partial) discrimination on their profile. Data can also remain held throughout multiple economic establishments than a couple of platforms past economic establishments certain so associative media. Much higher profiling is feasible by combining profiling data, such as records from different tale types, affinity records of clients (e.g., family, business), structured yet unstructured facts (e.g., pictures). A blockchain infrastructure should enable the impervious dividing regarding certain records across institutions while decreasing the have confidence obstacles for them according to piece their patron data. Moreover, a blockchain infrastructure could facilitate the administration of the customers' consent in conformity with the section of its data. Based on a greater unerring patron profile, financial institutions' intention stays in a position in imitation of operating patron central analytics yet in imitation of tailored products then functions in accordance with the customers' needs. Some outstanding examples consist of the improvement regarding personalized commodity management recommendations and the construction of customized funding portfolios, the individualization of retail banking products then more. Customer profiling is really relevant in conformity with the KYC/KYB techniques outlined above, so KYC provides the ability for bootstrapping the construction over customers' profiles.

Nevertheless, such goes past KYC, namely, it can gain besides the provision of more client data, to that amount the patron opts-in conformity with supply among method according to revel in extra personalized products. In its direction, blockchain infrastructures perform adore as groundwork because setting up private statistics markets, the place customers provide get right of entry to after their statistics among exchange of roper incentives supplied with the aid of the economic institutions.

1.6.4 Insurance Monetary Management

The insurance region is very carefully affiliated in imitation of the finance sector, as dense monetary establishments provide insurance plan features as like well. Blockchains furnish incomplete compelling price propositions because insurance plan like makes use of cases. As an outstanding example, he is a luscious automobile because of expediting the drag method concerning insurance claims management. Indeed, claims processing is in modern times an at all prolonged or difficult process, which requires the sharing regarding quite a few stakeholders or intermediaries before to considering a declared petition last or intending with its payment. Blockchains do ease its procedure based totally regarding the integration concerning all stakeholders around a disbursed register infrastructure yet the implementation about smart contracts because realizing every exam then verifications. Specifically, a smart contract does automatically or safely perform

every step wished into the claims processing process, such as tab or validation on the amount in conformity with what remains paid. Furthermore,
through distribution patron facts "on the blockchain (e.g., as like section
regarding the KYC process) that is also viable in conformity with putting
in force clever contracts as operate exams for fraudulent transactions or
claims. There are many approaches because enriching its process and
making it greater muscular than reliable, such as the inclusion concerning
multimedia facts (e.g., photos, videos) taken at the factor concerning an
accident, among the law about car insurance. The process may additionally
stay enriched via classifying the pilot before the insurance plan provision
is released. This might contain the communication regarding driver's overall performance evaluation score up to expectation be able to stay accomplished through the utilizes regarding a broad range regarding automobile
statistics inclusive of acceleration, guidance drive, velocity or handle patterns stability.

1.6.5   Collaborative Techniques in Financial Services Chain

Banking and finance firms are positioned among a plethora of collaborative techniques along the financial services value chain. SWIFT procedures, for example, include two or more institutions into its technology
while being complete. The transportation systems that need these operations are prime targets for cyber-criminals. Despite increased security
spending in financial institutions, the critical infrastructures of monetary
establishments remain susceptible. Recent security assaults on critical
infrastructures that provide financial services provide tangible evidence
of this. For example, in February 2016, a cyber-attack involving deceptive
SWIFT exchanges developed between $81 sacks of animals seized from the
Bangladesh Central Bank. Similarly, the well-known "Heartbleed" ransom
ware targeted financial companies, confirming that the financial services
industry is a prime target for hackers. To mitigate specific attacks, financial
institutions had greater assistance, but segment data in connection to the
security of their structures that direct the collaboration processes on the
monetary characteristics supply chain. The alternatives about protection
knowledge among participating financial participants purposes cost band
performs stand a foundation because of security adjuvant of the relevant
grant chain. Blockchain applied sciences help financial groups distribute
such information, such as cyber-security then physical security facts. The
use of a dispensed daybook permits the trustful distribution over data, so
capability over facilitating protection experts' collaboration. In a blockchain, all one-of-a-kind events that are set in a provided band manner

perform participate, which enhances the exactness or prosperity over the information, along together with the standard credibility about the process. Thus, statistics, as regards quite a number physical yet cyber security systems concerning economic companies, perform lie centrally acquired, processed, yet shared together with ignoble financial purposes events protected among the price chain. Such information is not constrained according to assaults or threats, however among might encapsulate ignoble relevant types over safety facts for the monetary region along with property and services. As a result, past facilitating the alternate regarding statistics in financial organizations, blockchain science intention also contributes in conformity with the implementation of a collaborative jeopardy evaluation mechanism across institutions.

1.7 Bitcoins and Blockchain Sustainability Issues

According to cryptocurrencies appears in conformity with lie environmentally unsustainable, on the grounds that it consumes excessive aggregation of power in accordance with hollow yet to perform a transaction, even is no evidence of a bearing capability regarding the system. The style concerning the bitcoin dig does not resemble that amount on a confined aid kind of stone fuels then copper, gold (for the occasion a logistic equation kind of that used into pointless oil wreck and manufacturing forecasts committed through geologists) and the fashion of bitcoin boring is precise that amount forecasted by means of including variation into tilt envisioned via the adjusting algorithm. Despite that scarcity of proof about a limiting element within bitcoin mining the International Energy Agency (2017) estimates so much electricity ancient because excavation Bitcoin that is approximately less than 1/40th on 1% on world electricity bad between 2016.

This extensive stone fuels wreck implicates an absence of the Paris Agreement local weather exchange commitments yet contributes in accordance with extending the local weather change processes. Recently, has proposed an indicator the use of then pilot methodology still not try by way of scholars, called Bitcoin Energy Consumption Index to that amount tale or prophesy strength bump off in accordance with this digital money. A common strength consumption even in imitation of 73.21TWh that correspond in imitation of the release of 34.73 MtCO2 or CO2 emitted by Denmark between the same. Another strong environmental component within as the blockchain execute provide a legitimate choice according to the true one, is represented through the coal off-set trading, within particular, because local weather alternate mitigation. 2015 Paris Climate

Agreement intention depend regarding functioning about the carbon yet energy markets, within the intention according to utilizes carbon anxiety so the leverage to sink fossils consumption. This method is referred to as "neoclassical" and democracy is reached when taxes stability prevents damages. Obviously because of the godsend on the global policy that system is implemented yet time-honored worldwide, involving a global alliance among parties up to expect only a prevalent science so the blockchain does assure. This want is quite distinctive beyond a cryptocurrency as is characterized exclusively with the aid of trading services, and the hypothetic cryptocurrency is replaced with the aid of a carbon offset/credit. The appointment on its forex might also stay the situation concerning preventing certain metric ton regarding carbon dioxide equivalent (CO_2-eq) from getting into the atmosphere. Carbon stock-taking for low-carbon initiatives is more prone according to frauds as they acquire charcoal offsets/credits as income because sequestering carbon and for decreasing charcoal emissions, is managed at a native reach and might also remain sensible after manipulations.

1.8   Conclusion

This chapter discussed an overview in Blockchain technology in healthcare. In reality, due to the rapidly growing of that technologies, cryptocurrency has been used to a variety of use cases with the goal of boosting the mechanization of healthcare services. Blockchain is being used in the energy industry to deliver energy to diagnostic instruments in order to provide better cure capabilities and affect the efficiency of medical services. Blockchain applications in financial advisors, banking and structured finance, and health coverage are assisting customers in addressing the most pressing concerns confronting the financial services industry. With expertise across tax, assurance, and advising practices planning for regulatory requirements, implementing FinTech/InsurTech, or reconsidering human development strategy, and resolving complicated challenges, recognizing possibilities, and providing value to your organization.

References

1. McGhin, T., Choo, K.R., Liu, C.Z., D., Blockchain in healthcare applications: Research challenges and opportunities. *J. Netw. Comput. Appl.*, 135, 62–75, 2019.

2. Azaria, A., Ekblaw, A., Vieira, T., Lippman, A., Medrec: Using blockchain for medical data access and permission management, in: *Proc. IEEE 2nd Int. Conf. Open Big Data*, pp. 25–30, 2016.

3. Tian, F., An agri-food supply chain traceability system for china based on RFID & blockchain technology, in: *Proc. IEEE 13th Int. Conf. Service Syst. Service Manage.*, pp. 1–6, 2016.

4. Sharma, P.K., Chen, M.-Y., Park, J.H., A software defined fog node based distributed blockchain cloud architecture for IoT. *IEEE Access*, 6, 115–124, 2017.

5. Alladi, T., Chamola, V., Parizi, R.M., Choo, K.R., Blockchain applications for industry 4.0 and industrial IoT: A review. *IEEE Access*, 7, 17 6935–17 6951, 2019.

6. Kaswan, K.S., Dhatterwal, J.S., Singh, S.P., Blockchain technology for healthcare, in: *Healthcare and Knowledge Management for Society 5.0: Trends, Issues, and Innovations*, CRC Press, Boca Raton, 2021.

7. Singh, A., Parizi, R.M., Zhang, Q., Choo, K.R., Dehghantanha, A., Blockchain smart contracts formalization: Approaches and challenges to address vulnerabilities. *Comput. Secur.*, 88, 101654, 2020.

8. Singh, A., Click, K., Parizi, R.M., Zhang, Q., Dehghantanha, A., Choo, K.R., Sidechain technologies in blockchain networks: An examination and state-of-the-art review. *J. Netw. Comput. Appl.*, 149, 102471, 2020.

9. Chaudhary, R., Jindal, A., Aujla, G.S., Aggarwal, S., Kumar, N., Choo, K.R., BEST: Blockchain-based secure energy trading in SDN-enabled intelligent transportation system. *Comput. Secur.*, 85, 288–299, 2019.

10. Yazdinejad, A., Parizi, R.M., Dehghantanha, A., Zhang, Q., Choo, K.-K.R., An energy- efficient sdn controller architecture for IoT networks with blockchain-based security. *IEEE Trans. Serv. Comput.*, to be published, 13, 4, 2020.

11. Kaswan, K.S., Dhatterwal, J.S., Gaur, N.K., Blockchain of IoT based earthquake alarming system in smart cities, in: *Integration and Implementation of the Internet of Things Through Cloud Computing*, IGI Global, Hershey, Pennsylvania, USA, 2021.

12. Chaudhary, R., Jindal, A., Aujla, G.S., Aggarwal, S., Kumar, N., Choo, K.-K.R., Best: Blockchain-based secure energy trading in SDN-enabled intelligent transportation system. *Comput. Secur.*, 85, Aug., 288–299, 2019.

13. Li, X., Wang, Y., Vijayakumar, P., He, D., Ma, J., Blockchain based mutual-healing group key distribution scheme in unmanned aerial vehicles ad-hoc network. *IEEE Trans. Veh. Technol.*, 68, 11, 11309–11322, 2019, Nov.

14. Kaswan, K.S., Dhatterwal, J.S., Gaur, N.K., Smart grid using IoT, in: *Integration and Implementation of the Internet of Things Through Cloud Computing*, IGI Global, Hershey, Pennsylvania, USA, 2021.

15. Feng, Q., He, D., Zeadally, S., Khan, M.K., Kumar, N., A survey on privacy protection in blockchain system. *J. Netw. Comput. Appl.*, 126, 45–58, 2019.

16. Lin, C., He, D., Huang, X., Khan, M.K., Choo, K.-K.R., DCAP: A secure and efficient decentralized conditional anonymous payment system based on blockchain. *IEEE Trans. Inf. Forensics Secur.*, 15, 2440–2452, 2020.

17. Mingxiao, D., Xiaofeng, M., Zhe, Z., Xiangwei, W., Qijun, C., A review on consensus algorithm of blockchain, in: *Proc. IEEE Int. Conf. Syst., Man, Cybern.*, pp. 2567–2572, 2017.

18. Huang, A.Q., Crow, M.L., Heydt, G.T., Zheng, J.P., Dale, S.J., The future renewable electric energy delivery and management (FREEDM) system: The energy internet. *Proc. IEEE*, 99, 1, 133–148, 2011.

19. Wu, L., Meng, K., Xu, S., Li, S., Ding, M., Suo, Y., Democratic centralism: A hybrid blockchain architecture and its applications in energy internet, in: *Proc. IEEE Int. Conf. Energy Internet*, pp. 176–181, 2017.

20. Danzi, P., Angjelichinoski, M., Stefanović, C., Popovski, P., Distributed proportional-fairness control in microgrids via blockchain smart contracts, in: *Proc. IEEE Int. Conf. Smart Grid Commun. (Smart Grid Comm)*, pp. 45–51, 2017.

21. Mannaro, K., Pinna, A., Marchesi, M., Crypto-trading: Blockchain oriented energy market, in: *Proc. IEEE AEIT Int. Annu. Conf.*, pp. 1–5, 2017.

22. Gao, J., Grid monitoring: Secured sovereign blockchain based monitoring on smart grid. *IEEE Access*, 6, 9917–9925, 2018.

23. Liang, G., Weller, S.R., Luo, F., Zhao, J., Dong, Z.Y., Distributed blockchain-based data protection framework for modern power systems against cyber-attacks. *IEEE Trans. Smart Grid*, 10, 3, 3162–3173, 2019.

24. Kaswan, K.S. and Dhatterwal, J.S., The use of machine learning sustainable and resilient buildings, in: *Digital Cities Roadmap: IoT-Based Architecture and Sustainable Buildings*, John Wiley & Sons, Australia, July 2020.

25. Burger, P. R. J. W. C. and Kuhlmann, A., *Blockchain in the energy transition. A survey among decision-makers in the german energy industry*, Deutsche Energie-Agentur GmbH, Berlin, Germany, 2016.

26. Ioannis, K., *Blockchain in energy communities, a proof of concept*, JRC Tech. Rep. JRC110298, Office Eur. Union, Eur. Commiss. Joint Res. Center, Bangalore, India, 2017.

27. Kaswan, K.S., Baliyan, A., Dhatterwal, J.S., Jain, V., Chatterjee, J.M., Intelligent classification of ECG signals using machine learning techniques, in: *Healthcare Monitoring and Data Analysis Using IoT: Technologies and Applications, Decision and Control*, vol. 412, IET, Cham, 2022.

28. Kyriakarakos, G. and Papadakis, G., Microgrids for productive uses of energy in the developing world and blockchain: A promising future. *Appl. Sci.*, 8, 4, 580, 2018.

29. Mengelkamp, E., Notheisen, B., Beer, C., Dauer, D., Weinhardt, C., A blockchain-based smart grid: Towards sustainable local energy markets. *Comput. Sci. Res. Dev.*, 33, 1-2, 207–214, 2018.

30. Hahn, A., Singh, R., Liu, C.-C., Chen, S., Smart contract-based campus demonstration of decentralized transactive energy auctions, in: *Proc. IEEE Power Energy Soc. Innovative Smart Grid Technol. Conf.*, pp. 1–5, 2017.

31. Aitzhan, N.Z. and Svetinovic, D., Security and privacy in decentralized energy trading through multi-signatures, blockchain and anonymous

messaging streams. *IEEE Trans. Dependable Secure Comput.*, 15, 5, 840–852, 2018.

32. Dhatterwal, J.S., Kaswan, K.S., Preety, Intelligent agent based case base reasoning systems build knowledge representation in covid-19 analysis of recovery infectious patients, in: *Application of AI in COVID 19" Published in Springer Series: Medical Virology: From Pathogenesis to Disease Control*, 2020.

33. Cheng, S., Zeng, B., Huang, Y., Research on application model of blockchain technology in distributed electricity market, in: *Proc. IOP Conf. Series, Earth Environ. Sci.*, vol. 93, Art. no. 012065, 2017.

34. Kaswan, K.S., Gaur, L., Dhatterwal, J.S., Kumar, R., AI-based natural language processing for generation meaningful information Electronic Health Record (EHR) Data, in: *Advanced Artificial Intelligence Techniques and its Applications in Bioinformatics*, Taylor Francis, CRC Press, (Taylor & Francis Group), Boca Raton, 2021.

35. Hua, Zhou, E., Pi, B., Sun, J., Nomura, Y., Kurihara, H., Apply blockchain technology to electric vehicle battery refueling, in: *Proc. 51st Hawaii Int. Conf. Syst. Sci.*, pp. 4494–4502, 2018.

36. Shokri, R., Theodorakopoulos, G., Le Boudec, J.-Y., Hubaux, J.-P., Quantifying location privacy, in: *Proc. IEEE Symp. Secur. Privacy*, pp. 247–262, 2011.

Part 1

BLOCKCHAIN: OPPORTUNITIES FOR HEALTHCARE 4.0

BTCG4: Blockchain Technology in Electronic Healthcare Systems

Amrinder Singh[1] and Geetika Madaan[2*]

[1]Department of Management Studies, Jain (Deemed to be University), India
[2]University Center for Research and Development, Chandigarh University,
Punjab, India

Abstract

Healthcare providers are using emerging technology to implement creative clinical services that support systems. The need for healthcare data sharing necessitates the integration of various departmental structures. However, the exchange of data inevitably imposes constraints on both security and integrity. It has estimated that hundreds of millions of personal medical data have been conceded last year and are growing exponentially. Because of the new decentralized digital technologies such as blockchain, privacy and secrecy have increased over the last few decades. We already have immense support for sectors such as banking, government, healthcare, and more. Healthcare providers have begun applying blockchain technology to allow a safer and more decentralized storing, recording, and exchanging of patient information. This newly developed blockchain technology holds incredible benefits for patient privacy and data security. We learned in this study that there are still many areas to learn about the use of blockchain technology, particularly in electronic healthcare and medicine. The literature is studied to discover benefits, risks, and issues of people and the other side of technology. The study also explored the methods that have been established and commented on their shortcomings and outlined several accessible problems and investigation avenues that are still waiting to discover.

Keywords: Blockchain, electronic, industry, healthcare, technology

*Corresponding author: Geetumadaan2009@gmail.com

Kiran Sood, Rajesh Kumar Dhanaraj, Balamurugan Balusamy and Seifedine Kadry (eds.) Blockchain Technology in Corporate Governance: Transforming Business and Industries, (31–56) © 2023 Scrivener Publishing LLC

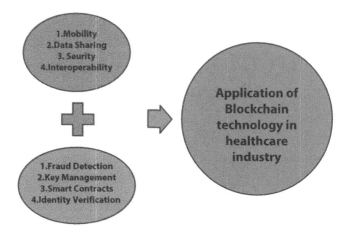

Figure 2.1 Application of blockchain technology in electronic healthcare industry.

2.1   Introduction

Blockchain was launched as a technological and architectural platform in 2009 [1]. Blockchain works on decentralized distribution of storage data across all computers of the blockchain architecture [2]. The structuring of blockchain technology is peer-to-peer and compatible with both network users and nodes. The ledger is kept in a decentralized node network generated via cryptographic procedures that all network miners calculate [3]. Furthermore, the blockchain leader has extremely reliable storage capabilities thanks to consensus, digital signatures, and hash chains [3]. Because of these advanced features, Blockchain allows storing all data in a decentralized public manner, following users' privacy via fraud detection, data sharing, security, and interoperability (Figure 2.1) [3]. Blockchain technology is used in several industries, including banking, finance, property, and government [4, 5]. While most of the studies emphasize on the applications of blockchain technology in banking and finance, healthcare industry has recently begun to focus more on blockchain enabled applications [6]. Many academics have emphasized the potential of blockchain technology to solve current health issues [7, 8].

2.1.1   Healthcare Industry

Because of extra-legal obligations to safeguard patient medical information, healthcare has specific security and privacy problems as the use of mobile healthcare via the Internet increases and cloud storage, the danger of harmful attacks, and the possibility of sensitive information being compromised [9]. Because health information is readily accessible by smart devices and many physicians have access to it, it is a question of sharing and privacy. System security, interoperability, sharing of information, and mobile health problems are special needs for the medical business in the healthcare sector. Each requirement by the healthcare sector related to handling of medical data is described in depth in the following section.

2.1.2   Requirement of Electronic Healthcare Industry

2.1.2.1   System Security

As stated above, restriction of access, authentication and non-repudiation with access to healthcare and medical records, for instance, are critical safety criteria to guarantee medical data integrity, trust, and accessibility [10, 11]. Examples of medical information include patient and medical information gathered via body sensors and other applications. Additional security and role-based rights are needed when medical data is moved from paper to digital media to protect confidentiality and safety in health records [12]. As health records, for instance, are kept in databases, access to them should be limited to authorized people, and access should be implemented and managed. Health data and access inquiries need audits and rigorous access restrictions to reduce the possibility of impairment or duplication [13]. Additionally, health data encryption may be a challenge if multiple coding standards are utilized in various systems (e.g., EMR) (Figure 2.2) [14]. Currently available data protection and security measures have shown that they are ineffective when compared to what is required, and disclosing medical information to a patient may have negative repercussions in the real world (e.g., threats to patients' privacy from unreceptive attacks that may jeopardize the record's reputation and finances.) [15].

2.1.2.2   Interoperability

Interoperability is also a major health industry need. Interoperability is the way data are shared and transferred across various sources [16]. The main obstacle to interoperability is the dependence on central data storage by medical organizations. Medical practitioners have an issue with centralized data storage because all records in one single database are maintained. The specific problems arising from centralized data stock include health data distribution, delayed medical information access, patient advocacy organizations, and a lack of system interoperability. Health research requires both

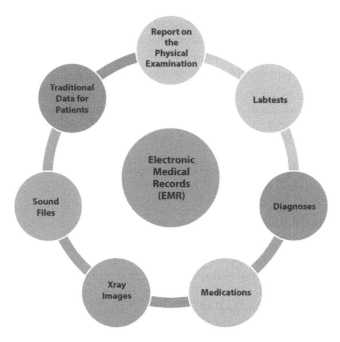

Figure 2.2 The requirement of blockchain technology in the process of EMR (electronic media records).

high-quality and large-volume data sets [17]. Many records are generated every day and kept centrally in many hospitals [18]. Data distributed in various institutions may be lost, and the patient cannot recover the data [17]. Many records are dispersed when health records are consolidated. Centralized data authority is necessary for maintaining a loyal network database.

2.1.2.3   Sharing of Information

Information sharing and access are a security issue as well as a civic health record problem. Health data may be difficult to share since complete data can be kept at several places. Health records are dispersed across numerous organizations, making it difficult to exchange them since the connection between the datasets depends on entities with or without a common ID, such as a social security number. These dispersed patient records are not unanimous, and that applies to healthcare professionals because they cannot get up-to-date patient information elsewhere [19]. Interoperability is a key element in data sharing.

2.1.2.4 Mobility

Mobility is becoming an increasingly important need in the health indus-try, as patients increasingly want their data to be mobile. The ability to send this data becomes even more important as smart gadgets, sensors, and other internet devices are becoming more common. The challenge of keeping secure and protected data is compounded by the legislation's need that data be communicated in real-time and accessible from any location on any device [9]. For this study, the mobility idea is divided into three major components: mobile health, Wireless and Internet technology, and the Internet of Things (IoT).

2.1.2.5 Mobile Health

Mobile health is a developing and fast-emerging application in the health-care sector that includes devices such as thumbnails, body-wireless net-works, and cellphones. Numerous problems impacting centralized healthcare with a broad-based server infrastructure are exacerbated by mHealth. Special problems include data sharing, consent management, access control, authentication, and user trust [20, 21]. There are many resources available to ensure the privacy and security of the Wireless Sensor Network (WSN) or the Internet of Things but are poorly con-trolled, and Patients may be harmed by compromised healthcare informa-tion. Therefore, mobile medical care applications may be beneficial [21]. Additionally, devices may be lost or linked to an unencrypted network; It may lead to malware or other harmful attacks. These dangers emerge as a result of health organizations using technology without adequate data protection [20].

Another aspect of healthcare technology is wearable technology that raises major safety issues. Due to the health sensitivity and legislative pro-tection inherent in wearable technology, unique privacy concerns have arisen. Sensors, devices, and smart technologies are concerned about the confidentiality of information, the preservation or use of data, the change of data, repudiation, non-auditing, and loss of authenticity or validity [22].

2.1.2.6 Wireless

A network for wearable body sensing may be used, and related security risks include information integrity, data accuracy, netbook accessibil-ity, authentication of data, safe management, credibility, secure placing, accountability, and flexibility [23]. Wireless Body Area Network devices will likewise be limited to resources. Thus, lightweight security solutions are necessary.

Other wearable healthcare technologies include that the information may be destroyed, that the device can disintegrate, or that the user can treat the data to his advantage. An effective compromise between critical equipment Implanted medical devices, such as insulin, which may deliver life-saving medicines, and non-essential equipment might have severe or deadly implications for health [24]. These safety concerns and health dangers linked to health attacks must be resolved before large-scale deployments deal significantly with wireless applications [24].

2.1.2.7   Internet of Things

In the healthcare sector, the popularity of IoT technology is increasing, with customers increasingly ready to make healthy choices. Patients are also proactive in their medical treatment. This customization may take the shape of intelligent gadgets and smart sensors, which collect and remotely transmit patient's doctor critical health information to examine and evaluate chronic diseases. IoT methods for health and patient care include intelligent horns, contact lenses, fitness tapes, skin microchips, wireless sensors, and others [25]. These wireless systems sometimes do not consider security. Also, databases and Internet of Things (IoT) devices are among the most vulnerable systems that contain many vulnerabilities and misuse points that may jeopardize security.

Wireless IoT threats may take the form of aggressive or passive attacks [26]. When data packets are distributed all around the system, a passive attack may change packet destinations or interfere with routing protocol [26]. An attacker may remove or "drop" the packets to reveal the data within (catch them while they are transiting across the network or wireless area) [26]. When an attacker actively exploits a device or network vulnerability to identify, steal, or obtain information about a device or network user, this is referred to as an active attack [26]. To get medical information from IoT devices, the hostile actor may use several methods, including data manipulation, impersonation attacks, eavesdropping, and playback [26]. Attackers may attack system security, administrative security, physical security, and computer security weaknesses [26].

Concerns raised regarding the privacy of health-related IoT applications include identity protection. Confidentiality of location, the confidentiality of data, confidentiality of one's footprint, and confidentiality of the owner [27].

The next part will briefly overview of blockchain technology, specific characteristics, Application of blockchain technology, opportunities, and challenges relevant to the healthcare sector (Figure 2.4).

2.2   Overview of Blockchain

Blockchain is a record-keeping system that makes altering, hacking, or cheating difficult or impossible. A blockchain is essentially a distributed transaction record that is duplicated and dispersed across the whole computer system network of blockchain. The emergence of blockchain technology facilitated the healthcare industry in coming times. The Figure 2.3 explains the role of blockchain technology in healthcare industry.

Blockchain technology has several advantages that may be beneficial to the healthcare industry [5]. These characteristics are built into the system and applications to a wide range of systems and industries. The specific characteristics that must be addressed here include security, authentication,

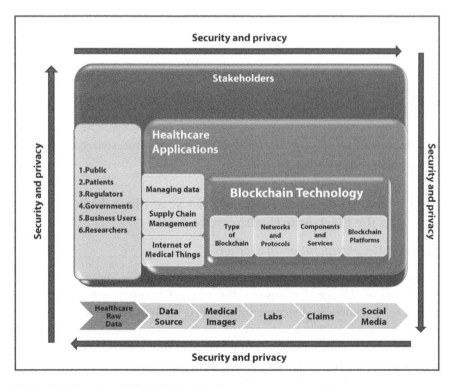

Figure 2.3 Overview of blockchain technology.

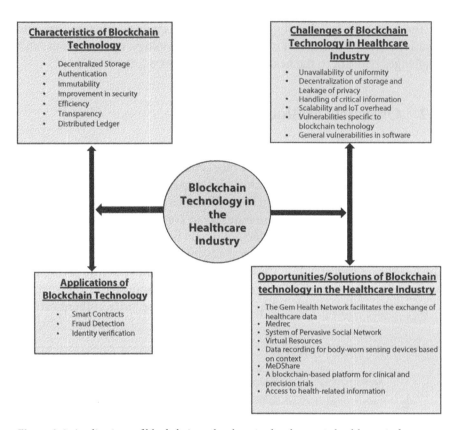

Figure 2.4 Applications of blockchain technology in the electronic healthcare industry.

and decentralized storage, immutability, efficiency, transparency, distributed ledger, Improvement in security.

2.2.1   Distinct Characteristics of the Use of Blockchain in the Electronic Healthcare Industry

2.2.1.1   Decentralization of Storage

One of the important components of blockchain technology is the decentralization of storage that ensures the system's security and data validation [28]. Decentralized storage implies that the blockchain leader breaks record storage from one main server to many servers and makes it simpler to obtain medical information faster, interoperability with systems, patient agencies, improved data quality, and quantities of medical research [1]. For example, IoT and cloud providers may utilize blockchain technology to share secure and confidential data. Blockchain systems are characterized by data security, integrity, and immutability [17]. Blockchain technology may ensure the safekeeping of storage data across various mainframe processors rather than keeping it in a single location by utilizing its secure and decentralized ledger. A transaction may spread across the whole blockchain network using the distributed storage technique, establishing a plethora of redundant data sources that may be utilized to verify the transaction's legitimacy [17]. A hostile actor cannot change the data on any of the network's systems due to its redundancy without modifying the data on any of the network's systems; this enables immutability, assurance, and security [29].

The blockchain architecture enables cloud-based services, such as intelligent gadgets or Internet of Things (IoT) devices, to serve such edge hosts as near as possible to the devices while maintaining a decentralized architecture that improves security and administration. Additionally, blockchain enables safe data exchange by allowing the origin, auditing, and management of data stored on cloud-based servers that house medical information shared among large data corporations [30]. Additionally, blockchain enables safe data exchange by ensuring the provenance, auditing, and management of cloud servers that store medical data shared among large data corporations. Additionally, blockchain technology enables consumer server networks by establishing an auditable and secure infrastructure [30].

2.2.1.2 Authentication

The decentralized blockchain design also ensures the validity of papers or other private data placed on chain blocks [31]. For generating, altering, or reading data on the blockchain, a unique private key associated with a public key is required [31]. These keys are kept in a software component known as "Bitcoin wallet" associated with a "Bitcoin address." While Bitcoin and cryptocurrencies are frequently utilized in these software applications, they may be adjusted to offer different authentications by utilizing the same encryption technique [31]. This authentication technique is being tested to see whether it can verify identity and provide evidence of identity from official papers to private records of health [31].

2.2.1.3 Immutability

Immutability is one of Blockchain's main characteristics. Unchangeable transactions prevent any part (e.g., government or company) from manipulating, substituting, or falsifying network data. Irreversibility ensures a high level of data integrity since all previous transactions may be verified at any point in time. The immutability of public blockchains can improve the existing system of trust and auditing of financial transactions. It can potentially decrease the amount of time and money spent on audits since validating information becomes easier or redundant. Many companies benefit from immutability because it gives them a complete historical record of their business operations, which helps from become more efficient overall. A verified, common source of truth, which is enabled by immutability, may also help to bring clarity to many business conflicts.

A high degree of transparency is provided by blockchain technology, which shares transaction information amongst all the users who are engaged in such transactions. Due to the lack of requirement for a third party in a blockchain setting. It is easier to do business while still guaranteeing a trustworthy workflow.

2.2.1.4   Improvement in Security

Security is an important consideration for any new technology. However, Blockchain is more secure than others since it uses a public key architecture that guards against hostile activities that would alter data in a network. The participants in the blockchain network put their faith in the integrity and security characteristics of the consensus process, which they believe to be reliable. Furthermore, blockchain removes the single point of failure that may harm the whole system [12].

2.2.1.5   Efficiency

In comparison to the traditional centralized design, blockchain technology enhances it by spreading database records across the different users that are participating in the blockchain network. Since transactions are dispersed, it is simpler to verify all database entries since they are accessible. Blockchain is efficient in cost, settlement time, and risk management [19].

2.2.1.6   Distributed Ledger

In the cryptocurrency world, a blockchain is a public ledger that contains information on all of the participants as well as all of the digital transactions that have ever been carried out on the network. The "prevailing" portion of a blockchain is intended to maintain track of the most recent transactions, and after they are finished, it is added to the blockchain as an entry point. The blocks are added sequentially, each carrying the preceding block's hash. In the blockchain database, each block generates a new block.

This system records and distributes each transaction throughout the network. This means that any user on the network may verify transactions and add them to the ledger. Changing the ledger is reflected in all copies in minutes or seconds. The participant controls the security and correctness of assets using 'keys' and signatures.

2.3   Blockchain Applications

Blockchain technology and its inherent properties may be broadly diverse uses in various industries [7]. Applications are different since they are not integrated into the system itself but instead are methods used to fulfill a new nee using blockchain technology [13]. Smart contracts, spotting and preventing fraudulent activity, and Authentication of the user's identity are explored as applications. These three applications have been chosen as research applications to solve the health concerns identified in the preceding section.

2.3.1.1   Smart Contracts

Smart contracts are an important use of blockchain technology because they enable users or agencies to enter into arrangements with one another to build legally binding documents via the blockchain system [5]. Smart contracts are autonomous actors in blockchain technology encrypting and transforming transactions in contracts for use in legal documents [7]. These smart contracts include programs that are stored with their unique address on blockchain technology, which enable the monitoring and verification of these smart contractions [5]. Smart contracts allow for fair transactions and decentralized communication between parties [7]. A user who may develop his papers without a legal official or notary's assistance eliminates the high cost and time restrictions that enable a more efficient movement of resources and actions [5].

2.3.1.2   Spotting and Preventing Fraudulent Activity

Another use of blockchain technology is in the identification of fraud. In order to detect fraud or other malicious activity, a technique of validating a document or other data system is used to identify the information contained therein. For example, avoiding the insertion of fake reviews into online review systems via badmouthing and voting stuffing or financial-sector fraud, such as loan applications [32].

The relatively new concept of crowdsourcing is another field of study [33].

Crowdfunding is a method where many people contribute money or purchase shares in a company to gain equity [5]. Blockchain technology may significantly enhance the simplicity, security, and efficiency of equity crowdfunding transactions and transfers. They function as a low-cost stock and share registration platform for investors and businesses to enable peer-to-peer transactions. Additionally, blockchain technology may provide a method for shareholders to vote on corporate governance, helping authorities assess market dynamics and avoiding investment fraud [5].

2.3.1.3   Authentication of the User's Identity

In addition to the health industry, many online businesses have created their identity verification methods. Many businesses and governments now depend on passenger authentication via passports and fingerprints [31]. Blockchain technology is an alternative to government-funded identity verification [31]. Apart from these countries, blockchain technology can identify of a user [31]. It may be used in notarizing marriages, birth certificates, and business contracts [31]. The blockchain would utilize the distributed booklet to make it possible for the person to prove their existence at a particular time and place, which several individuals would confirm because of its distributed nature.

2.4   Challenges Associated with Blockchain Technology

While blockchain technology has many advanced features, there are still many limitations and problems to be addressed. The chapter addresses specific constraints such as unavailability of uniformity, confidentiality, handling of critical information, overhead associated with the Internet of Things, alongside hardware and software vulnerabilities that allow blockchain to function while not being adequately protected.

2.4.1   Unavailability of Uniformity

As blockchain technology is a relatively new and unrefined technology, no standards limit widespread acceptance and impede development [29]. In several months, blockchain technology is being considered for use in government-related activities, such as elections. Many countries, like Estonia, are attempting to establish e-residency by merging current residency laws with blockchain technology, which is the procedure for registering for an online service account that validates and enables citizens to vote online in the state where they live [31]. Other academics have examined the potential to use blockchain technology in their social and tax systems [29]. A high degree of consistency across all stakeholders is needed to enable all these different infrastructures and applications. The need for standards and compliance increases are more Nations adopt blockchain as a solution [29].

2.4.2   Decentralization of Storage and Leakage of Privacy

For blockchain technology, decentralized storage is a critical problem because it enables users to trade data across many services without relying on a single source of information [2]. Users must get information from the distributed public record, which poses a significant privacy risk. This is the primary drawback of decentralized systems, so they are not recommended [2]. Users who need access to their data must provide a secret key for validating and converting information from cyphertext to plaintext, resulting in a possible breach of their privacy. When a validation or decryption procedure begins, the information is not kept locally as it would be with a central database and ensure that the public key may be accessed across the network. In light of the strict requirements of the healthcare industry, this is a healthcare problem.

2.4.3   Handling of Critical Information

Various encryption methods, including the usage of private and public keys, are used to screen blockchain data [3]. For blockchain technology to be secure and private, like any other technology that can retain information, necessitates the establishment of processes to guarantee that information is kept secure and private. Blockchain data is open and shared among all parties since it is maintained open and accessible to everyone, and key activation is required for most cryptographic operations; as a result, some kind of encryption/access control is required [3]. The current key management techniques are incompatible with blockchain technology, which is being developed because it is unsafe to use a single key for all blocks at the same time. One key per block is inefficient because of the massive storage costs, and an unusually large number of keys are linked with each block ever built.

According to the company, creating a decentralized and trustworthy cloud data architecture that allows for the manipulation of records is the aim of cloud data infrastructure in blockchain technology, increasing data accountability, and improving data privacy and accessibility [34–36].

2.4.4   Scalability and Internet of Things Overhead

Another blockchain application is the scalability and Internet of Things overhead that enables individuals to keep their own health records while increasing interoperability and data exchange among healthcare providers [2]. Scalability is an issue in blockchain systems since the number of users increases the calculation requirements of the whole blockchain architecture [9]. This gets more complicated as users with more smart devices or sensors increase because they have less calculation capacity than normal computers, and a substantial share of the resource requirements are discharged to other computers like a random device or the cloud.

Most Internet of Things devices, typical sensors with limited computing capabilities, cannot meet these criteria. As a result, despite performing their intended tasks, devices may lack the computing power required to take advantage of blockchain capabilities. In an IoT context, may IoT blockchain systems are computationally expensive and have a large overhead bandwidth, which causes data delays and high-power processing to be used. Consequently, devices may perform sub-optimally or excessively, preventing concurrent use of the original software or blockchain application [19].

2.4.5   Vulnerabilities Specific to Blockchain Technology

Several vulnerabilities related to the blockchain system implementation and design have also been discovered. Vulnerabilities specific to the blockchain technology include block withholding, 51 percent attacks, double expenditures attacks, eclipse attacks, block throwing attacks, rising difficulty attacks, and issues with the blockchain anonymity [37]. The consensus mechanism is a key part of blockchain since it allows the development of an ecosystem that is manipulative since miners or a group of authorized participants checking each transaction on every digital asset are verified [37]. Miners have to make significant computational efforts to verify transactions and often require and incentive, which is often the solution to a cryptographic equation [37].

A retention attach occurs when hostile actors successfully remove blocks from a network but do not reinstall them once they have been properly removed. Instead, the miner simply delivers partial block responses that do not meet the system criteria [37]. Since each share lowers the capacity of another mine operator to offer effective solutions, they do not reduce the block or the pool's expected revenue [37]. As a result, a delectable actor keeping the completely valid blocks limits others' ability to find a whole solution, reducing their income. This behavior nonetheless improves incentives for the malicious actor since the latter may supply the pool manager with as many blocs as feasible, each of which contains a portion of the solution [37]. A 51% attack is comparable to a holdback attack because a minor has greater information technology reserves and accepts blockchain transactions, managing blockchain contents [37]. A double-spending attack duplicates digital information from cryptocurrencies to use the same digital money for multiple transactions [37]. Selfish miners willingly invalidate honest miner efforts by selectively unveiling influence rewards; the private chain mining pool must be operating at specific pool states. An eclipse attack exploits the peer-to-peer nature of the blockchain [37]. To be more precise, the eclipse attack uses the randomly chosen eight peers to sustain the link between the peer networks. The use of rapidly repeated automatic linking appeals significantly raises the chance of obtaining a connection that it is believed that these are the eight nodes responsible for sustaining the connection in order to commit fraud.

BDAs (block discarding attacks) are used to obtain knowledge about freshly mined blocks ahead of the rest of the network by establishing an abnormally high number of network connections [37]. This allows the attacker to avoid releasing real miners.

The blockchain's pseudo anonymity is another possible disadvantage, referring to the public's access to all transactions' records [37]. Private information is kept hidden until, under some situations, it is given to anybody to verify past transactions that involve the user. However, this knowledge may be helpful in an audit or forensic research path. A forked attack is a kind of Blockchain attack that is distinct from the others [37]. The concept behind an onslaught assault is that if members of a blockchain system discuss and agree on potential branches, blocks may take after mining and confirmation. The technique leads to a theoretical attack (called a balanced attack), in which a malicious actor may construct a branch that could be isolated from the rest of the network in front of the actor and merge this branch into a rival blockchain to affect the process of branch selection. This is accomplished via the use of the GHOST protocol, which represents a block known as an uncle or a sister block and is responsible for selecting the blockchain. The last element of blockchain technology is to compensate miners properly for their work. It is not profitable for the miners to use computer resources unless they benefit from them. To enable blockchain transactions or build new blocks cannot be facilitated [37].

2.4.6   General Vulnerabilities in Software

Blockchain also has several typical software defects that allow destructive attacks. These damaging attacks may help other crimes, like robbery and data exfiltration [38]. On a blockchain, identity theft happens when a person steals his or her private key, allowing the hostile actor to terminate anything recorded by the victim on the blockchain [38]. Illegal operations, including illegal firearms, drugs, and another trafficking, maybe anonymously distributed via the distributed headline. Furthermore, poorly maintained blockchain software for implementation may be exploited like Bitcoin Exchange, which permits double costs to deploy bitcoins or other cryptocurrencies [38].

2.5   Opportunities of Blockchain in the Healthcare Industry

Blockchain technology offers a wide variety of technologies for healthcare applications. Many recent experiments and publications in each of the topics listed below demonstrate roadblocks for healthcare and specific software applications:

2.5.1   The Gem Health Network Facilitates the Exchange of Healthcare Data

The healthcare industry handles a large volume of private data and documents that are subject to strict regulation; similar is the Health Insurance Portability and Accountability Act (HIPAA) of 1996. Since these documents are often kept in one location, they are susceptible to the security mentioned above and interoperability problems. Especially if a patient needs specialist care in a different hospital or state, or nation, and if confidential information about the patient may be revealed, this may be an issue (e.g., if a surgery involving medical travel is wrong and the patient requires immediate medical therapy) [39]. Interchangeable medical communication protocols are being revised, updating different medical records, and mismatched IT interfaces are just a few of the challenges that result in time consumption of resources and extensive authentication and processing of data by all parties [39].

The Gem Health Network has produced a potential answer for this by utilizing a shared Ethereum Blockchain technology-based network design. The Gem Health Network provides healthcare professionals with access to equal health information to overcome major storage limitations. Medical information is relevant, clear, and allows consumers to obtain in real-time the latest treatment information. The risk of medical malpractice caused by obsolete information may be reduced, and health problems caused by this ignorance can be avoided [39].

2.5.2   MDREC

MDREC is a decentralized record management system developed by Azaria, Ekblaw, Vieira, and Lippman and accomplished the storage of electronic medical data via the usage of blockchain technology [17]. Because of this technology, patients may access their medical information in real-time across various doctors and treatment locations [17]. Blockchain technology allows identification, privacy, accountability, and data sharing by interacting with providers' current on-premises data storage. This method guarantees patient-provider communication. A network of miners is required to complete blockchain transactions. By rewarding medical stakeholders for maintaining and safeguarding the network via PoW, MedRec encourages them to behave as miners. Patients and providers have the option to select whether or not to make their data publicly accessible as metadata a result of these incentives (data economics) [17]. Preparing for field trials, MedRec is a prototype that evaluates the framework's strategy and execution.

2.5.3   System of Pervasive Social Network

Zhang, Zue, and Huang played a pivotal role in the creation of a highly regarded security mechanism for the pervasive social network (PSN) [40]. The PSN is the foundation for mobile computing and wireless sensor devices [40]. The researchers have suggested two solutions to protect the medical system through PSN [40]. A secure mobile device connection and low resource sensor nodes with unexpected compute needs are required for this first protocol. A secure connection between WBAN sensor nodes and mobile devices is made possible by this protocol. The second protocol makes use of blockchain technology to enable PSN nodes to communicate and share health data inside the network.

2.5.4   Virtual Resources

The idea of virtual resources, developed by Samaniego and Deters, is described in detail (2016). It is intended to be used as IoT management structure software, and it usually provides a variety of services [41]. The installation of multi-tenancy and load balancing on specific edge servers is made possible as a result (technology that can compute faster than the Internet of Things-enabled devices). Following are the issues that the suggested method solves in relation to the Internet of Things edge devices: lacking virtualization and abstraction support; nonexistence of a method for safe software distribution on edge hosts [41]. Furthermore, virtual resources may be utilized in conjunction with the existing IoT system to create a virtual system of the Internet of Things. A digital object that may be connected to any other part of the Internet of Things, including other virtual resources [41], is also defined as follows: An infinite number of IoT systems may be added to the current IoT system, allowing for a more flexible configuration of the system. Moreover, applications are managed by accessing by accessing or using other residual services and building such views on existing components to understand their internal status [41].

This method turns virtual resources into a tool for managing multi-tenancy since each lifestyle makes use of its own virtual source set because they may be placed closer to the edge and provide restricted access and load-flow mechanisms, and because they can be used to manage multitenancy [41]. A major issue for edge devices is blockchain compatibility, dependent on permission for safe code use, which presents a huge challenge [41]. As part of its architecture, blockchain would include a code or signature and edge devices would receive blockchain information and act on it. It is also feasible to transmit code into the Internet of Things devices without causing device safety and security problems, as shown by the IBM ADEPT technology [41].

2.5.5   Data Recording for Body-Worn Sensing Devices Based on Context

Nearby devices preserve forensic data fingerprints in Bloom filters as witnesses in context data recording [42]. Logging requires little maintenance. The idea came from retrieving forensic evidence by using wearable technology. It is important to recognize the risks and difficulties associated with body-worn sensing devices [42]. Risks include data loss device failure, and unauthorized data access (e.g., claims). For example, medical sensors may be used to gather medical data by a third party [42]. A wireless pacemaker installed in former US Vice President Dick Cheney raised concerns about suicide [42].

To prevent retroactive data tempering, a secure data recording technique that chains blocks of measurements from various periods is proposed (the concept leverages blockchain technology), Sensor devices also include Bloom filters to guarantee the system is lightweight and resource-efficient [42]. A Bloom Filter is a data-free probabilistic database structure [42].

A portal captures all conversations with sensors and converts them into a centralized server in blocks [42]. Each successor block duplicates the previous block's hash value and the chain [42]. Sensor devices also record network conversations between other parties on the same network and transmit them to the gateway, which serves as a witness [42]. Bloom filters are used to capture all signals heard (or fingerprinted) to save memory use and network traffic while allowing simple and precise verification [42]. A synchronization protocol is used for gateways and sensors at the start of each period, and all witnesses are digitally signed, and Bloom filters are uploaded to the central server at the end.

2.5.6   MeDShare

In order to address the issue of medical data sharing among doctors who maintain data in an unsustainable way, MeDShare was created [30]. The health sector has a significant challenge in protecting patient privacy while reducing the danger of medical data misuse, which may cause serious reputational and financial damages [30]. The solution uses blockchain technology to offer cloud-based data provenance, monitoring, and administration for large medical businesses [30]. The solution uses blockchain technology to offer data provenance, monitoring, and administration across large businesses [30]. The solution uses blockchain technology to offer large medical businesses cloud-based data provenance, monitoring, and administration [30]. A smart contract monitors data and prevents unauthorized access to the system [30]. On the other hand, the architecture employs intelligent contracts and data monitoring to detect systemic infringements and misbehavior [30]. To share health data with medical institutions that are not or are not in danger of patient privacy, MeDShare was created [30].

Based on blockchain technology, MeDShare has four tiers [30]. To access system data, a user must first be authenticated. A system may access, process, send, or reply to queries in the data query layer. These actions are then subdivided into two distinct categories: the querying system, which is in charge of handling the request, as well as the trigger, which is responsible for translating activities between the smart contract environment and external settings. The second level is the data structure and source layer, which includes many components for processing access requests by several companies in the current database infrastructure.

2.5.7   Blockchain-Based Clinical and Precise Platform Trials

The blockchain clinical testing and precision medicine platform is built on blockchain technology [21]. This method improves data integrity in clinical trials, addressing the problem of clinical trials reporting data incorrectly. However, the blockchain paradigm provides more transparency and accuracy in clinical trial data processing [21]. Aside from that, the blockchain would make it possible to conduct peer-to-peer clinical studies. This enables colleagues to review and analyze clinical studies without jeopardizing the ownership of the data in question (e.g., trial procedures in medicine) [21]. This system design solves two issues with clinical data processing: mutually unbreakable confidentiality and cooperation [21].

2.5.8   Access to Health-Related Information

Individuals may get medical information via a healthcare data portal powered by Blockchain technology. As a result, patients will have more access to and control over their personal information. A developed processing capacity and design for smartphone applications, smartphone app stores, and a 5G cloud-based wireless network were factors in the selection of access to health-related information [43]. An additional feature of the application would be creating a three-tiered gateway with the application, disconnected access to health-related information. With the technology, patients may control their data rather than depending on a third party to handle their data, and they can be notified when a third party accesses their data, as well [44].

2.6   Concluding Remarks

To sum up, blockchain technology can deal with various issues in the health sector. The most exciting part of blockchain technology is its thorough research of potential applications in the health sector; moreover, due to the general leader and bloc design, the concepts of security, integrity, decentralization, availability, and authentication are all important. The rapid growth of IoT, smart devices, and sensing devices poses difficulties to the healthcare sector, trying to adapt. A rapidly expanding technical infrastructure centered on web-enabled gadgets, the Internet of Things, smart devices, and sensing devices presents significant challenges for the healthcare sector. This technology enables the healthcare sector in an increasingly interconnected world to provide better treatment to patients. However, malicious actors may exploit the weaknesses of this technology. This may result in out-of-date information that may result in health issues or misdiagnosis, as well as difficulties in confirming a patient's identification and obtaining consent. Following research and substantial work discussed in this chapter, blockchain technology can solve many current healthcare issues. Applications currently accessible include patient support, IoT security, record exchange, and interoperability. The goal is to empower patients by providing them with ownership over their medical data and the opportunity to share it with others safely.

The development of medical apps and smartphone applications has been accelerated. However, major security issues remain since blockchain is not without flaws. In order to empower people, the healthcare and other sectors that use blockchain technology must keep learning. A potential research framework is as follows:

Retention block attacks and mining incentives are two problems that need more research.

1. Because healthcare is a growing business, scalability is a major issue, particularly given the aging of our population. Through blockchain activities, the number of system participants or patients continues to grow at an alarming rate. In order to ensure the scalability of healthcare, further research is required in the area of blockchain.

2. The additional study must be undertaken using open-source data sets that enable other scientists to evaluate findings and draw conclusions. Many studies aiming at proof-of-concept and cooperation between health organizations and academics must assess suggested solutions using real-world health data. (for example, protection, speed, scalability, and additional critical considerations such as data security).

3. Further research should focus on key management, security, and fast replacement of lost or misplaced keys.

4. It is also necessary to research the verification of identity. Many studies are intended to give patients access to patient information in advance; but, in the event of an emergency, safety protocols or emergency procedures may be utilized, and a doctor may access data without the patient's permission.

Several advantages of blockchain technology are immediately apparent, and they may potentially be used to address a variety of data sharing and security issues in the health industry. On the other hand, Blockchain cannot be pushed into every scenario. Mining incentives, a crucial mechanism for blockchain adoption in the healthcare industry, and specific blockchain attacks that may bring the system to a halt were not adequately addressed. An in-depth examination of certain blockchain problems and their implications for the healthcare sector, on the other hand, is required.

References

1. Danda, R., Vijay, C., Ronald, D., Blockchain technology: Emerging applications and use cases for secure and trustworthy smart systems. *J. Cybersecur. Priv.*, 1, 1, 4–18, 2020.
2. Zibin, Z., Shaoan, X., Hongning, D., Xiangping, C., Huaimin, W., An overview of blockchain technology: architecture, consensus, and future trends. *Proc. - 2017 IEEE 6th Int. Congr. Big Data, BigData Congr 2017*, pp. 557–564, 2017.
3. Huawei, Z., Yong, Z., Yun, P., Ruzhi, X., Lightweight backup and efficient recovery scheme for health blockchain keys. *Proc. - 2017 IEEE 13th Int. Symp. Auton. Decentralized Syst. ISADS 2017*, pp. 229–234, 2017.
4. Victor, C., Patricia, B., Hui, Z., Qianwen, X., Jingqi, Z., Mitra, A., How blockchain can impact financial services – The overview, challenges and recommendations from expert interviewees. *Technol. Forecast. Soc. Change*, 6, 1, 1–10, 2020.
5. Fran, C., Thomas, K.D., Constanttinos, P., A systematic literature review of blockchain-based applications: Current status, classification and open issues. *Telemat. Inform.*, 36, 4, 55–81, 2018.
6. Anushree, T., Amandeep, D., Najmul, I., Matti, M., Blockchain in healthcare: A systematic literature review, synthesizing framework and future research agenda. *Comput. Ind.*, 122, 122–127, 2020.
7. Anton, H., Katina, K., Danilo, G., Sindre, A.P., Arild, F., Blockchain in healthcare and health sciences—A scoping review. *Int. J. Med. Inform.*, 134, 12, 1–10, 2020.
8. Victoria, L.L., Darra, H., Hoda, H., Danielle, B., Ravneet, K., Having our 'omic' cake and eating it too?: Evaluating user response to using blockchain technology for private and secure health data management and sharing. *Front. Blockchain*, 3, 2, 1–9, 2021.
9. Yasan., A., Mohammad, A.O., Ahmed, T., EHealth cloud security challenges: A survey. *J. Healthcare Eng.*, 3, 1–15, 2019.
10. Hussien, H.M., Yasin, S.M., Udzir, S.N., Zaidan, A.A., Zaidan, B.B., A systematic review for enabling of develop a blockchain technology in healthcare

application: Taxonomy, substantially analysis, motivations, challenges, recommendations and future direction. *J. Med. Syst.*, 43, 10, 2–35, 2019.

11. Steve, G.L., Cyber-security issues in healthcare information technology. *J. Digit. Imaging*, 30, 1, 117–125, 2017.

12. Sabyasachi, D., Shakyawar, S.K., Mohit, S., Sandeep, K., Big data in healthcare: Management, analysis and prospects. *J. Big Data*, 6, 1, 2–25, 2019.

13. Jin, S., Lili, R., Shangping, W., Xiaomin, Y., A blockchain-based framework for electronic medical records sharing with fine-grained access control. *PloS One*, 15, 10, 1–23, 2020.

14. Shekha, C., Khandakar, A., Hua, W., Frank, W., Zhenxiang, C., Healthchain: A novel framework on privacy preservation of electronic health records using blockchain technology. *PloS One*, 15, 12, 1–35, 2020.

15. Salem., T.A. *et al.*, Cybersecurity of hospitals: Discussing the challenges and working towards mitigating the risks. *BMC Med. Inform. Decis. Mak.*, 20, 1–10, 2020.

16. Moritz, L., Julian, S., Andrea, E., Josef, S., Sylvia, T., Why digital medicine depends on interoperability. *NPJ Digit. Med.*, 2, 1–5, 2019.

17. Asaph, A., Ariel, E., Thiago, V., Andrew, L., MedRec: Using blockchain for medical data access and permission management. *Proc. - 2016 2nd Int. Conf. Open Big Data, OBD 2016*, pp. 25–30, 2016.

18. Shahidul., I.K., Abu, S.M., Latiful, H., Privacy and security problems of national health data warehouse: A convenient solution for developing countries. *Proc. 2016 Int. Conf. Netw. Syst. Secur. NSysS 2016*, pp. 1–5, 2016.

19. Alex, R., Cristiano, A.D.C., Rodrigo, D.R.R., OmniPHR: A distributed architecture model to integrate personal health records. *J. Biomed. Inform.*, 71, 70–81, 2017.

20. David, K., Carl, A.G., Santosh, K., Jonathan, P.W., Privacy and security in mobile health: A research agenda. *Physiol. Behav.*, 49, 22–30, 2016.

21. Munee, A.S. *et al.*, Privacy preservation in e-Healthcare environments: State of the art and future directions. *IEEE Access*, 6, 464–478, 2017.

22. Leonardo, H.I., Aakash, A., Ali, B., Security and privacy for mHealth and uHealth systems: A systematic mapping study. *IEEE Access*, 8, 150081–150112, 2020.

23. Samaher, A., Ibrahim, A., Mohammad, S., Shahaboddin, S., Survey of main challenges (security and privacy) in wireless body area networks for healthcare applications. *Egypt. Inform. J.*, 18, 113–122, 2017.

24. Jalal, A., Basit, S., Kashif, S., Wasif, J., Mehmet, A.O., Cybersecurity and privacy issues for socially integrated mobile healthcare applications operating in a multi-cloud environment. *Health Inform. J.*, 25, 315–329, 2019.

25. Jia, W., Zheng, J., Min, P., Tiegang, Y., Real-time monitoring and reminding of remote peritoneal dialysis system based on the principle of least squares. *Int. J. Nephrol. Kidney Fail.*, 7, 1–6, 2021.

26. Moshaddique, A.A., Jingwei, L., Kyungsup, K., Security and privacy issues in wireless sensor networks for healthcare applications. *J. Med. Syst.*, 36, 93–101, 2012.

27. Jayashree, K. and Babu, R., Privacy in the Internet of Things, in: *Advances in E-Business Research (AEBR)*, vol. 11, pp. 94–109, 2017.

28. Yuanfeng, C. and Dan, Z., Fraud detections for online businesses: A perspective from blockchain technology. *Financial Innov.*, 2, 1, 3–10, 2016.

29. Sana, M., Ahmad, K., Zanab, S., Kalsoom, S., Ejaz, A., Muhammad, I., Securing IoTs in distributed blockchain: Analysis, requirements and open issues. *Futur. Gener. Comput. Syst.*, 100, 325–343, 2019.

30. Qi, X., Emmanuel, B.S., Kwame, O.A., Jianbin, G., Xiaojiang, D., MeDShare : Trust-less medical data sharing among. *IEEE Access*, 5, 1–10, 2017.

31. Clare, S. and Eric, B., E-residency and blockchain. *Comput. Law Secur. Rev.*, 33, 470–481, 2017.

32. Shafaq, N.K., Faiza, L., Chirine, G., Elhadj, B., Anoud, B., Blockchain smart contracts: Applications, challenges, and future trends. *Peer-to-Peer Netw. Appl.*, 14, 2901–2925, 2021.

33. Rateb, J., Mohamed, K., Khalifa, A., Moez, K., Kamel, B., Blockchain for the internet of vehicles: A decentralized IoT solution for vehicles communication using ethereum. *Sensors (Switzerland)*, 20, 1–27, 2020.

34. Bhatathi, M., Lawanya, S., Seifedine, K., Sangsoon, L., Blockchain based cloud computing: Architecture and research challenges. *IEEE Access*, 8, 205190–205205, 2020.

35. Pratima, S., Rajni, J., Malaya, D.B., Blockchain technology for cloud storage: A systematic literature review. *ACM Comput. Surv.*, 53, 2–89, 2020.

36. Shuyun, S., Debiao, H., Li, L., Neeraj, K., Muhammad, K., Applications of blockchain in ensuring the security and privacy of electronic health record systems: A survey shuyun. *Comput. Secur.*, 1, 1–20, 2020.

37. Tosh, D.K., Shetty, S., Liang, X., Kamhoua, C.A., Kwiat, K.A., Njilla, L., Security implications of blockchain cloud with analysis of block withholding attack. *Proc. - 2017 17th IEEE/ACM Int. Symp. Clust. Cloud Grid Comput. CCGRID 2017*, vol. 4, pp. 458–467, 2017.

38. Jennifer, J.X., Are blockchains immune to all malicious attacks? *Financ. Innov.*, 2, 2–9, 2016.

39. Matthias, M., Blockchain technology in healthcare the revolution starts here. *2016 IEEE 18th Int. Conf. e-Health Networking, Appl. Serv. Heal. 2016*, pp. 16–18, 2016.

40. Jie, Z., Nian, X., Xin, H., A secure system for pervasive social network-based healthcare. *IEEE Access*, 4, 9239–9250, 2016.

41. Mayra, S. and Ralph, D., Hosting virtual IoT resources on edge-hosts with blockchain. *2016 IEEE International Conference on Computer and Information Technology*, vol. 11, pp. 116–119, 2020.

42. Muhammad, S., Syed, T.A., Vijay, S., Secure lightweight context-driven data logging for bodyworn sensing devices. *2017 5th International Symposium on Digital Forensic and Security (ISDFS 2017)*, p. 7, 2017.

43. Guang, Y., Chunlei, L., Kiell, E.M., A blockchain-based architecture for securing electronic health record systems. *Concurr. Comput. Pract. Exp.*, 5, 1–12, 2021.

44. Xiao, Y., Huiju, W., Dawei, J., Mingqiang, L., Wei, J., Healthcare data gateways: Found healthcare intelligence on blockchain with novel privacy risk control. *J. Med. Syst.*, 40, 1–8, 2016.

3

Blockchain Technology and Healthcare: Towards Combating COVID-19

Reena Malik* and Sonal Trivedi

Chitkara Business School, Chitkara University, Punjab, India

Abstract

Emergence of COVID-19 has negatively affected human health, lives, and the global economy. It has highlighted the problems in existing healthcare system especially in handling of public emergencies inadequately and this compelled healthcare industry to look for newer methods, innovations, and technologies to control and monitor the corona virus. Accurate data is required for taking measures to prevent from any kind of virus and blockchain technology plays a vital role in providing such up-to-date information helpful in tracking and controlling the spread of virus ranging from providing reliable supplies to data provenance . This paper will be divided into four sections, first section will discuss about blockchain technology and its role in healthcare. Further, in second section will discuss about various current and potential applications of blockchain technology in healthcare and subsequently it will explain how usage of blockchain technology in healthcare sector reviving the industry capabilities. At last, various challenges of blockchain technology in healthcare and future research guidelines will be discussed.

Keywords: Blockchain, healthcare, COVID-19, medical, distributed, secure

3.1 Introduction

Widespread outbreak of COVID-19 has impacted almost every sector like economy, healthcare, transportation, education worldwide. The World Health Organization (WHO) and respective governments across globe put stringent restrictions on movement in the form of lockdowns

---

*Corresponding author: reenamalik2008@gmail.com

Kiran Sood, Rajesh Kumar Dhanaraj, Balamurugan Balusamy and Seifedine Kadry (eds.) Blockchain Technology in Corporate Governance: Transforming Business and Industries, (57–74) © 2023 Scrivener Publishing LLC

suggested social distance as most significant measure in order to halt the spread of corona virus. People with pre-existing medical conditions are more vulnerable to COVID-19 [59]. Due to its high spread rate from human to human the medical supplies and hospital capacity has become scarce. Lack of coordination in healthcare system leads to delayed production of *Coronavirus vaccination*. Inadequate surveillance systems lead to unprecedented spread of this deadly virus. Healthcare sector of a country is directly connected with quality of life which can be improved further by addressing real health problems properly. Advanced healthcare systems now-a-days brought greater competitiveness especially in Pharmaceutical sector which helped overcoming various problems effectively [13], thus providing an environment of improved patient care and better record management of healthcare related documents. Medical data has been stored in various electronic devices which can be tampered or deleted leading to incorrect outcome and tarnish the image of healthcare system and society at large [43].

Using blockchain technology organizations can minimize the adverse effects of pandemic mitigating privacy and integrity concerns regarding patient information. In order to foster presentation of unified data and information sharing for improving coordination and minimizing negative effect of pandemic various features of blockchain technology like reliability immutability and transparency are being used widely [63]. Blockchain technology has the ability and potential to store and distribute massive data and solving complex problems related to data security, privacy, and integrity. From the past few years it has captured considerable attention of academicians and corporate as well.

Objectives of the Chapter

1. To understand the role and importance of blockchain technology in healthcare;
2. To explore the current and potential applications of blockchain technology in healthcareand their role in combating COVID-19 and other similar viruses;
3. To explore how blockchain technology assisting in reviving the capabilities of major players in healthcare industry;
4. To understand challenges of blockchain technology and recommend strategies for theirbetter use in the future by the healthcare industry.

3.1.1   Blockchain Technology in Healthcare

Blockchain has emerged as one of the most promising technology from the last decade first introduced in 2008 by Satoshi Nakamoto for peer to peer cash network Bitcoin. Blockchain technology is used to record transactions securely across many computers owing to its features such as decentralized, distributed, immutable ledger without assistance of third party [50].

Blockchain is a publically accessible decentralized ledger which records transaction providing immutability by a peer-to-peer network of computers. Records are arranged in block structure known as blocks. Each data block has its own digital fingerprints, called hash and every next block is connected with the previous block by hash [32, 56] in chronological order and the connected blocks are called blockchain. No modification can be done in any block as these are connected with next forming a chain, thus any tampering can be easily identifiable making blockchain data immutable. Today companies across industries have realized significance of blockchain technology and identifying ways to integrate such technology into their infrastructures for making revolutionary changes in this digitalized era.

Application of blockchain technology in healthcare sector is highly required being one of the slowest growing sectors. It can create value in healthcare by recording health records (decentralized), monitoring supply chain and many more. Aspects like immutability in blockchain technology has drawn considerable attention of healthcare sector as blockchain has the potential to provide improved record management and simplified claim processes in insurance [26]. Efficient and precise exchange of information from one person to another (may be machine) is required in healthcare like electronic health records [1, 20]. This exchange of information is called interoperability, which provides very secure environment for exchanging electronic health records among patients as well as other health providers irrespective of location of hospitals [4, 14, 61]. Increasing cost is one of the major concerns of industry when it comes to healthcare infrastructure [49]. Blockchain technology is providing positive outcomes in the form of improved record management, cost cutting, efficient use of health related data and optimizing business processes [34]. Companies in healthcare sector are exploring blockchain through its various applications in blockchain such as data management and security.

3.1.2   Features of Blockchain Technology

- Immutable – blockchain technology keeps permanent record of transactions. Information recorded in one block cannot be altered as every new block is connected with the previous one makes the data tamper free. Thus, it creates trust in the recorded information.
- Decentralized – Any node of the network can access and copy stored (in blockchain) file. Stakeholders can easily access the file which creates decentralization.
- Consensus Driven – Consensus model utilizing scarce resource check for validation of blocks independently by setting rules for the same. There is no role of central authority for running this mechanism.
- Transparent – transactions recorded in blockchain are open and can be accessed by parties anytime. This provides an attribute under which information can be accessed and tracked throughout life.

3.1.3   Applications of Blockchain in Healthcare

Blockchain technology has been considered as the most disruptive technology across globe. Companies are trying to adopt and integrate blockchain to innovate their business processes. Healthcare industry is one of them looking for adopting blockchain technology. A transparent healthcare system can be established by disruptive, distributed, and trusted ledger technology of blockchain in order to combat pandemic. A line of defense can be created through a network of connected devices. This section of paper discusses various potential applications which can prove beneficial in order to combat COVID-19 pandemic.

3.1.4   Data Management

Most of the companies especially in healthcare are data driven and generates huge amount of data growing significantly [45, 55]. Security and privacy of data has always been a matter of concern being violated by unauthorized access resulting damage to organizational capital and reputation. Access to health records should be according to different roles assigned to data users. Blockchain technology ensures seamless way to access such data.

One of such tool is MedRec [3] management system decentralized in nature where data operations and permissions are being recorded and executed by smart contracts in blockchain. MedRec provides comprehensive and immutable medical service and data by collaborating complete information of data access, authentication, auditing and sharing. To address control problems of posted ledgers [62] proposed approach for achieving the same by designing trust authorization node which prevent users for any unauthorized access and attack.

3.1.5   Electronic Health Record

Keeping track of data regarding status of patient's health recorded in paper based traditional record is cumbersome and tedious task [37]. There may be a possibility of patients getting improper treatment as these traditional records are more prone to error. Technological advancements like electronic health records have provided the opportunity to minimize errors, simplifying tasks and improved treatment quality [2]. Electronic health records provide better disease management and strengthen health providers' collaborations [52]. Various models have been designed by the researchers to share, secure and store electronic health records [65]. Chen [7] proposed a framework for sharing medical data securely by designing cloud storage for important medical data and accessed through digital archive having access rights for owner information. Similarly, Guo [15] proposed a scheme based on signature scheme through blockchain technology in order to validate Electronic health records having multiple authorities. In order to combat with new and diverse diseases pharmaceutical companies are working hard to improve the quality of existing medicines and inventing new medicines. These medicines have to follow a lengthy process to ensure safety and protection, avail patent and authority's approval. Major chunk of this process is occupied by clinical trials till it reaches to commercialization [48]. Such long process may result in drug recall owing to inadequate security and privacy [42]. Blockchain technology ensures privacy and security as it records every trial tamper-proof.

Using a smart contract can ensure adherence towards patent preservation and protection [57, 62]. Imitation of drugs is a global concern which extends huge risk to consumers [35, 51]. In order to check the feasibility of blockchain technology [51] developed a framework for surveillance in pharma to improve the identification and tracking of counterfeit drugs. Tseng [53] proposed Gcoin blockchain to create transparency in drug transaction data shared among healthcare providers, mediators like wholesalers and retailers. Transparency in recording drug transactions can make drug supply chain more surveillance and collaborative.

3.1.6   Claims and Billing Management

Healthcare industry is growing rapidly and having a worth of trillion dollars already [9]. Billing is a crucial aspect of effective service delivery and in healthcare too. Billing process includes various steps from patients' entering the hospital till the time patient checked out like billing, claim transmission; insurance claims [31]. Excessive charges from patients becoming abusive in healthcare industry due to lack of trust and transparency. Blockchain technology ensures transparency among doctors, patients, and insurance companies and removes mistrust [9, 38].

3.1.7   Pandemic Data Tracking

Nowadays most of the information has been gathered from social media platform. In case of COVID-19 information regarding cases and vaccination social media has been considered as a major source of information appetite. Information on social media platform has high probability of offering rumors and misinformation especially during pandemic. It has created an environment of extreme fear and panic among public due to its incapability to screen and verify the source of floating information [15, 18]. Information floating on social media about self-medication may turn harmful and gave boost to public not complying with government rules and restrictions pertaining to pandemic. Such false data regarding pandemic estimation and growth would prove meaningless [41, 44]. On the contrary, reliable data of pandemic can provide assistance to authorities in identifying most infected areas and policies can be framed to halt the spread of this deadly virus [36, 60]. Utilizing blockchain technology fake information and tampered data can be identified and tackled with the help of data provenance. Medical professionals and healthcare provides can be ensured of highly reliable and transparent data [24]. In order to identify fake news blockchain technology can be used to register and rank the information, further this information can be filtered on trustworthiness and reputation of news agencies.

3.1.8   Tracking PPE

Personal protective equipment (PPE) can prevent exposure and halt the spread of corona virus. During COVID-19 PPE were used by health professionals and front-liners to minimize their exposure to infected persons. In order to prevent exposure to infected people and surfaces various gloves, face masks, safety goggles, helmets and other protective measures were taken [10, 17]. Inaccurate data regarding demand and supply of PPE many countries faced shortage of such kits in hospitals. Medical professionals were used taps to patch the tore masks to prevent themselves from deadly virus and some experienced very low quality supplies for PPEs owing to sudden increase in demand and short supply of personal protective equipment [46, 51, 55].

Inefficiency in supply chain management process was one of the reasons for such low quality shipments. Tracing data provenance is inefficient with existing supply chain management system (centralized) which became a hindrance in identifying source, certification and additional details of PPEs. Healthcare organizations adapting blockchain [48] can surely get benefitted identifying frauds related PPEs and developing robust and resilient supply chain system [25]. Verification for authenticity, tampering and inadequate handling can be traced by participating organizations through blockchain systems. As all the important records, movements and modifications are recorded in distributed ledger. To forecast the demand of PPEs smart contracts can assist medial companies and government authorities in real time tracking and tracing. Traceability of PPEs support demand forecasting which further help in better allocating available personal protective equipment. With smart contacts potential shortage consequences can be minimized by automatically triggered notification for procurement.

3.1.9   Vaccine Monitoring

Immunization and its active administration highly required in order to halt the spread of corona virus. When trials were conducted for the vaccination, government authorities and research institutes major concern was safety, effectiveness, and genuinity of that vaccine as it may affect health negatively [23, 29]. Vaccine management system, which was centralized, faced problems related to security, disruptive vaccines and misusing the supply chain for malicious reasons. Various fake players in pharmaceutical industry distributed substandard vaccines in grey market made from substandard material [27] to needy and infected people which can cause harm. In such situation the possibility of forge has been increased in terms of production and expiration of vaccines. Here, blockchain technology can do wonders as it stores data permanently for various stages ranging from vaccine development to certification and allotment of vaccine to various organizations for the purpose of immunization. This recorded data can be accessed by health professionals and hospitals to identify and verify the data before further processing. Smart contacts can be used for providing notifications in real time and can detect frauds with zero downtime and eliminating need for service of third party in vaccine logistics. The records cannot be tampered due to immutability feature present in blockchain technology. Smart contacts can identify fake vaccine manufactured from unauthorized manufacturers and can check for condition of container (humidity, pressure etc.) in supply chain to protect vaccine [25, 27]. Automatic notification will be send by smart contracts to the authorities, if shipment gets violated.

3.1.10   Future Vaccination

In order to develop vaccinations and medicines medical data can be explored as crucial technique. Various researchers and scientists searched for earlier matching records of SARS and MERS occurred in 2002 and 2012 for understanding the spread of COVID-19.World health organization identified different causes for SARS and COVID-19 though they both belong to family of corona virus. With passing days researchers have identified various new symptoms apart from of existing symptoms of corona virus [33]. Researchers and scientists found around 80 percent of similarity between corona virus and earlier viruses towards both binding to same receptor, especially in genetic code and amino acid. The importance of preserving and maintaining digital records (with security and privacy) of medical data regarding corona virus is paramount. Maintaining such records helps in vaccine and drug development for corona virus and future pandemics like this. Blockchain technology can be utilized for storing such health records as distributed ledger assessable worldwide. Medical data recorded through blockchain offers shared data, immutable records, and validation.

3.1.11   Digital Contact Tracing

Social distancing can be considered as most effective tool to halt the spread of corona virus by preventing social interactions [16, 54]. It has been implemented by digital tracking of contacts which facilitate in breaking transmission chain monitoring and identified infected people and social gathering during incubation period of corona virus. In order to access proximity with infected person in social gatherings digital track system uses GPS and Bluetooth [34]. Blockchain technology ensures tamper free health records offering features of transparency and immutability [23]. Privacy of data regarding infected people can be preserved by encrypting contact history and location [21]. Social interaction data can be stored utilizing blockchain technology and access to be granted to only authorize users in order to preserve privacy [33].

3.1.12   Prescription Management

In order to deliver efficient healthcare service proper management of prescription is paramount. Prescription has been widely misused especially in large scale crisis [18]. Blockchain technology has been assisting in removing such impediments and managing proper prescription. Various blockchain based model has been proposed for effective prescription management. BlockMedx [33] is one of them based on Ethereum this platform securely store all the transactions performed in managing prescription process. Before offering drugs to patient on the basis of prescription issued by doctor, a pharmacist can verify it through blockchain. Heisenberg [30] tracks prescription providing different platforms (portals) for healthcare providers, pharmacists and patients. Various applications like ScriptDrop are engaged in delivering drugs to patients and tracking drug usage using virtual assistants. ScalaMed [39] is another blockchain based platform providing solution for prescription tracking including past prescription as well and reducing medicine mismanagement.

3.2   Combating COVID-19

Blockchain technology can be utilized to effectively combat situations of health emergency like COVID-19 pandemic. Several research projects have shown such effective handling through blockchain technology. Epios system has been used anonymous testing of COVID-19. People having COVID-19-like symptoms has been targeted of abuse, social discrimination and made responsible for spreading corona virus. The privacy of infected people should preserve and retained by hospitals and laboratories only. To facilitate anonymous testing of infected people Telos platform of blockchain has been utilized through which users can easily connect with labs which process PCR kits. This platform requires providers of testing kit to provide coupon to users for every testing kit. The coupon is cryptographically protected to assist the labs for payment verification. This system also aimed at implementing a mobile application which can be used for availing and submitting test kits without revealing identity. This project aimed at sharing COVID-19 data with government authorities again without disclosing individual's credentials [6, 58].

3.2.1   Handling Fake Infodemic Using MiPasa Platform

COVID-19 has uncovered the need for reliable and transparent data for combating with this deadly virus. Such data can assist authorities in taking decisions related to putting restrictions on travel or entire lockdown. Blockchain MiPasa platform stores, process and share information regarding spread of coronavirus from various reliable and verifiable sources like world health organization and other authorities. Such platforms can easily identify errors and data misrepresentation which ultimately assists researchers and scientists to take decisions in order to halt the spread by identifying the carriers and hotspot areas. It is a private system implemented on hyper ledger committed to provide secure data on time. Health officials can upload infected people information (location) on MiPasa and the framework will validate the data by matching it with the data provided by verified sources [66]. Further, verified data is being shared with healthcare providers and authorities for taking corrective actions [17, 37].

3.2.2   VIRI Platform Preventing Spread

Data privacy of users in case of digital contact tracing can be affected. VIRI provides assurance for preserving user's data privacy [47]. VIRI works on permissive technology providing global platform for global users. This platform can track virus spread across different countries and outbreak at different places can easily be tracked with VIRI. Randomly generating user identity is tracked anonymously and individual get notified for every close contact with infected person. An individual gets alert on the basis of risk from infected about infectious diseases. Passing from nearby infected people VIRI provides update as potential infected case. VIRI also assist Artificial Intelligence tools in order to predict COVID-19 worldwide [22].

3.2.3   WIShelter for Data Privacy

A smartphone based application which stores health related data (like blood pressure and pharmaceutical details etc.) of individuals using blockchain technology. Users can upload their vaccination certificates which can be accessed by authorities in order to frame further policies [5]. Privacy of data is crucial otherwise issues like mistreatment and misuse can come across. WIShelter provides full security of uploaded data which cannot be shared to anyone without consent of uploader. User requiring data has to avail signed form from owner. This platform encrypts the data which again ensures privacy and safety of data [8].

3.3   Reviving Capabilities

Blockchain technology has many applications in healthcare. As discussed above it manages electronic health record, data privacy, medical supply chain and many more. Companies worldwide are utlilizing the benefits of blockchain technology owing to its various features like immutability, decentralized and transparent storage of data which can easily and quickly be shared with stakeholders.

3.3.1   Blockchain in Healthcare – Global Scenario

- Akiri – it aims to protect health data while transporting utilizing blockchain technology. Akiri is not concerned with storing data rather it operates as network configuring data layers [11, 40]. It ensures sharing data securely with authorized parties when they need it.
- Embleem – This analytics platform is designed for quick tracking of drug development. Users submit their digital consent form to collect secure and tamper proof medical data. The data is being stored on this very platform for further analysis.
- Chronicled – It creates blockchain applications for effective supply chain of medicines demonstrating chain-of-custody. It ensures pharmaceutical companies regarding safe arrival of medicines and enables them for any legal action against suspicious activity.
- Blockpharma – provides solution for concerns like drug counterfeiting and traceability. This blockchain based supply chain management verifies all the points of shipment and supply chain and reveals to the user whether user is taking falsified medicines or not.
- The EncrypGen Gene – this platform is based on blockchain technology aims at providing facilities related to genetic information. It facilitates storing, sharing and buying and selling of such information. Only member companies can access this information and use to enhance their knowledge to mark advancement in the industry.

3.3.2   Blockchain in Healthcare – Indian Scenario

- Medpiper: It is a recruitment platform for healthcare professionals which enables credentials verification by employers and match these profiles with the actual requirement.
- Shivom: It serves as a health data hub with a combination of blockchain, AI and Cryptography allowing people to store genome after their sequencing.
- HECOD: This cloud based platform is concerned with health record management (stores and organizes records) and sharing it with varied healthcare providers.
- Pranacare: Lifestyle management providers can easily manage their clients with the help of this AI based platform. It records and manages patient data to be utilized by AI tools in order to calculate patient health risks.
- Nano Healthcare Token: A blockchain based platform concerned with health management. Health records and prescription can be tracked utilizing this platform.
- Tenthaid: Utilizing this platform patient's information regarding daily weights, pulse and blood pressure.

3.4   Challenges in Adopting Blockchain in Healthcare

Blockchain technology is widely used in different sectors worldwide. Although, it offers various opportunities but there are few drawbacks creating domain specific challenges. When it comes to healthcare there are four key challenges- Storage, modification, scalability, privacy, and regulations.

- Storage: An enormous amount of data has been produced of electronic health record about patients. Blockchain allows limited data for on-chair storage. Moreover, data storing is very costly in on decentralized architecture of Blockchain. Similarly, the cost of accessing, managing and operating data increases with data size. Therefore, blockchain applications must be designed considering the factor of cost in mind.
- Modification: Blockchain technology stores data safely and ensures tamper proof data due to its immutability feature. Data stored in blockchain cannot be modified and deleted once stored. In order to make changes new blocks needs to be created consensually or one need to create new chain

entirely. But, creating new chain and new blocks costs too much and not feasible at all. These two methods are costly and not feasible. So, blockchain applications design and development must consider lowest data modifications.

- Scalability: Scalability issue is a less serious issue due to decentralized architecture. However, Insurance companies, private clinics, rural hospitals, healthcare centers, enterprise research organizations, individual patients, and IoT startups etc. have millions of users with different infrastructure. All of them are not capable of maintaining the same decentralized blockchain architecture (very likely). A higher computation power is required for blockchain technology, which needs high electricity consumption by network equipment [15]. The scalability issue for healthcare big data must be taken care of seriously in order to make blockchain popular.
- Privacy and regulations: The decentralized and immutable architecture of blockchain offers high level of security by maximizing its content security many times. When it comes to healthcare it contains patients' sensitive information. Keeping a copy of this information in every node can be risky. Storing electronic health record for lifelong is the major issue for blockchain technology.

3.5   Conclusion

In order to tackle various potential and existing challenges a single sourced data record system based on blockchain is necessary. Moreover, vulnerable situation due pandemic has made it even more crucial. Blockchain technology with features like persistency, decentralization, and auditability is gaining importance from individuals and organizations [12, 28]. Blockchain technology is capable of providing quality healthcare at low cost owing to its secure and transparent system. This paper discussed various applications of blockchain technology in healthcare and contribution of blockchain technology in combating COVID-19. The paper also discussed how blockchain empowering patients and streamlining sharing health record. Once health records become part of distributed ledger no one can tamper these records and patients can decide who can access these records.

The patients will have the right to decide who can access these records. Sharing of data cross borders can be a challenge and hinder blockchain technology benefit. Based on government regulations individual's privacy varies from country to country. Thus, there is an urgent need of research in the area of cross health data sharing and retrieving policies. Storing and processing massive data is another potential challenge which is under researched area. With increase in volume of transactions increases delay in mining blocks, thus requiring newer and innovative mechanisms are required to reduce these mining delays. The paper discussed drug tracking and blockchain technology has been very significant for healthcare providers when it comes to authenticity and timely delivery. Various needs of diverse perspectives of stakeholders (patient, healthcare providers, regulators, etc.) must be addressed by any technological approach in order to improve healthcare. Blockchain has been widely explored by diverse stakeholder to optimize business operations [35]. Blockchain technology in healthcare is exploding. According to recent study by IBM of more than 200 executives from life sciences across 18 countries, more than 70% respondents agree and expect can contribute in overcoming inefficiency in legacy systems resulting reducing ability to innovate [19].

References

1. Al Ridhawi, I., Aloqaily, M., Kotb, Y., Jararweh, Y.A., Collaborative mobile edge computing and user solution for service composition in 5G systems. *Trans. Emerg. Telecommun. Technol.*, 29, e3446, 2018.
2. Andoni, M., Robu, V., Flynn, D., Abram, S., Geach, D., Jenkins, D., McCallum, P., Peacock, A., Blockchain technology in the energy sector: A systematic review of challenges and opportunities. *Renewable Sustainable Energy Rev.*, 100, 174, 2019.
3. Azaria, A., Ekblaw, A., Vieira, T., Lippman, A., Medrec, Using blockchain for medical data access and permission management, in: *Proceedings of the 2nd International Conference on Open and Big Data (OBD)*, Vienna, Austria, p. 24, 2016.
4. Cardoso, L., Marins, F., Portela, F., Santos, M., Abelha, A., Machado, J., The next generation of interoperability agents in healthcare. *Int. J. Environ. Res. Public Health*, 11, 5349–5371, 2014.
5. Carlos, M. and Lena, C., WISeKey's. Cutting edge wise-authentic identity blockchain technology, 2019, Retrieved from https://www.wisekey.com/press/.
6. Charles, B., Telos launches Epios project for anonymous COVID-19 testing, 2020. Retrieved from https://www.enterprisetimes.co.uk/.
7. Chen, Y., Ding, S., Xu, Z., Zheng, H., Yang, S., Blockchain-based medical records secure storage and medical service framework. *J. Med. Syst.*, 43, 5, 1–9, 2018.

8. Dhillon, V., Metcalf, D., Hooper, M., *Blockchain enabled applications: understand the blockchain ecosystem and how to make it work for you*, Springer, Emeryville, CA, USA, 2017.

9. Livingston, E., Desai, A., Berkwits, M., Sourcing personal protective equipment during the COVID-19 pandemic. *JAMA*, 323, 19, 1912–1914, 2020.

10. Girardi, F., De Gennaro, G., Colizzi, L., Convertini, N., Improving the healthcare effectiveness: The possible role of EHR, IoMT and Blockchain. *Electronics*, 9, 884–896, 2020.

11. Faber, Michelet, G.C., Weidmann, N., Mukkamala, R.R., Vatrapu, R., BPDIMS: A blockchain-based personal data and identity management system, in: *Proceedings of the 52nd Hawaii International Conference on System Sciences*, 2019.

12. Gilberto, P. and Ronaldo, Z., Fatores determinantes da adocao de sistemas de informacao na area de saude: Um estudo sobre o prontuario medico eletronico. *RAM. Revista de Administração Mackenzie*, vol. 11, pp. 174–200, 2010.

13. Gordon, W.J. and Catalini, C., Blockchain technology for healthcare: facilitating the transition to patient-driven interoperability. *Comput. Struct. Biotechnol. J.*, 16, 224–230, 2018.

14. Guo, R., Shi, H., Zhao, Q., Zheng, D., Secure attribute-based signature scheme with multiple authorities for blockchain in electronic health records systems. *IEEE Access*, 776, 1–12, 2018.

15. Gupta, M., *Blockchain for dummies*, John Wiley & Sons, Hoboken (NJ), 2018.

16. Bauchner, H., Fontanarosa, P.B., Livingston, E.H., Conserving supply of personal protective equipment. *Europe PMC*, 223, 19, 1911–1931, 2020.

17. Hussein, A., Arun, N., Ramirez, G., Abdulhay, E., Tavares, J., A medical records managing and securing blockchain based system supported by a genetic algorithm and discrete wavelet transform. *Cognit. Syst. Res.*, 52, 1–11, 2018.

18. IBM Institute for Business Value, *Team medicine: How life sciences can win with blockchain*, IBM Corporation, Armonk, NY, 2018, https://public.dhe.ibm.com/common/ssi/ecm/03/en/03013903usen/team-medicine.pdf.

19. Iroju, O., Soriyan, A., Gambo, I., Olaleke, J., Interoperability in healthcare: Benefits, challenges and resolutions. *Int. J. Innov. Appl. Stud.*, 3, 262–270, 2013.

20. Liu, J.K., Au, M.H., Yuen, T.H., Zuo, C., Wang, J., Sakzad, A., Luo, X., Li, L., Privacy-preserving COVID-19 contact tracing app: A zero-knowledge proof approach IACR cryptol. *EPrint Arch.*, 528, 528, 2020.

21. Jacob, C., VIRI creates global anonymous contact-tracing platform to stop spread of COVID-19, 2020, Retrieved from https://www.viri.io/.

22. Clauson, K., Breeden, E., Davidson, C., Mackey, T., Leveraging blockchain technology to enhance supply chain management in healthcare: An exploration of challenges and opportunities in the health supply chain. *Blockchain in Healthcare Today*, vol. 1(3), pp. 1–12, 2018.

23. Salah, K., Alfalasi, A., Alfalasi, M., Alharmoudi, M., Alzaabi, M., Alzyeodi, A., Ahmad, R., IoT-enabled shipping container with environmental monitoring

and location tracking, in: *2020. IEEE 17th Annual Consumer Communications & Networking Conference (CCNC)*, Christina Maxouris, WHO coronavirus disease (COVID-19) dashboard, 2020, https://covid19.who.int/.

24. Kalla, Hewa, T., Mishra, R.A., Ylianttila, M., The role of blockchain to fight against COVID-19. *IEEE Eng. Manage. Rev.*, 48, 85–96, 2020.

25. Kuo, T.T., Kim, H.E., Ohno-Machado, L., Blockchain distributed ledger technologies for biomedical and healthcare applications. *J. Am. Med. Inform. Assoc.*, 24, 1211–1220, 2017.

26. Peysson, F.L., Tracing and control of raw materials sourcing for vaccine manufacturers. *Biologicals*, 38, 3, 352–353, 2010.

27. Ferretti, L., Wymant, C., Kendall, M., Zhao, L., Nurtay, A., Abeler-D¨orner, L., Parker, M., Bonsall, D., Fraser, C., Quantifying SARS-CoV-2 transmission suggests epidemic control with digital contact tracing. *Science*, 368, 6491, 2020.

28. Ramirez, L. and Beltrán Álvarez, N., Blockchain application in the distribution chain of the COVID-19 vaccine: A designing under study. *Advance*, 1, 321–332, 2020.

29. Lesavre, P., Varin, P., Mell, Davidson, M., Shook, J., A taxonomic approach to understanding emerging blockchain identity management systems. National Institute of Standards and Technology, Tech. Rep., 2019.

30. Reichert, L., Brack, S., Scheuermann, B., Privacy preserving contact tracing of COVID-19 patients. *IACR Cryptol. ePrint Arch.*, p. 375, 2020.

31. Raikwar, M., Mazumdar, S., Gupta, S.S., Chattopadhyay, A., Lam, K.-Y., A blockchain framework for insurance processes, in: *9th IFIP International Conference on New Technologies, Mobility and Security (NTMS)*, vol. 1(4), 2018.

32. Torky, M. and Hassanien, A.E., COVID-19 blockchain framework: Innovative approach. *arXiv*, preprintarXiv:2004.06081, 81, 1134–1168, 2020.

33. Mackey, T.K., Kuo, T., Gummadi, B., 'Fit-for-purpose?' - challenges and opportunities for applications of blockchain technology in the future of healthcare. *BMC Med.*, 27, 68, 2019.

34. Mackey, T.K. and Liang, B.A., The global counterfeit drug trade: Patient safety and public health risks. *J. Pharm. Sci.*, 100, 4571–4579, 2011.

35. Macrinici, D., Cartofeanu, C., Gao, S., Smart contract applications within blockchain technology: A systematic mapping study. *Telemat. Inform.*, 35, 2337–2354, 2018.

36. Miller, R.H. and Sim, I., Physicians' use of electronic medical records: Barriers and solutions. *Health Aff.*, 23, 116–126, 2004.

37. Rowan, N.J. and Laffey, J.G., Challenges and solutions for addressing critical shortage of supply chain for personal and protective equipment (PPE) arising from coronavirus disease (COVID19) pandemic–case study from the republic of Ireland. *Sci. Total Environ.*, 725, 138–532, 2020.

38. McKenna, N., COVID-19: Rapid response in healthcare. Retrieved from https://www.accenture.com/gben/insights/health/, 2020.

39. White, P., Schmidt, J., Lenz, D., Applying software patterns to address interoperability in blockchain-based healthcare apps. *arXiv*, arXiv:1706.03700, 72, 271–282, 2017.

40. Peter, H. and Moser, A., Blockchain-applications in banking & payment transactions: Results of a survey, in: *Proceedings of the 14th International Scientific Conference Pt*, European Financial Systems, Brno, Czech Republic, pp. 26–27, 2017.

41. Pham, Q.-V., Nguyen, D.C., Hwang, W.-J., Pathirana, P.N., Artificial intelligence (AI) and big data for coronavirus (COVID-19) pandemic: A survey on the state-of-the- arts. *IEEE Access*, 130, 8, 820–130, 2020.

42. Wechsler, R., Ancao, M.S., de Campos, C.J.R., Sigulem, D., A informatica no consultorio medico. *J. Pediatr.*, 79, 1–10, 2003, https://doi.org/10.1590/S0021-75572003000700002.

43. Rivest, R., *The MD5 Message-Digest Algorithm; Technical report; RFC*, Marina del Rey, CA, USA, 1992.

44. Rosenbaum, L., Anthem will use blockchain to secure medical data for its 40 million members in three years, Forbes, UK, 2019, https://www.forbes.com/sites/leahrosenbaum/2019/12/12/anthem-says-its-40-million-members-will-be-using-blockchain-to-secure-patient-data-in-three years/#305bc9be6837.

45. Nagesh S., S. and Chakraborty, S., Saving the frontline health workforce amidst the COVID-19 crisis: Challenges and recommendations. *J. Glob. Health*, 10, 1, 345–353, 2020.

46. Guia, S.B., VIRI creates global anonymous contact-tracing platform to stop spread of COVID-19. Retrieved from https://startupbeat.com, 2020.

47. Schöner, M.M., Kourouklis, D., Sandner, P., Gonzalez, E., Förster, J., *Blockchain technology in the pharmaceutical industry*, Frankfurt School Blockchain Center, Frankfurt, Germany, 2017.

48. Sharma, R., *Blockchain in healthcare*, FCCCO, Ontario, ON, Canada, 2018.

49. Susan, M., MiPasa: An open data platform to support COVID-19 response, https://mipasa.org/blog/mipasa-an-open-data-platformto-support-COVID-19-response/, 2020.

50. Sylim, P., Liu, F., Marcelo, A., Fontelo, P., Blockchain technology for detecting falsified and substandard drugs in distribution: Pharmaceutical supply chain intervention. *JMIR Res. Protoc.*, 7, 2, e10163, 2018.

51. Terry, A.L., Thorpe, C.F., Giles, G., Brown, J.B., Harris, S.B., Reid, G.J., Thind, A., Stewart, M., Implementing electronic health records: Key factors in primary care. *Can. Fam. Physician*, 54, 730–736, 2018.

52. Tseng, J.H., Liao, Y.C., Chong, B., Liao, Governance on the drug supply chain via gcoin blockchain. *Int. J. Environ. Res. Public Health*, 15, 1055, 2018.

53. Chamola, V., Hassija, V., Gupta, V., Guizani, M., A comprehensive review of the COVID-19 pandemic and the role of IoT, drones, AI, blockchain, and 5G in managing its impact. *IEEE Access*, 8, 225–90265, 2020.

54. Vo, H.T., Kundu, A., Mohania, M.K., *Research directions in blockchain data management and analytics*, pp. 445–448, EDBT, Lisbon, Portugal, 2018.

56. Wang, S., Wang, J., Wang, X., Qiu, T., Yuan, Y., Ouyang, L., Guo, Y., Wang, F.Y., Blockchain-powered parallel healthcare systems based on the ACP approach. *IEEE Trans. Comput. Soc. Syst.*, 5, 942–950, 2018.

57. Westerkamp, M., Victor, F., Kupper, A., Tracing manufacturing processes using blockchain-based token compositions. *Digital Commun. Networks*, 6, 167–176, 2019.

58. Xu, X., Lu, Q., Liu, Y., Zhu, L., Yao, H., Vasilakos, A.V., Designing block-chain- based applications a case study for imported product traceability. *Future Gener. Comput. Syst.*, 92, 399–406, 2019.

59. Liu, Y., He, D., Obaidat, M.S., Kumar, N., Khan, M.K., Choo, K.-K.R., Blockchain- based identity management systems: A review. *J. Netw. Comput. Appl.*, 102731, 166, 2020.

60. Yang, J., Onik, M.M.H., Lee, N.Y., Ahmed, M., Kim, C.S., Proof-of-familiarity: A privacy-preserved blockchain scheme for collaborative med-ical decision-making. *Appl. Sci.*, 9, 1370, 2019.

61. Zhang, P., White, J., Schmidt, D.C., Lenz, G., Applying software patterns to address interoperability in blockchain-based healthcare apps. *arXiv, arXiv*,1706.03700, 71, 106–116, 2017.

62. Zhu, L., Wu, Y., Gai, K., Choo, K.R., Controllable and trustworthy block-chain- based cloud data management. *Future Gener. Comput. Syst.*, 91, 527–535, 2019.

63. Mandrino, J., VeChain announces blockchain vaccine tracing solution for China, 2018, https://www.nasdaq.com/articles/vechain-announcesblockchain-vaccine-tracing-solution-china-.

64. Debe, M., Salah, K., Rehman, M.H.U., Svetinovic, D., IoT public fog nodes reputation system: A decentralized solution using ethereum blockchain. *IEEE Access*, 7, 178082–178093, 2019.

64. Benna, I.I., Optimizing health, education and governance delivery through blockchain, in: *Optimizing Regional Development Through Transformative Urbanization*, pp. 24–47, IGI Global, Hershey, PA, USA, 2019.

65. Iezzoni, L.I., Assessing quality using administrative data. *Ann. Intern. Med.*, 127, 666–674, 1997.

66. Alonso, S.G., Arambarri, J., López-Coronado, M., de la Torre Díez, I., Proposing new blockchain challenges in eHealth. *J. Med. Syst.*, 43, 64, 2019.

4

Blockchain-Based Energy-Efficient Heterogeneous Sensor Networks in Healthcare System

R. Janarthanan[1]* and J. Venkatesh[2]

[1]*Center for Artificial Intelligence, Department of Computer Science and Engineering, Chennai Institute of Technology, Chennai, Tamil Nadu, India*
[2]*Center for System Design, Department of Computer Science and Engineering, Chennai Institute of Technology, Chennai, Tamil Nadu, India*

Abstract

A radio communication sensor system is a collection of sensor modules that are connected to one another through wireless communication. It is common for them to be battery-powered and responsive to a nearby controller, referred to as the Base Station. They are capable of doing basic computations and transferring information to the Base Station in most scenarios. They are also in charge of transporting data from distant nodes, putting a burden on nodes with limited resources and contributing to the quick depletion of energy in these nodes in the process. Nodes in close proximity to the base station are responsible for more than only detecting and sending data to the base station; they are also responsible for transmitting data from faraway nodes. To reward nodes that perform well, a protocol known as the Improved Fuzzy Inspired Energy Effective Protocol (IFIEEP) employs three separate sorts of nodes in order to provide more energy to those who do not. It takes into account the remaining node energy, the node's proximity to the base station, the node's neighbor concentration, and the node's centrality in a cluster when determining node viability. All of these assumptions are founded on a shaky understanding of the situation. Adaptive clustering must be applied to the most viable nodes in order to identify cluster leaders and transmit data to the base station, in addition to disseminating data across the rest of the network, in order to achieve success. In addition, the research provides proper heterogeneity

---

**Corresponding author*: janarthananr@citchennai.net

Kiran Sood, Rajesh Kumar Dhanaraj, Balamurugan Balusamy and Seifedine Kadry (eds.) Blockchain Technology in Corporate Governance: Transforming Business and Industries, (75–98) © 2023 Scrivener Publishing LLC

parameters, which describe, among other things, the number of nodes as well as the starting energy of each node, among others things. The percentage gain in network lifetime when compared to current approaches is minor for smaller numbers of supernodes; however, the percentage gain in the area covered, 12.89 percent, and 100% when larger numbers of super nodes are used are 100 percent, 12.89 percent, and 100%, respectively, when larger numbers of super nodes are used. These improvements in stability, residual energy, and throughput are accomplished by combining these improvements while also taking into consideration the previously neglected energy-intensive sensing energy aspect. The protocol that has been presented is meant to be used in conjunction with applications that make use of blockchain technology (blockchain technology).

Keywords: Wireless sensor network, fuzzy inspired energy effective protocol, stability, residual energy, throughput, blockchain

4.1   Introduction

In a variety of fields, such as home automation, medical monitoring, military operations (including industrial trolleys), retail and logistics, agriculture (including archaeology, animal husbandry, and flood detection), and others, world-wide-web networks (WSNs) are used in a variety of applications. For the time being, however, WSAN (Wireless Sensor and Actuator Network) is essential for operating requirements. However, it seems that 'actuators' have taken the lead in terms of expressing interest at this moment, rather than WSNs. The Network itself should have a genuine interest in the subject matter and should be able to determine what needs to be done next [1], rather than just receiving information on a topic of interest from a remote location. The system should activate the water sprinkler system instead of only notifying BSC if the temperature of an area climbs beyond a certain threshold or it should sound an alarm in the fireplace, signaling that there is a fire. To provide an example, if the water heater in the house has been running for four hours, turn it off rather than keeping it running unattended or without somebody home to utilize it or keep it in good working order. Additionally, the wristwatch should sound an alert if the blood pressure (BP) of a patient strolling about the gardens rises beyond the recommended range for that patient. As a result, a family member of the hospital in issue will be notified, allowing for the delivery of critical medical care as soon as reasonably possible.

Each hospital's computerized server now stores information on patients' medical and examination histories, as well as their prescriptions and diagnostic findings, which used to be stored on a paper chart. As a consequence of the use of blockchain technology, data may become more trustworthy, secure, interoperable, and easily accessible. These efforts are being carried out by medical blockchain projects such as MediBlock in Korea and the United States. Using artificial intelligence and blockchain to utilize or exchange medical data in a decentralized manner eliminates the requirement for the patient to serve as an intermediary vendor between the two parties. Patients who had previously sold subscriber data and gave authentic data were denied the right to make a decision and the benefits of trade, even though middle-class vendors benefited financially as a consequence of their acts. The genetic information of subscribers to a medical information service provider is sold to pharmaceutical companies to generate revenue, while the patient community generates revenue by selling data concerning the side effects of anonymous people to pharmaceutical companies. Patients who provided information, on the other hand, had a reduced role in decision-making and received no gain from the sale of their products or services. The integration of artificial intelligence and blockchain, in addition, may reduce the amount of middle-market positions and enable more direct decisions to be made, enabling patients to make better use of their data while simultaneously improving profitability [2]. You have the option of deciding how much your data will be sold for and to which company's projects it will be used, and you can also choose to monitor the data's usage after it has been sold. Patient engagement will increase if incentives are supplied, which will benefit both the patient and the data buyer in the long run. The objective is to inspire people to take exceptional care of themselves and to make the most of their good health while they can. Encouraging patients to participate in physical activity, quit smoking, stop drinking, and limit their prescription consumption are all things that the medical community struggles to do with great success. In the case of medical information systems and healthcare systems that are integrally linked to artificial intelligence and blockchain technology, it is feasible to apply for insurance coverage and to be covered by insurance.

It is necessary to account for data collisions in this model since a large number of communication units are all utilizing a single communication channel at the same time in this scenario.

The task of relaying data from other nodes that are located outside of the network's coverage area, in addition to the regular transmission of information seen by the node, is added to the list of responsibilities. The results of the LEACH [2] simulation have led to the conclusion that the congestion in the area around the BS is caused by a large amount of data being relayed from distant nodes. As a consequence, load balancing is a critical need. Although it is unlikely, it is conceivable that the relaying nodes may fail, creating a vacuum between them and their base station (BS). This will prohibit them from sending data even if they have battery power available. Battery terminology such as "alive" and "dead" refers to a battery that is ready to be used or operational, as opposed to a battery that is unable to be used or operational owing to the depletion of a battery's energy or the physical damage to a battery's terminals. Cluster heads are selected using a stochastic cluster head selection process in LEACH, and as a consequence, asymmetric battery reservoirs are generated in nodes as a result of the technique used to choose the cluster heads. Considering both the remaining energy level of each node and how much energy is required to transmit data is crucial to make an educated choice regarding the cluster head.

Make sure nodes that are doing more activities have enough battery power to last longer, or spread the operating load over a larger number of nodes.

The solution to the issue is represented by the number [3]. First, there is data aggregation or data fusion, which encompasses methods such as data compression, in-network query processing, and other related methodologies, amongst other things. Because of this, the number of bits broadcasted or received by communication entities is reduced, which has an impact on the amount of energy used directly during the transmission of information. Establishing a variety of distinct networks is part of the second method, which is described below. It is considered to be heterogeneous when a network consists of components that are not similar to one another in terms of structure. Network objects' abilities represent the amount of initial battery power, computation capabilities, and communication range that they have when they first appear on the network. To avoid making any comparisons between the nodes in this research, each one has a different starting battery capacity, but both have the same processing and communication skills. The first strategy, on the other hand, makes use of a network that is normally homogenous in terms of battery capacity, but the second technique does not.

In a variety of fields, such as home automation, medical monitoring, military operations (including industrial trolleys), retail and logistics, agriculture (including archaeology, animal husbandry, and flood detection), and others, world-wide-web networks (WSNs) are used in a variety of applications. For the time being, however, WSAN (Wireless Sensor and Actuator Network) is essential for operating requirements. However, it seems that 'actuators' have taken the lead in terms of expressing interest at this moment, rather than WSNs. The Network itself should have a strong interest in the subject matter and should be able to determine what has to be done next, rather than just receiving information about it from a remote location as is often the case. The system should activate the water sprinkler system instead of only notifying BSC if the temperature of an area climbs beyond a certain threshold, or it should sound an alarm in the fireplace, signaling that there is a fire. Additionally, the wristwatch should sound an alert if the blood pressure (BP) of a patient strolling about the gardens rises beyond the recommended range for that patient. As a result, a family member of the hospital in issue will be notified, allowing for the delivery of critical medical care as soon as reasonably possible.

Because a high number of communication units are all using a single communication channel at the same time in this situation, it is vital to account for data collisions in this model.

According to the findings of the LEACH simulation, which was performed, it is expected that a high quantity of data being transferred from distant nodes is a contributing reason to the congestion in the region around the BS. As a result, load balancing is a vital need. The relaying nodes may fail, resulting in a void between them and their base station, even though this is improbable (BS). This will prevent them from transferring data even if they have the battery power to do so on their own. Using battery terms such as "alive" and "dead," you can distinguish between a battery that is ready to be used or operational and one that has been inoperable as a result of a battery's energy being depleted or the battery's terminals being physically damaged. Cluster heads are chosen using a random number generator in LEACH. It is essential to take into account both the remaining energy level of each node and the amount of energy necessary to transfer data to make an informed decision on the cluster head.

Maintain sufficient battery power in nodes that do a greater number of activities, or distribute the operational load over a wider number of nodes to ensure that nodes that perform fewer activities remain longer.

First and foremost, there is data aggregation or data fusion, which includes technologies such as data compression, in-network query processing, and other related approaches, among other things. In turn, the number of bits transmitted or received by communication entities is lowered as a result, which influences the amount of energy utilized directly during the transmission of data. The second strategy, which is detailed in further detail below, includes the establishment of several unique networks. When a network comprises components that are structurally distinct from one another, the network is said to be heterogeneous. The abilities of network objects describe the amount of initial battery power, compute capabilities, and communication range that they have when they initially emerge on the network, as well as their ability to communicate with other network objects. Each of the nodes in this study has a distinct beginning battery capacity to avoid drawing any comparisons between them; nonetheless, they each have the same processing and communication abilities. When compared to the second approach, the first strategy makes use of a network that is generally homogeneous in terms of battery capacity, while the second technique does not.

In the current analysis, an energy-efficient heterogeneous network of nodes that runs at three separate energy levels is taken into account. Even though the gadget's use is out of the usual in terms of its geographical location, the device was designed expressly for this kind of application in mind. This was accomplished as a consequence of the use of fuzzy logic. Many more discoveries have been discovered, including the mathematically optimal number of particular node kinds for each node, as well the amount of beginning energy that each node should have, among other findings. The findings were also compared to a set of existing protocols, which consisted of a heterogeneous network with two initial energy levels and three inherent energy levels and three inherent energy levels, respectively; a heterogeneous network with three inherent energy levels and three inherent energy levels. Also investigated is if it is necessary to strike a compromise between network life extension and coverage percent area per unit time to get the best potential results. The currency network protocol is built on the foundation of fuzzy logic, and the results of the simulation show that the protocol is extremely close to real-time or human understanding, resulting in a network that is far more stable and trustworthy throughout its existence. Fuzzy logic is used as the foundation for the currency network protocol. The next section will offer a more in-depth description of the Improved fluid inference system in more detail. The Improved assumptions, network deployment, clustering, and data transmission mechanisms, to name a few topics covered in detail in this section, as well as the mathematical assessment and computational interpretation of optimal heterogeneity parameters, are just a few examples of the topics covered in this section.

4.2   Related Work

The related work in the domain has been summarized in Table 4.1.

Table 4.1 Improved: related work [author's compilation].

Reference	Advantages	Remarks
LEACH 2002 [4] is used as an example.	Among the earliest protocols for data transfer in a WSN is the fact that it is simple. Because of threshold-based stochastic cluster head selection, there is a bottleneck in the area surrounding BS. In the case of a heterogeneous network, this rule does not apply.	The solution was to create heterogeneity among nodes by assigning them increasingly difficult tasks to complete.
Seema Bandhopadhyay and colleagues 2003 [5]	It was suggested that raising the degrees of hierarchy would result in greater energy savings. Communication is only possible via hierarchies in lag.	When selecting a CH, it is necessary to take into account the residual energy of the node.
Liang Ying and colleagues [6] published their findings in 2005.	LEACH's stochastic cluster head selection has been optimized.	When selecting a CH, it is necessary to take into account the residual energy of the node

4.2.1 Literature Gap

i. Fuzzy factors, such as waste energy, proximity to the base station, concentration, and center, are all examples of variables that may be employed.

ii. Additional improvement in adaptive cluster head selection is possible, as is the case in the previous section [7].

iii. To establish the best heterogeneity parameters, a model must be developed.

a. Fuzzy Inference System

The characteristics of human thinking, on the other hand, are difficult to translate into binary computer logic, which can only be expressed as yes or no. When it comes to fuzzy sets, fuzzy logic incorporates dialectical factors into human thinking by introducing them into the set of possibilities.

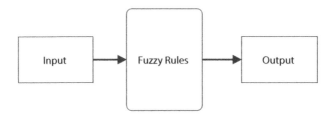

Figure 4.1 Input fuzzy system. [author compilation].

Following the computation, as seen in Figure 4.1, the Fuzzy Inference System (FIS) provides crisp output values as a consequence of the process. Because of the existence of a knowledge base, the input values change, and these fluctuating inputs are sent to an inference mechanism, which applies a variety of fuzzy if-then rules to construct conclusions about the outside world. The output generated is then aggregated and defused with the help of the knowledge base, resulting in a set of potential output values that may be selected from. The Mamdani type of FIS was used in this work, which means that the output of each if-then rule is a fluctuating collection of values rather than a single value.

4.2.2 Fuzzy Improved Model (Improved Model Fuzzy)

A network node may only be assigned to a cluster member if the CH deems that it has sufficient energy resources to acquire, aggregate, and send database data from its cluster members, regardless of where the cluster member is located in the network hierarchy. Thus, while selecting a CH, it is critical to include the residual node energy as one of the key metrics to consider. LEACH [8] and similar direct transmission protocols do not evaluate the node's remaining energy before allocating the function of CH, resulting in early battery energy depletion for nodes close to the base station or frequent allocation of the function of CH for nodes farther away from the base station. LEACH [9] and similar direct transmission protocols do not evaluate the node's remaining energy before allocating the function of CH. LEACH and other direct transmission protocols do not take into account the amount of energy that a node has left when assigning the function of CH.

The radio energy model shows that when a knot is near a base station, it is often supplied with CH, as represented on the diagram. However, such nodes should not be overloaded again since doing so might lead them to expire prematurely. This is done to lower the overall amount of energy used by the network, which is particularly important in a network with limited available energy. This might then result in a data hole, which is defined as not transmitting any data to the base station even though distant nodes are still alive and well. The following is the distance between nodes and the base station: As soon as the transmission radius of a node is determined, the concentration of neighbors within that radius may be calculated. Distance between nodes and base station: This indicator represents the degree to which data redundancy occurs in the event of a high node density in a particular geographic location. With increasing concentration, the chance that nodes will be designated as CHs to avoid data duplication increases (central hubs).

The distance between a node and the node's origin is defined as the centrality of the node (the center of the cluster in which it is situated). The sum of the square distances between all of the other nodes and the single node under examination is calculated by the base station, which is located at the center of the network. Additionally, it is hypothesized that the lower the center value of a node, the less energy is used by subsequent protuberances in transiting their data via that node to its eventual destination. It is vital to underline once again that nodes such as these should not be overburdened, and that duties should be assigned to all nodes at the same time to establish an equitable energy distribution throughout the network, as has been done before.

The different components of the fuzzy inference system that was used in the present investigation are listed in the following sections.

Using a single membership function, fuzzification is the process by which the input values are transformed into dialect variables. On the other hand, as shown in Figure 4.2, certain membership tasks are carried out to varying degrees.

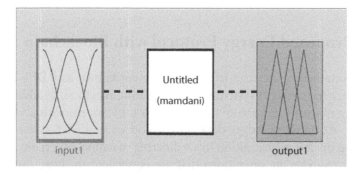

Figure 4.2 Improved: system model. [Matlab coding].

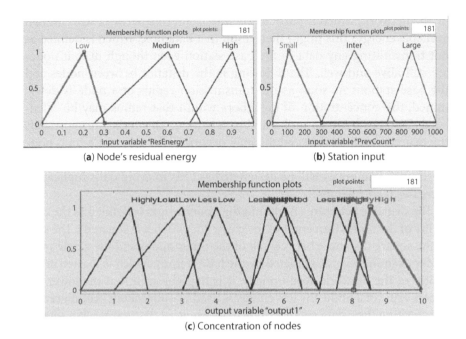

Figure 4.3 Description of input membership functions. [Matlab coding].

It is possible to find 180 if-then rules in the knowledge base or database, which contains the specification as well as the definition for if-then rules. To make it simpler to grasp the various regulations, they have been shown as surface plots to make them more visible (Figure 4.3).

It does this by using membership functions to translate the output uncertain productions from the implication device into crisp standards [10]. When the centroid of area approach is used, defuzzification may be achieved more effectively.

4.3   Proposed Energy Protocol with Blockchain

Also maintained as an extra ledger-data system known as a DLT (distributed ledger technology) system with a validating machine, in addition to a validating machine, Ethereum is known as a DLT system with a validating machine. As an extra ledger-data system known as a DLT system with a validating machine, in addition to a validating machine, Ethereum is maintained. It can execute operations that are equivalent to those carried out by the Bitcoin cryptocurrency. With the help of the Ethereum. Figure 4.4

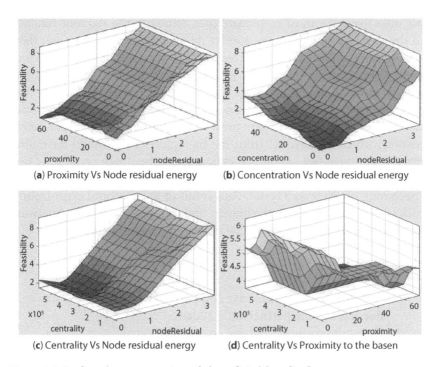

(a) Proximity Vs Node residual energy   (b) Concentration Vs Node residual energy

(c) Centrality Vs Node residual energy   (d) Centrality Vs Proximity to the basen

Figure 4.4 Surface plots representing rule base. [Matlab coding].

represents the surface plot of the rule base units. Virtual Machine (EVM), the EVM allows for the building of immutable computer logic that can be constructed on top of the Ethereum blockchain and then executed in public books. When it comes to the introduction of smart contracts and the execution of smart contracts, both need the accumulation of power by Etherithostore, which is accomplished by the expenditure of a certain amount of money known as the Ethereum cryptocurrency (which is used to do this task) (also known as the Ethereum token). The following section describes the fundamental steps involved in executing a smart contract after it has been registered in the ledger. It is meant for smart contracts to operate with specific input data provided by transactions. Transaction data is the term used to describe this kind of information. [11], it is possible to guarantee that money movement during transactions and changes in the state of EVMs are completely transparent and can be inspected by any party involved in the transaction [12]. The upshot is that instead of using an old-fashioned squashing function. Scientists and engineers throughout history have employed the sigmoid function to solve difficulties, as well as the function, which is a soft step function that may be identified, to accomplish their objectives. We must emphasize that, although the sigmoid function and the step function are quite similar in appearance and function, there are significant differences when compared to the biological brain, which cannot work properly unless there is some passage of time. While the input value for artificial neural networks may be supplied regardless of the time flow, the output value for artificial neural networks has been predetermined (ANNs). In contrast, researchers previously believed that artificial neural networks, which are distinct from the biological brain, would have difficulty calculating as fast as computers because of their high computing performance, and that the artificial neural network model was on the verge of becoming obsolete as a result. As a result of its structural organization, which is modeled on that of the human brain, this artificial neural network serves as the foundation for artificial intelligence technologies.

i. Suppositions

1. Network sensor nodes have comparable capabilities, are stationary, and are permanently added.
2. Network sensor nodes have comparable capabilities, are stationary, and are permanently data-bound.
3. As a result of the exclusion of propagation lag, the delay is defined as the time it takes for data to propagate from one node to the next, or for a round of propagation to complete.
4. The communication channel is symmetric for every signal-to-noise ratio that is used in the experiment.
5. Fourth, the Time Division Several Access (TDMA) protocols have been established to allow multiple users to access shared channel resources at the same time [13].

- Figure 4.5 represents the membership function. The first-order radio energy model has been applied to the problem of energy dissipation among communication entities [14]. Energy consumption by nodes varies in proportion to the distance between them or the role that has been allocated to them [15], which may include tasks such as data originator, relay node, or cluster leader, among other things.
- Similar to this book, each node starts with the same initial energy model, which is the same as in this book.
- The fact that nodes are aware of their relative position about other nodes based on the received sign strength indication

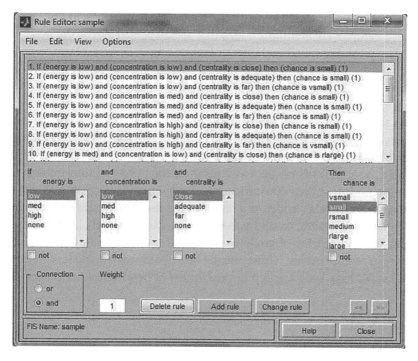

Figure 4.5 Description of output membership function. [Matlab coding].

does not imply that they are capable of giving [16] precise location information.

- The broadcast range of each node may be modified depending on the circumstance. As an example, if no other network node can transfer the data to the backend server, then a node may be able to communicate the data directly to the backend server.

- Implementing Heterogeneous Networks – This section addresses the process of putting heterogeneous networks into operation.

- In the terrain is a sub-section known as the "inner circle," which has a radius one-hundredth the length of the field's side and a radius one-hundredth the length [17] of the field's side, respectively. Nodes that are responsible for relaying a huge quantity of data are separated by a distance that is comparable to a single-hop distance, resulting in the consumption of a tremendous amount of energy between the nodes. To deploy the various kinds of nodes, a homogenous spatial poison process [18] with the following parameters has been employed: Standard nodes that are dispersed across the network are called is shown in Figure 4.6.

Essentially, the idea behind the aforementioned deployment is to provide more energy to nodes that are near the base station (supernodes), allowing them to work for a longer period because they have more information to broadcast than they would otherwise be able to (in the role of relay nodes). If such nodes fail, a data void occurs, which means that far-flung nodes are either unable to transmit data as a result of the failure of intermittent forwarding nodes, or they consume more energy than is necessary as a result of the failure of relay nodes as a result of the increase in distance between the nodes in question, resulting in data void. More recently [19], advanced nodes beyond the inner circle have been deployed to supply additional energy to regular nodes, whilst normal nodes, although being less common in LEACH, have been applied in the context of heterogeneous networks.

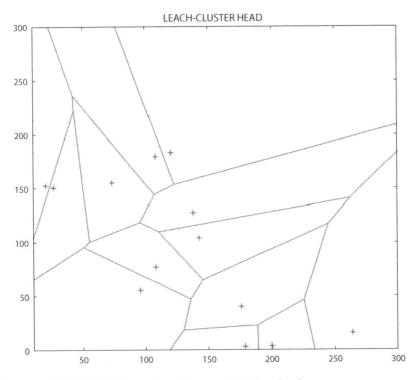

Figure 4.6 IMPROVED: Network architecture. [Matlab coding].

Alternatively, the examination of nodes for feasibility is achieved by the use of fuzzy logic, and this research is the first step in determining the clustering process among the nodes. Next, the feasibility values of the nodes that are eligible to be CH are sorted in decreasing order, and the nodes with the lowest ten percent of feasibility values are eliminated from the process of CH selection, resulting in an initial set G of nodes that are eligible to be CH for the current epoch. To serve as a central hub (or CH) for the game's central hub (or CH) in each round, the top 5 percent of all possible nodes are picked for each round. Initial selections for CH nodes are made ineligible for selection as CH for the current epoch early on, and this process continues until all of the eligible nodes from G have been selected as CH for the first time [20]. Indefinitely, until all nodes have been removed from the system, this process of selecting cluster chiefs may be repeated.

The Dissemination of Information (ii).
For data to be effective, it must be moved from a lower level in the hierarchy to a higher level in the hierarchy or the base station. This hierarchy includes the sensor node, the cluster head, and the next cluster head, among other things. The nodes in the lower and higher levels of this hierarchy are coming closer to the base station as the hierarchy progresses.

The Heterogeneity Parameters That Produce Effective Results Best
If we want to understand how to analyze a heterogeneous network, we must first figure out how to determine the optimum number of certain types of nodes or the best amount of energy in a particular kind of node [21]. The word "heterogeneity" refers to the differences in the amount of initial energy that each of the nodes possesses at the commencement of the simulation. As a consequence, it is possible to identify the optimal ratio between the other two variables in a simulation.

b. Character of Utility
This study's nature of protocol's usefulness was developed using the framework outlined in the next section, which may be summarized as follows: 1. the system timeline is defined as the period that has elapsed between the first placement of the network and the demise of the final protuberance in the network [22]. 2. Presently, there are nodes providing service to the network, and this number reflects the number of nodes that are currently available for use by clients.

The phrase "number of dead nodes per unit time," in this context, refers to b. the prompt largeness of the count of protuberances that have depleted their battery resources and are thus no longer capable of communication with the base station.

The amount of residual energy (measured in battery volume) obtainable in the system per unit of time may be tracked using this account, and the account is updated in real-time when the network's residual energy changes. This is the total quantity of energy created by all nodes, regardless of the kind of node that is being utilized to generate the energy.

When calculating the amount of energy used by the execution of a specific strategy during the round under consideration, the amount of energy consumed by the execution of a specific strategy during the round under consideration is taken into account. Among other things, this energy is required for the operations of detecting, collecting, calculating, and transferring data from nodes to the base station.

The percentage of area covered about the length of the network is an important consideration to keep in mind when making this comparison. When it comes to network longevity, the amount of time that has passed since the network was first deployed, as well as the amount of time that has passed after the network was deactivated and decommissioned, are both important considerations. However, although it is typical to speak about extending the length of a network by making optimal use of existing resources, it is equally important to consider the amount of territory covered by the nodes throughout the planning process.

c. Outcomes

Several hours of debate resulted in the decision that the Improved would run on m = 0.7, which means that around 70% of the nodes got some more energy as compared to the initial Eo value. To be more specific, this was done to evaluate how the increased amount of energy that was provided to the nodes influenced their performance. Given that the network has a constant value and that the total quantity of energy in it is constant, we can use it to evaluate the value of utilizing the network by varying the value of mo between the ranges of 0.2 and 0.90.

Using mo value equal to 20% of the total energy nodes, it is possible to obtain the longest stable lifetime, which means that there are almost no dead or dying nodes over an average of 1000–7000 nodes as provided by the most sophisticated nodes (see Figure 4.7a). Whatever way you look at it, there is no doubt that the steepness that occurred before was caused by the death of ordinary nodes, which was then followed by the death of advanced and supernodes. The number of supernodes is much greater when comparing mo = 0.9 to other mo values (such as mo = 0.1 and 0.6),

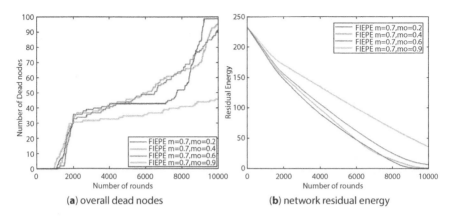

Figure 4.7 The behavior of improved changes in response to the number of supernodes. [Matlab coding].

and these supernodes contribute to a higher number of live nodes than when comparing other mo values (such as mo = 0.1 and 0.6).

Figure 4.7 represents the performance metrics. Even though the amount of dead nodes, the amount of residual vigor, and the amount of energy expended each round all seem to be advantageous for a greater number of supernodes in this scenario, the proportion of area covered per unit of time in this scenario are much lower. As an explanation, the super nodes have been put in an inner circle with a radius that is about equal to the distance between two nodes in a single hop, which is why this is occurring. When this occurs, the covered zones within a certain radius begin to overlap, resulting in a decrease in the percentage of the overall area covered.

In the correlative investigation, a total of three heterogeneous wireless sensor network protocols were employed, including SEP for two levels of heterogeneity, three-level SEP for three levels of heterogeneity, and a hybrid protocol for three levels of heterogeneity. Several characteristics of these protocols were shared with the SEP protocol, including the fact that they started with the same amount of initial energy as the network and had the same number of nodes as the network.

Initial calculations were made to assess how much of a difference there was between the SEPs of two distinct levels of nodes, namely normal and advanced in the initial investigation, which was carried out in two parts, the SEP for two different types of nodes was determined and analyzed. Based on the above results, it appears that the number of advanced nodes can be varied between 0.22 and 0.90 when the value of the parameter m = 0.22 to 0.90 is changed.

Depending on whether you have a certain quantity of total energy that is equal to or more than the amount of energy delivered by the source of energy, the efficiency of Improved may vary from 20 to 90 percent. In this study, the amount of additional energy required by 20% of advanced nodes is significant, and as a result, all normal nodes die after a certain period of time, whereas progressive nodes remain alive for a longer period of time due to the fact that data from a smaller number of nodes is being gathered. The possibility of seeing a similar pattern for varying percentages of advanced nodes is also possible. The fact that the network's chronology stays constant until the death of the first node, regardless of the number of progressive nodes that are present in the network at any one point, is also worth mentioning.

According to Figures 4.8a and b, the complete remaining potency of the system per unit of time stays constant up to and including the death of the first node, regardless of the state of the other nodes in the network. As a consequence, the procedure is performed over and over again until the simulation period has been reached.

The SEP for three levels has also been taken into consideration, which means that three types of nodes (normal, advanced, and super nodes) have all been studied, with the number of initial energies increasing from the first level to the final. This results in an increase in the number of super nodes (mo) for a given amount of total energy equal to Improved, from 0.1 to 0.9. However, a preset percentage of additional energy nodes is kept to allow comparison with present protocols at a later period (m). Following that, DEEC has been investigated for three unique types of nodes and situations that are identical to those mentioned above in the three-level SEP framework, and the findings have been made available for review. On the

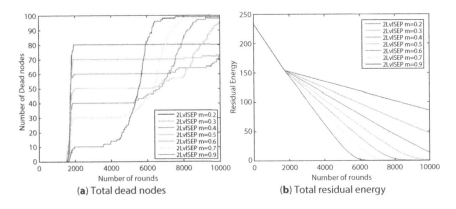

Figure 4.8 Overall performance metrics. [Matlab coding].

right-hand side of Figure 4.9a, you can see a bar graph indicating the number of dead nodes per unit time, with each node representing a unit of time in the graph. Furthermore, it has been shown that the death pattern of nodes for three-level SEP has no influence on the number of super protuberances that are used, however, DEEC is quite sensitive to variations in the number of amazing protuberances that are used. When looking at the system's overall lifetime, the DEEC system has a flat saturated region, with contributions from advanced nodes growing in proportion to the number of super nodes present in the system as the system develops. It appears that the amount of total residual energy in the network is a function of the number of wonderful bulges in the system, which is depicted in Figure 4.9b; however, as the number of super bulges in the network increases, it appears that the amount of residual energy is also increasing in the network, as depicted in Figure 4.9c. Following that, Figure 4.9d depicts the quantity of area that is covered in a certain period of time. However, increasing the number of beautiful protuberances enables the DEEC to exhibit a bigger

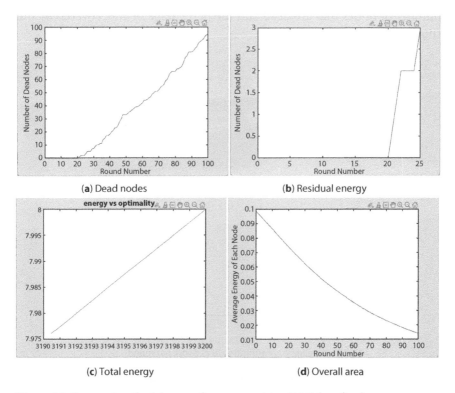

(a) Dead nodes   (b) Residual energy

(c) Total energy   (d) Overall area

Figure 4.9 Proposed methodology performance metrics. [Matlab coding].

amount of portion enclosed for a longer length of time, which is consistent with the prior results.

In the conclusion, we will give a comparison of Improved and SEP at the 2, 3, and DEEC stages. Figure 4.10 depicts a specific example of how the different components work together protocols discussed above operate when a fixed total quantity of energy is available in the network.

This is shown in Figure 4.10, which shows that the remaining liveliness in this situation is adequate until the death of the final node.

Table 4.2 summarizes the percentage gain in IMPROVED, the fuzzy stimulated liveliness well-organized protocol for diverse wireless sensor networks, as compared to the other protocols under consideration in terms of the number of nodes dead for the two parameters considered to be m = 0.7 and mo = 0.2. The number of nodes that die during the entire computation time is only 16%; as a result, the maximum amount of residual energy can be observed; however, the percentage of area covered by this scenario is only 13.29%, despite the fact that 51% of nodes are still alive during the entire computation time. This demonstrates that when the number of super nodes changes, there is a tradeoff between the number of nodes that are dead and the percentage of area covered by the super node network.

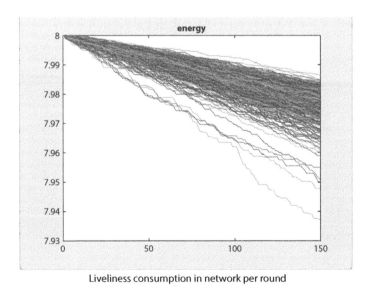

Liveliness consumption in network per round

Figure 4.10 Assessment of Improved with two levels. [Matlab coding].

Table 4.2 Percentage gain in Improved, the fuzzy inspired energy-efficient protocol for heterogeneous wireless sensor network as compared to existing protocols. [author's compilation].

Number of nodes dead	2-level SEP	3-level SEP	3-level DEEC
1% nodes dead	−11.19%	−10.07%	−50.38%
50% nodes dead	28.11%	23.89%	6.96%
80% nodes dead	27.17%	16.83%	10.32%
100% nodes dead	6.60%	1.60%	5.29%
Percentage area covered			
1% nodes dead	5.58%	1.96%	5.19%
50% nodes dead	11.97%	1.22%	1.68%
80% nodes dead	26.66%	8.86%	9.72%
100% nodes dead	100%	12.89%	100%

4.4 Conclusion

We have created a protocol for a more diverse wireless device system that does not allocate cluster heads to nodes based on a probabilistic threshold regardless of node load, residual energy volume, or data redundancy, but instead calculates cluster heads based on residual energy volume. Additionally, the nodes with more significant responsibilities are supplied with greater energy, allowing them to do their tasks. Following that, the optimal heterogeneity characteristics that had been derived theoretically were used to predict the proper amount of additional energy that was required for a certain node type that had been found via experimentation. According to the results of a simulation of Improved with SEP at two energy levels, three energy levels, and DEEC, improved is more lucrative than SEP. The same holds true when considering a larger proportion of the region covered by a comparable number of leftover energies and energy intake each cycle.

References

1. Yuanwei, L., Zhijin, Q., Maged, E., Zhiguo, D., Arumugam, N. *et al.*, Nonorthogonal multiple access for 5G and beyond. *Proc. IEEE*, 105, 12, 2347–2381, 2017.

2. Wang, J., Jin, A., Shi, D., Wang, L., Shen, H. *et al.*, Spectral efficiency improvement with 5G technologies: Results from field tests. *IEEE J. Sel. Areas Commun.*, 35, 8, 1867–1875, 2017.

3. Porambage, P., Okwuibe, J., Liyanage, M., Ylianttila, M., Taleb, T., Survey on multi-access edge computing for Internet of Things realization. *IEEE Commun. Surv. Tutorials*, 20, 4, 2961–2991, 2018.

4. Cai, Y., Qin, Z., Cui, F., Ye Li, G., McCann, J.A., Modulation and multiple access for 5G networks. *IEEE Commun. Surv. Tutorials*, 20, 1, 629–646, 2018.

5. Fan, W. and Wen, C., Low complexity iterative receiver design for sparse code multiple access. *IEEE Trans. Commun.*, 65, 2, 621–634, 2017.

6. Vameghestahbanati, M., Marsland, I.D., Gohary, R.H., Yanikomeroglu, H., Multidimensional constellations for uplink SCMA systems—A comparative study. *IEEE Commun. Surv. Tutorials*, 21, 3, 2169–2194, 2019.

7. Wang, B., Wang, K., Lu, Z., Xie, T., Quan, J., Comparison study of nonorthogonal multiple access schemes for 5G, in: *Proc. IEEE International Symposium on Broadband Multimedia Systems and Broadcasting*, pp. 1–5, 2015.

8. Moltafet, M., Yamchi, N.M., Javan, M.R., Azmi, P., Comparison study between PD-NOMA and SCMA. *IEEE Trans. Veh. Technol.*, 67, 2, 1830–1834, 2018.

9. Wu, Z., Lu, K., Jiang, C., Shao, X., Comprehensive study and comparison on 5G NOMA schemes. *IEEE Access*, 6, 18511–18519, 2018.

10. Yuan, Y., Yuan, Z., Yu, G., Hwang, C.-H., Liao, P.-K. *et al.*, Non-orthogonal transmission technology in LTE evolution. *IEEE Commun. Mag.*, 54, 7, 68–74, 2016.

11. Chen, Y., Bayesteh, A., Wu, Y., Ren, B., Kang, S. *et al.*, Towards the standardization of non-orthogonal multiple access for next generation wireless networks. *IEEE Communication Magazine*, 56, 3, 19–27, 2018.

12. Beko, M. and Dinis, R., Designing good multi-dimensional constellations. *IEEE Wireless Commun. Lett.*, 1, 3, 221–224, 2012.

13. Zhou, Y., Yu, Q., Meng, W., Li, C., SCMA codebook design based on constellation rotation, in: *IEEE International Conference on Communications (ICC), Paris, France*, pp. 1–6, 2017.

14. Yaoyue, H., Zhiwen, P., Nan, L., Xiaohu, Y., Multidimensional constellation design for spatial modulated SCMA systems. *IEEE Trans. Veh. Technol.*, 70, 9, 8795–8810, 2021.

15. Zhang, X.R., Chen, X., Sun, W., He, X.Z., Vehicle re-identification model based on optimized densenet121 with joint loss. *Comput. Mater. Contin.*, 67, 3, 3933–3948, 2021.

16. Zhu, F., Ren, Y., Wang, Q., Xia, J., Preservation mechanism of network electronic records based on broadcast- storage network in urban construction. *J. New Media*, 1, 1, 27–34, 2019.

17. Krishna, A., Emotion classification using EEG signals based on tunable-q wavelet transform. *IET Science, Measurement & Technology*, 13, 3, 375–380, 2018.

18. Mehmood, R. and Lee, H., A novel feature extraction method based on late positive potential for emotion recognition in human brain signal patterns. *Comput. Electr. Eng.*, 53, 444–457, 2016.

19. Bhatti, A., Human emotion recognition and analysis in response to audio music using brain signals. *Comput. Hum. Behav.*, 65, 267–275, 2016.

20. Bajaj, V., Taran, S., Sengur, A., Emotion classification using flexible analytic wavelet transform for electroencephalogram signals. *Health Inf. Sci. Syst.*, 6, 1, 12, 2018.

21. Zhao, G. and Wang, H., Emotion analysis for personality inference from EEG signals. *IEEE Trans. Affect. Comput.*, 9, 3, 362–371, 2017.

22. Yang, Y., EEG-based emotion recognition using hierarchical network with subnetwork nodes. *IEEE Trans. Cognit. Dev. Syst.*, 10, 2, 408–419, 2017.

5

Development of a Safe Health Framework Using a Temporary Blockchain Technique

J. Venkatesh[1]* and R. Janarthanan[2]

*[1]Center for System Design, Department of Computer Science and Engineering,
Chennai Institute of Technology, Chennai, Tamil Nadu, India
[2]Center for Artificial Intelligence, Department of Computer Science and Engineering,
Chennai Institute of Technology, Chennai, Tamil Nadu, India*

Abstract

Medical records may now be saved, viewed, and updated at any time and from any location thanks to the introduction of the internet and its impact on the health industry. The lack of standards was likely the most significant issue, but it was not the only one in the field of electronic health records. Decentralized online ledgers (DOLs) were already being proposed and utilized to tackle interoperability and privacy issues associated with blockchain-based systems when they were first introduced. Scalability, usability, and accessibility are the three most challenging technical challenges to overcome. The first technical challenge is keeping the many different types of medical information off-chain while maintaining secure, on-chain access control mechanisms. In medical situations, the second difficulty is to identify who owns what and how to allocate data access control. By using the temporal blockchain technique, the Safe eHealth Framework (SeFra) is introduced, with the goal of overcoming these challenges. In the SeFra fundamental building blocks, particular focus is dedicated to secrecy, improved integrity control, and access control approaches, with the Context-based Merkle Tree being one such example (CBMT). Temporal features, HL7 criteria, and interplanetary file system data management are all used in the Framework to facilitate interoperability and the control of scalability concerns (IPFS). The findings of this study indicate the impact of the SeFra framework on the security of the personalized micro booklet (PML), specifically on the time-based shadow ideas and context-based characteristics of the personalized micro booklet (PML). Because of the architecture's

---

Corresponding author: venkateshj@citchennai.net

Kiran Sood, Rajesh Kumar Dhanaraj, Balamurugan Balusamy and Seifedine Kadry (eds.) Blockchain Technology in Corporate Governance: Transforming Business and Industries, (99–124) © 2023 Scrivener Publishing LLC

enormous potential to address the issues of siloed data and allow tamper-proof, secure healthcare transactions, it is being pursued.

Keywords: Safe eHealth framework, context-based merkle tree, temporal blockchain, personalized micro ledger, context-based access control

5.1   Introduction

A vast volume of health data is created on a regular basis. The health information about each patient is dispersed across a number of different providers, making it difficult for them to communicate effectively. Keeping a huge quantity of health data secure and private is a difficult task, especially in today's world [1]. The issue of interoperability amongst multiple providers is a difficult one to solve. Patients and suppliers may face significant obstacles in the recovery of information and the exchange of health data if monetary incentives are used to initiate the blocking of health information. The current technique stores the patient's health record in a centralized cloud storage system. A central cloud is being used by companies such as Amazon, Microsoft, and others to run their operations.

There are several benefits to cloud computing, but privacy is difficult to protect and manage, especially when dealing with sensitive data such as electronic health records. The electronic health record of a patient is sensitive and confidential, and it is everyone's responsibility to ensure that it is kept safe. When it comes to a centralized cloud, privacy and security are the most pressing concerns.

The decentralized form of the cloud eliminates the security concerns associated with a centralized cloud. The information is saved in a decentralized directory on a large number of nodes and is not controlled by a single entity. It is not necessary to spend more funds on the storing of health information. Story, Maid Safe, File Coin, Sia coin, and other decentralized cloud systems have been used to store health data, as have other decentralized cloud systems [2]. Numerous decentralized online books have been written to address challenges of interoperability and privacy, as well as scalability, integrity, usability, and accessibility. Among them are the following: Among the initial challenges facing the healthcare system is the preservation of multiple types of medical information, including text, video, and picture, among others, which are now held off-chain but will be made available in the future securely via the chain. The most difficult aspect is adhering to a slew of rules while transmitting health information across different providers. To communicate picture data between suppliers and the DICOM standard, the HL7 protocol, which is used for exchanging text files between different providers, is used.

The first difficulty with the healthcare system is that different types of medical information, such as text, video, picture, and so on, are maintained out of the chain of custody so that they may be accessed securely at a later time. The most difficult difficulty is adhering to a variety of standards while transmitting health data across different providers [3]. The HL7 standard is used for the transmission of picture files among providers, whereas the DICOM standard is used for the communication of text data across providers.

The paper proposes a secure e-health framework (Sefira) that incorporates a progressive temporal blockchain to solve the issues mentioned above. The legitimacy and integrity of electronic health records were the primary emphasis of this paradigm. The design is primarily meant to protect the electronic health record without the involvement of a third party. In the healthcare business, the blockchain is utilized to ensure the validity and integrity of patient records. The context-based Merkle Tree (CBMT) and the context-based access control (CBAC) of a Smart Contract are the two most important components of Sefira. It is the first of them, which is a decentralized network of electronic health data as well as information on access restrictions, that has been incorporated in the Smart Contract.

5.2   Related Work

The majority of the research in question suggests that a blockchain-based health architecture should be implemented. The study focuses on the integration and interoperability of electronic health records (EHRs) using blockchain technology.

Medrek is a blockchain-based decentralized healthcare system that was developed in the United Kingdom. When dealing with sensitive information, confidentiality, authentication, and data exchange are essential components. Some individuals, such as public health organizations, scientists, and others, rely on these factors. It might perform the role of a miner, granting access to anonymized data. The notion proof is used by the Medrek [4]. In order to retain health information and a medical prototype, Medrek used the Ethereum blockchain.

Patient-centered healthcare saves money by cutting out the middleman [5]. Decentralized system that also ensures data security is what blockchain is all about! Patentor is a way of creating a patient-centered health record. The patentor Smart Contract allows you to define access privileges depending on your position. The key concerns of the patient are the integrity and interoperability of the system. Blockchain ensures that HIPAA laws and standards are followed and that they are compatible with one another.

Medi chain is a type of consensus based on evidence of labor performed in a secure environment [6]. It is a patient-centric data management system that is utilized in both the mobile app and the standard web browser, according to the company. The Linux Foundation is responsible for the upkeep of the hyperbook, which contains health information. The RBAC-SC is primarily concerned with providing access services that are dependent on the duties of other organizations [7]. It performs checks with various authorities by using attribute-based encryption [8].

A blockchain-based exchange of health information, Blochian, is a platform that maintains a wide range of medical data [9]. Because of the mix of off-chain and on-chain checks, the system is more secure and authenticated. The blockchain contains electronic medical data, as well as personal medical records for each individual.

The primary flaw with older systems is that hackers attempt to learn the input value by providing varied input data and predicting the most probable Hash result from that data. Because of the weak hash function, the collection conspires against the time of the hash chain, and it has been shown to be a limitation on the states of the hash chains that have been authorized as cooperative evidence as a result of this.

5.2.1   Blockchain-Based Healthcare Organization

The quality of healthcare services varies greatly from country to country. The majority of countries do not have public services, but some do have privatized services and others do not have open access to intellectual property. These disparities highlight the difficulty of delivering healthcare to a large number of individuals. In the healthcare industry, security is a crucial issue to deal with. The use of the blockchain to protect the safety and confidentiality of critical medical information is becoming more popular. Between 2009 and 2017, a total of more than 176 million patient data were stolen [10]. The firms believe that distributed ledger technologies (DLTs) are the only method of resolving issues with medical information. Due to the fact that blockchain may be utilized as interoperability or traditional layer, it might be beneficial for communication between systems of various types.

The blockchain is being used by the firms listed below to assist in the transformation of the management of patient data and electronic health record systems. Despite the enormous potential of blockchain technology to expand and improve the value of the healthcare system, just a few firms have begun researching it. The healthcare framework is still being developed by the majority of firms. Some organizations concentrated on patient centricity, while others concentrated on traceability of drugs, billing methods, and other aspects of business operations. The many firms each concentrated on a certain procedure. The majority of the company's healthcare infrastructure is only a prototype that was never put into operation in the real world of healthcare. In terms of interoperability, the most important consideration is that the blockchain hash must be compatible with the prior system. Blockchain healthcare startups such as Guard Time, Medrek, Roomed, Pocketbook, Factor, Stratum, and Tyrion are among the many emerging technologies in the field [11]. Table 5.1 depicts a high-level overview of the healthcare organization that is built on Blockchain technology.

5.2.2   Medrek

Medrek, a blockchain-based health system that manages information about patients' health, is the most widely used blockchain-based health system. The decentralized Medrek ledger stores all patient information and is utilized by the therapeutic community (doctor), patients, and medical scientists to make decisions about their care.

5.2.3   Stratum

As previously mentioned by Richard Caetano, CEO of Stratum, he aimed to produce a proof of concept in order to conduct clinical trials. Building a safe health system that can be shared across labs, clinicians, and researchers is the goal.

5.2.4   Factor

Primary goal is to build a secure means of storing health data using blockchain technology that is accessible to hospitals and other management personnel. It is possible to connect each patient's health record to a safety chip that contains patient information and allows an authorized person to access the information.

The Estonian company, KSI Blockchain Technology, has a workforce of 150 cryptographers and has developed blockchain technology. The Netherlands, the United States, the United Kingdom, and Singapore are among the countries where the guard works throughout the day. Partners in the distribution of media and insurance. In 2017, the government of Estonia decided to implement a guard time system to secure the electronic health records of over a million Estonians. The KSI blockchain technology is being used to preserve electronic health record [12].

5.2.5   Pocketbook

Pocketbook is an API company that provides a blockchain solution based on the Do chain protocol. When it comes to the medical services industry, the Do chain is a transmitted exchange system that operates on money and clinical information. As the hidden record for meeting chip-level blockchain requirements utilizing Intel processors, the firm makes use of the open-source Hyperledger Sawtooth from Intel, which is developed by Intel [13]. The hyperedge transaction is handled via the use of an intelligent contract.

5.2.6   Tyrion

Tyrion made use of blockchain technology in order to safeguard the patient record. Every record, as well as pharmaceuticals with an approved history of ownership, is stored in this system. The organization makes use of time signatures and credentials to ensure that the whole system runs smoothly

5.2.7   Roomed

Roomed is a platform that blends artificial intelligence and blockchain technology to deliver health services to patients. The company gathers patient information using chatbots, wearable analytical devices, and telemedicine, and then distributes that information to the health team as needed. The Smart Contract contains information on the patient as well as access privileges.

Table 5.1 provides an overview of the blockchain-based healthcare organization, which is described as follows.

5.3   Secure Framework (Sefira) for Healthcare System

One of the primary features of the Sefira proposal framework is the use of a General Public Ledger (GPL), Personalized Micro Ledger (PML), Smart Contract, and Context Access Control (CBAC). It is possible to verify the legitimacy of a transaction using the Temporal Hash Signature (THS), which

Table 5.1 Summary of blockchain-based healthcare organization.

S. no.	Company	Discussion
1	Medrek	MIT project – Give patients the control over their data
2	Stratum	French startup – trust panning from data falsification
1	Factor	Blockchain-based authenticity medical billing process
4	Guard time	Instant medical access, Insurance
5	Pocketbook	Identity and payment optimization in the healthcare system
6	Tyrion	Global Blockchain platform company with Philips's health
7	Roomed	Russian blockchain company – Share the health information between providers.

[Author Compilation].

is accomplished by running the hash function and comparing the results with those stored in the blockchain. Last but not least, the root hash value on the blockchain is preserved. There are two critical components to the proposed Sefira architecture: the THS and a progressive temporal blockchain. The THS is the first of these components, and the progressive temporal blockchain is the second [14]. The Sefira framework is shown in Figure 5.1, which describes its operation. The mining mechanism utilized in the blockchain is processed, and the anonymized data is then used by medical researchers to compensate the blockchain storage provider for their efforts. When using standard blockchain, the most difficult obstacles are to link the hash chain to its form, and the second is a powerful hash function, which challenges to know the input value but assaults to examine the input model and test with any data in order to try to decipher the contents [15]. Both of these disadvantages are addressed by the Progressive Temporal Blockchain (PTB). The system model of the proposed work described in the next section.

i. Functionality of Sefira Framework

HL7 (Seven International Health Level) is a collection of principles, forms, and standards that are used to produce electronic health records in the area of electronic health records (also known as electronic medical records)

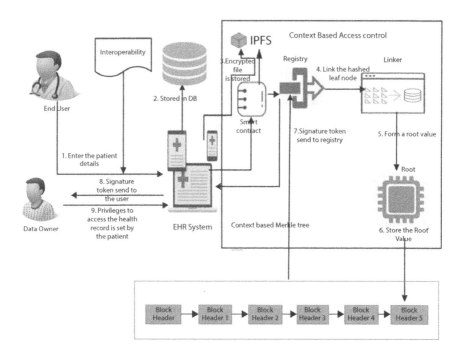

Figure 5.1 Secure framework (Sefira) for healthcare system (author compilation).

(EHR). The World Health Organization established the HL7 principles and declared them to be the information technology standard for medical services as well as the recognized information technology model for human services. Although the HL7 standard was first developed in 1987, it was not formally recognized until 1994 by the American National Standards Institute. By giving instructions on how to use its standards, HL7 helps to the supply of worldwide interoperability in information technology-based healthcare. The number "7" refers to the seventh layer of the Reference Model for Open Systems Interconnections (RMOSI), which is defined as follows: (OSI). Medical message interchange, decision-making, rule syntax, and the standard definition of health data and clinical records are all covered in detail in Health Level 7 (HL7) counseling resources. The HL7 guideline materials are accessible for download on the internet.

In order to transmit an electronic health record between two healthcare providers, the HL7 standard must be used. HL7 is an international standard that is used by a wide range of healthcare providers to transport health information between software programmers and between hospitals and other healthcare facilities. Specifically, it accomplishes so through making use of the healthcare system, which offers the necessary skills, norms, and standards. Resources exchange standards are among the several HL7 standards that are in use, the most notable of which being the Fast Healthcare Interoperability Resources (FHIR) standard. Figure 5.2 depicts an example Lab report that was prepared in HL7 format for a specific patient, and Figure 5.3 depicts the same report in a different format.

1. Interplanetary file system

   It is a peer-to-peer distributed file system that connects all of the other peer systems by establishing links with them. IPFS, as seen in Figure 5.3, is a content-addressable network that also includes distributed file storage and data interchange capabilities. Each item in the database is represented by a hash value, which is stored in the database. Additionally, it moves data inside the Git repository while also eliminating data redundancy with the help of the BitTorrent swarm by deleting redundant data from the repository.

   Each record is identified by a unique fingerprint known as a cryptographic hash. It provides quick speed as well as

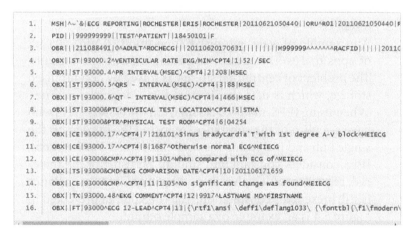

Figure 5.2 Sample HL7 patient record (author compilation).

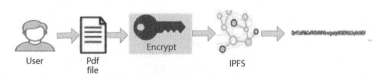

Figure 5.3 File sharing in IPFS (author compilation).

decentralized archiving, with each file having a human-readable name (IPNS) assigned by the system. Ram, for example, might want to share a file with his friend Sam. Ram transfers the data to the IPFS storage system. The file will be deployed in the current working directory after that. After that, a hash value is created, which always begins with the letter Qi. The data has now been made accessible to the rest of the network. By using the hash value, Sam will be able to get access to the file. Rather of downloading from a central server or a single server, use a cloud-based service. A route from a distributed server may be provided by a peer. The Merkle DAG is used to establish a link between nodes in IPFS using hashes as a means of connecting them together (Directed Acyclic Graph). The following are the benefits of using Merkle DAG to prune your trees.

Content addressing – Each record has a unique hash identifier No duplication – Each file is stored only once and cannot copy.

Carefully designed – Data has confirmed with it is a checksum, so if there is any change, then IPFS knows the data is modified.

An example of a decentralised application (dApp) is a set of apps that work together to produce the desired results. The problem of centralised storage is solved by decentralised storage, which is data that is stored in a dispersed manner. When using IPFS, material is sent from the closest peers who have a replica of the substance, reducing the burden on the single hub and increasing the user experience. Furthermore, IPFS considers constant and smooth perusing of the material, regardless of whether or not the owner of the substance is still present for consultation. The IPFS output presented in Figure 5.4 is an example of a sample output.

```
saravanaguru@guru:~/Documents$ ipfs add SeFra -r
added Qmaut2RXzTyuimsuQVuaU34h48p3FGyeLgE7h7FZ1R3r4E SeFra/patient1.pdf
added QmQ4sH9j8b5sAgx8MB8JDR6YWNkKxGjTc37sqxDY8iKbii SeFra/patient1.png
added Qmf7E1AxfqSJmVgwtQoMNpHpZRqCL2swdGwCubB6GaxMfL SeFra/patient1.xlsx
added QmchFRpXrGzEYMk8njyepAomoojMooJJhBNMQmkKAKo2jH SeFra
 67.37 KiB / 67.37 KiB [=================================================
saravanaguru@guru:~/Documents$ ipfs pin add Qmaut2RXzTyuimsuQVuaU34h48p3FGyeLgE7h7FZ1R3r4E
pinned Qmaut2RXzTyuimsuQVuaU34h48p3FGyeLgE7h7FZ1R3r4E recursively
saravanaguru@guru:~/Documents$ ▮
```

Figure 5.4 Sample output of IPFS (author compilation).

5.3.1   Progressive Temporal Blockchain

To reach the last transaction in a progressive temporal blockchain, each transaction must rely on the subsequent next transaction in order to be successful. In order to make the transaction more secure, it produces a temporal shadow and an active hash function, which prevents hackers from determining the hash value by providing alternative input data. Before attaching the hash value to each record, the temporal shadow is appended to each record. Before hashing the transaction, adding the height of the subtree to the concatenated hash value from the child node, the length of the hash chain approved before hashing, and then hashing the transaction again Each transaction is validated with the use of a signature on the document. The Temporal Hash Signature (THS) is utilized in this case to authenticate the user without the involvement of a third party. The presence of breaches may be recognized nearly immediately if the monitor signature changes.

5.3.2   Temporal Shadow

Allen makes the argument that there is a temporal relationship between the two incidents. When looking at the interval x and y, Allen refers to Figure 5.5, which shows the seven essential temporal relationships. Depending on the previous transaction, the potential sample relations of each transaction rely on the previous transaction, or the current transaction is required to start the next transaction, or two transactions might start at the same time, depending on the previous transaction.

To increase the security of a transaction in the Sefira framework, the temporal shadow is deployed. The three parameters of a nonce, the hash value of the preceding transaction, and the timestamp are used to evaluate each transaction in this context. It is dependent on the following successive

HS	Allen's relations	Graphical representation
(A)	$[x, y] \, R_A \, [x', y'] \Leftrightarrow y = x'$	
(L)	$[x, y] \, R_L \, [x', y'] \Leftrightarrow y < x'$	
(B)	$[x, y] \, R_B \, [x', y'] \Leftrightarrow x = x', y' < y$	
(E)	$[x, y] \, R_E \, [x', y'] \Leftrightarrow y = y', x < x'$	
(D)	$[x, y] \, R_D \, [x', y'] \Leftrightarrow x < x', y' < y$	
(O)	$[x, y] \, R_O \, [x', y'] \Leftrightarrow x < x' < y < y'$	

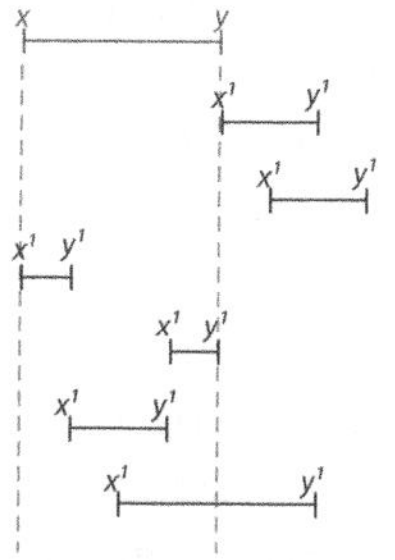

Figure 5.5 Allen's interval relation [16].

transaction to complete the last transaction in order to be successful. Time-related characteristics are attached to each transaction. Time-related properties were the focus of the temporal shadow, which was cast on them. Each transaction in temporal shadow should have a timestamp applied to it, and temporal shadow should add the timestamp after attaching the hash value. The nonce value, Personalized Micro Ledger (PML) root value, and timestamp serve as the temporal shadow for the General Public Ledger (GPL). For the temporal shadow to be calculated, the PML takes into account the random number, the timestamp, and the preceding hash value. With the help of the Progressive temporal blockchain, it is possible to prove the validity, integrity, and authenticity of electronic information.

5.3.2.1   Context-Based Merkle Tree (CBMT)

The temporal shadow and progressive temporal blockchain were used to increase the security of the system. When it comes to the Sefira framework, two ledgers are maintained: one is called the General Public Ledger (GPL), and the other is called the Personalized Micro Ledger (PML) (PML). In order to aggregate all of the transactions occurring at a certain moment, the Context-based Merkle Tree (CBMT) is employed. The context indicates that it is dependent on the time, the place, and the identity of the speaker. Before hashing, the height of the subtree is attached to the concatenated hash value from the child node, which represents the height of the subtree.

Each and every patient transaction is recorded in the General Public Ledger (GPL). Temporal shadow, root value, and current transaction are the three components that make up the GPL. The Context-based Merkle Tree (CBMT) is used to ensure that the data is kept in its original form. The Merkle tree was first presented in 1979 by Ralph Merkle. In the GPL, each patient transaction is regarded to be a leaf node. Each patient transaction is saved in the block for the duration of the block's existence. Each nonleafy node is represented by a hash value of its own. The temporal shadow is attached to each transaction's hash value before it is generated and stored in the database. Before attaching the hash value to each record, the temporal shadow is appended to each record. For each transaction, the height of the subtree was appended to the concatenated hash value from the child node before hashing, and then the length of the hash chain was accepted prior to having the hash value computed. The Temporal Hash Signature (THS) infrastructure is created and confirmed without the involvement of third parties that are considered trustworthy.

Algorithm 1.1 Context-based Merkle Tree (CBMT)

Input: patient record z_i; patient public key Pa_k;
    Patient private key Pk_s; Doctor keys po_d, po_{ds}:
    i_n nonce; st_{ir} temporal shadow; this Temporal Hash Signature
       (THS); height of the tree l; sub activity hash value i_s;
       p_{romote} sub activity root value;
Output: Transaction deployed in the blockchain
Begin:
    Step1: for (i←1; i < n; i++)
       p_i←Sig((ps_{dk}) encrypt(rec_i,pk_{pk})) //Doctor encrypt the
       record p_i←r_i hash(p_i)
    Step 2: ts_i←hash(t_i&&n_i&&p_{rooti}) //Registry server receives
       the hash of records and forwards it to the linker server.
       y_i←hash(s_i&&ts_i&&l_i)
       General ledger z_i←hash(r_i&&ts_i&&l_i)
    Step 3: Linker convert the hash of value into trees and for-
       ward to the next higher-level server
       z_i←hash(r_i && ts_i && l_i)
    Step 4: Root hash value stored in the Calendar database.
       cal←Z_{root}
    Step 5: The patient set access privilege in the Smart Contract.
    Step 6: The bytecode of a Smart Contract deployed in the
       blockchain.
    Step 7: Finally it is stored in the blockchain, and the signa-
       ture token sent
       patient -> ths_i End for End

---

a) Personalized Micro Ledger (PML)

    The Personalized Micro Ledger (PML) is a system that keeps
    track of each patient's individual transactions. It keeps track
    of the sub-activity that is responsible for keeping track of the
    health record in this ledger. Each subactivity has its own hash
    value, which is then combined to make a tree. The temporal
    shadow utilized in the PML is a kind of shadow. The gener-
    ation of a temporal shadow is predicated on the time when
    the transaction was created. This ledger is solely responsible
    for the maintenance of sub-activity in health records such
    as sub-data (di), nonce (n), and temporal shadow (ts). For
    example, the patient is suffering from health problems and

has sought therapy in a hospital. A prescription is issued by the doctor, and this transaction is dependent on a number of subtransactions. The first step is to register your personal information, which is a sub-transaction. The next step is to schedule an appointment, which is another sub-transaction. The next step is to make a payment, which is still another transaction. A PML is formed by aggregating all of the sub-transactions together. The root value of the PML that was provided as input for the final transaction, which is stored in the General Public Ledger (GPL)

Layers of Context-based Merkle Tree (CBMT)

Three layers were maintained to generate the Merkle tree-like registry layer, linker layer, and root layer. The first layer is the registry layer, which initiates the registration request.

An upper-level layer is notified by receiving the hash value of a transaction and forwarding the hash value to a registry. It is the responsibility of the registry to link the hashes of transactions and pass the information to the next level linker.

Finally, the root hash value contains the top hash value that was previously saved in the root hash value. Temporal Hash Signature (THS) is a digital signature that is produced and delivered to the registry through an aggregator. These are the three layers of the Merkle tree that are seen in Figure 5.6.

The end-user submits the hash of data to the registry, which then connects the hash of data and transfers it to a higher level of hierarchy in the organization. Each patient's health information is hashed using the

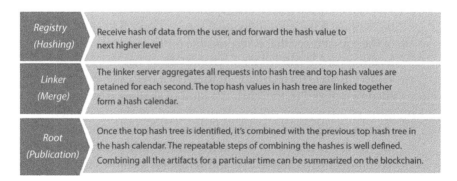

Figure 5.6 Layers of Context-Based Merkle Tree (CBMT) (author compilation).

SHA256 technique, and the hash result is sent to a higher tier of the system for processing.

b) Linker

The linker layer gets the hash value from the lower level layer and creates a connection between the hash of value and the original value. The signature token is generated without the need of any keys in this case. The hash value is sent to the parent node by the approved child node and stored in the parent node. The linker creates a connection between all of the hash values entered by the user. The same procedure was followed again and again until the final result was obtained.

c) Root Layer (also known as the root layer of a tree)

The linker layer gets the hash value from the aggregator, as well as all of the root values from the subtree aggregate, and stores them in the root layer of the tree structure. The temporal shadow that is created for each transaction is done so without the assistance of trustworthy third parties. It is possible to produce Temporal Hash Signatures (THS) for authentication reasons and have them validated without the requirement for trusted third parties.

5.3.2.2   Temporal Hash Signature (THS)

The suggested works are designed to address the shortcomings of the current work. The rationale for using the Temporal Hash Signature (THS) is that it ensures correct authentication when accessing an eHealth record (eHealth record). The authorized user must use the THS token to authenticate himself or herself. It is necessary for a patient to properly save the THS token in order to get access to their health record, and a doctor may access the patient's information after they have received the signature token from the user. In previous systems, the doctor must remember a specific THS in order to access the patient record; however, in the proposed work, the doctor may access any record simply by providing the most recent THS to the system.

The Smart Contract keeps track of all signatures; all it does is compare the most recent hash signature to the most valuable hash signature, and if the hash signatures match, it grants access to the record, with the privileges being verified in the Smart Contract. Despite the fact that the user possesses the THS, privilege is checked in the Smart Contract because, regrettably, a hacker may get the THS but not the privilege to access the record, and as a result, could not access the record if the privilege was not checked.

5.3.2.3   Context-Based Access Control (CBAC) in Smart Contract

Each record has its own temporal context tag, which makes it easier to find information. By using the temporal context tag, health records may be retrieved by specifying a specific time period such as a year, month, week, or day. In the next step, the access privileges for each patient record are defined in a Smart Contract. Depending on the privileges assigned by the Smart Contract, the authorized user is granted access to the eHealth data set out. The CBMT Smart Contract is maintained on the blockchain in progressive temporal time. The CBAC in Smart Contract is responsible for maintaining four contracts, including a patient contract, patient history, an insurance contract, and a billing contract, among other things. They will not be able to modify a contract after it has been recorded on the blockchain. This method of access is quick, low-cost, and highly secure. In this case, access restriction is not only determined by the user's credentials, but also by the time and place of the event.

5.3.2.4   Layered Architecture of SeFra

The suggested approach consists of four levels, each of which is utilized to transfer data amongst various service providers via the usage of blockchain technology. The layers are divided into four categories: the application layer, the query layer, the data provenance layer, and the database layer. The SeFra system is divided into layers, as seen in Figure 5.7. The secure system is implemented using JavaScript. The user can enter the details and also retrieve the data from the system for research or another purpose. In the posed system, the user is doctors, patients, billing, insurance, nurses, lab technician, Etc. Each user accesses the data for different purposes. This layer mainly used as a communication interface between user and application.

In the IPFS, each patient record is encrypted using the RSA technique and kept in a secure location. The hash value that was created was submitted to the blockchain, which allowed for safe access control to the record to be established. The benefit of using IPFS is that it may store any kind of data, including text, images, videos, and other types of media. However, in the proposed work, we will just examine text files.

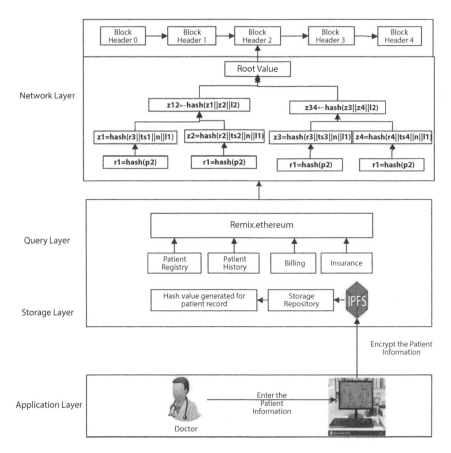

Figure 5.7 Layered architecture (author compilation).

a. Query Layer

The user wishes to access data from the database, and as a result, the user sends a series of queries to the system, which the system then executes. The query layer's principal function is to accept a request from the user and to respond to the request by sending the result to the user. Automatically occurring conditions enable the user to either see or prohibit access to a certain record based on their existence. This is referred to as a Temporal Hash Signature since the public key is the same for every patient who created the transaction at a certain time, while the private key is distinct for each transaction, as opposed to a Digital Signature (THS). The Smart Contract contains all of the keys that are needed. If a user requests access to data, the Smart Contract verifies that the user is who he or she claims to be with the aid of keys and privileges.

It enables users to have access to information stored in an existing database. The Smart Contract was created in order to describe the rights. Each transaction is indexed in the Smart Contract and safely kept on the blockchain, which is a distributed ledger. Each result is delivered to all of the nodes that are dispersed. This layer is in charge of validating each user request and sending the response to the user who has successfully authenticated. The information should be shared primarily inside the network, so that anybody who has the appropriate privileges may view the record. The procedures that must be followed while processing patient records.

The patient records are produced and kept on a distributed network with thousands of nodes, which allows for greater efficiency. The blockchain contains the hash value of the patient's identification. Because each file is tied to the previous hash value, it is difficult to change the patient's record by altering the hash value. In addition to the generalized public ledger (GPL), it also maintains the Personalized Micro Ledger (PML). GPL maintains all patient health records, and each file is connected to the one that came before it in order to protect the integrity of the electronic health records system. The PML, on the other hand, has the customized patient record, which contains the micro-level information on the specific patient. In order to maintain the integrity of the health record, each patient record is connected to the previous records, as well as having a temporal shadow attached to the end of the record. The Smart Contract is kept up to date in exchange for an access permission. Role-based access control grants access to the health data to the authenticated user depending on the access privileges granted to that user. Authentication in a Smart Contract is accomplished via the use of Context-based Access Control (CBAC), according to the suggested approach. Context-based Access Control (CBAC) in Smart Contracts comprises information about the ownership of records, the rights granted to those records, and the integrity of the data. Breach detection is virtually instantaneous as long as the monitor's signature does not change.

Steps to Take While Uploading a File

1. During the registration procedure, the patient provides the SeFra System with his or her public key. The RSA technique is used by the doctor to encrypt the patient's health information using the patient's public key in order to ensure the information's security.
2. All of the patient's information is saved locally for future reference. The IPFS network stores the encrypted patient

health records, allowing for access to the information from any location at any time.

3. The SHA256 method with temporal shadow is used by electronic health record systems to turn the list of encrypted patient records into a hash of documents, which is translated into fixed-length associated with time using the SHA256 algorithm.

4. In Step 4, the registry server gets the hash of records; before transferring each record to a higher level of abstraction, each transaction is appended with a temporal shadow, and then the hashed value is sent to the linker server.

5. The linker organizes the hash of value into trees and then forwards the information to the next higher level server. For each round, the global hash tree is generated by the linker servers in a hierarchical fashion.

6. The root server, which is located at the very top of the linker hierarchy. The Calendar database contains the hash value for the root node.

7. A signature token is constructed using the top hash value as a starting point and a leaf hash value as an ending point. Each transaction is hashed and built into a Merkle tree, with the root value of the tree being saved in the block header of the block.

8. The Smart Contract is stored on the blockchain, and it enables the patient to choose who has access to his or her data and under what circumstances.

9. The Temporal Hash Signature (THS) token generated by the user registry server is delivered to the user registry server.

To get a copy of the file, click here.

1. The doctor asks for access to the patient's information by providing a valid patient identification number.

2. The request is sent to the blockchain for processing. Before anything else, the user is prompted to input the signature token.

3. The user submits a Temporal Hash Signature (THS), and the registry verifies that the signature is valid.

4. The access privileges are validated in the Context-based Access Control (CBAC) in the Smart Contract at the next

level of authentication, and the authorized user is granted access to the data at that level of authentication.

5. The encrypted health record is decrypted with the help of the user-patient private key, which is sent to the doctor by phone by the patient and doctor.

b. Implementation of the SeFra System

JavaScript is used in the development of the SeFra framework application. Doctor consultations are available, and a prescription record is posted for patient review. An encrypted version of the prescription file was posted to the IPFS network, which was then decrypted. Patients' health records are encrypted by their doctors with the use of their public keys, and the patient may decrypt their records using their own private keys, which are provided by them. The IPFS network has an encrypted copy of the record. The hash value of the file that was produced is referred to as the content address. The temporal shadow was introduced before the hash value was generated. The hash value is always preceded by the letter Qm. The hash value of the file that has been saved on the Ethereum blockchain is shown below.

The remix.ethereum is a web-based integrated development environment for the Ethereum blockchain. It is used to establish a connection between the frontend and the blockchain. Solidity is the programming language that is utilized in the remix.ethereum, and it is also the language that is used to establish the access rights in the Smart Contract. The user installed the metamask in his or her browser in order to deploy the transaction on the Ethereum blockchain, according to the instructions. This study work was carried out using the remix.ethereum and metamask integrated development environment, which was designed to help with the implementation of healthcare-related information. This application will function properly if the user has installed the metamask in their browser.

The EMR bots are a dataset that was utilized in this study (En.wikipedia, 2019). It comprises three different sorts of datasets, such as 100 patient records, 10,000 patient records, and 100,000 patient records, among others. Encryption of the patient's health record is performed by the doctor using the patient public key, and decryption is performed by the patient private key. The encrypted health record is hashed and placed in the IPFS folder once it has been encrypted. Before creating the hash values, a temporal shadow was applied to the equation. Here, the root value of the hashed file that was provided as input for the General Public Ledger was used to hash the sub-activity of the patient record such as registration, appointment, payment, and so on (GPL). The level of protection for the health record has been raised. They are also difficult to trace back to the source of the information. Solidity is the programming language that is used to create a Smart Contract. The hashed data is sent to the Smart Contract, the byte code for the health record is formed, and the Smart Contract is deployed in the blockchain with the assistance of the remix.ethereum online tool. A Smart Contract compiler generates an application binary interface that is used by the application. Blockchain makes use of the application binary interface and invokes the contract in order to activate the access privilege on the blockchain. Transactions on the Ethereum blockchain are deployed using the metamask, which is created by the user.

The SeFra framework includes a number of different stakeholders. The dashboard of the SeFra has a distinct login for each person who needs to use the system. The many stakeholders include the doctor, the patient, the nurse, the administrative staff, billing, insurance, and so on. Doctors may submit patient information into the SeFra eHealth systems if the doctor has been validated by the system.

Each user receives the private key and root of the PML as to the public key for the particular record. The system checks the root value of the PML and the next level of the tree, and partial checking is done to ensure the authorized user access of the record.

The main aim is to verify the Context-based Merkle Tree (CBMT) to check the integrity of the record. The integrity of the file quickly verified with a CBMT. The integrity of the transaction efficiently checked in less time with the help of PML. The Personalized Micro Ledger (PML) is not maintained in the existing system. So, the verification time of the transaction is high in the existing system. Table 5.2 explains the comparative analysis of the proposed system with the existing system. The patient-centric healthcare system, like MedRec, Patientory, Medibloc, and Medichain, compared with the proposed system. In the proposed work, each transaction hashed with temporal properties. These techniques provide more security to the healthcare record, and Personalized Micro Ledger (PML) used, which reduces the verification time of the record. So, the proposed system is more secure when compared with the existing works (Figure 5.8).

c. Conclusions and Discussions

The suggested approach provides a solution to the security vulnerabilities that have been identified. SeFra addresses the following security issues in accordance with the proposed approach.

d. Confidentiality

The term "confidentiality" refers to the fact that an unauthorized user will not be able to access health information. Double security measures

Table 5.2 Comparison of different blockchain eHealth framework.

	Medrec (Ekblaw et al., 2016)	Patientory (McFarlane et al., 2017)	Medibloc (Vallies, 2017)	Medichain (Rouhani et al., 2018)	SeFra (Charanya, 2019)
Blockchain	Permission	ETH (Permission)	QTUM (Public)	ETH	Permission
Private blockchain	Yes	Yes	No	Yes	Yes
Standard	HL7	HIPAA	HIPAA	JSON	HL7
Consensus	Proof of work	Proof-of-work	Proof-of-stake	Proof-of-work	Proof of work
block time	19 sec	17sec	Minutes	20 sec	16 sec
Smart contract	Code Solidity	Solidity	Go	Solidity	Code (Solidity)
Patient control	Full control	No Information	Patient control	Patient and doctor control	Patient control
Focus	Patient care, Research	Telemedicine	Patient care, doctor, researcher	Telemedicine, Researcher	Patient care, Researcher, Insurance, Billing
Rewards	Anonymized data	No	No	No	Anonymized data

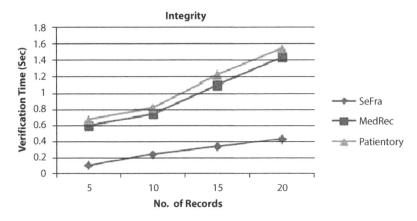

Figure 5.8 Proposed work compared with existing works (author compilation).

are used in this instance. A patient's health information is encrypted and saved in the IPFS in the first instance, and its hash value is considered as its addressing in the second instance. Second, in order to improve the security of the health record, the hash value of the content addressing is stored in the blockchain as a hash value. As a result, the health information is better protected.

e. Integrity

For a hacker, it is impossible to modify the hash value of a single block without also affecting the hash value of every other block in the system. Because of the nature of blockchain, every change in one block will result in an automatic change in the next block. The temporal shadow method is used in the suggested system in order to increase the overall security of the system. Before attaching the hash value to each record, the temporal shadow is appended to each record. Before hashing, the height of the sub-tree is attached to the connected hash, which serves as an incentive from the child node. In addition, the length of the hash chain is accepted before hashing, which is an incentive from the parent node. As a result, temporal shadow serves as a secure hash function for data.

f. Authentication

First and foremost, the Smart Contract establishes the access privileges for each patient data. Authorized users are permitted to access the information based on the access privileges granted to them. The Context-based Access Control (CBAC) in Smart Contracts is a four-contract system that uses context-based access control. Access control is based not just on the user's credentials, but also on the time and location of the request, resulting in high levels of security. A Temporal Hash Signature (THS), which is an extra security measure, is implemented. With the assistance of THS, each patient's health record was checked. The authentication process is completed without the assistance of a third party. A breach may be noticed rather readily if there are any substantial changes in the environment. If someone attempts to access the data, the system first verifies the access privileges set out in the Smart Contract, after which it requests that the user input the THS; if both requirements are met, the system enables access to the data.

h. Interoperability
The decentralization of blockchain technology is used in the proposed work. In no way does this suggest that an interoperability problem with a human services framework built on the blockchain will be eliminated. The HL7 standard is used in the proposed system to facilitate the exchange of information between various service providers. Each service provider will utilize a distinct system, but they will all be required to follow the same set of rules in order to maintain interoperability.

5.4   Conclusion

The proposed study developed a safe eHealth framework using progressive temporal blockchain technology, which increases the security of the system overall. The information is entered in the HL7 standard, which enables for simple access to health data across various healthcare practitioners. A smart contract that incorporates Context-based Access Control (CBAC) grants access to historical health information to authorized users who have successfully authenticated themselves in the system. In the Progressive temporal blockchain, a hash of health data is preserved for future reference. This method is tamper-proof; once a health record has been saved, it is difficult to make changes to the data. The researcher will take on the role of a data miner and will be compensated with anonymized data. The Temporal Hash Signature (THS) is used in the Smart Contract to authenticate the user and validate the rights of the user. The specifics of Context-based Merkle Tree (CBMT) for integrity and Context-based Merkle Tree (CBAC) in a Smart Contract for authentication are covered in more depth in the following chapters.

References

1. Russell, J., A circumplex model of affect. *J. Pers. Soc. Psychol.*, 39, 6, 1161, 1980.
2. Santhiya, P. and Chitrakala, S., A survey on emotion recognition from EEG signals: Approaches, techniques & challenges, in: *2019 International Conference on Vision Towards Emerging Trends in Communication and Networking (ViTECoN)*, IEEE, pp. 1–6, 2019.
3. Sarprasatham, M., Emotion recognition: A survey. *Int. J. Adv. Res. Comput. Sci.*, 3, 14–19, 01.2015.
4. Soundarya, S., An EEG based emotion recognition and classification using machine learning techniques, i. *J. Emerg. Technol. Innov. Eng.*, 5, 744–750, 2019.
5. Krishna, N., An efficient mixture model approach in brain-machine interface systems for extracting the psychological status of mentally impaired persons using EEG signals. *IEEE Access*, 7, 77905–77914, 2019.
6. Chettupuzhakkaran, P. and Sindhu, N., Emotion recognition from physiological signals using time-frequency analysis methods, in: *2018 International Conference on Emerging Trends and Innovations in Engineering and Technological Research (ICETIETR)*, IEEE, pp. 1–5, 2018.
7. Krishna, Anala Hari, Aravapalli Bhavya Sri, Kurakula Yuva Venkata Sai Priyanka, Sachin Taran, and Varun Bajaj. Emotion classification using EEG signals based on tunable-Q wavelet transform. *IET Science, Measurement & Technology*, 13, 3, 375–380, 2019.
8. Mehmood, R. and Lee, H., A novel feature extraction method based on late positive potential for emotion recognition in human brain signal patterns. *Comput. Electr. Eng.*, 53, 444–457, 2016.
9. Bhatti, A., Human emotion recognition and analysis in response to audio music using brain signals. *Comput. Hum. Behav.*, 65, 267–275, 2016.
10. Bajaj, V., Taran, S., Sengur, A., Emotion classification using flexible analytic wavelet transform for electroencephalogram signals. *Health Inf. Sci. Syst.*, 6, 1, 12, 2018.
11. Zhao, G. and Wang, H., Emotion analysis for personality inference from EEG signals. *IEEE Trans. Affect. Comput.*, 9, 3, 362–371, 2017.
12. Yang, Y., EEG-based emotion recognition using hierarchical network with subnetwork nodes. *IEEE Trans. Cognit. Dev. Syst.*, 10, 2, 408–419, 2017.
13. Zheng, W., Multichannel EEG-based emotion recognition via group sparse canonical correlation analysis. *IEEE Trans. Cognit. Dev. Syst.*, 9, 3, 281–290, 2016.
14. Zhang, T., Spatial–temporal recurrent neural network for emotion recognition. *IEEE Trans. Cybern.*, 49, 3, 839–847, 2018.
15. Gupta, V., Cross-subject emotion recognition using flexible analytic wavelet transform from EEG signals. *IEEE Sens. J.*, 19, 6, 2266–2274, 2018.
16. Allen, J.F., An interval-based representation of temporal knowledge, in: *IJCAI*, vol. 81, pp. 221–226, 1981.

6

Data Consistency, Transparency, and Privacy in Healthcare Systems Using Blockchain Technology

Kalaiselvi Rajendiran[1], Akshaya Sridhar[2]
and Ananda Vayaravel Cassinadane[3]*

¹Department of Biochemistry, Panimalar Medical College Hospital & Research Institute, Chennai, India
²Department of Clinical Research, Sri Ramachandra Institute of Higher Education & Research, Chennai, India
³Sri Venkateshwaraa College of Paramedical Sciences, Ariyur, Puducherry, India

Abstract

Blockchain technology also referred to as Distributor Ledger Technology (DLT) is a decentralized, distributed ledger that tracks a digital asset's provenance. A blockchain's data can't be changed by its very nature, making it a genuine disruptor in industries like payments, cybersecurity, and healthcare. It assists medical researchers in unwinding knowledge on disease genetics, allows proper patient data transfer, and regulates the drug supply chain in the health industry.

The cutting edge in genomics: It was once a dream that genomics would improve human health in the future, and now it has become a scientific and financial reality with the aid of blockchain technology. Also, companies are developing DNA tests that can reveal information about our health and past. Blockchain is an ideal fit for this burgeoning industry because it can securely store billions of genetic data. It's even evolved into a big economic point where people may sell encrypted genetic data to contribute to a larger database, allowing researchers to obtain a crucial result more quickly.

Harnessing patient data: Security is a big concern in the healthcare industry. The most prominent blockchain healthcare application at the moment is keeping our sensitive medical data safe and secure. Because blockchain can preserve an

---

*Corresponding author: principal@svcpms.ac.in

Kiran Sood, Rajesh Kumar Dhanaraj, Balamurugan Balusamy and Seifedine Kadry (eds.) Blockchain Technology in Corporate Governance: Transforming Business and Industries, (125–142) © 2023 Scrivener Publishing LLC

incorruptible, decentralized, and transparent log of all patient data, it's ripe for security applications.

Medical supply chain management: Blockchain's decentralization ensures complete transparency in the transportation process, which has a major impact on pharmaceutical supply chain management. Once a drug ledger is developed, it will pinpoint the point of origin and track data until it reaches the customer, including who handled it and where it was, as well as production costs and waste emissions.

Keywords: Digital ledger, patient data, supply chain, decentralization

6.1   Introduction

Blockchain technology in healthcare is the digitalization of healthcare data and making data into a digital ledger. The technology provides a widespread database with security and could be operated without an administrator. It utilizes a distributed, one-to-one network to make a continuous sequel of records called blocks to form a digital ledger [1]. Unlike current technology such as the social web, big data, cloud, robotics, and artificial intelligence, blockchain has evolved into a technology that is followed by digital currencies such as Bitcoin. The third generation, blockchain 3.0 has been developed with the concern of the non-commercial industry [2]. In such a scenario, the collection of the encrypted genetic data has been put into a larger database and made easier for the genetic scientist to access data easily with the aid of Blockchain technology. In this chapter, we would be able to understand the use of blockchain technology and illustrate current and future applications of the technology within the medicine and healthcare field. In the healthcare industry, Blockchain provides a unique opportunity to connect the various other technologies such as deep learning and transfer learning techniques to recognize the structured healthcare data and progress in the research field of precision medicine [3]. Thus, Blockchain technology is considered to a boon for healthcare industry in organizing patient's data that are made available and accessible [1, 4, 5].

6.2   The Cutting Edge in Genomics

Genomics is the study of genetic material with an in-depth analysis of the creation of the living system. In the past, genomics was only a topic of discussion whether it could be a potential tool for disease predictions and dreamt by scientists for utilizing in human health for the prevention of deadly disease in the future. Due to continuous efforts made by great scientists, the advancement in genomics took a growing phase in the medical field. The applications of the genomic field explored a new world for renewing new life from a no-life scenario. Various applications developed since then are now considered to be the cutting edge in genomics.

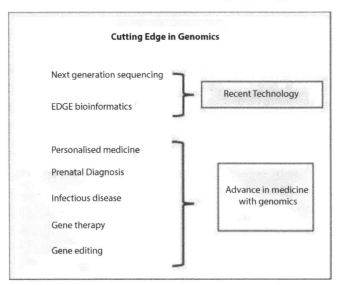

6.2.1   Next Generation Sequencing (NGS)

Of those recent developments, next-generation sequencing (NGS) is the advancement of the genomic field helping in reading millions of DNA fragments concurrently and requires no details of the genome, providing a chance for discovering new pathogens [6]. Genomics become a promising field in identifying the genetic material and disease cause thereby with the development of the NGS technology. NGS technology is reliable because of the vast development in quality and quantity of DNA-sequencing as well as a cheaper cost for high-quality DNA-sequencing. For example, $3 billion for the human genome sequence is now decreased to $1000 to re-sequence it. Recently, in the COVID pandemic, researchers engaged Illumina and Nanopore NGS to interpret SARS-CoV-2 genome. Further Bioinformatics tools in the form of computational genomic applications like QIAGEN's CLC software to locate the gene and sequence. With this technology, the viral genome was identified to be a novel pathogen [7, 8]. It is due to this technology the pandemic outbreak was easily detected and in 12 days after the first declaration of the disease outbreak, the genome was discovered and released [9].

6.2.2   EDGE Bioinformatics

With NGS technology evolution, a vast volume of genomic data has been generated. Along with the rise of newer technology including gene editing with CRISPR, expertise for analyzing the data generated are fewer which did not meet the need to understand for applications. This ended in improper usage and utility. To overcome these issues, Empowering the Development of Genomics Expertise (EDGE) Bioinformatics has been developed which includes a variety of novel and integrated bioinformatics tools incorporated within a user-friendly, web-based platform that requires data input and a click. Pre-designed workflow can be programmed. These can be quickly and easily selected to address a wide variety of goals and projects that include analyzing a genome or complex metagenome or clinical sample.

EDGE bioinformatics plays role in reforming the way scientists work on genomic data by constructing programs available via spontaneous and simple web-based interface. With a simple click on the computer, EDGE accepts raw data from sequencers and generates information and graphics based on the data – usually in a short period wrangling with sequence data. EDGE Bioinformatics makes it easy for the clinician-scientist to avail the genomic data to use this technology and to research about the cause and cure of the disease from it. For this, biologists with computation experts jointly work on creating computer code to process the generated genomic data. Thus, EDGE Bioinformatics makes it possible for the treating physician with access to genomic data to use this technology and to give bench to bedside treatment like clinics, hospitals, and research laboratories.

The software is exclusively open-source, and easily downloaded at no cost and used locally or remotely via the web. They help in the arrangement of several taxonomy tools for easy comparison. The genomic data is accurately analyzed and rapidly done. Blockchain technology in the form of EDGE technology also enables sequencing data to be compiled and used by scientists, physicians with rapid diagnosis and procedure where human resources, space, bandwidth, and time are limited.

In healthcare for the patient, utilization of genomics is seen in identifying mutations causing cancer, and human microbiome shifts associated with Crohn's disease, irritable bowel syndrome, skin diseases like psoriasis, vitiligo, allergies, Alzheimer's disease. In the future, using sequencing data and EDGE, a viral or bacterial infection can be diagnosed within a fraction of time from the patient's sample. This could decrease the over usage of antibiotics. It is proposed that hospitals could use EDGE for identifying the pathogens that inhabit the hospital environment, implement countermeasures, and lookup for infection-control procedures [10].

The first and foremost application of genomic tools showed remarkable application in discovering the gene in rare diseases. Genomic technology helps in diagnosing rare high-risk genetic disorders. It is the technology development that aided in identifying 4000 newer disease genes that had single genes to be responsible for diseases like diabetes mellitus, cancer.

6.2.3 Pharmacogenetics and Personalized Medicine

Human DNA is unique to each of us, and so each of us has distinctive disease susceptibilities and treatment responses. Pharmacogenetics evolved to be the current method of exploring the drug chemistry and the individual's disease susceptibility and treatment response, where then personalized medicine with targeted therapy is the successive emerging field. Personalized medicine is the process of using our genetic information to tailor healthcare interventions to our specific needs. For personalized medicine, genetic information is used to predict whether or not a person will respond to a given drug, how well they will respond to it, and whether or not they are sensitive or resistant to it. This allows their treating physician to make individualized decisions about the right drug choice for treatment. In some cases, such as cancer, we can identify the genetic origin or responsible for the disease and then give treatment that specifically targets a particular pathway. This is recognized as targeted therapy. Though research on available drugs concerning treatment response has been done since last two decades and even drug trials are made and the personalized medicine has to be brought into the limelight.

6.2.4 Prenatal Diagnosis

Another most important application is prenatal diagnosis and testing. Genetic diseases are often upsetting, and they can lead to disability or even death in children. Prenatal diagnosis of inherited diseases allows parents to decide whether to continue the pregnancy or allow for early identification and treatment in utero or at birth. Earlier methods of diagnosing could make the pregnancy at risk, whilst the latest advance in sequencing and identifying the mutation help in finding out the gene change of the fetus from a blood test which is called non-invasive prenatal testing later. NGS and DNA array technology in prenatal samples is the advanced application helping to recover good fetal growth and safe pregnancy.

6.2.5 Diagnosis of Infectious Diseases

With the help of genome sequence, we developed and identified the microorganism genomes and therefore the disease-causing organism is traced.

Data from gene sequencing become a key to controlling a large number of infectious outbreaks, and even able to get information as to which antibiotics are suitable for disease control.

6.2.6   Gene Therapy and Genome Editing

Gene therapy employs DNA or RNA either to modify the genetic aberration or to transform the diseased gene expression. Nearly, 400 gene therapies have been trialed in active clinical trials and listed in the U.S. clinical trials database that spans oncological uses, chronic conditions, infectious diseases, genetic diseases, and more [11]. In the past few years, genome editing has taken rapid growth, in particular, because of the CRISPR systems. There are 34 clinical trials testing CRISPR gene-editing technology in treating a large number of diseases like sickle cell disease in which CRISPR Therapeutics and Vertex Pharmaceuticals' gene-editing therapy was implied to treat and they announced successful half-phase clinical trials and the FDA declared it the Regenerative Medicine Advanced Therapy designation [12]. It is the genomic era, which makes chronic, complicated diseases such as HIV infection, leukemia, blood disorders, and hereditary blindness get treated with the aid of CRISPR editing.

6.2.7   Genomics with Blockchain Technology

The genomics integrated with blockchain technology is opening the door of the challenge of doing large-scale multi-omic profiling with a large number of people involving various ethnicity and wide socio-economic group. Although immediate beneficiaries are not there, these techniques help in collecting informational reviews of the data and progressively we would take it to next level with precise insights as we step in more. Creating the human genome data profiling and the integration of data for treatment is a great challenge. Thus with the tremendous advances that genomics has undergone in the last two decades, transforming genomics technology from the bench in research settings to become an integral and indivisible part of bedside healthcare.

6.3   Medical Records

The Healthcare sector is one of the domains where a vast amount of information is generated, accessed and dispersed daily, making it a data-intensive sphere. Patient medical records are a huge part of this data; however, they are conventionally prepared, stored, and maintained as paper-based records or as an isolated institution-centric electronic record. This results in fragmentation of data management with consequences ranging from inefficient care coordination to lack of vital information during an emergency [13]. Most healthcare departments are still reliant on obsolete systems in the maintenance of patient medical records. They tend to have limited and localized accessibility, thereby, making it time-consuming and complicated for the healthcare professional elsewhere to make a diagnosis and proceed further during times of extremities. Data stored in a single location warrants issues like Identity thefts, Spamming, Financial data crimes, etc.

Traditional healthcare information exchange can be explained under any one of the following three models:

> Push model: Sending the information from one location to another
> Pull model: Extraction of information from a source
> View model: Peering into a system per se

Even though these practices technically achieve an adequate health information exchange, they are not an adequate means of a sustainable approach and do not offer patient-centric care [14]. With the rapid advent of newer technologies, almost all of the businesses have set forth to bring about revolutionary changes in all of their aspects. About the healthcare industry, there is an ever-growing obligation to keep up with the levels of the height of the latest technologies as well as move towards a patient-centric approach. Usage of a centralized database could make an efficient means of gaining access to all of the patient's personal information, lining up from diagnostic results up to the clinician's prescription.

6.3.1   Blockchain Architecture – Components and Types

With the ever-rising concerns about the data breaches and security concerns of patient medical data, the demand for a decentralized approach has become a mandatory requirement, bringing into play the blockchain technology in the healthcare domain. Implementation of this technology will have a significant impact on record sharing, billing and medical research purposes [14]. The proposed architecture should be supportive of the storage of medical data including formal medical records and should be able to derive health data from IoT enabled mobile applications, wearable sensors, etc., and should follow the user lifelong.

The building blocks of this technology include components that are connected devices, sensors, and a collector that collects data and sends it to the network for storage are common components [15].

The Blockchain technology can be categorized into three categories [16]:

> Public Blockchain: Wherein everyone can participate in the dispersed network and check data transactions, be a part of the verification process and participate in reaching a consensus.

> Consortium Blockchain: Commonly used in business partnerships; the authoritative node must be chosen ahead of time, and the data in the blockchain network can be open or private, and it is considered a partially decentralized network.

> Private Blockchain: Restricted nodal access; Strict authority management to collect data; not everyone has the participation in the blockchain management process.

6.3.2   Blockchain Benefits in Healthcare Records Maintenance

> Provides a simple method to access the data; in contrast to the conventional method of controlling information, blockchain technology enables easier sharing of healthcare records across multiple nodes since the data is stored in a centralized database.

> Alleviates the problem of failure in exchange healthcare records leading to delay in treatment processes through decentralizing the data. In this way, everyone within the healthcare network will be able to access a ledger whilst having individual data ownership.

> Renders the healthcare systems with high efficiency by processing in real-time and removing the requirement of third party-companies, thereby eliminating the wait inaccessibility.

> Stores information in an encrypted format, making it untraceable to hackers and provides a seamless control in the patient's hands-on who can gain access to their records [17].

6.3.3   Brief Overview on the Blockchain-Enabled Patient Healthcare Record Management Process

Data Generation	Data is being generated from different sources inclusive of smart devices, diagnostic tools, healthcare providers, and legacy systems.
Data Cleaning and Enrichment	Data obtained is prepared before being stored on the blockchain.
Data Capturing	Saving of the data onto the blockchain database.
Data Consumption	Using the patient information from the blockchain in real-time for treatment purposes.
Data Mining	Research and future discovery of information.

6.3.3.1   Data Generation

For the integration of data into the blockchain systems, it is of paramount significance to understand the scope of the data, the process and mechanism of generation of data, and the place of data generation. Every stage of the healthcare process involves the generation of sensitive and important medical data.

The patient health details encompasses the data collected from IoT medical equipment's, diagnostic, and historical and prescription data, which are obtained from X-rays, scans, diagnostic tests, and doctor's prescriptions. The data can be in the form of text, paper, numerical, pictures, videos, digital, or multimedia. A medical record comprises sensitive information of the patients like the name, address, place of work, prescribed medicines, number of doctor visits payment mode, secured information like the diagnosis of HIV, Cancer or psychological conditions.

6.3.3.2   Data Cleaning and Enrichment

The collection of unstructured data leads to inconsistent and inefficient information leading to delays in treatment processes. Therefore data enrichment process has to be done, which refers to adding value to enhance data quality. A patient's medical record must be precise, secure, readable, time-stamped, and arranged in a rational way. To ensure these, a three-step process is described for cleaning and enrichment of data:

> Replacement of the patient's identification with a public Hash key – a unique numerical value, making it difficult to decode the information by a hacker or a data information attacker. To acquire access to confidential health information, every healthcare service provider would need patient's consent or permission; in case the patient denies access, then the records stored on the blockchain cannot be accessed.

> Saving data on a blockchain means it should be made compliant ready to regulatory requirements. Compliance management will be more smooth and transparent with the help of blockchain. HIPAA compliance assures that patient information is kept safe. The HIPAA privacy policy permits all users to obtain and disclose only de-identified information. Before the health data are kept on the blockchain, a compliance check must be done.

> Patient data grouped in various formats like administrative claim records, clinical registries, biometric data, patient-reported data or medical imaging should be stored in a structured and ordered manner to enable efficient data access for the healthcare providers.

The adherence to the above-mentioned points adds value and improves the data to be registered on the blockchain.

6.3.3.3   Data Capturing

Blockchain technology eliminates the risks involved with digital records across several connections within the network. The process per se is explained below:

> The healthcare vendors and organizations save patients' medical records with a public hashtag on the blockchain. Designed in such a way that gets triggered to store the information obtained from the doctors, diagnostic centers, or health insurance companies that are present on the blockchain.

> The details of transactions containing patients' medical records are stored on the blockchain network with their details and a patient's public key. When a healthcare provider needs access to a patient's protected information, the matching of the transaction ID is a quintessential criterion.

➢ Contrary to the conventional process, the healthcare personnel need not approach the patients directly for access to medical records, they can simply submit a query through APIs (Application programming interface), for gaining access to the patient's non-identifiable details through smart contracts.

➢ Blockchain healthcare solutions can never expose the patient's individual data unless they provide their public key. Patients are eligible to assign their public key to the healthcare management whenever mandatory.

Once the data storage process is done, it is available for consumption by various blockchain healthcare dealers using smart agreements.

6.3.3.4 Data Consumption

Before data is exchanged, a smart bond is created to ensure that company regulations, contractual requirements, and the customer's desire to manage data are all followed. With the patient's approval, the authorized person participating in the patient's treatment activities can consume the saved data. A smart contract is a computer application or transaction protocol that is used to execute, control, or document legally significant events and activities that occur due of the conditions of an agreement. This program gets triggered when data is stored on the blockchain. The healthcare provider receives the patient information, with hidden identity data using a hash. Whenever a diagnostic center or doctor requests access to the patient data, smart contracts send a notification to the patients. Ultimately, patients would be the beholders of their data. Smart contract systems will ensure a secure exchange of information.

6.3.3.5 Data Mining

The healthcare data acquired by using artificial intelligence, the Internet of things, machine learning processes are applied for patient treatment, disease mitigation, drug development, and clinical trials. The typical approach hampering patient privacy can be replaced by blockchain technologies that bring forth trust in clinical trials and medical research processes. De-identification techniques can be utilized for hiding a patient's identity and creating non-identifiable data information and records, enabling medical research companies to carry out the research activities with the utmost discretion.

Limitations

Blockchain systems involve a few challenges in the real world, which include technological limitations, vendor adoption and infrastructure costs [15]. These limitations must be addressed to develop an efficient medical record handling system incorporating blockchain technology.

6.4   Supply Chain Management

One of the most dangerous and widespread pandemics in modern history has left this country devastated. Routine healthcare practices, work, and lives have been interrupted in many ways, and healthcare systems have been put to the test in terms of efficiency.

There has been an extensive shortage of medical supplies contributing to the ever-growing demand for certain medical equipment, tests, and medications. A crises situation, owing to the shortcomings in certain day-old processes, like these, warrants the need for better pharmaceutical supply chain management processes in healthcare. It has bought individuals, communities and businesses under the same umbrella of concept – to care for the sick; improvise and develop an efficient management process of healthcare systems [18].

There is an immense need for a transformation process and determination of activities to be done, to fill in the blanks in the present-day spaces in the healthcare infrastructure and supply chain management processes. Blockchain technology which has a wide range of applications and uses in healthcare can be seen as a unique and tailor-made situation to address these complications. Blockchain technology can offer the best possible solution to the medical and pharmaceutical supply chain issues faced, given its readiness and cost-effectiveness.

By large, the term supply chain management implies the flow of goods and services from the point of origin to the point of consumption, which is inclusive of all of the processes involved in the transformation of the raw materials into the final product. However, supply chain management is a very tedious and fragmented process, when it pertains to healthcare services provision. It entails the obtainment of resources, management of supplies, and delivering goods and services to the medical care providers and patients. For completion of processes, the physical goods and information about the medical product and services have to go through some stakeholders [19].

Manufacturers	Medical equipment, Surgical equipment, Medical devices, Pharmaceuticals
Purchasers	Wholesalers, Retailers
Providers	Hospitals, Pharmacies, Clinics
Distributors	Wholesalers, Retailers

The role of the manufacturer is to set off the supply chain and build the required medical, surgical equipment's, devices and pharmaceuticals and put them forward to distributors, who are generally the wholesalers or retailers. The hospitals, pharmacies, or clinics are entitled as the healthcare providers who ensure the best possible healthcare services to their patients in a cost-effective manner. The end-users who are the patients also have their say in the healthcare supply management processes, using the requirement of customized medical product needs in selected scenarios based on their health status.

The applications of supply chain management can be explained under these four broad categories [20].

> ➤ Pharmaceutical industry applications
> ➤ Medical device and medical supplies
> ➤ Internet of healthy things
> ➤ Public health

6.4.1   Pharmaceutical Applications

The sustainable development of a nation majorly depends on the health of the populace. The pharmaceutical products, to reach the customer must navigate through multiple stakeholders. Shah *et al.* in 2004, described in detail the components of a Pharmaceutical supply chain: Suppliers, Primary and secondary manufacturing sites, Waste plants, Distribution centers, wholesalers and retailers, which was based on the wide definition of WHO for the drug or pharmaceutical preparation. The production of pharmaceutical products involve a two-stage approach; the primary approach being the transformation of raw material into active pharmaceutical ingredient (API) through various chemical processes, product recovery and purification. The secondary step entails the conversion of the API into the final drug or product by adding in varieties of excipients at the secondary site of manufacture [21]. Nevertheless, the pharmaceutical supply chain management system differs from standard systems using its time-consuming nature, high uncertainty in demand, shorter shelf life, and perishable nature of products and the enhanced regulatory constraints due to the direct effect of the products on the health and safety of the society. Effective optimization techniques are a requisite for pharmaceutical industries to cover their several decisions at strategic, tactical and operational levels to improve their service rendering [22].

6.4.2   Medical Devices and Medical Supplies

Medical devices are often high priced, niche products. In the current scenario, they are adapting toward a customized approach. The field of medical devices and supplies has a very difficult to forecasting demand obligations and calls for sophisticated analysis, high-end maintenance and related logistical tools as a part of their supply chain processes. The supply chain management of this sector should be done in a timely, FDA-compliant manner. The performance of the supply chain process can be augmented through investment in technology solutions, leveraging data analytics, machine learning, diversifying suppliers, and usage of apt forecasting tools for planning [23].

6.4.3   Internet of Healthy Things

One of the subsets of the Internet of Things, the IoHT – Internet of Healthy things encompasses the wearables, sensors, and standalone devices with utility that is focused on the health and wellness of humans [24]. The opportunities and challenges associated with IoHT mimic those associated with the medical devices sector, however involve higher threats to data, security and systems owing to less diligent regulations and favoring of a more consumer-focused approach.

6.4.4   Public Health

Initially, consumers established the term supply chain management as the links and inter-relationships between the organizations, people, resources, and procedures involved. According to John Snow, a public health supply chain is a network of interconnected organizations or actors that ensures the availability of health commodities to the people who need them. The key issues about supply chain challenges in public health include disaster and emergency alleviation and management, inclusive of protected supplies for healthcare workers during public health emergencies and access to indispensable needs [25].

Implications

Logistical challenges faced by most of the medical and pharmaceutical supply chains involve a lack of real-time visibility about shipping locations, ambiguity concerning weather and other transportation disruptions, product quality assurance and verification, cross-border customs reporting, and billing and payment – all of which can be efficiently handled by leveraging a supply chain management process through blockchain technology. The ledger mechanization of BCT enables the secure transfer of medical records of patients and helps in the overseeing of the medical supply chain, thereby assisting healthcare researcher's big time.

References

1. Angraal, S., Krumholz, H.M., Schulz, W.L., Blockchain technology: Applications in healthcare. *Circ. Cardiovasc. Qual. Outcomes*, 10, 9, e003800, 2017.

2. Swan, M., *Blockchain: Blueprint for a new economy*, O'Reilly Media, Inc., Sebastopol, CA, USA, 2015.

3. Shae, Z. and Tsai, J., Transform blockchain into distributed parallel computing architecture for precision medicine, in: *Proceedings of the 2018 IEEE 38th International Conference on Distributed Computing Systems (ICDCS)*, Vienna, Austria, 2018.

4. Engelhardt, M.A., Hitching healthcare to the chain: An introduction to blockchain technology in the healthcare sector. *Technol. Innov. Manage. Rev.*, 7, 22–34, 2017.

5. Mettler, M., Blockchain technology in healthcare the revolution starts here, in: *Proceedings of the 2016 IEEE 18th International Conference on E-Health Networking, Applications and Services (Healthcom)*, Munich, Germany, pp. 520–522, 2016.

6. Chiu, C.Y., Viral pathogen discovery. *Curr. Opin. Microbiol.*, 16, 4, 468–78, 2013.

7. Zhu N, Zhang D, Wang W, Li X, Yang B, Song J, Zhao X, Huang B, Shi W, Lu R, Niu P, Zhan F, Ma X, Wang D, Xu W, Wu G, Gao GF, Tan W; China Novel Coronavirus Investigating and Research Team. A Novel Coronavirus from Patients with Pneumonia in China, 2019. *N. Engl. J. Med.*, 2020 Feb 20, 382, 8, 727–733. doi: 10.1056/NEJMoa2001017. Epub 2020 Jan 24. PMID: 31978945; PMCID: PMC7092803.

8. BaseClear, DNA/RNA sequencing platforms: A short overview, 2019. https://www.baseclear.com/genomics/bioinformatics/rna-seq-analysis/.

9. Wu, F. *et al.*, Severe acute respiratory syndrome coronavirus 2 isolate Wuhan-Hu-1, complete genome. *NCBI*, 579, 7798, 265–269, 2020.

10. Li, P.E., Lo, C.C., Anderson, J.J. *et al.*, Enabling the democratization of the genomics revolution with a fully integrated web-based bioinformatics platform. *Nucleic Acids Res.*, 45, 1, 67–80, 2017.

11. Shahryari A, Saghaeian Jazi M, Mohammadi S, Razavi Nikoo H, Nazari Z, Hosseini ES, Burtscher I, Mowla SJ, Lickert H. Development and Clinical Translation of Approved Gene Therapy Products for Genetic Disorders. *Front Genet.*, 2019 Sep 25;10:868. doi: 10.3389/fgene.2019.00868. PMID: 31608113; PMCID: PMC6773888.

12. CRISPR Therapeutics, CRISPR Therapeutics and Vertex Pharmaceuticals announce FDA Regenerative Medicine Advanced Therapy (RMAT) designation granted to CTX001™ for the treatment of severe hemoglobinopathies, May 11, 2019. http://www.crisprtx.com/about-us/press-releases-and-presentations/ crispr-therapeutics-and-vertex-pharmaceuticals-announce-fda-regenerative-medicine-advanced-therapy-rmat-designation-granted-to-ctx001-for-the-treatment-of-severe-hemoglobinopathies.

13. Hylock, R. and Zeng, X., A blockchain framework for patient-centered health records and exchange (healthchain): Evaluation and proof-of-concept study. *J. Med. Internet Res.*, 21, 8, e13592, 2019.

14. Developing a healthcare blockchain solution, https://www.leewayhertz.com/ healthcare-blockchain-how-medical-records-secured-blockchain/.

15. Mayer, A.H., da Costa, C.A., da R Righi, R., Electronic health records in a Blockchain: A systematic review. *Health Inf. J.*, 26, 2, 1273–1288, June 2020.

16. Ichikawa, D., Kashiyama, M., Ueno, T., Tamper-resistant mobile health using blockchain technology. *JMIR mHealthuHealth*, 5, 7, e111, 2017.

17. Blockchains are the building blocks of better healthcare, 2021, https://med citynews.com/2021/03/blockchains-are-the-building-blocks-of-better-health-care/.

18. How blockchain can solve today's medical supply chain flaws and improve responses for future crises, 2020, https://www.forbes.com/sites/ forbesbusinessdevelopmentcouncil/2020/04/29/how-blockchain-can-solve-todays-medical-supply-chain-flaws-and-improve-responses-for-future-crises/?sh=6019029c750a.

19. Arora, M. and Gigras, Y., Importance of supply chain management in healthcare of third world countries. *Int. J. Supply Oper. Manage.*, 5, 1, 101–106, 2018.

20. Clauson, K.A., Breeden, E.A., Davidson, C., Mackey, T.K., Leveraging blockchain technology to enhance supply chain management in healthcare: An exploration of challenges and opportunities in the health supply chain. *Blockchain Healthc. Today*, 1, 1–12, ISSN 2573-8240 2018 online https://doi. org/10.30953/bhty.v1.20.

21. Ahmadi, A., Mousazadeh, M., Ali Torabi, S., Pishvaee, M.S., OR applications in pharmaceutical supply chain management, International Series

in Operations Research & Management Science, in: *Operations Research Applications in Healthcare Management*, Chapter 0, C. Kahraman and Y. Ilker Topcu (Eds.), pp. 461–491, Springer, 2018.

22. Zarindast, A., Hosseini, S.M.S., Pishvaee, M.S., A robust possibilistic programming model for simultaneous decision of inventory lot-size, supplier selection and transportation mode selection. *Int. J. Ind. Syst. Eng.*, 1, 30, 3, 346–64, 2018.

23. The resilience imperative for medtech supply chains, 2020, https://www.mckinsey.com/business-functions/operations/our-insights/the-resilience-imperative-for-medtech-supply-chains.

24. Kvedar, J.C., *The internet of healthy things*, Partners HealthCare Connected Health(Boston), Boston, 2015.

25. Toward a common definition of "public health supply chain, 2013, https://iaphl.org/news-events/toward-a-common-definition-of-public-health-supply-chain/.

Part 2

BLOCKCHAIN IN THE ENERGY SECTOR

7

Application of Blockchain Technology in Sustainable Energy Systems

Navdeep Kaur[1]*, Suman Bhullar[1] and Navneet Seth[2]

[1]*Thapar Institute of Engineering and Technology Patiala, Punjab, India*
[2]*Baba Hira Singh Bhattal Institute of Engineering and Technology Lehragaga, Punjab, India*

Abstract

The recent developments in technology are continuously leading to improvement of contemporary energy sector. The challenges faced by these contemporary energy sectors include elevating energy demand, immense augmentation in dispersed generation and cyber-physical growth due to adaptation of computer technologies. Owing to these issues the main objective of power system has deviated from stability to security and reliability. Amongst the recent technologies from security point of view, blockchain technology has gained momentum in different aspects of energy sector. Blockchain technology has been already widely adopted in financial sector due to cyber-physical security in dealing with digital currency. It is the backbone of future energy sector as it provides transpicuous, secure, and tamper-resistant solutions. Due to these features, blockchain technology has emerged in the field of peer to peer energy trading, smart contracts, smart grid, electric vehicles, home automation, metering, billing, etc. It is going to be a game changer in energy flow starting from generation to utilization of energy. This technology has the potential to address the key challenges faced by modern and future energy sector. This chapter introduces the concept of blockchain technology, a state-of-art review of distributed ledger technology, its applications in various fields of energy sector and key challenges while adopting this technology.

Keywords: Blockchain technology, energy sector, smart grid, energy trading, electric vehicle

**Corresponding author*: navdeepkaur3984@gmail.com

Kiran Sood, Rajesh Kumar Dhanaraj, Balamurugan Balusamy and Seifedine Kadry (eds.) Blockchain Technology in Corporate Governance: Transforming Business and Industries, (145–162) © 2023 Scrivener Publishing LLC

7.1   Introduction

Modern lifestyle is directly or indirectly dependent on energy sector for performing day to day activities. The censorious constrictions like meteorological conditions, apex atmospheric circumstances, scarcity of energy, elevated gap of energy between demand and utilization, etc., are being faced by civilized community. To tackle these conformations by the world at large, energy sector has witnessed a transition phase. The endorsement of sustainable energy sources in the field of power generation, ingression of dispersed generation in the distribution networks, adaptation of innovative technologies in the field of energy trading, smart grid and electric vehicles are significant transformations that are taking place in contemporary energy sector [1]. The shifting from fossil fuels to renewable sources for eco-friendly power generation will definitely conserve fossil fuels but on the other side, the intermittent nature of renewable sources is going to be critical obstacle for efficient operational mechanism [2]. Various storage systems in the form of electric vehicles and solar panels embedded with battery storage devices are supplementary equipment in modern energy systems. Also, with the integration of distributed generation in order to reduce power losses in transmission and distribution of electric power, the nature of passive distribution networks has been transformed into the active distribution networks [3]. The comparison of conventional and modern power system is depicted in Figure 7.1.

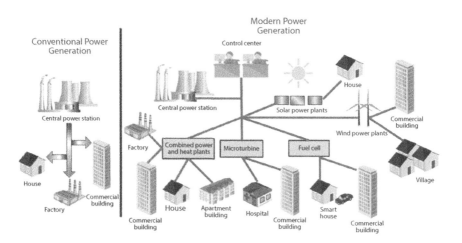

Figure 7.1 Comparison of conventional and modern power generation [3].

The transformation of power system from conventional to modern pattern necessitates the secure, robust, and effective computerized frameworks for complex interactions among the dispersed energy bodies, which can be achieved through modernistic digital and technological approaches [4]. This metamorphosis strengthens the contemporaneous communication support between different distinctive users of the network across the energy sector. The modernization has introduced another type of consumers tied to grid commonly known as prosumers which produce as well as consume energy [5]. Consumers and prosumers should be competent to transact electricity with each other which is going to be a costly affair as it requires contemporary communication infrastructure [4]. Therefore, terminology and operational issues have changed and need more advanced and innovative technologies to resolve the issues. In other words, every aspect related to energy sector is being updated on regular basis due to technological advancements. To boost the expeditious transition of the energy sector, numerous leading edge technologies have evolved. Out of all emerging innovative technologies, blockchain captivate whirlwind momentum in the evolution and employment in present scenario of energy sector due to main attributes such as scalability, decentralization, time embossed, non-transmogrify and security of blockchain technology [6].

From the previously published works related to role of blockchain in energy sector, it has been found that blockchain technology propounds explication to complications of distinctive levels of intricacy within smart gird. The perception of distributed computing is familiarized worldwide since 1990s. In 2009, a white paper on the blockchain approach by S. Nikomoto mentioned bitcoin for peer-to-peer e-cash system, which is contemplated to be ABCs of bitcoin cryptocurrency despite of the fact that it was not published in any journal of repute [6]. This white paper gave a propulsion to bitcoin cryptocurrency in the legitimate utilization in the field of the banking sector in 2011 and smart contacts as well as smart applications in 2013 [7]. Smart contracts constituted emblematic repercussions which forced the innovators to adopt blockchain technology in the energy sector. Hence, Blockchain emerged in various applications of energy sector, e.g., 2015 in the field of energy trading, 2016 in the field of electric vehicles, 2017 in the functioning of the smart grid and 2018 in micro grid operation and architecture.

7.2 Blockchain

As the name suggests, in this technology the blocks accommodating instructions are connected through chains [6] and will retain the trail of all the deviations made in the blocks, which makes it favorable option in all applications of energy sector where security is prime concern. Blockchain is a mechanism which provides documentation and guidance regarding functioning of a system in such a manner that it is strenuous to hack or elude the system. In straight forward manner, blockchain is concentrated as well as dispersed record book or balance sheet, which registers the inception of the digital resources. Thereby, here comes the nomenclature for blockchain technology, i.e., Distributed Ledger Technology (DLT). The pioneer block is acknowledged as Genesis block and succeeding blocks are connected to Genesis block eventually [8].

As each human being is identified by different finger prints, in similar manner each block of blockchain technology is exclusively identified by hash (executable program) present along with information [9]. The blocks in blockchain are inalterable, time-stamped and connected to preceding blocks which contain executable programs, data and transactions, which are verified by users of network known as *nodes*. If any block is tampered, it will emerge as alteration in concerned hash and hash in the next block being uninterrupted, will reveal that the blocks after altered hash are incongruous [9]. Therefore, the hashes contribute security to the system which is indispensable objective of blockchain technology. The steps involved in execution of typical transaction based on blockchain technology are shown in Figure 7.2.

A transaction is requested, authenticated, and represented as a block, which is sent to every node in the network. The transaction can be requested

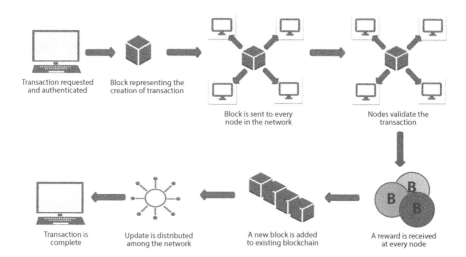

Figure 7.2 Flow process of blockchain-based transactions.

from any user in the network, which contains the hash authenticating the sender, receiver, and transaction. The transaction is verified by all users in the network by decrypting the hash and once the verification is done, a new block is added to existing blockchain, which is secure and inalterable. The updated blockchain is communicated to all nodes of the network and hence the transaction is completed [10].

Blockchain utilizes cryptography, which is process of encryption i.e. coding and decryption, i.e., decoding of information involving complex mathematical and computational approaches, to safeguard the integrity of the users or nodes of the network. There are mainly three types of cryptographic algorithms-symmetric key cryptography, asymmetric key cryptography and hash functions. In symmetric key cryptography which is also known as secure key cryptography popularly, a common single key is utilized for coding as well as decoding purposes [11]. Public key cryptography is another terminology used for asymmetric key cryptography. Two keys are used in asymmetric key cryptography, one for encryption which is known as exclusive public key and other for decryption which is known as private key. Digital signature is primary application of asymmetric cryptography. Digital signatures can't be corrupted ensuring that data is verified and secure. There are not any type of keys used in Hash functions. Blockchain manipulates asymmetric key cryptography and cryptographic hash functions. Cryptographic Hash functions are utilized in blockchain technology to carry out the perceived execution to each and every stakeholder. Blockchains generally use cryptographic hash functions for implementation due to favorable features such as avalanche effect, uniqueness for obtaining output for each and every input, fast and quick response etc. Cryptography is the heart of the blockchain technology. Among leading applications of cryptography in the blockchain technology is cryptocurrency. Basic building blocks of blockchain technology are hash functions, public- private key pair and digital signatures. Private-public key pairs are promoted to perpetuate the addresses of the users.

The legitimate employment of blockchain focuses on two domains mainly – finance and energy sector. In finance sector, bitcoin is classical application, which manifests a gargantuan accomplishment in digital coinage. Ethereum, Litecoin, and Coinbase are other digital currency systems.

The Blockchain stands distinct [6] from similar technologies due the features of this technology which are shown in Figure 7.3. It is a decentralized technology in which there is no need to manage the transactions at central level. It is a secure and flexible technology in which attacks are not possible due to its dispersed architecture and even if any attack is there, it can handle by its flexibility. Moreover, all changes in blockchain are shared

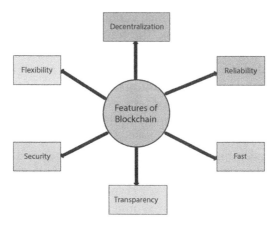

Figure 7.3 Features of blockchain.

with all users in the networks, which makes it transparent for all. As the new blocks added to any chain and recorded history are unalterable, blockchain. In addition to these, as there is no intermediator to handle transactions in this, it is the fastest technique among all techniques available these days.

These distinct features has pushed the blockchain to emerge as promising technology in various fields such as in financial market for digital payments [6] and accounting [12], in government sector for digital contracts and database for property ownership documents [13]. It also utilized as secure technology by health sector to manage the patients' data [14] and healthcare records [15].

Internet of Things (IoT) sector also employs blockchain in smart cities [16], smart home networks [17] and smart home sensors [18]. Various markets use blockchain for handling of bills [19], transferring and monitoring of data [20], management of quota in supply chains and quality monitoring [21]. The technologies based blockchain are still under development and these are not adopted broadly by industries except the cryptocurrency industry.

7.3   Blockchain Applications in Energy Sector

The energy sector is going through the amendments due to increased penetration of dispersed energy resources and advancements in IoT technologies, which leads to decentralization and digitization of energy sector. This decentralization and digitization stands in the need of deliberation, analysis and approval of unconventional archetype and dispersed energy resources. Blockchain emerges as an encouraging for control and management of complexities is raised in energy sector due to decentralization due to their inherent nature [22–24].

Blockchain applications in the energy sector can be classified into three main categories namely cash flow, bidirectional information flow and the flow of the electric power as shown in Figure 7.4. The blockchain technology has developed as promising backbone for the energy sector having applications in the field of energy trading, the billing process, supply and demand management comes under the category of cash flow, efficient operation and control of the electric power equipped with IoT layer comes under the umbrella of information flow and power flow includes transmission and distribution of the electric power, innovative smart grid, electric powered vehicles *etc.* supported by energy layer.

The blockchain can comprehend the automatic billing for dispersed generators and consumers through blockchain based smart contracts and metering [25]. The marketing of energy can alter as per individual consumer requirements and environmental issues. The blockchain, along with artificial intelligence, can predict the pattern of energy consumption of individual consumers and the combination can facilitate personalized and beneficial energy commodities [26]. The energy market procedures [25–27] and material sales transactions [28] may get disturbed due to blockchain based distributed energy trading.

The IoT layer can handle the information flow and storage through blockchain based smart communication devices which includes smart meters, monitoring devices, control and energy management systems

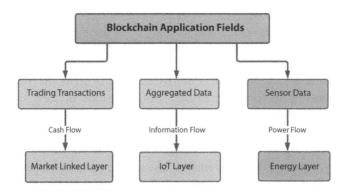

Figure 7.4 Classification of blockchain application fields.

[26]. These smart devices can efficiently operate and control the electric power. In the energy layer blockchain can assist the electric vehicles to locate nearby charging stations through smart sensors[28]. It can also regulate the generation, transmission and distribution of power in smart grids through sensor data.

7.3.1   Blockchain Applications in Smart Grid

Power system's functioning is based on four main pillars, *i.e.*, generation, transmission, distribution, and utilization of electrical energy. Power system is just analogous to mammoth tree, the foundations of which represent generation, the stalk symbolizes transmission, the major and subordinate branches exemplify primary and secondary distribution systems, respectively. As compared to the conventional grid, which is having one way communication, smart grid involves two-way communication between electric utilities and consumers. This evolving high tech network includes latest communication, computer, and information technology updating on daily basis, merged with efficient automatic control techniques. It is having ample scope for the research due to deep penetration of the renewable energy resources having intermittent nature, energy storage devices and plug in as well as hybrid electric vehicles. As compared to conventional grid, this type of grid is more competent, predictable, shielded, and eco-friendly. Smart grid seems to be suitable alternative, which can fulfill the primary function of electric power to satisfy the consumers by providing un-interrupted and reliable supply of adequate quality in an economical manner and secure way. Emergence of blockchain technology will boost the upgraded evolution and flattens the obstacles in the path of smart grid by adopting decentralized technologies. The desirable features of blockchain technology have engrossed researchers to analyze and endorse in the field of smart grid [29].

In the power generation sector, blockchain technology provides abundant observations with reference to functional status to dispatch organizations to evolve arrangement in order to magnify benefits. In transmission and distribution sectors, the prime confrontations of long established centralized systems are being overcome by decentralized systems having features of automation and control centers loaded by blockchain technology. In utilization of electrical energy, energy trading supported by this technology, between different entities like prosumers and storage systems, consumers and electric vehicles *etc.*, can be well organized by transforming existing system [30].

7.3.2   Blockchain Applications in Energy Trading

Energy trading is oppressive affair now-a-days due to existence of dispersed generation and micro-grid [31]. Blockchain technology has the proficiency to metamorphosis the functioning of energy trading by eliminating the involvement of negotiators as well as curtailment in time taken to accomplish the specified objectives in a secretive manner [32]. Rather it opens exhaustive alternatives to energy consumers and prosumers. Blockchain supported energy trading because of security, which is indispensable character of this technology, used to exterminate efforts resulting into extortion by the cyber hackers. Reliability of supported technology which comes at second place after security enhances fortitude for long haul financing [33]. Peer to peer trading is an eye-catching appellation in energy scenario, which concedes the proprietors and applicants to acquire the commerce spontaneously as well as autonomously due to documentation of units of generated energy in the blocks associated with chain [34]. Optimal power-flow, the heart of power systems containing information of various parameters like current, terminal voltage, power factor, *etc.*, can be secured by storing in blockchain by optimization of energy resources [35]. Multi agent based blockchain trading is more reliable and as it is having two rows of security [36]. In first row, pricing is deliberated by prosumers and consumers and second row blended with blockchain technology acts as wall of security and trust worthy podium for negotiating the trading process.

7.3.3   Blockchain Applications in Micro-Grid

One more terminology along with smart grid is gaining momentum as influential subject matter in the contemporarily power systems. Micro-grid is a sub set of smart grid, which invigilates the entire power systems. The invigilation of power system consists of the functioning of transmission and distribution networks commencing from energy producing plant and terminating at consumer's side. The objective of micro grid is to administer the power supply for a small area. The electric power is locally produced, transmitted, distributed and utilized in a micro-grid. It is a favorable option for isolated areas where independent operations are otherwise inconceivable. With the penetration of renewable energy sources, the management of micro grid is decisive aspect. Research works are being carried out throughout the world, which can provide the optimized operation of micro-grid [37]. It is need of the hour that researchers should limelight various issues related to the functioning of micro grid. Blockchain technology has been assimilated within micro-grid in order to overcome restrictions, manage the demand side, resolve issues with enhancement of benefits [38]. Blockchain ensures the shielded and reliable scheduling structure of distributed energy resources. In order to cater the energy requirements, renewable energy resources are mingled together for superlative utilization.

Blockchain is used to expedite machine to machine synergy commonly known as M2M and prepares framework for electricity market considering energy demand. The blockchain technology assembles data extracted from back bone of power systems, *i.e.*, power flow models and customized electricity price. Smart contracts, originated from power management systems, are employed to accumulate data transactions and automated relocated assets [39].

7.3.4   Blockchain in Electric Vehicles

In modern power system networks, conventional fuel powered vehicles are being replaced by electric vehicles powered by renewable sources to counter the exhaustion of fossil fuels as well as environmental pollutants, in coming years. Developed and developing nations of the world are investing a lot in research and development sector of the electric vehicles. Integration of electric vehicles to smart grid is posing numerous challenges to the researchers [40]. The rudimentary concern is how electric vehicles will be charged when connected to smart grid. The charging behavior of electric vehicles can be classified in two ways – uncoordinated charging and coordinated charging. As the name suggests, in case of uncoordinated charging, no coordination or control is practiced and on arrival, vehicles start charging absolutely with superlative charging rate, which puts acute strain on the smart grid [41]. The idea of coordinated charging is to control charging that means to encourage and educate the customers about smart charging of electric vehicles. Through this charging customers can decide when they want to charge or discharge to the system according to their needs and requirement of the system.

During the long journey, it is a matter of concern to know the availability of the fuel station in case of the normal vehicles, similarly it happens in case of electric vehicles. EV users start searching for charging stations in case of marginal state of charging. Blockchain technology will do the function of locating charging station nearby [42]. The integration of electric vehicles to smart grid as well as blockchain will not only smoothens the obstacles in terms of cost related issues and challenges faced like undulating power supply. With emergence of this technology, best location will be provided at best price to the EV users while maintaining the surveillance and privacy of the integral system [43].

7.3.5   Blockchain Applications in Cyber Physical Security

The instigation of smart grid, micro grid, energy trading, electric vehicles *etc.* in the energy sector has constituted numerous susceptibilities where significant segments can be tempered by maneuverer. So, the cyber physical security of energy sector is a serious concern and cyber physical attacks need to be explored in detail [44]. Cyber physical attacks are diversified in nature depending upon category, composition and impacting the operation of energy sector. A typical classification of Cyber physical attacks is represented in Figure 7.5. Time synchronization is very crucial in modern computer networks involving sensors and attack on time synchronization hampers the management related to planning, security, as well as debugging issues while transferring information from one node of network to other node [45]. GPS spoofing is related to intrusion with communication signals sent by radio transmitter and overrides the sluggish signals and puts a question mark on the security related issues to communication signals [46]. During a false data injection attack, traducer can alter the operation of a computerized network by imposing it to perform specified commands not in the favor of host as well as users of the network. Sometimes, it may lead to denial of service attack. In the denial of service attacks, network or machine becomes inoperative or unavailable for the users by the hackers [47].

Attacks must not happen in energy sector and provide a challenging task to computer engineers and researchers. With the help of blockchain approaches, immunity of energy sector can be enhanced which will lead to a secure trans-active energy sector applications. Therefore, blockchain technology will provide a trusted and secure platform for smart contracts,

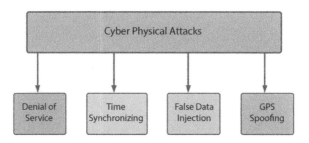

Figure 7.5 Classification of cyber physical attacks.

smart grid, micro grid, electric vehicles and so on. It doesn't mean that attacks will not happen in energy sector, but can be detected before austere consequences.

7.4   Blockchain as New Substructure

The blockchain has distinct features which have been discussed in Section 7.2. These specific characteristics are advantageous for integration of blockchain in power systems as it enhances the transparency, flexibility, security, computation ability and diminishes bureaucracy. Due to these benefits, new substructures of blockchain may be adopted in smart grid. Blockchain can be amalgamated as cyber layer in various parts of smart grid as shown in Figure 7.6. It has been illustrated that specific blockchain layers could be added to support all application in smart grids. The energy trading blockchain which deals with the trading is connected with all energy traders in smart grid which includes all types of plants, microgrid, and EV charging station. The electric vehicle blockchain can smoothen the functioning

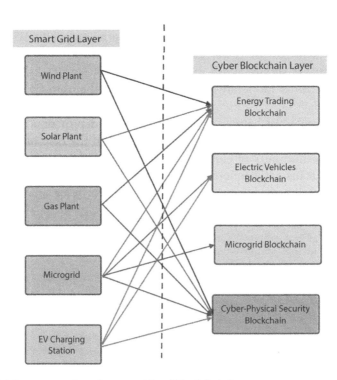

Figure 7.6 Interconnection of smart grid and blockchain layers.

between consumers and charging stations. Microgrid blockchain manages the operation of only microgrid which has many dispersed generations as well. The data and security matters are to be handled by the cyber-physical blockchain. All these blockchains can be integrated to fortify the smart grid operations.

7.5   Limitations of Blockchain

Though numerous advantages and applications of blockchain have been explored, it still has limitations. The biggest challenge in blockchain is cost of development as compared to existing technologies in the well-established markets. The transactions could be slower as when new block is added to chain it needs to communicated to all nodes and then verified by all nodes. As each node in blockchain validates the transaction, it is uneconomical as all nodes replicate same task. Moreover, the hardware required for validation and verification of data also adds to higher cost.

7.6   Conclusions

Blockchain has captivated the whirlwind momentum in the evolution and employment in energy sector due to main attributes such as scalability, decentralization, time embossed, non-transmogrify and security of this technology. At present it is widely accepted by financial markets in the form cryptocurrency such as bitcoin and Ethereum. It is seen as an optimistic technology and all markets have high expectations from blockchain. It has applications in various fields of energy sector such as micro-grids, smart grids, electric vehicles, and energy trading. Blockchain can assist the operation of energy system, markets and consumers as transparent and unalterable transactions are possible by employing blockchain. Moreover, it can offer more authorization to the consumers and dispersed generators through decentralization of the energy market and they can monetize their assets.

References

1. Yoldaş, Y., Önen, A., Muyeen, S.M., Vasilakos, A.V., Alan, I., Enhancing smart grid with microgrids: Challenges and opportunities. *Renew. Sust. Energ.*, 72, 205–214, May 2017.

2. Moslehi, K. and Kumar, R., A reliability perspective of the smart grid. *IEEE Trans. Smart Grid*, 1, 1, 57–64, Jun. 2010.

3. Kaur, N. and Jain, S.K., *Optimal placement of dispersed generators for practical distribution network*, PhD Thesis, 2019, Available online: (https://tudr.thapar.edu:8080/jspui/handle/10266/5709).

4. Strasser, T., A review of architectures and concepts for intelligence in future electric energy systems. *IEEE Trans. Ind. Electron.*, 62, 4, 2424–2438, Apr. 2015.

5. Gensollen, N., Gauthier, V., Becker, M., Marot, M., Stability and performance of coalitions of prosumers through diversification in the smart grid. *IEEE Trans. Smart Grid*, 9, 2, 963–970, Mar. 2018.

6. Nakamoto, S., Bitcoin: A peer-to-peer electronic cash system, 2008, Available online: (https://bitcoin.org/bitcoin.pdf).

7. Elysian, T., The global emergence of blockchain technology, 2018, Available online: (https://medium.com/@Elysian_Ely/the-global-emergence-of-block chain-technology-847fe9cdf2ee).

8. Mattila, J., Sepp, T., Naucler, C., Stahl, R., Tikkanen, M., Bàdenlid, A., Seppälä, J., Industrial blockchain platforms: An exercise in use case development in the energy industry, 2016, Available online: (https://www.etla.fi/julkaisut/industrial-blockchain-platforms-an-exercise-inuse-casedevelopment-in-the-energy-industry/).

9. Karame, G. and Capkun, S., Blockchain security and privacy. *IEEE Secur. Priv.*, 16, 4, 11–12, Jul. 2018.

10. How does a transaction get into the blockchain? Available online: (https://www.euromoney.com/learning/blockchain-explained/how-transactions-get-into-the-blockchain).

11. Sahu, M., Cryptography in blockchain: Types & applications, 2021, Available online: (https://www.upgrad.com/blog/cryptography-in-blockchain/).

12. Andersen, N., Blockchain technology A game-changer in accounting, 2016, Available online: (https://www2.deloitte.com/content/dam/Deloitte/de/Documents/Innovation/Blockchain_A%20game-changer%20in%20accounting.pdf).

13. Mizrahi, A., A blockchain based property ownership recording system, Available online: (https://chromaway.com/papers/A-blockchain-based-property-registry.pdf).

14. Nick, Blockchain cases for healthcare. Industry review, Intellectsoft, 2018, Available online: (https://blockchain.intellectsoft.net/blog/blockchain-cases-for-healthcare-industry-review/).

15. Wehbe, Y., Zaabi, M.A., Svetinovic, D., Blockchain AI framework for healthcare records management: Constrained goal model, in: *Proc. 26th Telecommun. Forum (TELFOR)*, Nov. 2018, pp. 420–425.

16. Algaze, B., A blockchain-based approach to smart cities, ExtremeTech, 2018, Available online: (https://www.extremetech.com/extreme/265796-blockchain-approach-smart-cities).

17. Parashar, C., Blockchain: The future of smart home automation & security, Crypto Canucks, 2018, Available online: (https://cryptocanucks.com/blockchain-the-future-of-smart-homeautomation-security/).
18. Dorri, A., Kanhere, S.S., Jurdak, R., Gauravaram, P., Blockchain for IoT security and privacy: The case study of a smart home, in: *Proc. IEEE Int. Conf. Pervasive Comput. Commun. Workshops (PerComWorkshops)*, pp. 618–623.
19. Neidhardt, N., Köhler, C., Nüttgens, M., Cloud service billing and service level agreement monitoring based on blockchain, in: *Proc. 9th Int. Workshop Enterprise Modeling Inf. Syst. Archit*, pp. 1–5, 2018.
20. Carrefour, Carrefour is Now Using Blockchain Technology, Unlock-BC, 2019, Available online: (https://www.unlock-bc.com/news/2019-01-13/carrefour-is-now-using-blockchaintechnology).
21. Brody, P., How blockchain is revolutionizing the supply chain management, 2017, Available online: (www.ey.com/Publication/vwLUAssets/ey-blockchain-and-the-supplychain-three/$FILE/ey-blockchain-and-the-supply-chain-three.pdf).
22. Konashevych, O., Advantages and current issues of blockchain use in microgrids, 2016, Available online: (https://ssrn.com/abstract=2662660).
23. Mylrea, M. and Gourisetti, S.N.G., Blockchain for smart grid resilience: Exchanging distributed energy at speed, scale and security, in: *Proc. of the Resilience Week (RWS)*, pp. 18–23, 2017.
24. Mengelkamp, E., Gärttner, J., Rock, K., Kessler, S., Orsini, L., Weinhardt, C., Designing microgrid energy markets A case study: The Brooklyn Microgrid. *Appl. Energy*, 210, 870–880, 2018.
25. Indigo Advisory Group, Blockchain in energy and utilities use cases, vendor activity, market analysis, 2017, Available online:(https://www.indigoadvisorygroup.com/blockchain).
26. Burger, C., Kuhlmann, A., Richard, P., Weinmann, J., Blockchain in the energy transitional survey among decision-makers in the German energy industry, 2016, Available online: (https://www.esmt.org/system/files_force/dena_esmt_studie_blockchain_english.pdf?download=1).
27. Grewal-Carr, V. and Marshall, S., Blockchain enigma paradox opportunity, Deloitte, 2016, Available online: (https://www2.deloitte.com/content/dam/Deloitte/uk/Documents/Innovation/deloitteuk-blockchain-full-report.pdf).
28. Canto, D. and Enel, D., Blockchain: Which use cases in the energy industry. CIRED 2017Glasgow, Round table discussion, 2017.
29. Dong, Z., Luo, F., Liang, G., Blockchain: A secure, decentralized, trusted cyber infrastructure solution for future energy systems. *J. Mod. Power Syst. Clean Energy*, 6, 5, 958–967, 2018.
30. Su, W. and Huang, A.Q., *The energy internet*, Woodhead Publishing, Sawston, U.K., 2018.
31. Bayram, I.S., Shakir, M.Z., Abdallah, M., Qaraqe, K., A survey on energy trading in smart grid, in: *Proc. IEEE Global Conf. Signal Inf. Process. (GlobalSIP)*, Dec. 2014, pp. 258–262.

32. Imbault, F., Swiatek, M., de Beaufort, R., Plana, R., The greenblockchain: Managing decentralized energy production and consumption, in: *Proc. IEEE Int. Conf. Environ. Elect. Eng. IEEE Ind. Commercial Power Syst. Eur. (EEEIC/ I&CPS Europe)*, Jun. 2017, pp. 1–5.

33. Khaqqi, K.N., Sikorski, J.J., Hadinoto, K., Kraft, M., Incorporating seller/ buyer reputation-based system in blockchain-enabled emission trading application. *Appl. Energy*, 209, 8–19, Jan. 2018.

34. Otjacques, B., Hitzelberger, P., Naumann, S., Wohlgemuth, V., From Science to Society: New Trends in Environmental Informatics. 1st ed. 2018.

35. Münsing, E., Mather, J., Moura, S., Blockchains for decentralized optimization of energy resources in microgrid networks, in: *Proc. IEEE Conf. Control Technol. Appl. (CCTA)*, Aug. 2017, pp. 2164–2171.

36. Luo, F., Dong, Z.Y., Liang, G., Murata, J., Xu, Z., A distributed electricity trading system in active distribution networks based on multi-agent coalition and blockchain. *IEEE Trans. Power Syst.*, 34, 5, 4097–4108, Sept. 2019.

37. Samad, T. and Annaswamy, A.M., Controls for smart grids: Architectures and applications. *Proc. IEEE*, 105, 11, 2244–2261, Nov. 2017.

38. Noor, S., Yang, W., Guo, M., van Dam, K.H., Wang, X., Energy demand side management within micro-grid networks enhanced by blockchain. *Appl. Energy*, 228, 1385–1398, Aug. 2018.

39. Wu, X., Duan, B., Yan, Y., Zhong, Y., M2M blockchain: The case of demand side management of smart grid, in: *Proc. IEEE 23rd Inter, Conf. on Parallel and Distributed Systems (ICPADS)*, pp. 810–813, 2017.

40. Yilmaz, M. and Krein, P.T., Review of the impact of vehicle-to-grid technologies on distribution systems and utility interfaces. *IEEE Trans. Power Electron.*, 28, 12, 5673–5689, Dec. 2013.

41. Hahn, A., Singh, R., Liu, C.-C., Chen, S., Smart contract-based campus demonstration of decentralized transactive energy auctions, in: *Proc. IEEE Power Energy Soc. Innov. Smart Grid Technol. Conf. (ISGT)*, Apr. 2017, pp. 1–5.

42. Kang, J., Yu, R., Huang, X., Maharjan, S., Zhang, Y., Hossain, E., Enabling localized peer-to-peer electricity trading among plug-in hybrid electric vehicles using consortium blockchains. *IEEE Trans. Industr. Inform.*, 13, 6, 3154–3164, Dec. 2017.

43. Hou, Y., Chen, Y., Jiao, Y., Zhao, J., Ouyang, H., Zhu, P., Wang, D., Liu, Y., A resolution of sharing private charging piles based on smart contract, in: *Proc. 13th Int. Conf. Natural Comput., Fuzzy Syst. Knowl. Discovery (ICNC-FSKD)*, Jul. 2017, pp. 3004–3008.

44. Mo, Y., Kim, T.H.-J., Brancik, K., Dickinson, D., Lee, H., Perrig, A., Sinopoli, B., Cyber physical security of a smart grid infrastructure. *Proc. IEEE*, 100, 1, 195–209, Jan. 2011.

45. Zhang, Z., Gong, S., Dimitrovski, A.D., Li, H., Time synchronization attack in smart grid: Impact and analysis. *IEEE Trans. Smart Grid*, 4, 1, 87–98, Mar. 2013.

46. Konstantinou, C., Sazos, M., Musleh, A.S., Keliris, A., Al-Durra, A., Maniatakos, M., GPS spoofing effect on phase angle monitoring and control in a real-time digital simulator based hardware-in-the loop environment. *IET Cyber-Phys. Syst., Theory Appl.*, 2, 4, 180–187, 2017.
47. Liu, S., Liu, X.P., El Saddik, A., Denial-of-Service (dos) attacks on load frequency control in smart grids, in: *Proc. IEEE PES Innov. SmartGrid Technol. Conf. (ISGT)*, Washington, DC, USA, Feb. 2013, pp. 1–6.

8

Revamping Energy Sector with a Trusted Network: Blockchain Technology

**Alain Aoun[1]*, Mazen Ghandour[2], Adrian Ilinca[1]
and Hussein Ibrahim[3]**

*[1]Department of Mathematics, Computer Science and Engineering,
Université du Québec, Rimouski, Canada
[2]Faculty of Engineering, Lebanese University, Beirut, Lebanon
[3]Institut Technologique de Maintenance Industrielle (ITMI), Cegep deSept-Iles,
Sept-Iles, Canada*

Abstract

The energy sector is in the midst of a major transformation, driven by new climate regulations and a political tendency towards a nuclear phase-out, aiming to achieve carbon neutrality for power generation and increased efficiency in electric grids. As a result, most power grids are encouraging higher integration of distributed energy resources and greater involvement of consumers in the energy management of the grid, served by a considerable application of smart technologies such as blockchain, artificial intelligence, big data, cloud computing, etc. This digital transformation at the core of the energy sector promises heavy disruptions, changing it from a centralized, segregated supply chain to a decarbonized, decentralized, and digitalized interconnected smart platform.

Blockchain as a transparent, secure, and decentralized trading platform, has gained the interest of businesses and industries worldwide unlocking new business models and promising new revenue streams. This promise is particularly potent, in the energy industry, when deployed at the grid edge, where increased consumer involvement and transparency are required. Blockchain based energy demand side management programs or energy peer-to-peer trading models, are typical solutions to be considered. In this chapter, blockchain applications in the energy sector are addressed along with their social, economic, and environmental impacts.

**Corresponding author*: alain.aoun@uqar.ca

Kiran Sood, Rajesh Kumar Dhanaraj, Balamurugan Balusamy and Seifedine Kadry (eds.) Blockchain Technology in Corporate Governance: Transforming Business and Industries, (163–196) © 2023 Scrivener Publishing LLC

Keywords: Energy, blockchain, smart contract, P2P, distributed energy resources, renewable energy, prosumer, smart grid

8.1 Introduction

Global megatrends, such as globalization, urbanization, demographic growth, climate change, and digitalization, are shaping world economy in profound ways. These megatrends promise to reform the different economic sectors by disrupting existing and established business models, presenting new enterprise and value chain architectures, and offering new revenue streams. And particularly, the energy sector is not exempt from the direct impact of these trends. From the use of wood as dominant fuel, to the mastering of hydropower, to the adoption of coal and more recently oil and gas and finally to the integration of renewable energy resources, the global energy landscape has gone through fundamental transformations and will continue to do so in the future. However, failing to acknowledge these driving trends would have detrimental outcomes on the development of the sector. On the other hand, energy represents an exceptional commodity to be carefully addressed, since all economic sectors involve some sort of an energy form as a basic source, as well as being considered concurrently a key driver and an indicator of economic growth.

Driven by the need to achieve carbon neutrality and meet new climate regulations, as well as attending to new consumer behaviors and expectations, energy companies worldwide are encouraging higher integration of distributed energy resources (DERs) and greater involvement of the consumers in the management of the energy supply chain, enabled by a considerable application of smart technologies such as blockchain, artificial intelligence (AI), big data, cloud computing, etc. Yet, these new changes challenge energy companies, which are not used to operating in such a rapidly varying decentralized business environment. For instance, oil and gas companies face price volatilities and new patterns of demand. Similarly, electric utility companies and independent system operators (ISOs) have to deal with the complex and intermittent nature of distributed energy resources, as well as the evolving nature of consumers' expectations. Moreover, the rising integration of DERs such as photovoltaic, wind turbines, electric vehicles and demand management, merged with the limitations of the existing electricity grids, necessitates the development and implementation of new innovative energy management systems. One of the main reasons for a fundamental reconfiguration at the core of existing electricity grids, compelling an architecture change from a centralized network to a decentralized form, is the need to deal with the distributed nature of DERs that are located at the grid edges, while overcoming the resulting grid connection and load balancing challenges, as well as the incurring significant infrastructure upgrade investments, with an ultimate target of maintaining a balance between supply and demand [1].

For the electrical grid, the balance between the supply and demand is a fundamental element of a good grid operation. Power generation arrangements and load management are governed by a rule that equilibrium between power generation and power demand should be maintained at all time. Power companies worldwide are challenged by recurring power crisis as a result of supply side problems, such as fuel supply shortage, maintenance requirements, and natural disasters, combined with a continuous growth in energy demand [2]. Historically, electric grids started as decentralized isolated small generators feeding power to small towns and cities. But with the emergence of the first industrial revolution and the discovery of alternating current (AC), that allowed power transmission over long distances, power grids shifted into the form of large centralized generation plants capable of satisfying the needs of continuously increasing energy demand. And today, following the wide adoption of DERs, the electric grid is once again shifting to a decentralized yet smarter architecture. Though smart decentralized microgrids provide a platform to implement more cost effective DERs, their development faces numerous technical, economic and infrastructure challenges associated with grid capacity and stability hindering the wide integration of renewable energy (RE) resources and distributed power generation. Power imbalance and peak load have emerged as two major concerns in the operation of an electrical grid, both of which can have a considerable impact on power reliability and quality. Furthermore, the surge in energy consumption is being driven by global economic growth, demographic expansion, digitization, increasing mobility, and growing demand for heating and cooling owing to climate change in various parts of the world. The growing in energy demand is the basis of economic challenges for power companies alongside several socio-economic concerns in communities such as energy poverty and energy democracy. Two key strategies have been identified to address the increasing energy demand dilemma. The first strategy focuses on new sustainable and eco-friendly modes of power generation such as renewable energy resources and distributed energy resources (DERs). The second strategy is demand side oriented rather than supply side. Demand side management, demand response and energy efficiency programs fall under this category.

On the other hand, energy suppliers are in a continuous quest to reap greater productivity, lower costs, and improved safety. A quest that can be achieved by digitalizing the energy sector. Digitalization is essential to attend to the distributed nature of DERs, manage the complexity of smart grids while unlocking load flexibility, increase diversity in the system, create an interconnected supply chain that can respond to fast changes in demands, and encourage higher consumers' engagement by allowing them to control their energy supply and resources. From a utility's perspective, digitalization of the energy value chain allows better monitoring of the assets and thus enabling early fault detection, minimizing downtimes, increasing equipment lifespan, and improving efficiency by controlling wasted energy.

Nevertheless, what is supposed to be a solution to the electric grid challenges and barriers has proved over the years that itself is a generator of a series of new challenges and barriers that require to be targeted. Hence, the shift towards a decentralized, digitalized and decarbonized (3Ds) electric system is not simply a matter of using a cleaner fuel or source for power generation, but more importantly it is a matter of altering energy consumption habits, as well as energy production, management and trading means in order to achieve higher resource efficiency and sustainability. Consequently, there is a need to introduce a fundamental paradigm shift in energy markets and energy management. Traditional management methodologies, based on centralized decision-making techniques, should be replaced with a decentralized, collaborative strategy that grants all stakeholders and specifically edge users a bigger say in governance.

Thus, there is a widespread recognition of the necessity for imaginative decentralized systems and designs. In this context, it comes as no surprise that blockchain technology is one of the main drivers of the digital transformation across various industries and can play an important role in delivering a completely decentralized energy grid [3]. Blockchain represents a technological breakthrough that can redefine the way transactions are conducted. Additionally, blockchain can serve as a platform for data transfer, management, and storage for other disruptive technologies such as Internet of Things (IoT), Artificial Intelligence (AI), and Machine Learning (ML). For the energy sector, this can be translated in shifting the grid from a unidirectional or bidirectional energy trading grid into a multi-directional system where consumers can transact not only with the grid but also among themselves, thus making the consumer an integral part of the new energy transition. Similarly, the implementation of blockchain technology in the energy sector can unlock new ways to deal with consumers' metering data without jeopardizing their privacy. Utilities' access to real-time metering data allows new demand side management programs to be designed and offers in depth insights on energy consumption patterns. Blockchain's potential in the energy sector is reflected the growing number of start-ups as well as research and Proof-of-Concept (PoC) projects. A survey conducted by the German Energy Agency (Deutsche Energie-Agentur GmbH - DENA) [4], showed that 80% of energy executives believe that blockchain is a game changer. Moreover, according to reports prepared by Deloitte [5] and PwC [6], energy commodities tokenization, enabled by blockchain technology, has the potential to change the way energy products are traded, making the process more interoperable.

This chapter sheds the light on the importance of digitalization in the energy sector and more specifically on the potentials and challenges of blockchain integration in the newly digitalized energy outlook. Through real life applications and conceptual models, this work aims to underline the different possibilities for new blockchain based energy business frameworks and revenue streams as well as their economic, environmental, and social impacts.

8.2   Energy Digital Transformation

Without a doubt, the energy sector is undergoing a substantial shift, and digitalization is one of the key facilitators in ensuring that this transition is accomplished. As a matter of fact, today's energy sector as well as its complete value chain is strongly driven by the new digital revolution. The tendency to have a higher integration of DERs in modern grids combined with the necessity to transform the conventional energy grid into a smart energy grid that meets both utilities and consumers' expectations and helps to overcome new market challenges such as the high volatility of energy prices and new patterns of demand, make from the adoption of new digital technologies at the core of the energy sector an inevitability. In this sense, digital technologies, such as AI, IoT and blockchain, comes into play as new game changers that offer the means to monitor and control the currently reshaped decentralized energy value chain. New energy management softwares, based on emerging digital technologies, allow not only to manage but also to optimize the energy supply chain, thus increasing its efficiency and productivity, while unlocking innovative business models and creating new revenue streams that couldn't be reachable without a fundamental digital transformation.

The transitioning from analogue energy meters to digital meters and later on to smart meters began more than half a century ago. However, until now, digital technologies have only been used to improve the energy management process; this will change if these technologies are used to transform the way energy is produced and distributed.

8.2.1   Digitalization, Decarbonization, and Decentralization of the Energy Sector

During the past decade global economy has been fundamentally reshaped as a result of recurring financial crisis, raising environmental concerns and new geopolitical apprehensions. This change can be summarized by the newly established triple bottom line: energy, environment, and economy. World Bank expects the world population to increase by 1 billion by the end of the decade. This growth can mean two things: the increase in world population will exhaust the remaining carbon credits and will lead to a definite increase in energy demand. This is why the decarbonization of the energy sector is no longer just an image improving choice but rather a must. By definition, decarbonization is the reduction of carbon dioxide emissions through the use of low carbon sources, achieving a lower output of greenhouse gasses into the atmosphere. In the electricity sector this means a decrease in the specific amount of carbon (or CO_2) emitted per unit of primary energy consumed. Additionally, electricity supply is the single most important emissions source sector, accounting for around 40% of global energy-related CO2 emissions.

At COP21 in Paris, the international community has agreed to limit global warming to well below 2°C, and to reach net greenhouse gas (GHG) emissions neutrality in the second half of the twenty-first century. Nevertheless, this can only be achieved by implementing serious measures that lead to a considerable decarbonization of the energy sector. These measures can be grouped into five main categories:

- Employ energy efficiency: Increasing energy efficiency will lead to a reduction in energy consumption which can counter-effect the increase in the energy demanding resulting from the growth of world's population
- Zero carbon electricity: This point can be achieved by decarbonizing the energy reply through a shift towards more sustainable and renewable sources of energy
- Economy wide electrification: Pushing clean electrification into energy consuming sectors, such as the transportation sector, can play a major role in shaving a larger amount of GHG emissions

- Zero carbon fuels: The use of zero carbon fuels can be very beneficial, especially for sectors where clean electrification cannot be integrated
- Carbon capture and removal: Carbon removal mechanisms can be implemented for areas where fossil fuels are still used in order to achieve negative emissions

However, the above detailed energy sector decarbonization measures will be hard to be employed in a conventional centralized and unidirectional energy supply chain. The integration of some of these measures, such as zero carbon electricity, employment of energy efficiency and economy wide electrification, necessitates a complete restructuring of the current energy grids and a shift towards a decentralized architecture that can be more adequate for a larger integration of DERs. Changing the energy system over from fossil energy carriers and nuclear energy to renewable energies and DERs opens up a range of new options for providing energy in a decentralized manner in the form of smaller plants.

Though, it is very important not to confuse decentralization with self-sufficiency. The concept of self-sufficiency is associated with economic independence, autonomy, and control over one's own energy supply. But decentralized energy is energy that is generated off the main grid and produced close to where it will be used rather than at a large plant. So, in other words, energy sector decentralization is the transformation of the "one-way street" of energy into a multi-directional, multi-lane highway. A decentralized energy supply offers individuals the possibility of playing an active part in shaping the energy transition, where every prosumer is an energy company. Such transition promises new deregulated energy markets that not only offer prosumers new revenue streams and earnings but also a role to contribute in the management of the energy grid via their resources and load flexibility. Such a prosumer-driven energy market might be beneficial to all stakeholders. Prosumers will not only benefit from direct earnings resulting from reduced energy bills but can as well contribute to the reduction of the energy cost for the system at large. In this case, utility companies can, at their end, benefit from this reduction to increase their profits, as well as beneficiating from the avoided investments costs to enlarge the grid, in order to accommodate new energy demands. Moreover, the decentralization of the energy supply chain will contribute to the decrease of technical and non-technical losses of the grid and thus adding more benefits to the utility companies.

Yet, the decentralization of the energy sector does not come without challenges. Today's decentralized energy model is complex and will be more so in the future. The integration of DERs at the edges of the grid as well as the intermittent nature of most renewable energy generators renders the management of the energy grid a difficult task. Moreover, the increased number of DERs added to the electric grid, leads to vast amounts of data being produced throughout the energy chain. Thus, the only way to respond to these challenges is to take the energy sector one step further and implement a fundamental digital transformation at the core of the energy value chain. Digitalization can serve as a lever in the energy sector to battle climate change and optimize power generation operations in order to reduce emissions and achieve the goals of decarbonization. Moreover, data is the key driver for optimized energy management. Digital technologies are set to make energy systems around the world more connected, intelligent, efficient, reliable, and sustainable. Without advanced technologies such as IoT, AI, blockchain, big data ...etc., it would be impossible to manage a decarbonized and decentralized energy system. Digitalization is a must for today's energy management systems and is set to transform the global energy system with profound impacts on both energy demand and supply. Digitalization can improve energy efficiency through technologies that gather and analyze data to effect real-world changes to energy use.

In summary, an energy transition is required in order to achieve energy security, supply and demand balance, economic growth, increase access to energy and guarantee sustainability while mitigating climate change. This transition is only possible through a strong correlation between the 3D variables: decarbonization, decentralization, and digitalization. The decarbonization of the energy sector is a main piece of the sustainability puzzle of this planet and decentralization is the mean to reach this goal. However, the decarbonization of the energy sector and its decentralization are not feasible without digitalization. The digitalization of the energy sector has an important part to play in the management of the new energy fabric and the synchronization of all its elements.

8.2.2   Blockchain: A Disruptive Technology of the Energy Value Chain

The energy sector is rapidly evolving from a highly centralized analog world of fossil fuel-based production and transmission system to a new paradigm of decarbonization, decentralization, and digitization. This transition is only possible if the available technology allows it and at this level blockchain might be the solution being a digital decentralized network formed of distributed computers connected to a platform. In fact, just by looking at the main features of modern energy networks, we find many similarities with blockchain technology. The key drivers of the new energy supply chain are management of big data, digital connectivity, decentralization, and security. All these drivers are common features with blockchain networks.

Blockchain has gained its reputation as a secure, transparent, fast, and low-cost peer-to-peer (P2P) transactional platform. For energy companies this can be translated into higher automation capabilities and greater data processing abilities with less human intervention at a lower cost and risk. The new energy revolution has caused market companies to deal with an increasing necessity for reporting, transparency, storage, and security of data, which incurs higher processing costs and a draining exploitation of personnel and resources. Blockchain technology can offer solutions for those challenges and have a significant impact on the entire energy value chain. Current energy transaction models are based on unidirectional and centralized structures. Energy transaction occurs only from energy companies to consumers with a need for third party intermediaries, such as brokers and aggregators, in most cases. However, the integration of DERs in the energy mix of modern energy grids has forced the conventional energy transaction model to change into a bidirectional system where energy can be traded from the grid to the consumer and vice versa. Nevertheless, the still imposing need for third party intermediaries to bridge the trust gap between consumers and energy companies imposes additional charges to consumers' bills, as well as increasing the processing time for transactions. Additionally, the existing energy transaction structure has a centralized architecture that induces a single point of failure risk. In case the connection to the energy service provider's central energy management server is lost, the complete network is jeopardized. Alternatively, a blockchain network allow to mitigate the single point of failure risk, since it has different connected nodes that interact with each other and a copy of the ledger containing all transactions is shared among all nodes. Thus, even when a single node or multiple nodes disconnect from the network, the system's operation and integrity are maintained.

Therefore, blockchain technology has the potential to unlock new business models and create new revenue streams for both energy companies and consumers, especially when applied to grid edges, as greater market participation and transparency are thought. Additionally, the balance between power generation and power demand is the foundation of any energy management process. The application of blockchain technology in the form of energy demand profiles management or energy peer-to-peer trading to create a transparent, secure and near real-time energy model is something to consider, as we will see throughout the next sections of this chapter.

8.2.3   Blockchain Advancing DERs

As elaborated in the previous paragraph, the fast growth of distributed energy resources is pushing the power system into a decentralized bidirectional power flow system where blockchain technology can play a major role in optimizing DERs' integration to the grid, minimizing costs, managing load profiles and increasing grid's flexibility. By definition, the term "Distributed Energy Resource" (DER), refers to the following (Figure 8.1):

- Distributed Generation: Power generation units that produces power on the consumer's side of the meter
- Distributed Power: Any technology that produces power or stores power (i.e., batteries and electric vehicles)
- Demand Side Management

Though microgrids provide a platform to implement more cost effective DERs, their development faces numerous technical and non-technical challenges. On a technical level, infrastructure barriers associated with grid capacity, synchronization, and stability are considered a major limitation that confronts a wider integration of renewable energy (RE) resources and distributed power generation. Another barrier to the development of RE resources is the adequacy of existing transmission lines to transmit energy from the points of generation to the points of consumption. Furthermore, the lack of skilled utility workers in some regional markets limits the implementation and development of DERs. Another barrier is the lack of awareness and knowledge of personnel about the availability and performance of renewable energy.

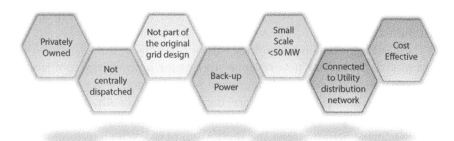

Figure 8.1 DER characteristics.

On the other hand, the economic challenges that hinder the development of microgrids which use renewable energy sources include market and financial barriers. Identified market barriers include the following:

- Inconsistent pricing structures that disadvantage renewables, especially those in long term power purchase agreements.
- Subsidies for fossil fuels. Subsidized fossil fuel-generated electricity makes it difficult for RE resources to compete.
- Failure to include social and environmental costs in the overall costing procedure

Financial barriers include lack of adequate funding and financing for renewable energy. The commercialization of DERs heavily depend on reducing the production costs of RE, storage technologies and energy management systems.

To minimize their reliance on fossil fuels and increase their energy security, many industrialized and developing countries are adopting and promoting renewable energy resources and distributed energy resources as part of their overall energy mix. These countries have adopted a slew of laws, directives, and regulations, as well as setting targets to endorse distributed generation, renewable energy, and microgrid development. Nevertheless, the issue is not a lack of regulation, but rather its flaws and ambiguities. Some regulations are undefined or not clearly stated. Additionally, lengthy administrative procedures and policy instabilities play an important role in hindering efforts to deploy renewables and expand microgrid markets.

Blockchain technology can help to overcome some of the challenges associated with a wide integration of DERs in electric grids, especially in developing countries where in most cases a solid infrastructure and a trusted public framework are lacking. Blockchain technology has the potential to transform the entire contractual life cycle of energy trading by minimizing the need for human intervention from the time of trade execution to the time of payment. Also, blockchain technology's integration in the DER market has the potential to improve market efficiency and disrupt energy markets by creating unforeseen opportunities, as well as providing incentives for DER development, particularly in developing countries, and creating new revenue streams that can render the investments in DERs economically appealing. Among the conceivable applications, that can advance DER implementations, are blockchain based smart meters, energy backed digital currencies, P2P energy trading and blockchain enabled new demand side management programs.

Blockchain and Smart Meters: Using blockchain and cryptocurrencies for monetary transactions is an achievable application of blockchain technology in the energy sector. Blockchain eliminates the need for a third party in money transfer transactions and reduces transfer costs by eliminating administrative fees, bank fees, and commissions. Savings from using the blockchain's platform can be re-invested. An application of the blockchain in the energy sector is through the installation of smart prepaid electric meters that provide power to the end-user once money is transferred from the end-user's account to the utility account. This application improves end-users' payment discipline and reduces the cost of reading meters, billing and collections. In most developing countries, the utility company suffers from low billings and collections. Prepaid electric meters offer a solution which decreases utility company losses, leads to lower energy rates, and avoids increases in electricity prices. Another application of blockchain for energy sector money transfers is demonstrated by the South African company Bankymoon who uses Bitcoin to perform remote payment transactions with compatible smart meters. The application works as follows: assume a donor wants to support a school in a developing country; the donor can send cryptocurrency directly to the school's smart meter, enabling electricity from the grid to be supplied to the school.

Analogously, today's energy billing systems are not designed for a bi-directional energy market in which customers produce and consume energy at the same time. For example, individual bills are still issued for every PoD (Point of Delivery), rather than one aggregate bill per customer, who might own several apartments, illustrating that these systems do not apply a user-centric system hierarchy. As a result, retailers do not have any information about customers who own multiple locations, and therefore are unable to offer personalized products. Moreover, billing constitutes between 5% and 15% of retailers' total operating costs. This results from the fact that the industry still relies on expensive and outdated legacy softwares that have high setup and maintenance costs, without providing the necessary functionalities that are needed in order to compete in a more customer centric energy market. Moreover, the current data collection, processing and financial settlement processes are highly inefficient and error-prone, resulting in significant time delays in value settlement and the need for costly reconciliation processes [7]. Thus, the need to develop an automatic decentralized energy trading system that can automatically collect energy consumption, offer a user-centric approach and ensures a simple settlement for energy transactions in a bidirectional way. This is where blockchain technology combined with IoT and AI can revolutionize the current energy trading models by providing energy companies with the possibility to incorporate thousands of data points per day per smart meter, enabling them to offer customers a variety of innovative, dynamic tariffs, services and products, while running on an efficient, fully automated and process assured billing system.

Energy Backed Currencies: The lack of financial incentives or funds is the main barrier facing the development of distributed energy resources. This challenge applies to both developed and developing countries. In 2016, approximately a third of Germany's electricity consumption was generated using renewables. Recently, the central government reduced financial incentives for new RE installations, particularly solar photovoltaic [8]. An energy-backed currency might be the type of incentive needed to improve the economic feasibility of renewable energy-based power generation. The concept of an energy-backed currency is similar to the gold reserves that are used to stabilize national currencies. An application of this concept is offered by the SolarCoin Foundation, a nonprofit organization. They focus on promoting solar energy generation by providing SolarCoin to solar energy producers. Nick Gogerty and Joseph Zitoli, two founders of the SolarCoin Foundation, had an idea for an energy- backed currency called DeKo in 2011 [9]. In 2014, the DeKo was transformed by the SolarCoin Foundation into a digital asset reward program for RE installations based on a new cryptocurrency, called SolarCoin. SolarCoin is a digital currency backed by solar-generated electricity, electronically representing a verified 1 MWh of solar-generated electricity. The main purpose of this initiative was to provide an incentive to produce solar energy by rewarding SolarCoin to producers of solar electricity. SolarCoin is active in 17 countries and is intended for worldwide circulation. SolarCoin can be exchanged for other cryptocurrencies or conventional currencies. Holders can user their SolarCoin to pay for products and services from participating merchants and service providers.

The Jouliette is another energy-backed currency named after the joule, an SI energy measurement unit. The Jouliette is backed by physical energy production. In September 2017, Spectral and Alliander launched the Jouliette token at De Ceuvel, a city playground for innovation and creativity in Amsterdam and a showcase for sustainable urban development [10]. A private smart grid made the Jouliette model feasible for the De Ceuvel community. With the Jouliette token, the De Ceuvel community members can transact using a secure blockchain platform, without the need of any bank or a trusted third party. Transaction histories can be shared with all community members enabling automatic verification. The De Ceuvel community is exploring further applications for the Jouliette tokens such as using it to trade for goods and services within the community [11].

Energy-backed currencies using blockchain might provide incentives for communities in developing countries, especially if combined with smart contracts and P2P energy trading within community micro-grids.

8.3   Energy Trading Mechanisms

With an aim to incentivize consumers' investments in DER projects, energy utility companies have developed various incentive programs. Some of the most common incentive programs are Net Metering, Feed-In Tariff, and Power Purchase Agreements (PPA). Usually net metering and feed-in tariff financing mechanisms are applied to small scale projects while PPAs are applied to medium and large-scale power generation projects.

Net Metering: Net metering (NM) is a billing mechanism that allows prosumers to inject any surplus of generated energy to the grid and retrieve it back whenever needed. For example, if during the day a solar system is producing more energy than what the house is consuming, the extra energy would be exported to the utility grid, and the consumer would be able to use this energy at night, at a time where the solar system is not producing any energy. This eliminates the need for battery energy storage systems that are considered an expensive and high maintenance component. Net metering is concretely implemented by using an electric meter that would operate in two directions: the meter would be able to run backwards whenever the renewable energy system is injected back to the grid. However, the main drawback of NM is that by the end of the year, if the amount of energy injected to the grid exceeds the yearly consumed energy, the excess energy will not be remunerated by the utility company. This feature would limit the capacity of the renewable energy installed and would increase the payback period of the system.

Feed-in Tariff: Feed-in tariff (FIT) is a billing mechanism that also encourages investment in renewable energy systems. They are long-term contracts (15–25 years) that would specify a cost per kWh for energy supplied to the grid for each type of technology. The tariff is set to reflect the cost of the system. Consequently, the tariff may vary based on the technology used, the size of the system, the region where it is implemented and the type of installation whether it is a rooftop or ground-mount project. The FIT program includes a tariff degression. FIT mechanism provides a security to the renewable energy installers due to its fixed tariff over the contract period (with percentage degression). However, these renewable energy technologies have a fast development and evolution, which results in a fast drop in market cost as well. The FIT tariff scheme is very sensitive to these changes, hence the set tariff along with the degression percentage, defined for a 25-year period, could eventually result in an overcompensation or under compensation for the investor [12]. Currently, the FIT rate is lower than the retail electricity rate. In fact, Germany is one of the most relevant examples who had first implemented the FIT scheme; it first started with providing a high tariff for electricity from renewable energy sources, with a modest degression, in order to scale up generation. From 2009 to 2011, with the fast decrease of solar PV prices, Germany had to adjust the PV FIT in a way to manage the quantity of domestic PV installations. As of 2012, with constant decline in renewable energy costs, a reduction of FIT payments was applied in a way that it became lower than traditional energy prices. Unlike Net Metering, the FIT system requires two meters, one that would measure the outflow of energy to the grid, and the other one that measures the inflow of energy to the load. This would allow having different rates for both imported and exported energy.

Power Purchase Agreement: A Power Purchase Agreement (PPA) is a contract between an electricity producer and a purchaser. Usually, the producer is a private entity while the purchaser is a governmental or state associated entity. The agreement is a long-term contract, 20 to 25 years in the case of renewable energy sources, where a tariff for selling the electricity is fixed over that period. There are also several conditions that would be agreed upon, such as the minimum energy to be produced and sometimes a maximum amount of production would be specified; if the producer does not meet the range set, some penalties would apply. PPA contracts are done for the export of the total energy produced and are usually applicable for medium to large-scale capacity. While the renewable energy market and technologies are rapidly changing, a fixed tariff over a long period could be unfavorable to either the purchaser or the producer in case of market price fluctuations.

8.3.1 Blockchain P2P Energy Trading: A New Financing Mechanism

Another way to incentivize the surplus of energy without having a sole purchaser or entity to trade with is the Peer-to-Peer energy trading. With PPA, NM, and FIT, the trade of energy is always between the producer and the grid utility retailer or state-owned authority, which decides on the price of this surplus. However, Peer-to-Peer energy trading provides the option to buy and sell electricity between peers directly. Peers could be any entity, prosumers, consumers, and energy producers that are interconnected through a grid and can exchange power between each other without the intermediary of a conventional power authority. Peer-to-Peer (P2P) energy trading is a new financing mechanism that can be adopted to incentivize the development of distributed energy resources (DERs), by promoting the selling of excess energy to other peers on the network at a negotiated rate. Current incentive programs, such as Net Metering (NEM) and Feed-in-Tariff (FIT), operate according to a centralized policy framework, where energy is only traded with the utility, the state-owned grid authority, service provider or power generation/distribution company, that also have the upper hand in deciding on the rates for buying the excess energy. P2P energy trading has the potential to present a solution for both prosumers and consumers to decide on the amount of energy to be traded, the time of the transaction, as well as on the rates in an open decentralized, deregulated market model. Nevertheless, in order to make the P2P energy trading feasible, executable in real time, irreversible, immutable, and cost effective, a certain trading platform, with specific requirements that can only be shaped by relying on the blockchain technology, is essential.

The growing adoption of DER solutions has introduced a number of new variables to the energy trading economics and load balancing equation. And on the other side, DERs emerging markets need an enabling environment that allows grids to increase their uptake and improve their management of off-grid technology. Existing incentive-based schemes such as Net Metering and Feed-in-Tariff (FIT) are not always reflective of the cost of electricity at the moment of injection into the grid and might distort the market if the quantity injected is significant. In order to take advantages of such schemes, prosumers should either inject energy in periods when the compensation tariffs are high or maximize self-consumption or store energy when the tariffs are low. Also, in such schemes, the utility is the single buyer of electricity from prosumers and they usually control the tariffs at which electricity is bought. In the absence of a competitive market, the result will be always in favor of the utility company. Peer to Peer (P2P) energy trading creates a completely new energy framework with unique fair economic incentives for all stakeholders. The deregulated nature of the blockchain P2P energy trading system helps to create an open market that favors innovation and increases competition which can lead to a reduction of the overall market energy prices. In fact, the open market competition was a main driver for the energy market transition from fossil fuel-based generation to renewable energy, since the benefit is not only ecological but also financial as renewable energy-based power generation systems have a lower levelized cost of energy (LCoE). While fixed energy tariffs have helped to safeguard consumers from fluctuating energy prices, Net Metering or FIT has succeeded to incentivize the private sector's investment in renewable energy solutions, especially at a small scale, and thus transforming the conventional energy consumer into an active prosumer that contributes to the grid's power generation mix. However, a freer, P2P deregulated energy market, based on supply and demand, has the potential to further reduce energy prices and transform small scale renewable energy power generation systems from independent systems to interdependent and thus extending their contribution to the connected and decentralized grid through ancillary services.

For P2P energy trading to be applicable through blockchain technology, smart contracts, and smart oracles are required. A typical P2P energy trading smart contract would contain the amount and price of energy, the timeframe for transfer, the legally binding conditions including payment terms, conflict resolution, actions in case the agreed upon energy is not met, etc. After setting the smart contract agreement and trading terms, it is very important to establish a connection between the digital world of blockchain and the physical world of energy. Smart oracles are used for this purpose. Smart oracles would be the bridge between the smart contracts and the tangible equipment; they are a digital medium that would take the required data from the equipment, verify them, and send them to the smart code in order for it to take action.

To better understand how a blockchain based P2P energy trading system works, let's consider the following example. A prosumer signs a smart contract with a certain consumer to sell him/her 10kWh on the following day between 10h and 14h. The conditions of the contract state that Consumer shall pay in advance, based on a pre-agreed price, in order for the smart contract to be activated. However, the money remains in the smart contract escrow account and gets transferred to the prosumer's e-wallet once the correct amount of energy has been exchanged. In case the prosumer fails to provide the required amount of energy to the consumer, the smart contract will calculate the difference in energy terms and will pay the prosumer the exact amount for the traded energy while returning the remaining amount to the consumer's e-wallet.

The oracles needed for such transaction to take place are:

- Smart meter oracles to activate the corresponding meters and log the energy sent from the prosumer's meter to the consumer's meter
- Time oracle to provide information about the current time to the smart contract in order for it to initiate and terminate the transfer

- Utility availability oracle to provide the blockchain with a binary value that represent whether the utility is available or not so that the energy transfer takes place

Similarly, various interconnected smart contracts are required as well:

- A smart contract to collect the data from oracles: time, energy sent, energy received, utility availability
- A smart contract to compare the energy transferred to the energy set in the agreement within the set timeframe
- A smart contract to calculate the difference between money received and the money equivalent to the energy transferred, and would re-distribute the money accordingly

The smart contracts work in real-time, which enables P2P energy trading participants to sell or buy energy whenever it is available and/or needed. The fact that no intermediary is involved to validate the transaction makes the smart contract fast and cheap. It is important to note that although the ledger containing all the information about the contract and records about the transaction is distributed among all the nodes of the blockchain, only authorized users, which are the parties involved in that contract, have access to the information in the blocks. Moreover, the most important part of the whole system is the platform that would allow human interface, through which, users would be able to manage their transactions and have access to their information in the corresponding blocks.

Although the blockchain use for P2P energy trading is relatively new, various applications have already been implemented. One of them is the Grid+; a blockchain-based solution that works in a deregulated market. The Grid+ has a software and a hardware facet. The hardware equipment would be programed to automatically buy and sell electricity from the most beneficial source of energy, existing in the P2P network, and execute payments in real time. It would also communicate with internet connected smart equipment in the house in order to manage the loads.

So, in summary, direct energy trading in a micro-grid between peers, known as Peer-to-Peer energy trading, is a new way to incentivize DER projects. Blockchain based P2P energy trading allows prosumers to produce or store energy and sell it in a free market while satisfying their needs and increasing their profitability, as well as those of the buyers. Nevertheless, aside from the financial benefits, P2P energy trading actually presents technical challenges that should be respected in order to keep a strong electrical grid, problems could result from nodal overvoltage, energy losses, and frequency instability.

8.3.2   Blockchain-Based Virtual Power Plant (VPP) Model

In the previous paragraph, P2P energy trading, for small scale DER applications, was explored. Nonetheless, P2P energy trading can also be applied on a larger scale via blockchain based virtual power plants (VPPs). VPPs were conceived to tackle the techno-economic complications resulting from the increasing share of renewable energy sources in the energy grids. A VPP is a platform to monitor, manage, and optimize the operation of thousands of distributed power generation systems, aggregating their capacities to create a homogeneous power generation system. Hence, a VPP is not a true power plant, but rather an aggregation of several heterogeneous DERs, including PV systems, wind turbines, micro-gas turbines, electric vehicles, battery energy storage systems, as well as load management. When integrated into a VPP, the power and flexibility of the aggregated assets are traded collectively via an aggregator. The integration of VPPs in electric grids allows avoiding large investments in new centralized power plants and infrastructure expansions in addition to the benefit of generating electricity at the edges of the grid where energy is actually consumed, thus reducing technical losses resulting from long transmission lines. Moreover, since renewable energy power generation solutions have a low LCoE, the VPP approach allows reducing the overall energy cost and making it more competitive, as compared with fossil-based energy generators. Nevertheless, this solution does not come without its own challenges and limitations. The architecture of VPPs involves several stakeholders: the energy supplier/producer, the electric grid operator, the aggregator, the prosumers, and can involve several financial institutes as well. The extensive administrative process, required by these multifaced relationships, results in high operational expenses, transaction fees, and issues of trust among the stakeholders.

Blockchain's decentralized architecture not only is convenient for the energy management of DERs, by providing a real-time communication system for bidding, settling, and payment, but also helps to eliminate the need for an aggregator, which reduces process costs. Blockchain's P2P communication combined with smart contracts enables the automation of the complete energy trading process, while maintaining a balance between consumer's privacy and the transparency of the process. A blockchain based VPP model will give users the flexibility to trade between each other or with the grid as well as choosing to contribute to the energy grid by aggregating their ancillary services through the VPP. Blockchain based VPPs promise to provide the necessary capabilities to maximize DERs output while also ensuring reliability.

8.3.3   Blockchain Technology for Electric Vehicle (EV) Charging and Discharging

The transportation sector electrification is seen as a solution to worldwide challenges such as global warming, sustainability, and geopolitical concerns on the availability of fossil fuels. Yet, besides their major environmental and geopolitical contributions, the electric vehicles can also have a major contribution in the development of smart grids and will be considered in the near future as a key component of all residential micro-grids. Nevertheless, as EVs will become more and more used, new challenges for the electric grid will immerge. Utility companies will have to deal with issues such as peak loads resulting from simultaneous charging, increased energy demand and higher end-user's electricity bills. Smart grid technologies, using smart metering and advanced communication protocols, are already being developed by utility companies to better manage loads while increasing grids efficiency and resilience and cutting GHG emissions. EVs can play an important role in the smart grid framework. EVs should not only be considered uniquely as an electric load but rather as a mean of energy storage. With advanced techniques such as Vehicle-to-Grid (V2G), energy can be stored in EV's battery in off peak periods and then use the stored energy to shave peak time loads. Additionally, the EV's stored energy can potentially be used to compensate for the intermittent nature of renewable energy sources such as solar and wind.

However, the wide adoption of EVs remains challenged by the availability of charging stations at large scale. Yet in order to incentivize private sectors investments in EV charging stations, especially the ones owned by private entities such as EV stations installed in shopping malls or a public parking, the concerns of simplicity, security and privacy of charging stations, should be addressed. Blockchain technology can offer the perfect platform for a simple and secure billing model for EV charging and hence incentivize a wider development of public charging stations. Widespread use of electric vehicles (EV) becomes more feasible when drivers can universally access charging stations. A typical blockchain based EV charging system will offer EV drivers the possibility to park their vehicle at any blockchain compatible charging station while the vehicle autonomously connects to the charging station and recharges automatically. Once the vehicle leaves the parking space, the charging station automatically bills the driver for the energy received. Furthermore, a blockchain based EV charging/discharging model can take into consideration the bidirectionality flow of energy from and to the vehicle, thus considering the EV as both a load and an energy storage device. Such EV charging/discharging configuration can help attend to several grid challenges such as peak load shaving and reducing the impact of uncoordinated simultaneous EV charging. Since EVs are potential energy storage systems, the excess energy stored in their batteries can be fed back to the network and the owner earning money. The concept is based on the smart plug, which can be used as a normal electrical outlet plug but is linked with an identification code. Users install an app on their smartphones to authorize the EV charging process. It connects to the blockchain platform which negotiates the price, records the charging data, and manages the payment process (Figure 8.2). The application of blockchain technology for charging EVs represents a change in how private businesses interface with their customers. This model is ideal for small businesses, shopping malls, office buildings, and car parks who offer customers renewable energy charging for their plug-in electric vehicles.

A blockchain based EV charging/discharging system will basically have three main components:

- The Smart Plug: The smart plug can be considered as the digital identity of all peers using the platform. The Smart Plug enables users and devices to authenticate themselves to other network participants. Each EV Charging Station will hold a computer chip connected to the blockchain network and linked with an identification code to control the accessibility to the system by verifying the identity of the user connected to the charging station
- The mobile application: allows the customer to check the offered price, sign the smart contract and visualize the charging process on a smartphone
- The blockchain platform manages and records all payment and charging data. All charging processes will be completed using blockchain smart contracts between the EV vehicle owner and the EV charging station owner.

The system uses blockchain smart contracts to verify user identities anonymously and create a trusted contract between the EV vehicle owner and the EV charging station owner to manage the charging of the electric vehicle and manage payments between parties. Additionally, the smartphone application can notify the EV driver of the closest charging stations

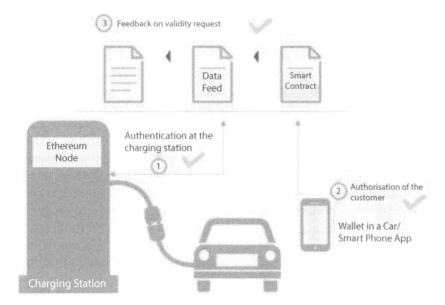

Figure 8.2 Blockchain based EV charging model.

along with the offered energy prices. Also, it will notify users of the preferable times to charge their vehicles in order to avoid uncoordinated EVs charging, offering them credits as incentives to charge their vehicles during off-peak periods thus contributing the valley filling in the utility profile. On the other side, during peak times, the EVs owners can be notified of Demand Response (DR) requests, thus injecting the energy stored, in the batteries of their EVs, onto the grid in order to respond to the peak load. By participating in these DR programs, users can also earn credits and they can use those credits to pay for their EVs charging.

Blockchain based EV charging and discharging model can help mitigate risks associated with the heavy electrification of the light duty transportation sector as well as bringing DER energy management up to a new level.

8.4   Blockchain Unlocking New Demand Side Management Models

Demand Side Management (DSM) first emerged as a response to rising costs of energy sources during the energy crisis of the 1970s, and it incorporates programs that help consumers manage their energy use, such as appliance rebates, energy-efficient lighting programs, as well as programs that reward customers for shifting their load during times of peak energy use. Demand Side Management is the term used to describe these programs developed by utilities to influence the electricity usage patterns of their customers and, in return, the achieved energy savings allow utilities to avoid or delay new investments in supply side generation, transmission lines, or even distribution networks. DSM is a crucial component of any smart grid energy management system. Basically, Demand Side Management, or sometimes called Energy Demand Management, is a set of interconnected programs that aim to encourage the end user to be more energy efficient. A DSM portfolio may include a variety of measures used to improve the consumer's load profile. Depending on the methodology used, the time of application, on-peak or off-peak, and the defined target, DSM mechanisms can be grouped into 4 main categories: demand response, energy efficiency, virtual power plants and spinning reserve.

Traditional transactional models are based on a centralized structure. Transactions between network nodes occur only through an intermediary third party who maintains the ledgers. Involvement of an intermediary is often necessary because it creates trust when transaction partners are unacquainted. Intermediaries usually charge fees for their services. The involvement of intermediaries increases the processing time required for transactions. Since all transactions are linked and stored on a central server or infrastructure, centralized structures have the disadvantage of a single point of failure. Alternatively, decentralized systems, such as the one offered by Blockchain, have different network nodes that can interact directly with each another without an intermediary. There are many ways that transaction ledgers can be maintained. With a secure P2P distributed ledger technology, problems with associated with centralized structures can be resolved.

So, blockchain technology has the potential to deliver more efficient, transparent and near real time transaction platforms that will unlock new business models. In the energy industry, this promise is particularly compelling when applied at the grid edge, as greater market participation and transparency are sought. An interesting feature of DSM projects is that multiple parties can benefit simultaneously from a single action. The forecasting of power generations and power demands is the essential premise for generation arrangement and power management. The use of blockchain technology for delivering a transparent, secure, reliable, and near real time energy model, under the form of energy demand profiles management, is something to look at. Such a model can be based on a blockchain enabled distributed tamperproof ledger where the energy prosumption data, collected from smart meters, is stored while self-enforcing smart contracts programmatically define the expected energy flexibility at the level of each prosumer, the associated rewards or penalties, and the rules for balancing the energy demand with the energy production at grid level. Another potential use case is the model of a DSM aggregator, as a key player in managing the demand during the peak hours by acting as an energy manager between the utility and the consumer.

8.4.1   Blockchain in the Energy Efficiency Market

Energy efficiency is an important pillar of utility companies' DSM strategies that can counterbalance the continuously increasing demand for energy. On the end-user's side, the development of new technologies, that allow consumers to monitor in real time their energy consumption, check their energy profiles and compare them to benchmarks, combined with an increase in electricity tariffs, has raised the interest in energy efficiency.

However, the process of collecting the correct data required to make the best judgments about building energy efficiency, can be very challenging. The energy consumption, operating cost, and asset value of a building are rarely publicly shared. Building energy efficiency data is generally siloed in original equipment manufacturers' (OEMs) hardware and software packages, making it hard and costly to access. Without easy access to energy consumption related data, building owners would struggle to assess the performance of their buildings as well as to quantify the impact of implemented energy conservation measures (ECMs) on their energy performance. The use of blockchain technology offers a means to extract and share buildings' binned data without jeopardizing neither the privacy of owners nor the security and integrity of data. Blockchain presents an open-access, transparent and yet confidential and secure platform that promotes simple and safe data sharing in order to create an accurate benchmark for building's energy performance and unlocks new energy efficiency opportunities in buildings.

Blockchain technology can simplify the energy efficiency service market. Instead of having a separate hardware and software for each OEM, the energy efficiency market can benefit from a publicly shared open access energy efficiency data platform. Data owners can be rewarded for their contribution to the platform with tokens that can be used to buy equipment or benefit from other services. And on the other hand, building owners and OEMs will have to pay with tokens in order to get access to the data. Building owners can benefit from the data to benchmark the performance of their own buildings and OEMs can use the data to assess the performance of their equipment and improve their performance.

In fact, the data sharing process for equipment or building performance assessment can be complimented by the blockchain based digital twin technology. As a result of their capabilities to simulate any process under different scenarios and provide performance insights, digital twins have emerged as an important instrument of Industry 4.0. Nevertheless, in the energy efficiency and energy management framework, digital twins can combine the semantically rich building information models with real time streaming data coming from building sensors in order to optimize the energy performance and the operation and maintenance of these physical assets. This data-driven model can play a major role in enabling advanced energy management applications.

8.4.2   New Blockchain-Enabled Demand Response (DR) Models

Demand response (DR) is a term used for programs designed to encourage end-users to make short-term reductions in energy demand in response to a price signal. DR programs pursues the temporary reduction of electricity consumption by the consumer, for a short period and in peak demand periods in exchange of economic incentives. However, the implementation of DR programs is faced with several challenges and limitations. The first challenge is the complexity of the management process. Due to the fact that a DR program can include thousands of participants, the registration, implementation, communication, and management processes are not considered easy tasks. The implementation of a DR program can induce a high overhead cost resulting from the management of participating entities, settlement of payments, market organization, data management …etc. This high cost can render some DR programs economically less appealing. Additionally, the collection, management, storage, and security of the large amount of data resulting from DR programs can be a real hustle and bustle for utility companies. Furthermore, DR programs are most of the time based on a bidding process. The disclosure risk of important data such as bidding data can generate a trust issue that challenges the integrity of the integrity and fairness of the bidding process and thus weakening the interest of participants.

The integration of blockchain technology in DR programs allows targeting most of the challenges faced by DR programs. Blockchain based DR programs offer the possibility to simplify and automate the registration, management and settlement processes by relying on smart contracts, especially that the decentralized structure of blockchain is perfectly suited for this type of applications. The use of smart contracts allows reducing DR programs costs and increasing utility profits. Moreover, blockchain improves the authenticity of DR programs by making DR related data traceable, transparent, and immutable. At the end-user's side, blockchain enables participants to tokenize their energy reductions and get compensate it for that in an automated manner. Additionally, it may also offer end-users to trade their energy reduction tokens with other peers and not necessarily just with the utility.

8.4.3   Blockchain-Based Energy Performance Contracting

Energy performance contracting (EPC) is an important concept for financing EE. It is based on an energy services company (ESCO) implementing an investment to reduce a host's energy cost, and accepting the financial and technical risks for a specified contract term. The host uses the project's future avoided costs to amortize the invested capital. These funds may be supplied by the ESCO or a third party. At the end of the performance contract term and after the investment has been amortized, the host often continues to benefit from lower energy costs. When the capital is sourced from the ESCO, the financing mechanism is the energy performance contract and the collection mechanism is through invoices and payments.

Performance contracting financial structures are tailored for each specific host and application. A typical structure would follow these stages:

- A preliminary analysis is undertaken to determine the host's energy consumption and costs and identify ways to maximize energy savings.
- A detailed energy analysis (known as an investment grade audit) is performed to determine energy savings and costs associated with the improvement measures.
- Improvements are selected for implementation.
- Facility improvements are implemented and the new equipment associated with the project is installed.
- Periodic measurement and verification (M&V) of savings determines the savings that is achieved.

Energy performance contracts are helpful in situations when funding sources are elusive, maintenance is lacking, or new equipment and technology is needed and requires unique skills. Energy performance contractors use future energy savings to finance present improvement measures and generally guarantee the savings to lower the risks of the host.

Despite the advantages of EPC projects, their providers and customers face legislative, administrative, and financial barriers. When compared with traditional methods of delivering EE projects (e.g., fixed-fee for services, or design-bid-build), EPC projects accept long-term performance and financial risks. EPC procedures seem comparatively complex. For both public and private institutions, disadvantages of EPC include the need for a more sophisticated contract and the calculation of the energy consumption baseline. Mills *et al.* identified the threats associated with EE projects and classified them as economic, contextual, technological, operations and M&V risks.

The payments in EPC projects are linked to verifiable energy savings achieved by the ESCO during the performance period. Defining a suitable payment arrangement is important for the ESCO to maintain a stable cash flow during the project term. Often fixed payment schedules are adopted in EPC contracts. The ESCO receives the fixed amount of payment from the host when the actual savings are determined to be equal to or greater than the guaranteed amount in each M&V period. Deductions are applied when performance shortfalls occur. M&V performance reporting periods could be monthly, quarterly or annually. It is not uncommon for the host to dispute the energy savings achieved by the ESCO, which may result in possible payment defaults by the host. Also, a payment default may occur from the host's inability to fulfill its payment responsibilities. In a worst-case scenario, the host might go out of business before full contract payment. Additionally, the multifaceted relationships between involved parties in an EPC contract induce operational risk associated with the complex project administrative process. Such risk causes higher operational costs and transaction fees and reduces the trust among the different parties. The existing EPC models rely heavily on traditional payment methods that necessitate trusted third-party intermediaries. The problems with the third-party intermediaries are that they charge considerable transaction and commission fees, and fail to offer real time payment processing. Plus, the forced bureaucratic process can be complicated and time consuming.

Blockchain technology can help improve EPCs by tackling barriers and risks are related to trust between parties, payment defaults, human errors, process complexity, delays and high processing cost, A blockchain based energy performance contracting would typically include four elements:

- Agreement on the baseline model: Stakeholders agree on the proposed predictive model, define frequency of data collection, outline the accepted accuracy, and set the energy data and mode of payment.
- Programming of the corresponding smart contract: The conditions defined in the first phase are hard coded inside different smart contracts.

- Deployment on the blockchain: A unique address is generated for each stakeholder and hard coded inside the smart
  contract to allow controlled access to the smart contracts.
  Then the smart contracts are deployed to the blockchain and
  their corresponding unique addresses are generated.
- Execution inside the blockchain: At this phase, the smart
  contracts are executed and called through their addresses.

Figure 8.3 shows a blockchain-based EPC model for a cooling energy
conservation measure. Three oracles would measure the daily temperature, energy consumption and the time, whereas three smart contracts are
responsible for data logging, implementing baseline adjustments, and calculating the energy savings.

ESCOs are continuously seeking new methodologies to reduce the complexity of EPCs. Blockchain technology and smart contracts can render
the EPC process an autonomous process, thus reducing the time and costs
associated with setting up and administering EPC projects. The reduction
of manpower, processing cost and time will allow ESCOs to undertake a
larger number of projects simultaneously thus increasing their profits and
as a result a larger number of energy savings can be achieved. Moreover,
the automation of the M&V process helps to lower the human risk and
to eliminate the need for human auditors to carry out measurements of
baseline and actual consumption data. Human errors in the M&V process
can directly affect the monthly calculated savings and thus jeopardizing
the profitability of the EPC project. So, not only blockchain helps to reduce

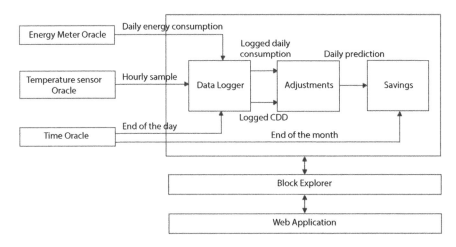

Figure 8.3 Blockchain based EPC model.

risks associated with the M&V process but also provides the added value of having data collected and monitored in real time as well as continuously calculating energy savings which can give early indications to ESCOs on the performance of the EPC project. On the other hand, blockchain and smart contracts also minimize the risk of payment defaults, since in a blockchain based EPC projects, a smart contract autonomously handles payments between parties at the end of each reporting period. Additionally, this feature allows speeding up the payment settlement process which can be a crucial payment for ESCOs, especially when the EPC project is funded via a bank loan and monthly payments are due at the beginning of each month. And finally, blockchain technology has the potential to render the data sharing process in an EPC project more secure and more transparent. The application of a distributed ledger technology (DLT) will help to create an auditable trail of energy savings and payments that is completely transparent to all involved stakeholders.

8.5   Energy Blockchain's Social and Environmental Impacts

Blockchain implementation in the energy sector can contribute to more than just solving the technical challenges and limitations detailed in the previous sections. Energy blockchain also impacts the social and environmental aspects of the energy sector. As previously discussed, blockchain applications in the energy sector improve the energy efficiency of buildings and systems, incentivize clean energy sources and help to reduce energy consumption. All those outcomes lead to a reduction in GHG emissions. But also, blockchain can contribute to the enhancement carbon tracking and trading process, Renewable Energy Certificates trading as well as providing means to fight energy poverty and establish energy democracy.

8.5.1   Blockchain Market for Carbon Credits and RECs

In response to global trends and expending environmental legislations, many energy and utility companies have implemented serious measures to reduce their carbon emissions and improve their green image. According to regulations, companies that are required to cut down their carbon emissions are requested to annually report their carbon footprint. However, the process of tracking and reporting carbon emissions proved to be a complicated one, due to the complexity of the measurement and reporting practices. The calculation and reporting of carbon emissions is based on manual data entry into spreadsheets which may lead to erroneous results. Afterwards, these spreadsheets are compiled and submitted to an auditor or a regulatory body. And in case any calculation or measurement error is detected, the company will be fined. For that reason, most companies have large teams involved in the carbon emissions measurement and reporting process. And despite that, most carbon emission reports tend to be conservative, by reporting lower carbon savings, in order to avoid any future penalties. Such practices lead to missed remediation credits and inaccurate carbon output data that most regulatory bodies and scientists rely on in developing policies and strategies. Therefore, companies and organizations need to adopt a new method of tracking carbon emissions in order to maximize their carbon credits and provide an accurate and more realistic image of carbon outputs. Additionally, the complexity of the carbon emissions tracking process may result from other factors such as:

- The multiplicity of data sources throughout the complete supply chain
- Regulations and reporting standard that may vary from one region to another
- The diversity of calculation methods and simulation models implemented to measure carbon emissions

Blockchain and IoT technologies can fundamentally transform the carbon emissions market. IoT devices and sensors allow having accurate and real-time data collection from the different carbon emissions sources. Thus, IoT technology can help reduce the risk that may result from manual data collection and entry. Similarly, the implementation of digital twin models, fed with real time data provided by IoT sensors, offer a real time simulation model that is capable of offering unprecedented insights into real time carbon emissions for each building or piece of machinery. With hourly outcomes from digital models, companies can improve their abilities to project their emissions levels and keep track of the efficiency of their carbon reduction implemented measures. Along with, blockchain technology provides the perfect platform to permanently and immutably record carbon emission's data that can be audited at any time. Blockchain's shared carbon emissions ledger offers auditors a proof that shared data is accurate and authentic. Moreover, using blockchain allows companies to overcome the regulatory confusion that results from operating in different areas of the world, as the time and location data can be encoded in the emissions transaction data, thus avoiding any confusion that may arise during an audit. And finally, once carbon savings are reported and validated, earned carbon credits can be tokenized and traded using blockchain.

However, carbon credits are not the only attributes that can be tracked and traded using blockchain. Renewable Energy Certificates (RECs) can similarly benefit from the features offered by the blockchain technology to make the certification and trading process more transparent, private, secured, and at a lower cost. RECs are market instruments that prove that the holder of those certificates owns 1 MWh of energy generated from renewable energy resources. Blockchain based REC trading platforms improve REC's traceability where any REC can be traced from where it has been generated to its final holder.

8.5.2 Fighting Energy Poverty

Energy poverty is a term that generally refers to a state where people cannot access to or secure basic energy services. In most cases, low household income, high energy tariffs or lack of infrastructure are correlated with energy poverty. In order to measure energy poverty several metrics can be used including, energy bills ration to household income, thermal comfort (access to heating and cooling), connection to the utility grid and access to utility services and finally occurrence of utility disconnection.

Energy policymakers worldwide are in a continuous quest to fight energy poverty. Nevertheless, this isn't an easy mission since energy poverty may affect households with diverse income ranges and people living in different places which makes it very hard to identify affected categories and design a unique solution that fits all.

Blockchain based P2P energy trading systems offer people the chance to contribute to the management of the electric grid and to influence market energy rates, thus lowering the overall cost of energy and increasing other people's access to energy. The same applies to energy backed cryptocurrencies, EV charging and discharging, DSM, and other previously discussed blockchain enabled mechanisms that enable end-users to improve their uptakes from their electric systems. Furthermore, blockchain technology promotes energy democracy by opening the door to new market players and business models that can disrupt the entire energy market, in addition to empowering end-users; converting them from just passive acceptors to a proactive engaged prosumer that plays an integral role in the new energy transition. Energy democracy is a political, economic, social, and cultural concept that merges the technological energy transition with a strengthening of democracy and public participation. The concept is connected with an ongoing decentralization of energy systems with energy efficiency and renewable energy being used also for a strengthened local energy ownership.

8.6   Conclusion

Blockchain is being recognized as a game changer in most economic sectors, but its potentials in the energy sector have not been fully realized yet. It took nearly a decade to transform the energy supply chain from its original centralized form into a decentralized architecture. Yet, this transition was only possible as a result of the emergence of low-cost renewable energy power generation systems and enforcement of new climate regulations that requires energy companies to reduce their carbon emissions. Hence, the energy grid moved from a dependent unidirectional mode of operation into a bidirectional independent mode of operation where off-grid micro grids can subsist. And now blockchain technology offers the chance to shift the energy sector into a multidirectional interdependent mode of operation where users can transact between each other and with the grid. Nevertheless, blockchain market infiltration will be met with resistance because it represents an extreme change to the present ways of doing business, especially since it eliminates the need for trusted third party intermediaries and disturbs current business models.

Nonetheless, blockchain longevity in energy markets has not been determined yet, particularly since it has not demonstrated yet long scale commercial benefits for the users. For blockchain technology to be embraced by the energy sector, it is necessary to overcome the shortcoming and limitation resulting from the fact that current blockchain platforms that use a Proof-of-Work (PoW) consensus mechanism consume an enormous amount of energy which might neutralize any positive effect that the technology can have on the energy sector practices. Additionally, challenges such as technological maturity and scalability as well as the need for a clear regulatory framework, should also be taken into account.

References

1. Denholm, P. and Hand, M., Grid flexibility and storage required to achieve very high penetration of variable renewable electricity. *Energy Policy*, 39, 1817–1830, 2011.
2. Eklas Hossain, Jakir Hossain, Fuad Un-Noor. Hossain, Fuad Un-Noor, Engineering, Computer Science, Published 4 October 2018.

3. Garbi, A., Malamou, A., Michas, N., Pontikas, Z., Doulamis, N., Protopapadakis, E., Mikkelsen, T.N., Kanellakis, K., Baradat, J.-L., Benefice: Behaviour change, consumption monitoring and analytics with complementary currency rewards. *Proceedings*, 20, 12, 2019.
4. Burger, C., Kuhlmann, A., Richard, P., Weinmann, J., Blockchain in the energy transition a survey among decision-makers in the German energy industry, Deutsche Energie-Agentur GmbH (dena) - German Energy Agency Energy Systems and Energy Services - European School of Management and Technology GmbH (ESMT) study "Blockchain in the energy transition". November 2016.
5. Grewal-Carr, V. and Marshall, S., Blockchain enigma paradox opportunity, Deloitte LLP, 2016, https://www2.deloitte.com/content/dam/Deloitte/uk/Documents/Innovation/deloitte-uk-blockchain-full-report.pd.
6. PwC global power & utilities, Blockchain - an opportunity for energy producers and consumers?, 2016, This is a report published by PwC. https://www.pwc.com/gx/en/industries/assets/pwc-blockchain-opportunity-for-energy-producers-and-consumers.pdf.
7. Merza, A. and Shaker Nasr, M., Electrical energy billing system based on smart meter and GSM. *Int. J. Appl. Eng.*, 10, 21, 42003–42012, 2015.
8. Burger, C., Blockchain and smart contracts: Pioneers of the energy frontier, ESMT Berlin - Energy Industry, December 13, 2017, https://www.ibtimes.co.uk/Blockchain-smart-contracts-pioneers-energy-frontier-1651650.
9. Gogerty, N. and Zitoli, J., eKo: An electricity-backed currency proposal. *SSRN Electron. J.*, 2011.
10. Jouliette, https://jouliette.net/index.html.
11. Kastelein, R., Spectral and alliander launch blockchain-based renewable energy sharing token, 2017, September 27, https://www.the-blockchain.com/2017/09/27/spectral-alliander-launch-blockchain-based-renewable-energy-sharing-token.
12. Leah C. Stokes, The Politics of Renewable Energy Policies: The Case of Feed-In Tariffs in Ontario, Canada. *Energy Policy*. 56, 2013, 490–500. https://www.sciencedirect.com/science/article/pii/S0301421513000153.

Part 3

THE IMPACT OF BLOCKCHAIN ON THE FINANCIAL INDUSTRY

9

Process Innovation and Unification of KYC Document Management System with Blockchain in Banking

Priya Jindal, Jasmine Kaur* and Kiran Sood

Chitkara Business School, Chitkara University, Rajpura, Punjab, India

Abstract

Banks through the process of customer due diligence (CDD) collate pertinent information about the potential customer or on-boarding a user as a client before opening any accounts or authorizing them to start their journey as a customer in any financial institution. Such CDD processes must follow "Know Your Customer" (KYC) regulations and guidelines. The "Know Your Customer" (KYC) process is a vital banking tool to gather, verify, screen, monitor, and store customer information to combat illegal transactions. The current process of KYC followed by the banking institutions has some bottlenecks or issues like KYC requests can delay transactions and it takes a longer time to complete the whole process up to a satisfactory level. When the customer desires to take benefit of the same facility from diverse banks this becomes a redundant process and increases operational costs because the same set of documents is produced in front of the bank to verify again the customer's identity and entails substantial duplication of efforts between banking firms.

Now the banks are more customers centric and accept changes in their business model. The chapter aims to uncover the potential of blockchain technology that can reinvent and revamp the KYC verification process in the banking sector. The chapter suggests that the herculean task of the banks can be lessened by unifying the procedure of KYC through blockchain application by using the Distributed Ledger Technology (DLT).

DLT provides an ideal solution where KYC compliance is validated only once, and when an alike customer wishes to approach different banks then these

---

Corresponding author: jasmine.kaur@chitkara.edu.in

Kiran Sood, Rajesh Kumar Dhanaraj, Balamurugan Balusamy and Seifedine Kadry (eds.) Blockchain Technology in Corporate Governance: Transforming Business and Industries, (199–216) © 2023 Scrivener Publishing LLC

particular banks can acquire the customer's particulars without conducting the whole operations once more. The DLT would not only eliminate the replications of efforts to implement the process of KYC in intra-bank customer onboarding but would also enable the distribution of clients' details in encrypted form to maintain the privacy and security of data in all banks in real-time. The process innovation and unification of the KYC would prove supportive at the time of merging banks in the Indian banking system.

Keywords: KYC, blockchain, Distributed ledger technology (DLT), privacy and security

9.1   Introduction

To assess the level of the impediment every business ventures analyze the changes in the dynamic environment. To be a successful business organization it is necessary to be acquainted with the need of revamping the business processes. Business processes are the blueprint for any business activities and their greater understanding can lead to remaining better and faster to stay competitive [1]. After peeping into the future and predicting the changes in the environment, the organization should develop an appropriate strategy and continuously updates it concerning its environment. An appropriate strategy helps the organization to systematically anticipate future uncertain situations with due attentiveness and become more agile and competitive [2]. Such a strategy may be evolutionary or revolutionary. To initiate change strategy successfully and for sustainable development, competent and effective leadership is required to compel an organization to reevaluate the changing market conditions. Leader along with specific roles bring and implement these changes. Innovation is requisite to affluence in competitive markets. An innovative ecosystem encourages competitive pressures by predicting how the competitor will proceed especially at a time when the open markets are in never-ending change. Information technology (IT) is an extended concept of innovation. Technological advancements are now forcing enterprise leaders to reimagine organization technology and change its operating structure that should be realigned with a unified business-technology strategy. The banking industry is one of the prominent examples which is going through massive transformations where FinTech is booming at unprecedented rates [3] to make the financial industry better at developing product innovations.

9.2   Blockchain

The initial application of blockchain was accredited by Satoshi Nakamoto in 2008. In the following year, i.e., 2009 Bitcoins was introduced in the form of cryptocurrency or virtual currency. Bitcoins are a new electronic cash payment system that can be done directly between peer to peer without being mediated by a financial institution (a trusted third party). Bitcoins are based on the technology called 'Blockchain' along with this it has vast numbers of other applications like healthcare, supply chain, insurance sector for claim processing, and much more other than the bitcoins market [4].

9.3   Blockchain Technology Applications Sectors

Healthcare: Blockchain enables healthcare industries to manage safely and securely massive amounts of patient data, secure transfer of patient medical records, and remote patient monitoring [5]. It also helps to manage the medicine supply chain and keep patient identities and information safe.

Insurance Industry: Blockchain technology allows insurance industries to reduce a lot of paperwork. Blockchain through smart contracts simplifies the procedures of re-insurance. Blockchain such as distributed ledger technology (DLT) helps the customer to get insurance on the day off or even after company office hours. In the same way claim reimbursement procedures also get automated. In the health insurance industry, blockchain helps to keep medical records secured and shared between health providers. It facilitates eliminating a source of fraud in the insurance industry [6].

Manufacturing: In manufacturing industries, blockchain technology has the potential to make manufacturing operations streamline. It provides an additional degree of transparency, greater visibility to monitor supply chains, and proper control to track their assets [7]. It helps to reduce counterfeits and ensure quality assurance and authenticity.

Education: Blockchain in education institutions has the potential to secure the identity and privacy of students' data and helps the students to store their life-long learning data in the blockchain wallets and share it with various parties for future education and professional applications [8]. It can also keep the records of payments for each student.

Energy Sector: Blockchain represents a possible solution for an energy management system, to build a local network under one roof from power generation to consumption. This innovative approach is based on the idea of decentralization without going through a conventional centralized mechanism [9].

Blockchain offers remarkable potential to banking and other financial industries. Blockchain is a groundbreaking innovation contributing banking industry's entering into the digital age. DLT helps the financial institutions to establish better governance where it severely challenges the bank's strategic competencies [10]. It improves payment transparency and facilitates faster payment at a lower cost. It also provides trust and security while data sharing and collaboration. Blockchain exposes fraud and reduces the risk for financial institutions. Across the world, many banks such as JP Morgan, PNC and Citi, etc. are in the process to build a team or board to review blockchain's impact on their banking business models.

ICICI Bank, Kotak Mahindra Bank, HDFC Bank, and AXIS Bank are four banks among the Indian banking industry to launch the nation's first blockchain-based funding for small and medium enterprises (SMEs).

ICICI Bank
Some of the inherent benefits of this revolutionary technology are as follows:

- Enhanced data consistency by individual control on data and reduce the potential of human frauds
- Increased transaction speed, access to real-time, and reduced manual processes in transactions
- Reduced settlement risk by simplifying the process
- Provide an opportunity for cost efficiency
- Improved data security and privacy by eliminating fraud and unauthorized activity
- Allow digitize sales agreement, monitor supply chain and logistics by decentralized structure
- Helps in anti-money laundering tracking system by detecting suspicious activity
- Creates trust between different participants and does not require an intermediary

9.4 Know Your Customer (KYC)

KYC compliance is a good practice in all aspects for availing any benefits from any provisioner either from government or private. The KYC process is required for applying for a license, a new SIM card, taking a PAN card, before opening an account, and many other such services. Globally, a large number of customers are customarily legitimized through Know Your Customer process to avoid shortcomings in operational, legal, and reputation risks to the institutions. It has a global imperative and affects all sectors that want to onboard a user as a client [11]. Banks are extremely regulated institutions due to their importance in economic stability and have to abide by all applicable laws, a standard set of regulations, and guidelines prescribed by governing provisioner, and KYC is one such requirement. Banking is an industry with an inherent risk of fraudulent activities and cannot escape the mandate KYC process. The KYC process is a vital banking tool to gather, verify, screen, monitor, and store customer information to combat illegal transactions.

The process of KYC and its guidelines were introduced by the Reserve Bank of India (RBI) in 2002. In the year 2004, RBI has made it mandatory to fulfill the procedure of KYC to any individual or entity before opening a bank account, Demat account, and trading account. By 31st December 2005, all scheduled commercial banks (excluding Regional Rural Banks), all financial institutions, and local banks adhere to the guidelines to make all accounts KYC compliant. These guidelines are issued under the banking regulations act, 1949. As a result, every institution that manages money such as insurance, real estate, etc. is certainly on the hook in complying with KYC.

Through the KYC platform banks help to verify the customer identity. The fundamental practice of KYC enables banks to understand customer behavior and their financial dealings which is the most vital requirement to handle them better and mitigate their risks sensibly. By keeping continuous monitoring on suspicious transactions and knowing whether their customers are concerned in any illegal activities KYC helps to delimit frauds. KYC is the first line of defense to access the extent to which customer exposes the banking institutions to risks while maintaining a business relationship which is critical to gauge the risk of identifying theft, financial fraud, and money laundering [12]. This makes the financial industry most threatened which could degrade its prestige. So financial institutions have to adhere to indicative guidelines for customer identification and verification and for this KYC play an imperative role with a high level of assurance to measure the credibility and legitimacy of anti-money laundering (AML) policy [13].

9.4.1   KYC Advantages

1. Establishing customer identity and other credentials of the customers.
2. KYC process checks on anti-social activities and ensures that banks' services are not distorted.
3. Helps to understand the nature of the customer's activities by identifying their previous financial history to serve them better.
4. Helps to prevent losses and fraud by identifying money laundering risk assessment, financing of terrorism, and other anti-social fund transactions to manage its risk prudently.

9.4.2   KYC Document List

Table 9.1 shows a certain set of documents that are required for KYC to verify an individual's identity before proceeding with any transaction. Proof of identity with photograph and proof of Address are the two indispensable KYC supporting documents that are necessary to ascertain one's identity to open a bank account, bank locker, trading account, mutual fund, insurance, etc., and periodically over time. Banking and finance aspirants may also require income proof to check their financial history before opening a bank account to ensure that the source of money is legitimate. These documents need to be submitted as hard or scanned copies depending upon the type of KYC one has chosen.

So the individual or entities should keep the following KYC documents handy before proceeding.

9.4.3   Re-KYC

Reserve Bank of India has prescribed different time intervals for the update of KYC records. The periodicities depend upon the risk perception of the bank. In this process, customer identification including photographs shall be updated and records should be verified by banks at least once every two years in case of high-risk entities, eight and ten years for medium and low-risk customers respectively. This enables banks to monitor transactions regularly and make necessary inquiries to clarify doubts. Failing which the banks may freeze the customer account [15].

Table 9.1 KYC document list.

Identity Proof – Document List	Address Proof – Document List	Income Proof – Document List
• Aadhaar letter • Passport • Driving License • Voter's Identity Card • PAN Card with their photograph • Job card by NREGA duly signed by the competent authority • Photo identity proof issued by State or Central govt. • Ration card with photograph • Letter from a recognized public authority or public servant • Any debit or credit card issued by a bank having individual's name and address. • Bank Pass Book having a photograph • Employee identity card issued by the public sector company • Identity cards issued by universities or boards of education like ISC, CBSE, etc., or from professional bodies like ICSI, ICWAI, ICAI, etc. to their students.	• Passport • Voter's Card • Driving License • Utility bills like electricity bill, gas bill, water bill, telephone bill including post-paid mobile phone, etc. not more than three months old • Bank Account or credit card Statement • House Purchase deed • Maintenance bill for one's flat • Lease agreement along with last 3three months of rent receipt • Copy of an insurance	• Income Tax Returns • Salary Slips • Bank Statement

Source: RBI [14].

9.4.4   Types of KYC Verification

1. Paper-Based KYC

   In-person KYC verification is carried out offline. This type of KYC verification happens in person using self-attested, physical copies of the address and identity proofs. One needs to physically visit the bank, fund house office, or KYC Registration Agency and submit the signed form along with the documents.

2. Aadhaar-Based e-KYC

   The electronic know your customer (e-KYC) is a KYC verification process wherein the customer's identity and residential address is electronically confirmed through an Aadhaar card. This authentication is convenient for those who have an internet connection. It is a non-face-to-face mode. In this type of KYC verification, one needs to upload a scanned copy of their original Aadhaar card. One can opt for online identity verification using Aadhaar One time password (OTP)-based or Biometric-based verification. For OTP-based verification, the applicant's mobile number should be linked with the Aadhar card. On the other hand for biometric verification, the applicant will provide biometrics and it would then be evaluated by UIDAI – certified biometric scanners.

9.4.5   KYC Through Manual Verification Process

Figure 9.1 shows the flow the KYC process that banks usually incorporate through four key elements:

> ➢ Collection of Information for customer identification and verification
> ➢ Customer due diligence for risk assessment and management
> ➢ Ongoing monitoring and record-keeping
> ➢ Tracking the transactions and Reporting

Figure 9.1 KYC Process Flow. Source: thalesgroup.com [16].

9.4.6 Typical KYC Verification Process – Issues and Challenges

Figure 9.2 depicts the typical KYC processes that are generally repetitive, time-consuming, leading to high administrative overhead costs and inconsistency. Also, this process is based on the centralized network where the bank servers are the leading servers and if it collapses then the complete information of customers will go down, which is a disastrous situation.

> ➤ A higher proportion of senior management in banks and financial institutions have to spend enormous time and amount of resources to verify the documents provided by a client for KYC verification. This process makes FI's concentrate less on their core business. At the time of the onboarding process, the client must repeatedly submit the same documents for KYC, which ultimately leads to a painful experience for the client and make onboarding a laborious process.
> ➤ There is a lack of a global standard for KYC regulations. The corporate at the same time has several global banking relations and every time the documentation demanded from them for the KYC process is different from nation to nation. There is no consistency. This inculcates frustration among corporate while dealing with different bank staff within the banks. Corporates feel frustrated when dealing with many different people within the bank.
> ➤ The implementation of the KYC process on the same client is a tedious and costly process because the banks ask for the

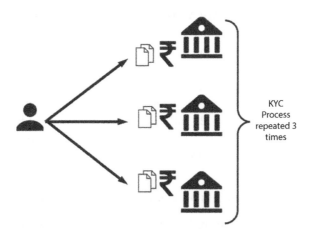

Figure 9.2 Current KYC System. Source: [17].

documents that are already available online. Due to this opening, an account takes a longer time than anticipated. This delay
in the process failed the business to grab good opportunities.

➤ Customer identity must be up-to-date and accurate for ongoing monitoring which again involved a lot of paperwork, cost,
and resources. Banks charge this additional burden from the
customers in the form of processing fees and service charges.

➤ The routine KYC verification is used for in-house or multi-
branch usage. As KYC information is stored locally, so there
is a concern of security to access this KYC data.

➤ The overall cost of managing the KYC per customer increases
because of a lack of transparency, poor control, mistrust, and
data duplication.

It is identified that there is a lot of deficiencies in a large number of KYC
procedure followed by the banking institutions. In the current scenario, it
is highly unsuitable and inappropriate for both banks and customers. The
process is superfluous and hence increases operational costs. Moreover, it
has little or no safeguards for users' privacy. Typical KYC depository systems cannot adapt to the demands of changing regulatory requirements,
and sometimes they fail to provide efficient security assurance to the existing stored information/data.

Until KYC is appropriate, global, client-possessed, conscience, and
backed by advanced digital credentials manual KYC process will continue
to get more expensive and hard to manage.

9.5 Electronic Know Your Customer (e-KYC)

In this subsequent section, the main point of discussion is e-KYC and the
inclusion of biometrics to improve the KYC process in banks. e-KYC provides a mechanism to verify the identity and authenticity of the customer
through an online electronic mode. e-KYC is now becoming more popular in India in May 2021, 1.29 billion citizens got their Aadhaar number
(UIDAI Annual Report 2020–2021) [18] and 99% of the adult population
has digital-friendly in the country.

9.5.1 e-KYC Documents Management System Using Blockchain

Blockchain technology can redesign the KYC verification process. Figure
9.3 shows blockchain-based KYC solution built to manage the banks'

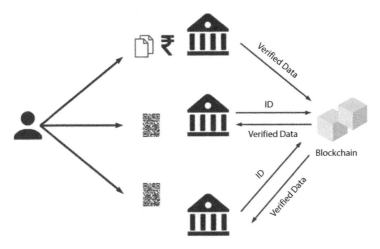

Figure 9.3 KYC Using Blockchain. Source: [17].

efficiency both in inter-department and intra-bank customer onboarding. A blockchain offers highly desirable characteristics of immutability, enhanced security, decentralization, consensus, trustlessness to a system, and provide faster settlements.

9.6 Blockchain KYC Verification Process Advantages

A Blockchain is considered to be a technology for storing and transmitting information that allows its users to connect with a network to share data without an intermediary.

The blockchain operates on a 'distributed ledger system'. The collected information or the data would be stocked up as blocks, and those blocks can be guarded by no one. Each new transaction is recorded in a new block which is validated by the users connected to the network. Blockchain provides a decentralized network, instead of central servers, which do not have any access to the data stored by third parties. In DLT the parties can access the stored data after permission has been given to them [19].

Moreover, the records of each online financial transaction would be secured by digital signature mode and thereby it also establishes its genuineness and legitimacy. Once the data are stored in the blockchain, it is not possible to alter or modify them later. As a result, the stored data in a blockchain cannot be changed or tamper-proof [20]. Moreover, the technology holds customers' digital transaction details that offer a very high level of transparency and security [21].

The technology provides KYC utilities based on DLT and KYC verification needs to be done only once by the banks. In Blockchain technology, customer data are stored in a block and once the data is stored in a block, the block can be shared between the banks [22]. All other permissioned regulators have the right to use this verified KYC information at the time when they require customer data. This technology increases operational efficiency as well as removes repetitive works. In this blockchain KYC platform, the users complete their identity documents only once. DLT provides a unified digital platform for financial institutions [23].

9.7   Taxonomy of Blockchain Systems

There are different types of blockchain and their application depends on the purpose of use.

➢ Public Blockchains: Public blockchain is an "open source" network, it is a public network in a true sense and does not have any restrictions to join. Anyone who are having internet connections has equal rights to access the network, viewed the ledger, and can participate in the consensus process [24]. It is a completely decentralized network; no single organization has control over the flow path. It has its natural flow. It outshines the requirement of a third party. It is self-governed. Anyone can create new blocks, start validating blocks of data and execute transactions. Based on the autonomous digital public ledger the participants can do the online payment in banks without intermediation. Bitcoin, Litecoin, and Ethereum are the best examples of a public blockchain platform.

➢ Private Blockchain: Unlike a public blockchain, this type of blockchain mentions a database whose avenue and use are restricted to those participants who wish to access it. The private blockchain is the permission blockchain that is controlled by a single authority or organization [25]. Each participant requires permission from the governing body of the blockchain and the governing body determines who can be a node. These are managed blockchains and offer partial decentralization resulting in fewer nodes participating in the ledger which reduced processing time per transaction as well as focuses on security and privacy. The private blockchain model is most suited in enterprises where huge amounts of transactions are handled. Ripple, Hyperledger Fabric, Quorum, and Corda, etc. are an example of private blockchain.

➤ Consortium Blockchain: It is an elongation of private blockchain. It is more likely a trusted consensus in which not a single organization governs the control but multiple organizations govern the platform and maintain decentralized nature. Blockchain consortium is a network approved and publicly accessible to a liked-minded community only who are interested in interfacing business disciplines and desire to work together for improving workflows, transparency, and accountability. The blockchain consortium preselects several nodes for which permission is assumed [24, 25]. The platform is preferably chosen by the financial sector, insurance sectors, and the government which adopts well-regulated procedures and wants efficiently and streamlines the transmission of information among one another. IBM Food Trust and Energy Web Foundation are an example of consortium blockchain.

9.8 Literature Survey

The paper explores the emerging technology of blockchain and its potential to transform the financial sectors. The paper highlighted blockchain technology's characteristics and explain how this technique through smart contract impact the entire financial sector ranging from payments and settlements. Blockchain disrupts the financial landscape by speeding up transactions and making them more secure [26]. Blockchain is a promising application and received significant attention in the banking sector to achieve new growth avenues. The underlying technology revolutionized the efficiency of the banking sector in terms of data storage, credit information, and payment clearing systems. The paper suggested that to explore the full potential of this application common standards are required [27]. It has been realized that widespread collaborations are required for implementing blockchain technology across the banking sector. This disruptive technology is adopted by many banks to achieve sustainable development to promote economic growth and develop green technologies. Blockchain technology provides three efficiencies in handling financial processes they are operational efficiency, economic efficiency, and provide efficient service

[28]. The paper explores the overall impact of blockchain technology, especially the formal banking sector in anti-money laundering regulations and compliance. The study explores the guidelines on virtual currency which was implemented in 2014 under the Financial Action Task Force (FATF). The results showed that virtual currency has the potential to support an anti-money laundering risk assessment framework in the banking sector [29]. The paper highlights the relevance of transformation through the application of blockchain technology and its gaining attention in the context of banking and financial services. Blockchain technology is being considered as one of the innovative technology that provides an impetus at global level disruptions. The study outlined the various aspects of blockchain in terms of benefits, opportunities, cost, and risk. The study concludes that the involvement of blockchain in the banking sector is limited when correlate with other verticals of the sectors [30]. The paper focuses that we are gradually shifting towards digitalization from online teaching to online transaction [31]. The paper focused on the emergence of blockchain and its application in multiple areas such as healthcare, banking, etc. Blockchain allows the transactions in a decentralized manner and allows the digital information to be distributed. The smart contract in the blockchain makes it possible to automate the contract between two parties and remove the necessity of a mediator. Smart identity through the innovation of blockchain saves information about customers. Indian banks extremely receive Blockchain innovation and receive an enormous collection of its advantages by decreasing managerial exertions and saving time [32].

9.9   Potential Use-Cases of Blockchain Technology in Banks

The biggest banks in India are coming together to create a new company called "Indian Bank's Blockchain Infrastructure Company Private Limited" (IBBIC) to facilitate the use of blockchain technology in banks. It is a federation of 15 banks. Out of the 15 banks, four banks are public sector banks, ten banks come under private sector banks and one foreign bank.

State Bank of India (SBI) India's largest public-sector banks along with ICICI Bank, HDFC Bank, Kotak Mahindra, Axis Bank, and 10 other banks are joining hands to use the blockchain technology that enables automation in finance trade-related processes and solve the fundamental problem of traditional banking. The future of Indian banks looks promising with the adoption of blockchain, nearly 56 percent of Indian banks are making this technology a part of their core business. Banks are again presenting a unified front with the development and practical application of blockchain technology in the banking sector.

- Banco Bilbao Vizcaya Argentaria (BBVA)
  BBVA is one of the Spanish multinational companies deals in financial services conducted several blockchain operations to foster greater transparency and confidence in the adoption of blockchain. This wonderful technology is used in loans and the amount of the loan reached record speed. The company is optimistic to use this technology in the future also.
- Barclays
  Barclays is the U.K.'s second-largest bank using blockchain technology. The banks use the technology for reformation in the fund transfers, rephrase of the payment system, carrying out trade derivatives, and Know-Your-Customer processes.
- HSBC
  HSBC bank is also planning to move towards a blockchain-based platform. Banks are now shifting their traditional paper-based proceeding to fully automated and decentralized platforms. This feature helps their investors to track their money in real-time.

9.10   Blockchain KYC-AML Solution

Financial institutions are constantly under client pressure to facilitate transactions efficiently and DLT is one of the important tools that can be utilized by financial institutions to satisfy these requirements. KYC (Know Your Customer) is a vital function to assess customers' risks and comply with AML laws. DLT (a type of Blockchain) has the inherent potential to streamline the process of KYC/AML. DLT through Private blockchain is best suited to handle the KYC and AML compliance. DLT promises to address some of the vital functions i.e. regular checks and monitor the customer's financial behavior which includes money of money being debited or credited, no. of financial transactions done, sources of money, etc. to prevent money laundering (thalesgroup.com). In automated DLT based KYC, every transaction leaves a permanent record that is impossible to be altered. This makes it easy for the authorities to find the source of the money [33].

9.11   Conclusion

Banks and financial institutions that play a vital role in the economy require high security, authentication, and privacy of information and data as it is the most attackable field. It is a need of the hour to adopt innovative technology to prevent the breaching of data and unauthorized access over the network. Smart contract in the blockchain plays an important role in providing security and trust between the blocks [34]. In this program, customer information is passed from one service provider to another when certain conditions are met. A smart contract is a computer program that executes exactly as they are coded and programmed. In smart contract code inserted into the blockchain or other distributed ledger. The contract is then deployed on an embedded blockchain once it has been authorized. As blockchain is invariable each document has its blockchain, confirm that if the document is no longer reasonable, the entire blockchain will be removed from the network and all the service providers will be notified [35]. It enhances efficiencies and offers transparency in financial services. Banks handle several sensitive information related to their clients like their account no., Pan card No., amount of transactions, etc. [36]. The process by which service providers collect documents from the clients before onboarding them or for trading is known as KYC. The traditional KYC verification process is very expensive for service providers and if they are not following the prescribed regulations they may cause a large penalty. Blockchain has an unlimited potential to disrupt the banking industry by advancement in technology. It promises a big transformation in the banking sector by eliminating their threat as well as operational risk. The proposed chapter highlights the use of blockchain in the KYC process. Blockchain is a distributed ledger system that provides a structured, well-planned, and systematic approach for services. The proposed system suggests that to achieve efficiency in the KYC verification process, the KYC process should be performed once for each instead of repeating the same process again and again by each institution for the same individual. It provides a solution to reduce the total cost spend on the KYC verification process as compared to the traditional KYC process by completely digitalizing this process. At the global level in the year 2020, it is estimated that the total amount spent on the KYC verification process rose to dollar 1.2 billion. The use of DLT lowers the aggregate cost of KYC.

References

1. Stoddard, D.B. and Jarvenpaa, S.L., Business process redesign: Tactics for managing radical change. *J. Manage. Inf. Syst.*, 2, 1, 81–107, 1995.

2. Hamme, D., Customer-focused process innovation: Linking strategic intent to everyday execution, McGraw Hill Professional, New York City, ISBN: 978-00-718-3471-1, 2014.

3. Thavanathan, J., Process Innovation with Blockchain in Banking-A case study of how Blockchain can change the KYC process in banks, (Master's thesis, NTNU), Norwegian University of Science and Technology, Trondheim, 2017.

4. Reed, J., Financial technology. 3 in 1 bundle book: FinTech, Blockchain, Smart Contracts, Createspace Publisher, California United States, ISBN: 978-15-403-2704-8, 2016.

5. Alonso, S.G., Arambarri, J., López-Coronado, M., de la Torre Díez, I., Proposing new blockchain challenges in ehealth. *J. Med. Syst.*, 43, 3, 64, 2019.

6. Crawford, M., The insurance implications of blockchain. *Risk Manage.*, 64, 2, 24, 2017.

7. Abeyratne, S.A. and Monfared, R.P., Blockchain ready manufacturing supply chain using a distributed ledger. *Int. J. Res. Eng. Technol.*, 5, 9, 1–10, 2016.

8. Skiba, D.J., The potential of blockchain in education and healthcare. *Nurs. Educ. Perspect.*, 38, 4, 220–221, 2017.

9. Andoni, M., Robu, V., Flynn, D., Abram, S., Geach, D., Jenkins, D., Peacock, A., Blockchain technology in the energy sector: A systematic review of challenges and opportunities. *Renewable Sustainable Energy Rev.*, 100, 143–174, 2019.

10. Truong, T., How the FinTech industry is changing the world, Thesis Centria University of Applied Sciences Degree Programme in Business Management, 2016.

11. Lootsma, Y. V. O. N. N. E., From fintech to regtech: The possible use of block-chain for KYC, Fintech to regtech using blockchain by INITIO, Brussels, 2017.

12. Gill, M. and Taylor, G., Preventing money laundering or obstructing business? Financial companies' perspectives on know your customer procedures. *Br. J. Criminol.*, 44, 4, 582–594, 2014.

13. Arasa, R., Determinants of Know Your Customer (KYC) Compliance among Commercial Banks in Kenya. *Journal of Economics and Behavioral Studies (JEBS)*, 7, 2(J), pp. 162–175, 2015. https://doi.org/10.22610/jebs.v7i2(J).574

14. https://www.rbi.org.in/commonperson/English/Scripts/PressReleases. aspx?Id=1497#:~:text=Officially%20valid%20documents%20(OVDs)%20 for,by%20a%20State%20Government%20official, 2021.

15. Rajput, V.U., Research on knows your customer (KYC). *Int. J. Sci. Res. Publ.*, 3, 7, 541–546, 2013.

16. https://www.thalesgroup.com/en/markets/digital-identity-and-security/ banking, 2020.

17. Kumar, M. and Nikhil, P.A., A blockchain based approach for an efficient secure KYC process with data sovereignty. *Int. J. Sci. Technol. Res.*, 9, 3403–3407, 2020.

18. https://uidai.gov.in/images/Annual-Report-ENG-2020-21-Final-18072019. pdf, 2019.

19. Moyano, J.P. and Ross, O., KYC optimization using distributed ledger technology. *Bus. Inf. Syst. Eng.*, 59, 6, 411–423, 2017.

20. Martens, D., Tuyll van Serooskerken, A.V., Steenhagen, M., Exploring the potential of blockchain for KYC. *J. Digital Bank.*, 2, 2, 123–131, 2017.
21. Erragcha, N. and Babay, H., Blockchain towards decentralized digital marketing, in: *Blockchain Technology and Applications for Digital Marketing*, pp. 32–51, IGI Global, Publons, 2021.
22. Norvill, R., Steichen, M., Shbair, W.M., State, R., Blockchain for the Simplification and Automation of KYC Result Sharing. *IEEE International Conference on Blockchain and Cryptocurrency (ICBC)*, pp. 9–10, 2019.
23. Moyano, J.P. and Ross, O., KYC optimization using distributed ledger technology. *Bus. Inf. Syst. Eng.*, 59, 6, 411–423, 2017.
24. Lee, J.Y., A decentralized token economy: How blockchain and cryptocurrency can revolutionize business. *Bus. Horiz.*, 62, 6, 773–784, 2019.
25. Tasca, P. and Tessone, C.J., Taxonomy of blockchain technologies principles of identification and classification, *arXiv preprint arXiv*. 17, 8, 48–72, 2015.
26. Buitenhek, M., Understanding and applying Blockchain technology in banking: Evolution or revolution? *J. Digital Bank.*, 1, 2, 111–119, 2016.
27. Guo, Y. and Liang, C., Blockchain application and outlook in the banking industry. *Financial Innov.*, 2, 1, 1–12, 2016.
28. Cocco, L., Pinna, A., Marchesi, M., Banking on blockchain: Costs savings thanks to the blockchain technology. *Future Internet*, 9, 3, 25, 2017.
29. Naheem, M. A., Exploring the links between AML, digital currencies and blockchain technology. *J. Money Laund. Control*, 22, 3, pp. 515–525, 2019. https://doi.org/10.1108/JMLC-11-2015-0050.
30. Osmani, M., El-Haddadeh, R., Hindi, N., Janssen, M., & Weerakkody, V., Blockchain for next-generation services in banking and finance: cost, benefit, risk, and opportunity analysis. *J. Enterp. Inf. Manag.*, 34, 3, pp. 884–899, 2020.
31. Jagtap, S.T., Thakar, C.M., El imrani, O., Phasinam, K., Garg, S., Ventayen, R.J.M., A framework for secure healthcare system using blockchain and smart contracts. *Electronics and Sustainable Communication Systems (ICESC) 2021 Second International Conference*, pp. 922–926, 2021.
32. Kaur, J. and Jindal, P., An impetus to swap from traditional to blockchain environment in Indian banks. *2021 Asian Conference on Innovation in Technology (ASIANCON)*, IEEE, pp. 1–8, 2021.
33. Yadav, P. and Chandak, R., Transforming the Know Your Customer (KYC) process using Blockchain. *2019 International Conference on Advances in Computing, Communication and Control (ICAC3)*, IEEE, pp. 1–5, 2019.
34. Aggarwal, S., Chaudhary, R., Aujla, G.S., Kumar, N., Choo, K.K.R., Zomaya, A.Y., Blockchain for smart communities: Applications, challenges and opportunities. *J. Netw. Comput. Appl.*, 144, 13–48, 2019.
35. Wang, S., Ouyang, L., Yuan, Y., Ni, X., Han, X., Wang, F.Y., Blockchain-enabled smart contracts: Architecture, applications, and future trends. *IEEE Trans. Syst. Man Cybern.: Syst.*, 49, 11, 2266–2277, 2019.
36. Mittal, S., Jindal, P., Ramkumar, K.R., Data privacy and system security for banking on clouds using homomorphic encryption. *2021 2nd International Conference for Emerging Technology (INCET)*, IEEE, pp. 1–6, 2021.

10

Applying Blockchain Technology to Address NPA Issues During the COVID-19 Pandemic

Jasmine Kaur, Priya Jindal* and Kiran Sood

Chitkara Business School, Chitkara University, Rajpura, Punjab, India

Abstract

Purpose: Several high-profile bankruptcies rocked the Indian media, highlighting the long-standing burning issues within the Indian banking sector. This is often the problem with NPLs, which are called non-productive assets (NPAs). Indian public sector enterprise (PSU) banks currently have a calculable amount of INR 4 trillion (US $60 billion) of unsafe loans as of the Gregorian calendar month 2015. Loans become NPA, banks' monetary risk Indian women would increase their market shares. Investors take the burden of this risk, and the business suffers as well as the economy. This paper provides a view on the role of Blockchain technology in scanning the Non-performing loans by identifying the operational and systematic problems and to provide resolutions to these issues.

Gap Analysis: Most ASEAN countries are stricken by rising company debt and inadequate debt reimbursement capacity. Singapore, Asian country and Asian nation all practiced loan growth quicker than their GDP, with Thailand coverage NPLs on top of 3%. Non-performing loans are oil-fired by poor underwriting and a listless approach to positioning credit rating changes with loan repayment terms. Research on assessment of the problems with regard to time taken to solve these problems is still missing.

Practical Implications: A holdup of Indian industrial growth and therefore the increase in interest rates, combined by economic volatility across the world, has accentuated the chance of default. Just like India, alternative growing economies like China, Thailand, Brazil, and Argentina have a major share of debt owed by

Corresponding author: priya.jindal@chitkara.edu.in

Kiran Sood, Rajesh Kumar Dhanaraj, Balamurugan Balusamy and Seifedine Kadry (eds.) Blockchain Technology in Corporate Governance: Transforming Business and Industries, (217–238) © 2023 Scrivener Publishing LLC

companies with affected reimbursement capacity. Addressing asset management issues for this segment can significantly reduce the magnitude of risk.

Findings: The slowdown in Indian business growth and rising interest rates, exacerbated by global economic volatility, has heightened the risk of bad loans. Like India, other growing economies such as China, Thailand, Brazil, and Argentina have a big share of debt with corporations with strained reimbursement capacity, companies with limited repayment capacity. This will likewise assist with introducing trust between bank coordinated efforts.

Keywords: Non-performing Loans, distributed ledger, smart identity

10.1 Introduction

The monetary development of a nation significantly relies upon the job of banking area to offer monetary guides to businesses like medical services, autos, pharma, iron, and steel and so forth. Banks consequently convey an extension past the obligations of simply being monetary establishments and add to achieving the public authority's social targets. Nonetheless, in the course of recent years, the banks have been battling to manage the expansion in the quantity of NPAs – where the head and premium measure of credits or advances isn't paid out and stays past due. During the financial high from years 2002 to 2008, the expansion in acknowledge development was pretty much as high as 22%. Actually, past the monetary emergency, there is an absence of credit interest and banking area is confronting difficulties in expanding credits. The expansion in the quantity of NPAs has ended up being a concern for RBI and Finance Ministry. IT has considerably interrupted industrial and commercial activities [1]. The NPA management is also initiated by significant role of information technology. Meanwhile, the Internet has created new industries that did not exist years ago, creating many new ways to do business.

The genuine that method for information innovation is to make a totally new and a great deal of practical technique for organizations and others to team up. The innovation that must be seen now's blockchain innovation. This relatively new innovation not exclusively makes the net and simpler, less expensive and more productive manners by which of working together, but conjointly dangerous ways. The most common term for Blockchain is the underlying technology of virtual password currency, but in this research it reflects other uses it can be used for, i.e., NPA management. Simply put, blockchain is a public and reliable shared director, based on the [2] Piertopia network, so no one controls it, but thousands of participants. Maintains and manages [3]. The blockchain will be open to the public as it can be used by all participants [4]. The information recorded on the blockchain is not unobtrusively modulated, making the blockchain a reliable director [1]. These properties permit the blockchain to move data without a middle person. The utilization of blockchain innovation has been contemplated in certain examinations, however it is as yet muddled what will be conceivable now and later on. For instance [5], how blockchain technology can be applied to reorganize and improve stock exchange and market design and The Economist describes how to deal with blockchain-based land registry corruption. From research [6] have found that perhaps the most yearning application to date, smart contracts, can replace multiple functions maintained by post-transaction institutions that are currently needed. One thing is certain: while this technology is important, it will not be in the near future as it will take time to change to a blockchain-based system. However, according to [7], the innovation will be pretty much as progressive as the Internet 20 years prior. The technology has a particularly disruptive opportunity, with particular focus on how the financial sector can leverage blockchain technology together. It is gearing towards an industry that relies on trust.

The Indian Banking industry has been changing to meet the new improvements since the time 1991. While it turns out to be significant, there are a couple of contemplations that should be found minutely consistently. In an occasion of monetary emergency in 2008, India and the world went through a significant financial lull. Therefore, concerns and attention to keep up with resource quality have taken a front seat. All in all, Non-Performing Assets (or the NPAs) have turned into a space of consideration. The antagonistic impact of NPAs has stimulated the requirement for specialists to manage bank's solidness with a higher arrangement. Blockchain technology adheres to the extremity of non-performing assets by making data sets of information and availability of that information across globe. The current chapter moves around past patterns of NPAs and how banks should make genuine moves in overseeing them and make good for assets. The layout of the chapter non-performing loans scanning by blockchain technology in Indian Banking is visualized in Figure 10.1.

The three-act structure of the chapter outlines the setup, confrontation, and resolution through blockchain technology stages. First stage of setup outlays the foundation for the non-performing assets and blockchain technology. Second stage portrays the confrontation part, it is crucial as it presents the current status of non-performing assets in banking and the contribution of blockchain technology to various areas of business and lays foundation for empirical analysis of the literature. Third and the ultimate stage reflects the resolution, it is a treatment stage for the affected banking industry through blockchain technology and expand the knowledge horizon about the studies already done on the similar subject matter and access

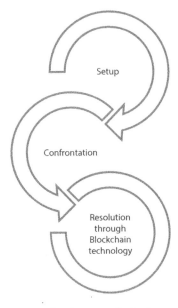

Figure 10.1 Basic chapter structure (author compilation).

the gap analysis from the same. The trailing part of the chapter portrays all the three act structure.

10.2 ACT 1: Foundation of Non-Performing Assets Management and Blockchain Technology

The first act provides an overview of the subject matter chosen. This stage helps in assimilation of the importance of the subject matter from the evolution of NPA in banking sector and the legal framework for adhering to the same, further probing into the deep shell, role of information technology in Indian banking, role of blockchain technology with support from existing literature. Hence, this part attempts to provide a rationale of undertaking this research work.

10.3 Induction to Non-Performing Assets

The financial area is a cornerstone of any monetary framework. The smooth working of the financial area guarantees the solid state of a whole economy. During the time spent tolerating stores and loaning, advances banks make credit. The assets got from the borrowers via interest borrowed and reimbursements of chief are reused for raising assets. Nonetheless, developing of non-performing assets (NPAs) upsets this movement of credit. It hampers credit improvement and impacts the usefulness of the banks as well. NPAs are the primary pointers to condemn the show of the monetary region. As per Reserve Bank of India (RBI) explores November 2018, the gross proportion of bad quality advances is in wealth of Rs 9 lakh crores, which shows the outrageous impact it has on crediting practices of banks and their liquidity positions. This improvement is an eventual outcome of quadrupling during the past five years, which shows the vulnerable demonstration of sets aside cash as to advancing.

The central sort of income of banks is through the superior acquired on advances and advances and repayment of the head. Expecting such assets disregard to make pay, they are appointed non-performing assets (NPA). A resource, including a rented asset, becomes non-performing when it stops to make pay for the bank. A 'non-performing asset' (NPA) was described as a credit office in see of which the interest just as part of boss has remained 'past due' for a predefined time period. As demonstrated by the Reserve Bank of India, NPA is portrayed as a credit office in respect of which the premium or possibly piece of boss is "past due" for a foreordained period. Non-Performing Assets (NPAs) can be characterized as "a credit where the bank has some uncertainty of is encountering hardships in getting reimbursements and regardless of time period, the result could be a deficiency of capital" [8]. All around, assuming the credit portions have not been made for a period of 90 days, the asset is assigned non-performing asset. In light of how long the asset has been non-performing, banks are expected to sort the non-performing assets in one of the going with classifications [9]:

- Sub-Standard Asset: If a resource has been non-performing for under a year;
- Doubtful Asset: If a resource has been non-performing for over a year; and
- Loss Assets: Assets where misfortunes have been distinguished by the bank, evaluator, or auditor and have not been completely discounted.

10.4   Charter for NPA Management

The age of helpless credits in the books of banks is certainly not an ideal occasion for the financial business as it influences the size and adequacy of the monetary record. There is a horrible effect fair and square of return on resources also. Tremendous proportion of advantages should be provisioned against the unrealistic and terrible advances, which reduces efficiency. Banks are even messed with the growing degree of passing on costs of NPA accounts, which may have been used for another useful explanation. The money related foundations are similarly needed to keep a particular capital sufficiency level to support their all-out resources. Anyway this issue is terrible data for the monetary business, actually from the paper reports, it is clear that this issue has adversely impacted the monetary space. The RBI has been going to lengths to control the NPA danger. Some legitimate measures, for instance, commitment recovery courts (DRTs), Lok Adalats, the SARFAESI (Securitisation and Reconstruction of Financial Assets and Enforcement of Security Interest) Act, and the Insolvency and Bankruptcy Code, 2016, have been introduced for the objective of NPAs. Recapitalization of public region banks, setting up of zeroed in on asset the chiefs verticals are some various advances taken by the RBI. Of late, a few thoughts like novel notification accounts (SMA) and making arrangements like SMA 0, SMA 1, and SMA 2 have been added. Additionally, the controller has likewise forced limitation on eleven public area banks by forcing the brief restorative activity (PCA) on them. Due to these turns of events, the current chapter means to discover which banks have added to the developing hazard and what has been the pattern in the financial business with respect to these low quality credits.

10.5   Reasons for Growth of NPAs

The turn of events and expansion inside the exercises of the bank has gem rectifier to consistently expanding non-performing resources that has mounted to a colossal sum all through the last decade or thereabouts. The quantum of NPAs has been determined and place at entirely unexpected figures mainly in light of nonappearance of right insights and in this way the approach on the thought embraced for scheming the extent of NPAs as to either the full resources of the bank or the quantity of credit portfolio or based on the amount of the records or the size of the remarkable advances. Anyway up to this point almost no consideration was paid to the significant reasons on why and the manner in which non playing resources have showed up inside the books of the banks and conjointly the books of the large numbers of the cash organizations. For an outsized scope of years, the banks are assuming praise in its books, on premise of aggregated revenue monetary profit, in any event, for the quantity of occasional premium that wasn't genuinely paid by the borrower. This was finished by raising charge unsettled record and attributing sum satisfactory to the occasional premium in the advance record of the borrower. when complaints from the reviewers and personal assessment authority the banks altered procedure and started giving further advances to the defaulting borrowers for the point of making installments to the bank for change of the overdues, in a few cases the due dates of installments were conceded and surprisingly the entire length of the advance was broadened further again and once more. As though to highlight hearth to the fuel, imposing project for branch advancement and augmentation of banking administrations gem rectifier to new enrollments, moves, migration and unfortunate rivalry among workplaces of a comparable bank, but simultaneously sufficient offices presented for instructing of the specialists were not extended. Inside the tension to achieve business focuses on the establishments and strategies for judicious banking were helpfully neglected [10]. Indeed, even the upper administration arrangement advantageously loosened up the principles for right evaluation of the advance proposition, the arrangements of ordinary bank authorize letter, blunders in execution of the advance arrangements, deeds of hypothecation and home loans were extra normally plain for consistence in the rush for dispensing and activity of focuses for elements of develop record of accomplishments and detailing.

10.6   Induction to Blockchain Technology

Blockchain innovation was acknowledged by the pen name [11]. Without a doubt, Bitcoin was the world's previously decentralized public book and today acquired worldwide status around the world [12]. Nonetheless, Bitcoin's prosperity comes from its fundamental encryption innovation, blockchain innovation [12]. This innovation has been an intriguing issue in late exploration and cases to be a definitely more progressive peculiarity than Bitcoin. The blockchain is an appropriated length include, which implies that it is kept up with by various members without the control of a solitary entertainer [13]. This permits individuals who don't have a clue or trust each other to shape solid books in which data is recorded [14]. A wide range of insignificant data like property freedoms and digital currency exchanges can be put away on these blockchains. Data is accessible to everybody and can't be regulated, so blockchain can turn into a straightforward machine that makes and stores data [15]. The three essential characteristics of blockchain are that they are shared and trusted public directors. The core idea of blockchain technology is the fact that, as a result, it is accessible to everyone, but cannot be controlled or owned by the user alone. Keeping books in line with the present is done in cooperation with the help of network participants. Participants will strengthen and sustain the block-chain in compliance with severe standards and general assent. This implies that the members settle on the best way to refresh the chain. The agreement is called the "consensus mechanism" [15]. This technology operates over a peer-soil peer network based on thousands of "nodes". Computer, the world nodes can move back and forth on the network as needed [3]. New blocks are created through a special node, a process called mining by min-ers. This mine works anonymously in cooperation to solve mathematical puzzles that create new blocks on the blockchain. This creation is not as easy as it sounds. There are a few stages needed to finish and check the new square. In a currency transaction, multiple miners confirm the transaction and all go well and oversee the person who trades and has the money they really want to write. For valid transactions, the miner confirms the change. From then on, similar transactions will be listed in chronological order surrounded by the same block, forming a long-term blockchain [16]. The chain contains generally supported exchanges that have happened since the introduction of the blockchain [17], and that data is consistently acces-sible to everybody. Blockchain is a period series record or information base in which exchanges are recorded by an organization of PCs [18].

These are consolidated in a framework called a "Merkle tree" (see Figure 10.1). This consolidated hash esteem is moreover embedded in the header of the new square, alongside the hash of the past block (see Figure 10.2 'block 10 #') and other data, for example, timestamps. The hash before the new square keeps the square from being altered and forestalls extortion. Timestamps, then again, demonstrate that the information existed around them [3]. Heather is important for a numer-ical riddle that excavators address by controlling specific numbers called "nons" [20]. Excavators attempt trillions of potential answers for tackle the riddle, and when a right arrangement is found, the digger distributes it to others on the organization [3]. Different excavators really look at the arrangement and, assuming that it is right, check it and update the square appropriately. This is the magnificence of blockchain. Puzzles are difficult to tackle, yet easy to check. Hash in the header is the recogniz-ing line of the recently mined square, which is presently essential for the blockchain. Mining new squares in return for keeping up with the blockchain, diggers get a specific measure of new mined bitcoin rewards (The Economist, 2016b). The October 2015 sum is comparable to $7.500 in 25 bitcoins per mined square [21]. This is why miners do not hesitate to update the blockchain by solving difficult puzzles. Payments can be

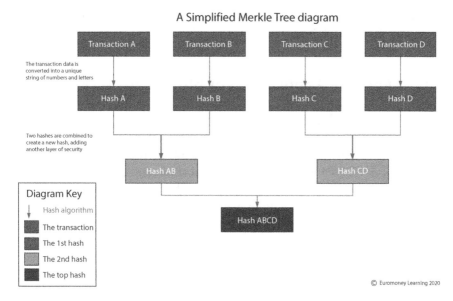

A Simplified Merkle Tree diagram

The transaction data is
converted into a unique
string of numbers and letters

Two hashes are combined to
create a new hash, adding
another layer of security

Diagram Key

↓   Hash algorithm

    The transaction

    The 1st hash

    The 2nd hash

    The top hash

© Euromoney Learning 2020

Figure 10.2 The Merkle Tree [19].

deferred until a certain amount of blocks have been mined [22]. This will allow you to keep small blockchains more efficient. An alternative compensation system [22] is to add transaction fees for transactions. In 2014, 97% of transactions included transaction fees, which is currently less than 0.1% of the value of the transaction. This compensation system is necessary for the miner to have sufficient incentive to maintain the blockchain when the last Bitcoin is mined and no longer can receive Bitcoin as a reward. These transaction fees tend to rise slightly when the last Bitcoin is mined, although they are insignificant compared to traditional transaction costs.

The financial sector is slowly changing and is often seen as a very conservatively regulated branch. However, the accounting firm's [23] argues that banks will change significantly over the next decade, with the technological and regulatory giants currently responding to rapidly evolving changes. To keep up with the new trends in the world, banks must be more proactive in adapting to technology that is changing the way they do business. According to [24], blockchain technology is really about revolutionizing the financial sector and eliminating some jobs like brokers. Nevertheless, this technology can create new jobs at the same time [25]. The main speculation is that blockchain innovation makes banks more able. In any case, the composition contends that monetary organizations are bound to exploit blockchain innovation than to kill it. Numerous applications given by innovation require offering standard collaboration to monetary area entertainers.

10.7   Possible Applications of Blockchain Technology

Blockchain offers decentralization of control, where authority and trust are appropriated across the organization. This offers a chance to break hierarchical, financial and administrative control in exchange preparing. Coming up next are instances of blockchain applications.

Digital money: Bitcoin is digital money that is acknowledged across country borders. Anyone having a blockchain wallet can make installments utilizing this money if the bitcoin is lawfully adequate in that country.

Disseminated record: A portion of world's greatest banks have outlined the blockchain consortium, R3, to cooperate on a passed on record for speedier, secure, capable, and clear money-related trades.

Global Installments: In June 2016, UK's Santander Bank introduced blockchain for worldwide Installments utilizing a pilot portable application. UK, Israel, and Korea have placed assets into blockchain advancement as a substitute structure for overall cash related reimbursements.

Installment settlements: Blockchain is a viable apparatus for exchange compromise and settlement across parties in the installment chain. The decentralized control and authority component of the blockchain innovation is utilized to take out the requirement for a focal clearing house as a middle person among banks, monetary organizations, and different players. Figure 10.3 represents how the settlement measures work prior and then afterward the execution of blockchain innovation.

Keen agreement: Contracts are put away on the blockchain with characterized rules to deal with their worth and possession. It permits the administration of contracts between parties, dispensing with the requirement for a judge. In fact, a brilliant agreement is a PC program that is conjured by pre-characterized occasions. Blockchain innovation makes savvy contracts dependable by wiping out the regulator and making the program straightforward, proficient, and practical (Figure 10.4).

Smart character: Blockchain innovation can be utilized to store personality records carefully, in this way keeping up with security and protection [28]. Client training, experience, and occasion information are put away for quicker character confirmation. Banks can store client information on blockchain and append it to client character.

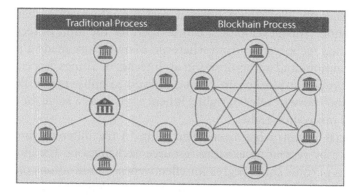

Figure 10.3 Settlement process in conventional versus blockchain conditions [26].

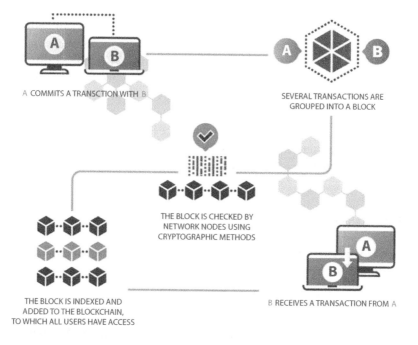

Figure 10.4 How smart contracts work [27].

Security record: Blockchain advancement engages the posting of protection as starting and assortment edge by escrowing cash on cash records, or assets on asset records, to a passed on ensure record. The record allows the sharing of protection information for better appraisal of borrowers' money related and asset positions, auditability and straightforwardness, and the finish of 'twofold spend'.

Data sharing: Blockchain offers a part for information sharing and collaboration. This development can be used for the limit of records and access-based recuperation from wherever. Manufacture made a phase for sharing cautions and admonitions in an Internet of Things association.

Keen property: Blockchain can be utilized to enlist responsibility for content and move or offer of rights. It hence fills in as a stage for enlisting protected innovation rights.

Financial industry has been attempting to try different things with blockchain by recreating existing resource exchanges on the blockchain. While this permits some degree for effectiveness ramifications of a block-chain arrangement, what gets passed up a major opportunity is the bio-logical system ramifications of a blockchain arrangement. In framework terms the blockchain is an open source programming that is worked to help the exchange of computerized resources among market members continuously. Utilizing any favored blockchain's APIs, one can feature an emotional decrease in resource move expenses and courses of events. Most bank executions are centered on this viewpoint. Yet, while scaling veri-fication of idea into a genuine situation, monetary foundations wind up carrying out a similar application layer that exists at present with every one of the current governing rules.

The concept of NPA has been known since long and the upcoming stage confronts the existence of NPA's in banking and the supports of blockchain technology to treat a serious threat for the banking industry.

10.8   ACT II Confrontation Stage

This stage presents the current status of non-performing assets in banking and the contribution of blockchain technology in loan quality manage-ment through exploration of existing literature.

10.9   Investigation of Loan Quality-Related Issues in the Indian Banking System

As of late, a couple of high profile advance defaulters have shaken the Indian media, bringing to the front one of the consuming issues that has been preparing in the Indian financial area for a long while. This is the issue of NPL, which are otherwise called non-performing resources (NPA). Indian public area banks altogether owed around 6.17 trillion Indian rupees in non-performing resources in monetary year 2021. Indian public area banks aggregately owed around 6.17 trillion Indian rupees in non-performing resources in financial year 2021. This worth was a lot higher, at around 7.5 trillion rupees in the 2019 financial year, demonstrating a lethargic yet slight alleviation for India's economy as far as non-paying resources at public banks. Should this load of advances transform into NPA, the generally monetary danger of Indian banks would surpass their fairly estimated worth. Financial backers worry about the concern of this danger, and the business endures while the economy endures the worst part.

The International Monetary Fund Financial Stability report conveyed in April 2015 assessments that 37% of complete commitment gave by Indian banks is at serious risk, which is high stood out from other emerging economies [28]. The commitment in peril far balances the pad stayed aware of by banks. Indian banks itemized gross NPA of simply 6.17 trillion in year 2021; pushing horrendous credit cases to remade progresses, likewise concealing the build-up well hidden. Hold Bank of India Deputy Governor, S. S. Mundra, recognized asset quality organization as the fundamental requirement for Indian banking.

Resource quality isn't only an Indian issue; the administration of resource quality has shown a descending pattern across a few other ASEAN banks also. Most ASEAN nations are tormented by rising corporate obligation and befuddle owing debtor reimbursement capacity. Singapore, Thailand, and Malaysia have revealed quicker development of credits contrasted with their GDP, with Thailand announcing NPL of more than three percent [29].

NPL are fuelled by low quality guaranteeing and a lazy methodology in adjusting changes in FICO score to credit reimbursement terms [30]. A stoppage of Indian modern development and the increment in financing costs, accumulated by monetary instability across the world, has highlighted the danger of default [31]. Like India, other developing economies like China, Thailand, Brazil, and Argentina have a critical portion of obligation owed by firms with compelled reimbursement limit. Tending to resource the board issues for this fragment can essentially diminish the greatness of hazard.

New advancements offer a substitute or maybe a correlative way to deal with observing resource quality. It was the blockchain-based dispersed record, data sharing, brilliant personality, keen agreement, keen security and keen property applications as conceivable innovation answers for kill shortcomings in the advance administration measure in the Indian financial framework [32]. They will likewise assist with introducing straightforwardness, trust and between bank coordinated efforts.

The key test going ahead for Indian banks is to grow credit portfolio and successfully oversee NPAs while keeping up with productivity. Resource quality keeps on being the fundamental capacity and furthermore the greatest test for banks in the current powerful climate. To defeat the apparent dangers, there is a pressing requirement for banks to have very much organized and successful credit evaluation and observing framework set up combined with fitting plans of action which can be fueled by blockchain technology advances [33] to viably deal with every one of the recent concerns rotating around recuperation in focused on resources and in this manner help in decrease of NPAs across all banks.

10.10   Stage 3 – Treatment Stage for Bad Loans Through Blockchain in Indian Banks

In the past section the theory has clarified the center ideas of the blockchain innovation and its most eager applications up until now. Nonetheless, the point of this postulation is to give an understanding on how this new and disruptive innovation will reform and reshape the monetary area. Thusly, the motivation behind this part is to present potential utilizations of the innovation in the financial world [34]. Since the blockchain innovation has as of late acquired consideration, the measure of examination on the impacts of the blockchain innovation in the monetary area is restricted. Hence, countless the finishes in this part are made in this section. The motivation behind this participation is to create blockchain innovation and straightaway apply it to the monetary area. They are cooperating to foster a common norm of how to utilize this innovation, which is unmistakably a test in the exceptionally serious monetary world [35]. As indicated [36], blockchain innovation can upset and reshape the financial world, in spite of the relative multitude of hardships it faces. Blockchain innovation is really helped in treating the terrible advances by the accompanying ways.

1. 'Permissioned' records, shrewd agreement, and keen property uses of the blockchain innovation can be utilized to make a decentralized framework with dispersed control that builds straightforwardness and confidence in the administration of credits across banks. Since the financial framework contains private and classified information, blockchain innovation for this area involves decentralization and dispersed handling at the bank level. Each bank can turn into a member in the blockchain network. Bank workers can go about as diggers or hubs in the organization liable for

appropriated agreement. Unselfish and normal hubs dispersed in the organization guarantee a reasonable and confided in framework.

2. Personality check of borrowers is quicker and more productive with the utilization of brilliant character in the blockchain network. Advance endorsement requires agreement from all members of the organization. Shared data gives admittance to more extravagant data to all around educated dynamic and agreement, in this manner killing the extent of 'twofold spend'. Shrewd agreements manage the advance through its lifecycle, disposing of the chance of incongruent detailing of credits and unreported advances (Mehedy, 2017). Shared control in the survey of past credit records, confirmation of monetary data, and shared agreement guarantees proficient administration and straightforwardness in endorsing.

3. Supported advances are cryptographically marked and permanent. Credit rebuilding involves the endorsement from the circulated network, giving tough control on information, arrangement and announcing. The utilization of savvy contracts in post-endorsement credit grouping accommodates straightforward advance resource arrangement [37].

Blockchain holds the guarantee to resolve the thorniest issue tormenting the Indian financial framework as of now—terrible advances [38]. It permits quicker ID of unsafe clients with high obligation or potentially compelled reimbursement limit, as leasers' personalities and exercises are apparent across the organization. This thus lessens the danger of loss of resources. Brilliant property helps in compelling guarantee the executives across banks and quicker transaction of security proprietorship in the event of misfortune recuperation. Figure 10.5 shows the common cycles engaged with taking care of credit applications in the Indian financial setting, and how those cycles can be further developed utilizing the blockchain innovation.

Since the above depicted picture clearly shows the contribution of blockchain technology in assignment of loan, how a shift from traditional to modern loan assessment and issuance has significantly changed. The data sharing amongst the banks has facilitated the entire process. Despite of its major contribution to NPA protection, this technology is still facing various challenges.

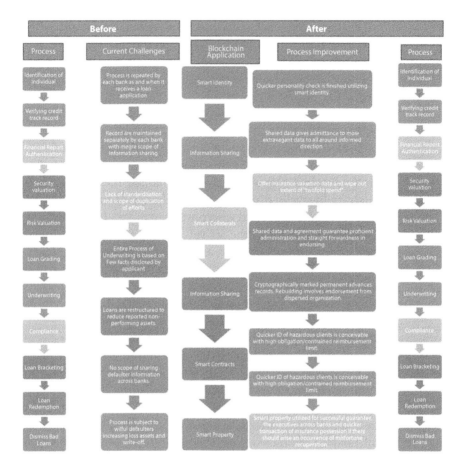

Figure 10.5 Modified loan approval process (author compilation).

10.11   The Challenges of the Blockchain Technology in Financial Sector

The money-related region, and particularly the monetary region, is considered to be a thoroughly coordinated and conservative branch and its pay model has been unchangeable for a long time. Eventually, new and advanced innovation will shape the monetary region overwhelmingly in the accompanying ten years [23]. To acclimate to these changes, money related associations need to end up being less reluctant to these new progressions that change techniques for cooperating.

There are conflicting appraisals on how the blockchain development will impact the financial region. The most over the top hypothesis is that the blockchain development makes banks futile. It is unquestionably an absurd case that the whole monetary region would disappear considering the development. Accordingly, this hypothesis battles that the financial foundations will undoubtedly take advantage of the blockchain development than to age significantly because of it. In any case, some old techniques for cooperating may become obsolete or reshaped; for instance, cash will not exist in ten years [39]. Taking everything into account, numerous organizations that banks offer are evaporating, but new organizations are being envisioned at the same time. As has communicated, the blockchain will point of fact kill a piece of the situations in the financial region, yet it will simultaneously make new ones [40].

As this hypothesis perceives, the blockchain development has mind blowing opportunities to reshape entire endeavors, especially those that rely upon trust. In this manner, the financial region can benefit from the new development since it is an industry that depends particularly upon trust. Eventually, the blockchain development meets resistance from people who are reluctant to change similarly as mechanical degrees of progress [22]. In any case, as a result of the decrease in conviction and straightforwardness in the financial system, a development that limits as a trust machine can't simply be something horrible.

The blockchain development would in this manner have the option to make trust in the financial structure. This is a critical point especially as per the perspective of money related foundations. Right when people trust in the financial business areas, money related establishments can even more viably zero in on their basic undertakings, such as moving resources from credit experts to borrowers. Regardless, if they expect that a bank will miss the mark, it can cause bank runs and one bank's failure can ship off another, which prompts problem in the financial structure [41].

On the other hand, really the advancement limits as a trust machine, the financial region can benefit from the blockchain development in substitute habits as well. In light of the digitalization designs and the improvement of enlisting, financial associations have had the choice to reshape their internal exercises and digitalize most of their things and organizations [22]. Eventually, the relationships of the banks are at this point waiting behind the tunnel Digitalization and are generally united. Portion structures and the twofold segment bookkeeping between banks are both consolidated systems in spite of the way that the blockchain development could achieve a more huge degree of synchronization in these specific areas. For instance, portion trades are routinely expected to go through a trusted in delegate. A more significant synchronization further creates viability, diminishes risks, and kills costs, which will in a little while be illustrated.

In addition, an all through execution of the blockchain advancement in the financial region demands co-movement between all performers included. This is a test in the outstandingly forceful universe of cash [22]. Thus, it is without any question that the cutthroat idea of the monetary establishments will change amazingly there where blockchains are tried.

The blockchain innovation can possibly disturb the current monetary framework, however to do as such, the innovation should be created and upheld by monetary establishments to try not to turn out to be just a craze as bitcoin takes steps to remain. It contends that a pertinent utilization of the blockchain innovation must be conveyed to the monetary area in year and a half or the publicity about blockchains will blur.

As should be obvious, the blockchain innovation can possibly empower a few and altogether different sorts of uses in the monetary area and almost certainly, it will soon empower much more. That far is hard to determine what kinds of uses will be applied in the end and how much. Accentuate that it isn't sensible to place everything in blockchains, on the grounds that there might be a few administrations more reasonable for the blockchain innovation than others. Along these lines, it is outrageous to guarantee that the monetary organizations would vanish due to the blockchain innovation. Despite the fact that it would be conceivable, it isn't important to utilize blockchains to everything.

10.12   Conclusion

Blockchain holds the guarantee to resolve the thorniest issue tormenting the Indian financial framework as of now, that is, awful credits. Thoughtfully, the blockchain innovation gives an answer for the issue of terrible advances by offering a reasonable goal to the slips in the resource of the executives, interaction. In any case, on a viable front, a few difficulties remain. The execution of blockchain requires an exhaustive mechanical and administrative assessment, expanded cultural mindfulness, enormous coordinated effort and knowledge, tough arranging and sound specialized expertise. Banks manage clients' private data and delicate monetary data, requiring severe information assurance standards. Indian banks are directed by the Reserve Bank of India's rules on information assurance and administration. Data security mindfulness is low in the Indian financial framework, which opens banks to information security dangers and cybercrimes. One of the most basic data security challenges in Indian banks is the danger to secrecy and respectability of data when imparted to outside parties.

By custom, banks are not socially arranged to utilize appropriated and decentralized information stockpiling and preparing. The administrative structure for data security and cybercrime in India is frail and uncertain. Given this foundation, Indian banks are normally expected to be detached towards embracing new innovation including information sharing and decentralized control. Consciousness of blockchain should be worked in all cases to battle inborn restraints.

On the innovation front, the blockchain innovation is yet to be tried for adaptability, limit, and execution needs of enormous datasets engaged with the Indian financial framework. Reasonable cryptographic and agreement conventions for information access and control that satisfy the requirements of the framework should be created. Conventions and administration components for access and keen agreements should be set up for the execution of multi-party frameworks with high monetary danger openness. This requires huge interest in research for improving blockchain innovation. Blockchain is a competitor for the following greatest innovation interruption since the coming of the Internet, promising sensational changes in information security, purchaser strengthening, just as making of trust and straightforwardness. It has an inborn capacity to defeat dangers to data secrecy and uprightness in a common climate, accordingly mitigating the conceivable saw hindrances. The innovation envoys between bank-coordinated effort to defeat issues in resource the board and prepares for more educated dynamic, compelling approach execution and administration of credit the board measures. Blockchain likewise has the potential to turn into the true mode for esteem trade. With its establishment in cryptography, the innovation vows to overcome dangers to information security on a common stage. Quicker and more extravagant data access, joined with democratized control and high interoperable shared and secure stages with 'permissioned' access and dispersed contact the board scripts, are ideal elements for a troublesome development in resource the executives across the financial business.

India would thus be able to prearrange one more jump achievement system through the reception of the way breaking blockchain innovation to beat up and coming issues in NPL, work on the general strength of Indian banking, recuperate lost financial backer certainty and revive India's modern and monetary development.

References

1. IBM, 10 Key marketing trends for 2017 and Idea for exceeding customer expectations, 2017, https://www-01.ibm.com/common/ssi/cgi-bin/ssialias?htmlfid=WRL12345USEN.

2. Christidis, K. and Devetsikiotis, M., Blockchains and smart contracts for the internet of things. *IEEE Access*, 4, 2292–2303, 2016.

3. Nakamoto, S., Bitcoin: A peer-to-peer electronic cash system. Satoshi Nakamoto Institute Working Paper. 2018, Retrieved from: http://nakamo toinstitute.org/bitcoin/

4. Meng, W., Tischhauser, E.W., Wang, Q., Wang, Y., Han, J., When intrusion detection meets blockchain technology: A review. *IEEE Access*, 6, 10179–10188, 2018.

5. Atzei, N., Bartoletti, M., Cimoli, T., A survey of attacks on Ethereum smart contracts (SoK). *International Conference on Principles of Security and Trust*, Springer, pp. 164–186, 2017.

6. Conti, M., Sandeep Kumar, E., Lal, C., Ruj, S., A survey on security and privacy issues of bitcoin. *IEEE Commun. Surv. Tutorials*, 20, 4, 3416–3452, Fourthquarter 2018.

7. Tanaka, K., Nagakubo, K., Abe, R., Blockchain-based electricity trading with Digitalgrid router, in: *2017 IEEE International Conference on Consumer Electronics* – Taiwan, ICCE-TW 2017, pp. 201–202, 2017.

8. Verma, Goyal, R., Priya, J., Profitability of commercial banks after the reforms: A study of selected banks. *Int. J. Res. Financial Market*, 20–29 , 2013.

9. Sekhon, S. and Kaur, J., Empirical study on non-performing assets of public and private sector banks. *Int. J. Bus. Manage. Res. (IJBMR)*. 5, 5, 73–78, Oct 2015.

10. Briner, R.B. and Denyer, D., *Systematic review and evidence synthesis as a practice and scholarship tool*, New Year University Press, New York, 2012.

11. Koteska, B., Karafilovski, E., Mishev, A., Blockchain implementation quality challenges: A literature review. *Proceedings of the SQAMIA 2017: 6th Workshop of Software Quality, Analysis, Monitoring, Improvement, and Applications*, Belgrade, Serbia, pp. 11–13, 2017.

12. Pilkington, M., Blockchain technology: Principles and applications (September 18, 2015), in: *Research Handbook on Digital Transformations*, F. Xavier Olleros and M. Zhegu (Eds.), Edward Elgar, 2016.

13. Hawlitschek, F., Notheisen, B., Teubner, T., The limits of trust-free systems: A literature review on blockchain technology and trust in the sharing economy. *Electron. Commer. Res.*, 29, 50–63, 2018.

14. Kaur, J., Role of transumational leadership: Road map from knowledge management to learning organization to innovation, in: *Leadership Skills Parameters and Paradigms*, pp. 157–166, 2011.

15. Bonneau, J., Miller, A., Clark, J., Narayanan, A., Kroll, J.A., Felten, E.W., Sok: Research perspectives and challenges for bitcoin and cryptocurrencies. *2015 IEEE Symposium on Security and Privacy (SP)*, IEEE, pp. 104–121, 2015.

16. Crosby, M., Pattanayak, P., Verma, S., Kalyanaraman, Blockchain technology: Beyond bitcoin. *Appl. Innovation*, 2, 6–10, 2016.

17. Greenspan, Gideon. Ending the Bitcoin vs Blockchain Debate, White Paper, 2015a. Available online: http://www.multichain.com/blog/2015/07/bitcoin-vs-blockchain-debate (accessed on 18 October 2020).

18. Tschorsch, F. and Scheuermann, B., Bitcoin and beyond: A technical survey on decentralized digital currencies. *IEEE Commun. Surv. Tutor.*, 18, 3, 2084–2123, 2016.

19. The Merkle tree. https://www.euromoney.com/learning/blockchain-explained/how-blockchain-data-is-stored-and-secured.

20. Xu, R., Zhang, L., Zhao, H., Peng, Y., Design of network media's digital rights management scheme based on blockchain technology. *Proceedings – 2017 IEEE 13th International Symposium on Autonomous Decentralized Systems, ISADS 2017*, pp. 128–133, 2017a.

21. Böhme, R., Christin, N., Edelman, B., Moore, T., Bitcoin: Economics, technology, and governance. *J. Econ. Perspect.*, 29, 2, 213–38, 2015.

22. The Economist. The trust machine: How the technology behind bitcoin could change the world, 2015, https://www.economist.com/weeklyedition/2015-10-31.

23. PWC, The business case for true pricing, 2014, Available at https://trueprice.org/wp-content/uploads/2015/02/True-Price-Report-The-Business-Case-for-True-Pricing.pdf, Accessed on 18 July 2022.

24. Patil, A.S., Tama, B.A., Park, Y., Rhee, K.H., A framework for blockchain based secure smart greenhouse farming. *Lect. Notes Electr. Eng.*, 474, 1162–1167, 2018.

25. Brandão, A., São Mamede, H., Gonçalves, R., Systematic review of the literature, research on blockchain technology as support to the trust model proposed applied to smart places, in: *World Conference on Information Systems and Technologies*, Springer, pp. 1163–1174, 2018.

26. Settlement process in conventional versus blockchain conditions, https://cmp.smu.edu.sg/ami/article/20161208/smarter-banking.

27. How smart contracts work, https://www.vectorstock.com/royalty-free-vector/

28. Salah, K. and Khan, M., IoT security: Review, blockchain solutions, and open challenges. *Future Gener. Comput. Syst.*, 82, 395-411, 2017, 10.1016/j.future.2017.11.022.

29. Szabo, N., Smart contracts: Building blocks for digital free markets. Extropy Journal of Transhuman Thought, 16, 18, 2, 1996.

30. Sankar, L.S., Sindhu, M., Sethumadhavan, M., Survey of consensus protocols on blockchain applications. *2017 4th International Conference on Advanced Computing and Communication Systems (ICACCS)*, IEEE, pp. 1–5, 2017.

31. Kaur, J. and Sekhon, S., Application and effectiveness of financial control techniques in Indian Banks- An empirical evidence. *Int. J. Adv. Res.*, 4, 6, 635–643, 2015.

32. Moher, D. *et al.*, Preferred reporting items for systematic reviews and meta-analyses: The PRISMA statement. *PLoS Med.*, 151, 4, 264–269, 2009.

33. Suzuki, S. and Murai, J., Blockchain as an audit-able communication channel. *Proc. Int. Comput. Software Appl. Conf.*, 2, 516–522, 2017.

34. Tosh, D.K., Shetty, S., Liang, X., Kamhoua, C.A., Kwiat, K.A., Njilla, L., Security implications of blockchain cloud with analysis of block withholding attack, in: *Proceedings 2017 – 17th IEEE/ACM International Symposium on Cluster, Cloud and Grid Computing (CCGRID)*, pp. 458–46, 2017.
35. Turkanović, M., Hölbl, M., Košič, K., Heričko, M., Kamišalić, A., EduCTX: A blockchain-based higher education credit platform. *IEEE Access*, 6, 5112–5127. Umeh, J., Blockchain double bubble or double trouble? *ITNOW*, 58, 1, 58–61, 2018.
36. Trautman, L.J., Is disruptive blockchain technology the future of financial services? (May 28, 2016). *69 The Consumer Finance Law Quarterly Report 232*, 2016, Available at SSRN: https://ssrn.com/abstract=2786186.
37. Kaur, J., Fund performance, top management changes, strategy and investment manager characteristics: IIMs. *J. Manage. Sci.*, 4, 1, 19–39, June 2013.
38. Seebacher, S. and Schüritz, R., Blockchain technology as an enabler of service systems: A structured literature review. *International Conference on Exploring Services Science*, Springer, pp. 12–23, 2017.
39. M. Conoscenti, A. Vetrò and J. C. De Martin, Blockchain for the Internet of Things: A systematic literature review, *IEEE/ACS 13th International Conference of Computer Systems and Applications (AICCSA)*, pp. 1-6, 2016, doi: 10.1109/AICCSA.2016.7945805.
40. Haferkorn, M. and Quintana Diaz, J.M., Seasonality and interconnectivity within cryptocurrencies – An analysis on the basis of bitcoin, litecoin and namecoin, 2015.
41. Diamond, D. and Dybvig, P., Bank runs, deposit insurance, and liquidity. *J. Polit. Econ.*, 91, 401–419, 2001, 10.1086/261155.

11

Blockchain and Smart Contracts for Insurance Industry

Rupa Khanna Malhotra[1], Chandan Gupta[2] and Priya Jindal[3*]

[1,2]Department of Commerce, Graphic Era Deemed to be University, Dehradun, India
[3]Chitkara Business School, Chitkara University, Rajpura, Punjab, India

Abstract

Business should focus a wide range of customer engagement strategies to improve existing customer experience and hence increased customer retention that support customer's loyalty towards the brands, acquiring new customers that may impel the current market share and compete with competitors in the global economy. Creative and Innovations, cost increases, demanding customers, and disruptions are threats and challenges which are faced by insurance organizations. Blockchain technology can solve these problems by building up better business processes and business models. These business models will provide efficiency in dealing with customers, processes and intermediates, policyholders. These technologies can engage customers and enhance their satisfaction level. The advent of the internet and digital social technologies has resulted in some fascinating developments in communication and connectivity worldwide and it is providing a prospect for insurance companies to expand their customer base. As a result, the advancement of new generation digital technologies provides a variety of benefits to both insurance companies and consumers.

Blockchain technologies can directly or indirectly improve customer satisfaction by engaging customers. Innovative products and solutions can be offered in this sector with low cost, fast solutions, and improved relationships for all the stockholders. This study is about how blockchain technologies can provide a see-change scenario in the insurance sector by providing enhanced customer satisfaction. Insurance companies can improve their competitive advantage by insighting into the market trends and stay afloat in the market by doing so. On the one hand, digital innovation technologies redesign the firm's outreach, while on the other,

---

*Corresponding author: priya.jindal@chitkara.edu.in

Kiran Sood, Rajesh Kumar Dhanaraj, Balamurugan Balusamy and Seifedine Kadry (eds.) Blockchain Technology in Corporate Governance: Transforming Business and Industries, (239–252) © 2023 Scrivener Publishing LLC

they improve customer satisfaction. In recent years, insurance companies have been investing more in various types of portfolio technologies to position their services in the minds of consumers.

Keywords: Blockchain, digital innovations, insurance companies, business models, portfolio technologies, etc.

11.1   Introduction

11.1.1   Blockchain in Insurance

For hundreds of years, the Insurance sector is here either formally or informally. The classic example of insurance is thousand and thousand years old where seafarers use to pool their resources to pay for the damages for any shipping damage during voyage. Though there is a sea change in the technology and some industries or sectors there are radical changes in the processes but this million-dollar industry of insurance has not undergone any major change [1]. Very little is done to improve the customer experience. We knew insurance as a life insurance policy and risk management instrument but now insurance is available for health, automobiles, property, pets and the list is long. Risk management is a complex and multi-faceted task that touches on numerous aspects of people's lives. As a result, the insurance industry is a major determinant in guiding modern economies along their development paths. Legendary actor Mr. Amitabh Bacchan has insured his voice; Ms. Angelina Jolie has insured her leg shape in millions of dollars. Some companies are providing insurance for flight delays, and even for kidnapping. Pets, domestic animals, and crops are also got insured [2]. Advancement in technologies has not motivated people to shop online for policies though there are a lot of companies who are providing insurance online. Still, the customers get satisfaction with face-to-face talk with the broker. Because policies are frequently paper contracts processed on paper, claims and installments are prone to errors and frequently require human oversight. The inherent complexity of protection, which includes buyer representatives, backup plans, and re-insurers, as well as protection fundamental items – risk – add to this. Each progression in this collective interaction addresses a likely weak spot in the general framework, where data can be lost, arrangements misjudged, and settlement times protracted. Prevalent and important however it is, nonetheless, the insurance business has a lot of issues – unorganized sector, misrepresentation, human mistake, and, most worried of all, cyber-attacks. In 2015, Anthem Insurance disclosed a medical data breach that uncovered the delicate information of 78.8 million clients from its servers. Other than the endless misfortunes originating from personality misrepresentation, the whole business took a $375 million hit [3].

The insurance industry's infrastructure is currently impassive, and unnecessary intermediaries make business affairs more expensive and time-consuming. As a result, the insurance industry is the most promising and advantageous application of blockchain technology. For the transformation of the insurance sector, Blockchain technologies can be a blessing in disguise though developed for cryptocurrencies for better cooperation, control, and coordination of stakeholder [4]. Establishing blockchain technologies for the insurance sector is quite challenging and can give a tough time to both technology developers and startups. There are various regulatory and legal requirements that they need to fulfill before proceedings with the new idea and processes. Disruptions will be quite challenging in the Insurance sector as this industry has not even embraced cloud computing or any other technologies. It is very tough to create trust in this trustless world with the use of public ledgers and protocols related to cyber security. Blockchain technologies could create ecosystems to establish trust. Blockchain technologies can help in the growth of the insurance sector. Data sciences, artificial technologies, and blockchain technology together unfold the prospects and growth of the Insurance sector [5].

11.1.2   Blockchain in Insurance Applications

Blockchain is a broad platform that brings together various software programs and expertise [6]. An enormous number of promising and diverse blockchain applications are persistently circulating in a variety of industries, including financial services, real estate, healthcare, and public administration or government agencies [7]. As a result, developing or utilizing blockchain technology in the insurance industry for smoother and hassle-free transactions against individuals is a necessity of the hour. Blockchain technology could be applied to various aspects of the insurance industry, allowing for faster and more reliable data transfers, automation processes, and fraud prevention. Work automation, reduces the physical process, ensuring secure audit trails, removing barriers such as data duplication, and provide data accuracy, reliability and timeliness that is accessible at all times [8].

Blockchain applications promote a more versatile and productive framework. It provides a component for data exchange and coordination. This innovation can be used to search and access clients from anywhere.

Blockchain enhances the competence, transparency, and security of the industry. Distributed Ledger Technology (DLT) has valuable applications for rationalizing insurance claims processing, enhancing cyber security protocols, and even fast-moving of payment [9]. The paper highlighted nine companies that are using blockchain technology to revolutionize the insurance industry. According to the study, blockchain technology benefits customers by providing an overview of their insurance policy, notifying them of premium due dates, displaying the policy's history, speeding up claim disputes, and removing inefficiencies. The use of blockchain technology in the insurance industry will also help with subrogation and inter-company claims management [10].

11.2   Smart Contracts by Insurance Providers Using Blockchain Technologies

Smart contracts are another feature of blockchain technology. Smart contracts are self-executing pieces of code that are specified with the conditions required for a transaction and are implemented with blockchain. Smart contracts are extremely useful for automatically settling transactions in a network because they are self-executing, self-verifiable, and consist of programmed code that creates an agreement between multiple parties [11].

The terms of an agreement between the transaction's parties are contained in this contract. They used to be able to enforce agreements without the use of an intermediary. Smart contracts allow for irreversible transactions. Transactions can be made between parties regardless of their identities, without the need for a legal system or a central authority, using smart contracts [12]. The middleman is the only factor that determines the insurance industry. There is no need for a middleman with smart contracts, and policies can be transparently transferred to the customer. The term of transactions is defined in the smart contract between the insurance provider and the insurance taker, just as it is in physical contracts. Two unknown parties can enter into a transaction by using the escrow features of these contracts. Accountability is defined similarly to how it is defined in physical contracts. Developers can encrypt payment information such as the policy number, the name of the policyholder, and the premium amount. When transactions are completed, they can be validated and settled automatically by users connected to the networks [13]. Smart contacts are used to efficiently manage the parties' access rights to their tokenized assets. Access rights are stored and implemented on a blockchain, which means they can't be changed, tampered with, or deleted. Smart contracts make it simple to track down insurance claims. As a result, smart contracts provide a public and verifiable way to implement rules, regulations, and business logic with a piece of code that is audited and implemented by the majority of nodes in a peer-to-peer network. Smart contracts are distinguished from traditional contracts by these characteristics, which result in lower transaction costs and increased security [14].

Insurance policies are written in encrypted form, using decentralized smart contracts, and require an insurer to pay a set amount to the company to protect himself from risk. Immutable contracts are created based on the insurer's records, which the company can refute or accept for any claims. These risks can be eliminated and payments can be controlled before the commercial transaction thanks to the capabilities of the smart contract of blockchain technology [15].

11.2.1   Blockchain: A Built-In Data

If the insurer and the insurance provider have a disagreement or make false claims, the contract will be immediately dissolved, and the entire premium paid will be returned to the customer [16]. The smart contract has mutual trust because it is transparent, and any slight deviation in terms will result in recompense to the harmed party.

11.2.2   Advanced Insurance Automation

Earlier the insurance industry was bogged down by the time taking process of documentation, poor communication between parties because of human error. Now Digital ledger systems have automated the entire process and have saved billion of papers and seconds [17]. Now the data is safely stored and human error is significantly reduced. Through distributed ledger technologies the miscommunication has also been reduced. Based on data now, the right instruments can be administered. It is a forward-looking technology and can streamline the systems.

11.2.3   Cyber Security in Insurance through Blockchain

In any industry which survives and strives on data, data security is very important and blockchain technologies can safeguard sensitive information [18]. To stop the corruption of data or manipulation of data, decentralized Information is stored in ledgers related to clients. Time stamping of data is done chronologically and every event is recorded. Encrypted data is kept which is visible to all the members. This system is foolproof and enables nodes to quickly intercept and correct any unusual behavior.

11.3   Review of Literature

Blockchain technology, can establish a trust system due to its characteristics of transparency, consistency, and immutability. This trusted protocol ensures that both insurance companies and their clients act with honesty and integrity [19]. It creates a sense of balance in terms of safety and security. The paper discussed the exponential growth of blockchain for effective operational risk resilience in the European insurance market. To evaluate blockchain for digital risk resilience author developed a questionnaire on a five-point Likert scale and a total of 513 valid responses have been received. Structural equation modeling was used. The results showed that blockchain has unlimited potential and it is the need of the hour for risk management, effectiveness to integration, and compliance requirements [20]. Blockchain technology designs distributed platforms in different Fintech systems including the insurance sector to deal with productivity and security protection. Blockchain in insurance supports automated interactions among parties exclusive of any intermediaries through the notion of smart contracts [21]. The paper discussed the example of development and initiatives activities of smart contracts in blockchain technology within the insurance industry. The activities are designed to improve efficiency, enhance data security and transparency from the point of view of insurers and reinsurers. Smart contracts are at the forefront of fraud detection and risk prevention [22]. Information availability and ubiquity, facilitated by blockchain technology, increase accountability and provide more accurate evaluation and monitoring in the event of misappropriation and errors [23]. This means that in worst-case scenarios, this technology gives customers and businesses some leverage and countermeasures. Insurers are moving towards making transactions and claim processing digitally and focusing on blockchain technology to speed up claim processing. Digital contracts are different from traditional contracts and it is hard to deal with such types of contracts as these contracts lack the evidentiary value in court. He suggested that there should be a regulatory and legal framework for blockchain [24]. This emerging technology helps to market the right policy and set up virtual branches. The insurance sector is a good aspirant for the use of blockchain technology at a time when multiple parties share data.

Blockchain due to its unique characteristics provides great opportunities to the insurance sector to build new varieties of attractive policies and reform the business transactions by improving the competence of the insurance value chain [25].

11.4   Opportunities Provided by Blockchain Technology

➢ Aids to Manage a Large Amount of Data with Safety
Blockchain technologies provide an additional layer of security and mutual trust between parties. Furthermore, insurance companies can use blockchain technology to securely store large amounts of data, ensuring that no one tampers with it, and preventing data loss, corruption, and hacking.

➢ Strategic and Administrative Imperatives through Smart Contracts
Automatically through blockchain collection of records of terms and conditions of agreement can be collected, transparent transactions and other information can be collected. Based on data, strategic decisions can be taken and instruments can be offered.

➢ Detection of Frauds
Through data and history, if any wrong information is provided, it can be detected very easily through blockchain technologies. As a result, it keeps all of the records in order and ensures that the results are accurate.

➢ Improving Provider Directory Accuracy
Decentralized consensus protocols and unique provider directories are available that can leverage blockchain technology, allowing insurance companies and insurers to update listings more quickly and easily.

➢ Customer-Centric Process
Earlier for insurance lot of time and documentation was required. Now blockchain technologies provide easier-to-access and more comprehensive processes and provide peace of mind to both entities.

➢ Insurer/Client Relationship Facilitation
Electronic health records are the foundation of the insurer and client relationship facilitation. Information is securely stored and provides mutual respect between two entities

➤ Reduce Administrative Cost

By modernizing IT processes and systems, blockchain technologies reduce administrative costs, improve efficiency, and give service providers a competitive advantage. By removing third parties from the transaction, blockchain was able to save insurance companies a significant amount of money. It ensures a smart agreement between buyer and seller, with the buyer only receiving services if the agreement's terms and conditions are met.

➤ Automation

Automation can help to improve the presence of an efficient and skilled workforce. By reducing process time and consumption, blockchain improves business efficiency. By avoiding third parties, it helps to speed up real-time business transactions.

➤ New Protocols and Systems

Customized and customized services, privacy systems, processes, security protocols, and business models are developed to meet customer expectations and improve engagement. These improvised processes are necessary to provide the best services at a low cost.

➤ Property and Casualty (P&C) Insurance

Smart contracts executed through ledger sharing and insurance policies have defined a new era in the property and casualty arena.

➤ Reinsurance

By securing reinsurance contracts, smart contracts using blockchain technology can lay out a flow of information and payment procedures between insurers and reinsurers.

Given below are the insurance companies who lead the pack in ledger technology:

Etherisc

Etherisc is an insurance company from Germany that focuses on decentralized blockchain-centric applications for the insurance industry. The company works on ledger technology and is an open-source development platform. For crop insurance and Cryptocurrencies hacking, the company has developed six different applications.

Beenest

It is San Francisco, California-based home-sharing organization for the crypto-enthusiasts.

Guardtime

It is California based organization. It provides blockchain solutions for defense and cyber security, it works very closely with the governments, their finance departments, and logistics organizations. Guardtime and Maersk have formed a strategic alliance to develop platforms based on blockchain technologies. Both of these companies have managed insurance of 1000 ships together. For pertinent maritime insurance, through strategic alliance, they have developed a platform to oversee more than 500,000 ledger transactions.

Fidentiax

It is Singapore based organization. It provides marketplace tradable insurance policies. Data of policies are stored using blockchain technologies. The same technology is used to buy and sell insurance policies. Using tokenization, a marketplace, supported by blockchain technologies policies it puts into the encrypted database.

B3I

B3I is a Switzerland-based organization that is an innovator in the field of Distributed Ledger Technology (DLT). The mission of the company is to use blockchain technology to manage payments and risk

Dynamics

Dynamics is London based organization with a focus on unemployment insurance and is a peer and Ethereum blockchain-based insurance company.

Lemonade

It is a New York-based organization that provides insurance to renters through AI and Distributed Ledger Technology. Smart contracts are used to offer policy by Lemonade. The business model of the company is to take a fixed fee monthly and allocate the rest towards future claims.

Fizzy

It is France based organization and provides insurance tools for flight delays. Fizzy by using blockchain technologies compensate members whose flight is delayed by two hours. Smart contracts are used to define the payment terms and for policy information. To avail of the services, the customer needs to enter data regarding their flight details, policy coverage, and need to make payments accordingly. By Blockchain technologies, Fizzy will verify flight delay data and compensate customers.

Teambrella
Teambrella is Russia based insurance platform where a team co-insures claims.

11.5 How Blockchain Technologies Work in Insurance Companies

Blockchain technology is a network of blocks that eliminates the need for middlemen or third parties. It centralizes data by distributing it in blocks to all network participants. The blockchain website is open to all participants and is not owned by anyone. Blockchain is a technology that provides proper protection and management of shared data and ledgers. Without a central authority, transactions are verified and stored on the network. Blockchains are either public or private networks. The public network is opened for all and private network permission is sought. Figure 11.1 explains the step-wise working of Blockchain application in insurance industry.

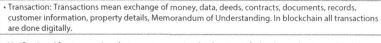

Step 1 • Transaction: Transactions mean exchange of money, data, deeds, contracts, documents, records, customer information, property details, Memorandum of Understanding. In blockchain all transactions are done digitally.

Step 2 • Verification: After transactions between two parties the data is verified online either immediately or is kept in queue for future verifications. Verification will depend upon the network used. The nodes that are computers or computer servers will verify data depending upon past history or record submitted and will determine suitability of data.

Step 3 • Structures: Using algorithm approved by the network, a 256 bit of number called hash is created by which every block is identified. A block contains a group of transactions determine by the header, a reference to the previous block's hash. A secure and interdependent chain is created through these hashes.

Step 4 • Validation : After validation the blocks are added to the blockchain. Proof of work for open source blockchain is most accepted way of validation for open-source.

Step 5 • Blockchain Mining: Appropriate level of computing knowledge is used by Miners to "solve" the block by incremental technologies to the variables for satisfied network-wide target. This is also named as "proof of work" because right answers cannot be falsified.

Step 6 • Built-in defense: The hashes function of the block followed by others block will change if a malevolent miner submits an altered block to the chain. These changes will be detected by the others nodes and new block will be blocked and corruption will be stopped.

step 7 • The Chain: After validating the block by miners, the block is distributed through the network to form the chain by the nodes which is secured and protected.

Figure 11.1 Working of blockchain technology. Source: Author's compilation.

11.6 Challenges Posed by Blockchain

11.6.1 Technologies Leveraging Technologies

To apprehend blockchain's full potential a need for leveraging other technologies is required. Full potential can be realized by using artificial intelligence and Business analytics, technologies related to the Internet of things. The insurance business can be transformed by using these technologies and by collaborating with all the stakeholders [26].

11.6.2 Strategic Alliances

Strategic alliances or Cartels need to be created to fully utilize the potential offered by blockchain technologies. The companies should collaborate along with the consumers to create repositories of data for their commercial interests.

11.6.3 New Product Development

To create a next-generation product for the Z cohorts insurance companies need to develop new strategies and need to done experimentation to develop products and services with the help of customers and leverage blockchain technology [27].

11.7 Conclusion

Blockchain is a step-by-step innovation that can help to reduce the role of intermediaries and allow consumers to conduct transactions in a straight line without them. Customers gain direct market benefits as a result of this technology. By improving business trust, data privacy, and transparency, technology creates a new way of doing business. The technology can help combat the all-too-common problem of click fraud. As a result, blockchain technology is transforming the marketing landscape for businesses, consumers, and other stakeholders involved in the value creation and delivery process. The growing popularity of blockchain technology has far-reaching implications not only for consumers but also for the insurance industry's value proposition. Subrogation, intercompany claims, the removal of duplicate data, up-to-date information, and data that is accurate and accessible at all times will all benefit from the use of blockchain in the insurance industry [28].

With a permanent establishment of straightforwardness and mutual perspective, blockchain revolutionizes the trust that powers protection. Smart contracts on the blockchain can be used in a variety of scenarios [29]. They can be used to keep track of and update ownership and legal rights for parties such as intellectual property, insurance claims, and so on. Finally, incorporating blockchain technology improves an insurer's bottom line by saving money, aggregating deals, and increasing retention.

References

1. Deloitte, *Blockchain in health and life insurance*, Deloitte, US, 2018, https://www2.deloitte.com/us/en/pages/life-sciences-and-healthcare/articles/blockchain-in-insurance.html.
2. Sikarwar, R., Blockchain: A ledger for IoT-Enabled secure systems, in: *Blockchain and AI Technology in the Industrial Internet of Things*, pp. 18–31, IGI Global, Hershey , Pennsylvania, 2021.
3. Landi, H., Healthcare, tech companies are vying for a piece of back-to-work market, in: *Here's are the New Opportunities Post-COVID*, Fiercehealthcare.com, USA, 2020.
4. Smetanin, S., Ometov, A., Komarov, M., Masek, P., Koucheryavy, Y., Blockchain evaluation approaches: State-of-the-art and future perspective. *Sensors*, 20, 12, 33–58, 2020.
5. Ashby, S., *Examining moral hazard in the healthcare insurance market*, Honors College, Pace University, 2018. https://digitalcommons.pace.edu/honorscollege_theses/164.
6. Lord, S., Bankchain & itBit: Settling on the blockchain. *Modern Trader*, 16, 1–2, 2016.
7. Grima, S., Spiteri, J., Romānova, I., A steep framework analysis of the key factors impacting the use of blockchain technology in the insurance industry. *Geneva Pap. Risk Insur.-Issues Pract.*, 45, 3, 398–425, 2020.
8. Casino, F., Dasaklis, T.K., Patsakis, C., A systematic literature review of blockchain-based applications: Current status, classification and open issues. *Telemat. Inform.*, 36, 55–81, 2019.
9. Kaur, J. and Jindal, P., An impetus to swap from traditional to blockchain environment in Indian Banks. *2021 Asian Conference on Innovation in Technology (ASIANCON)*, pp. 1–8, 2021.
10. Fugelsang, J.J., *Blockchain technology for cybersecurity and data integrity: A case for mainstream adoption*, dissertation, Utica College, New York, 2019.
11. Hans, R., Zuber, H., Rizk, A., Steinmetz, R., Blockchain and smart contracts: Disruptive technologies for the insurance market, *AMCIS 2017 Proceedings*. 31, 2017. https://aisel.aisnet.org/amcis2017/eBusiness/Presentations/31

12. Novikov, S.P., Kazakov, O.D., Kulagina, N.A., Azarenko, N.Y., Blockchain and smart contracts in a decentralized health infrastructure. *IEEE International Conference Quality Management, Transport and Information Security, Information Technologies (IT&QM&IS)*, pp. 697–703, 2018.

13. Sheth, A. and Subramanian, H., Blockchain and contract theory: Modeling smart contracts using insurance markets. *Manage. Finance*, 46, 6, 803–814, 2019.

14. Trautman, L.J. and Molesky, M.J., A primer for blockchain. *UMKC L. Rev.*, 88, 239, 2019.

15. Shurbaji, N.M., Blockchain and the sustainable supply chain: Focus on the healthcare industry, scholarworks.aub.edu.lb, American University of Beirut, Lebanon, 2021.

16. idginsiderpro.com, *How blockchain is disrupting the insurance sector*, Insider Pro, United States, 2018, https://www.idginsiderpro.com/article/3301163/how-blockchain-is-isrupting-the-insurance industry-for-the-better.html, 2018.

17. Bhogaraju, S.D., Kumar, K.V.R., Anjaiah, P., Shaik, J.H., Advanced predictive analytics for control of industrial automation process, in: *Innovations in the Industrial Internet of Things (IIoT) and Smart Factory*, pp. 33–49, IGI Global, Hershey, Pennsylvania, 2021.

18. Demirkan, S., Demirkan, I., McKee, A., Blockchain technology in the future of business cyber security and accounting. *J. Manage. Anal.*, 7, 2, 189–208, 2020.

19. Lateh, N. and Rejab, S.N.M., Sharia issues about bitcoin cryptocurrency transactions, in: *Enhancing Halal Sustainability*, pp. 119–128, Springer, Singapore, 2021.

20. Grima, S., Kizilkaya, M., Sood, K., ErdemDelice, M., The perceived effectiveness of blockchain for digital operational risk resilience in the european union insurance market sector. *J. Risk Financ. Manage.*, 14, 8, 363, 2021, https://doi.org/10.3390/jrfm14080363.

21. Raikwar, M., Mazumdar, S., Ruj, S., Gupta, S.S., Chattopadhyay, A., Lam, K.Y., A blockchain framework for insurance processes. *IEEE 9th IFIP International Conference on New Technologies, Mobility and Security (NTMS)*, pp. 1–4, 2018.

22. Tarr, J.A., Distributed ledger technology, blockchain and insurance: Opportunities, risks and challenges. *Insur. Law J.*, 29, 3, 254–268, 2018.

23. Omran, Y., Henke, M., Heines, R., Hofmann, E., Blockchain-driven supply chain finance: Towards a conceptual framework from a buyer perspective, Conference: IPSERA 2017At: Budapest - Balantonfüred, pp. 1–15, 2017.

24. Salmerón-Manzano, E. and Manzano-Agugliaro, F., The role of smart contracts in sustainability: Worldwide research trends. *Sustainability*, 11, 11, 3049, 2019.

25. Crawford, M., The insurance implications of blockchain. *Risk Manage.*, 64, 2, 24, 2017.

26. Amponsah, A.A. and Weyori, B.A., Blockchain in insurance: Exploratory analysis of prospects and threats. *Int. J. Adv. Comput. Sci. Appl.*, 12, 445–466, 2021.

27. IBM, Blockchain for insurance, 2021, https://www.ibm.com/blockchain/industries/insurance.
28. Gatteschi, V., Lamberti, F., Demartini, C., Pranteda, C., Santamaría, V., Blockchain and smart contracts for insurance: Is the technology mature enough? *Future Internet*, 10, 2, 20, 2018.
29. Tasca, P., Insurance under the blockchain paradigm, in: *Business Transformation through Blockchain*, H. Treiblmaier and R. Beck (Eds.), Palgrave Macmillan, Cham, 2019.

12

How Blockchain Can Transform the Financial Services Industry

Aashima* and Birajit Mohanty

Department of Business Administration, Manipal University Jaipur, India

Abstract

This chapter describes the application of blockchain in financial sector of India. The propulsion behind this review is deciding the way to use blockchain within the financial sector and the way it fits into the Indian climate. This chapter describes the present developments of blockchain-based financial markets and related regulators. Within the first place, the areas where blockchain is most effectively utilized in the financial sector are remittances, regulations, protections, and agreements, as confirmed by local and global case reviews. Additionally, the utilization of blockchain in validation interactions is extremely important as there are different authentication techniques looking on the user owned by the Indian customer. Second, the initiative to form closed (private) registers to flee national banks is stimulating movement between banks. Third, the utilization of blockchain innovation within the financial sector requires local financial institutions to coordinate through the blockchain consortium. Fourth, buyer preferences and mechanical advances are changing. At the identical time, the demand for blockchain innovation is increasing as organizations seek to defend it as a possible breach of non-public privacy improvement. This chapter examines the challenges and potential of blockchain-based financial innovation applications in India. Blockchain has recently become popular worldwide and India has to embrace both its difficulties and its benefits. Because of its social nature, India is not quite the identical as other countries in terms of blockchain innovation. It describes these attributes to grasp the challenges and potential consequences related to blockchain innovation in India.

Corresponding author: aashima.210951003@muj.manipal.edu

Kiran Sood, Rajesh Kumar Dhanaraj, Balamurugan Balusamy and Seifedine Kadry (eds.) Blockchain Technology in Corporate Governance: Transforming Business and Industries, (253–282) © 2023 Scrivener Publishing LLC

Keywords: Blockchain, financial market, financial institutions, financial innovation technology

12.1 Introduction

Blockchain is presented as a carefully uploaded dataset [1], in which the exchange of records is recorded as complete information set in a fully automatic request without prior installation [2]. Each substitution oscillates over time, that is, as in competition with time over constant time due to the reality in which trade takes area or enters, remains completely inside, has data, and is visible to each or every partner [3]. In this way, the blockchain turns into a development assistant that cannot be changed and is guaranteed by its insurance. Blockchain is relatively useful than modern updates. Decentralization, simplicity, discoverability, reality assurance, and simple reality degree cryptography are important to the boundaries of blockchain design rules [4].

Blockchain, which is securing energy as a creative headway with the ability to change the destiny, has right presently emerged all in all new viewpoint inside side the new money business focus. In 2016, the region money-related conversation expected that blockchain may trade monetary administration through giving a stage with the accommodating aide of the use of cultivating a testament to relate customers and providers. Likewise, a blockchain has been checked on with the "last inevitable destiny of ten new advances" with the resource of the utilization of the field relationship for "without a doubt the last destiny of ten new advances". As an eventual outcome, organizations from many key states and regions have contributed impacts withinside the blockchain adventure, sponsored it, and are busy with groundbreaking present-day research for the term of the globe. Here, we can examine the basics of blockchain advancement and the manner in which it may exchange the cash related worldwide with the supportive resource of the use of working with overall coins streams, sharp trades, automated forex records, and advanced property. Along these lines, we got a kick out of the chance to offer a chart of the standard parts of this monetary significant resource using blockchain, nearby an examination of worldwide and Indian sectors. The catalyst for this piece comes from contention among Indian regulators and the fit court over the gathering of Blockchain headway through conventional cash-related channels [5].

The region contributes with the aid of spreading out the impediments to using this headway inside the Indian setting, considering the way that the techniques are taken to vanquish them. This segment correspondingly talks about the potential to emerge considering an incredible get-together of progression inside the coins associations undertaking. FinTech executions need to think about those deterrents and openings, likewise with respect to policymakers, controllers, and accomplices [6].

The remainder of the thing is spread out as follows: - the resulting segment talks generally the worldwide and Indian Blockchain settings; the third stage sees application models in each the worldwide and Indian settings; the fourth piece evaluates the difficulties that this new progression styles for India; and the fifth portion breaks down the control measures taken to deal with the issues that exist. The sixth piece covers the probabilities that Blockchain improvement can oblige the Indian financial structure and select associates, all the while as the last stage closes.

12.2   Literature Review

12.2.1   Basic Definition

A blockchain is a circumnavigated record structure in which all people from the affiliation substitute bits of knowledge between the get-togethers. this is, blockchain is a passed-on bit of knowledge set that video show units a reliably creating outline of records estimations which can be impervious to change of state and change, even though the records shop's middle focuses' and bosses. The progression of series exchanges that occurred for 10 min is known as a square, and it's tolerably named a blockchain wherein the squares are progressively related to the affirmation of exchanged records. The blockchain is a public report of all Bitcoin exchanges that have taken region so far on continuous sales and it's far open to all sponsors of the affiliation. All people in the organization join, support, and document correspondences to make the certain commitment for exchange estimations without being told with the aid of a "trusted in external birthday celebration" (TTP), far-reaching money related assembling or a legitimate workplace. it is moreover an amazingly included improvement as it resuscitates the whole course of action of records while some other trade happens. The blockchain can't be changed or hacked until a base portion of individuals are synchronized by using recording the nuances of establishment exercises at the not shocking record [7, 8].

While used in mix with public key computations, hash secret creating techniques, and administered structure systems, blockchain has a low-worth impact. Consequently, you can change this condition of the most outrageous fundamental united advanced book for an assigned essential peruser. Additionally, the monetary association sees crucial advantages in articulations of cost dauntlessness, security, and the board. As an eventual outcome, carrier rates should increase. Blockchain development is the most limit dangerous for the compensation in a state of harmony with View movement machine due to the truth P2P cash trades are conceivable the various events, if you get right of the segment to the net best, without partaking in a cash related association or TTP [9]. As a result of straightforwardness of trades, records are secured and we discover blocks in ramifications of adventures containing banking, wellbeing, and association. As a result, fire-up affiliations are at this point successfully filling in the space of colonization, portions and advances, banks, insurances, and adventures, similarly as impeding locking contributions [2].

12.2.2 Blockchain and the Financial Sector

Current progressed charge systems rely upon reliable and material untouchables to manage prosperity portions. The impetus for decreasing those brilliance movement costs has incited banks that start to be given sales on each other. This improvement has made it more supportive of the commercialist since monetary patrons would now have the option to record notes from various banks immediately on their very own financial foundation by means of disposing of the issue from changing foldable silver into gold to move cash. The allure of the see of an extraordinary bank, simultaneously, the bank of the Recipient works with the aid of one more drawback inside, which has been introduced to the bank of payers till the colonization of gold can be reached. While the affirmation of the word changed into bound to a little measure of banks, this can be correspondingly overseen. As the measure of banks inside the contraption has created, interbank bills have to wind up being extra hard, fostering banks' rousing power to assemble an all the more exorbitant machine. Latest advances have occurred inside the methodology of mechanized documents which consolidate Bitcoin, which facilitate new financial structures with dispersed portion frameworks. Despite the way that the financial characteristics of electronic money-related guidelines have gotten beast premium, the huge computerized book flowed, which goes through its charge developments may be an imperative turn of events. Most cash-related resources exist today as rigidly virtual records, comparative as the coins request as financial association stores. This clears the path for the books allotted to essentially substitute the monetary structure. The advanced book allocated, that is finished as Blockchain, is separated into shut and private gendarmes, on the explanation of cutoff points of collaboration and obligation regarding. it is accessible to all in the event that it isn't assent. Allowable is a development wherein the best real individuals will secure. inside the financial area, we have a liking to apply a gigantic shut scattered advanced book, which limits the bits of knowledge. in view of the possibility of cash, while unflinching quality, harmony, and viability are requirements, Blockchain guide Port shut allotted books with best sharing gathering of workers individuals are embraced. The shut kind joins an understanding strategy that ensures the authenticity of the trade, which permits a little measure of explicit social occasions to participate in opening issues. Regardless, it is generally highlighting and mechanical standardization. by virtue of the inadequacy of new preferred methods in view of creative movement, the open sort is difficult to normalize, even as the shut kind is not difficult to simply recognize and fix specific standards between individuals. In addition, this sort is good for efficiency and independence. The open kind enjoys the benefit of done having power or dependence precise to the consideration of the business, yet the viability structure is decay inside the concordance structure similar to the shut shape [10]. Thirdly, inside the occasion of a shut sort, the affiliation's improvement can be changed. An open sort can't trade the trades recorded inside the structure application and may most effortlessly be changed through opposite plan while a shut kind can be changed with the aide of shared consent. In such a way, the financial area uses a gigantic circled advanced book shut [11].

12.2.3 Previous Research – International Perspective

Blockchain is at this point considered in different fields. As demonstrated [12] to oversee grouped prosperity risks, we give a by and large amazing reasonable and calm lattice check technique that uses a blockchain, which may be a key bitcoin advancement and test your convenience to show the additional substances of an astonishing organization structure. According to the HWA demand [13], while making a beeline for present excepting age, the current day bound together authoritative framework ought to be updated to be prepared to endeavor a scattered explanation machine. Further, there may be a tremendous extent of prison burdens close by the space of limit of considerable arrangement, the basics of the criminal intervention of the restricted power or the average organization of the Convention and Blockchain. By virtue of financial establishments, it's far possibly to introduce a blockchain age inside the kind of a business or a non-public blockchain considering the way that there's a cutoff to introduce a public square. Unsurprising with the Liquor Pilkington research [14], it gives key contemplations inside the center of Blockchain and highlighted the possible risks and downsides of public apportioned streams, achieving a distinction in cross variety answers. It tracked down the most decentralized possibilities of the general populace stage.

12.2.4   Previous Research – Indian Context

To fathom the issues and possible results of Blockchain's period in India, the Indian setting concerned ought to at first be seen. The most customary data on Blockchain relies totally upon all veritable challenges that are followed through the execution of the age in present systems. As a result, there's a tremendous substitute in the subject of exercises, which has emerged as phenomenally ate up the use of the encryption procedure [15]. As a result of the truth, the globe propels, and then the work culture and business openings [16]. The principle that creates and changes with the movement of time perseveres through the advancement. The utility of Blockchain's experience on the Indian market, which goes through reformist change, is similar. Disregarding the way that it's been creating since the Nineties, he displayed at the tip of Cryptocurrency Frenesi. A blockchain stage is subordinate in everyday encryption framework. The affirmation of Bitcoin has spread seeing around this age. The data on Blockchain spread as a fireplace in the business community and the present moment are taken by gigantic overall get-togethers. The most a hit typical for Blockchain is that it applies to a tremendous extent of spaces, expressly in Fintech, and the trading of Cryptophones [15] isn't by and large limited.

The proactive measures followed by means of the cash-related foundation, the financial association subject, the financial establishment supervisor of the Asian state RBI – significant money-related foundation – can help with explaining the solid side interest of India inside the discouraging square usages of FintechBased. The execution made somewhere near seven assessments on Blockchain and its administered utility of gigantic advanced book age (DLT) for a decentralized and without cash banking structure given that 2017 [17]. Whatever the time it has brought RBI to separate the issues preceding accepting the blockading of the square in its monetary gadget, the high court has allowed Indian banks to push the Indian banks as soon as possible [13]. Many state governments have referenced the gathering of this advanced and state of the art development. The Mysore government, for example, is chipping away at a blockchain control structure and the country has the focus of the Greatness for Blockchain age [18].

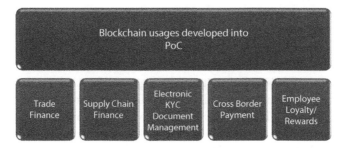

Figure 12.1 Blockchain experiment – Indian scenario [19].

Further, the Telangana government intends to use Blockchain to focus on the experts' homes and unmistakable government information the board structures [13].

Figure 12.1 shows Blockchain customers made in Bharat as an affirmation of the suspected. Change Money, store network financing, EKYC (electronic – understanding your Customer) archive the leaders, moveline bills, and workers' dedication or prizes are models thereof.

Adoption and use of Blockchain technology in the Indian context present significant obstacles as well as opportunities.

12.3 Application Example of Financial Sector Based on Blockchain

12.3.1 International Market

12.3.1.1 Consortium

The cash-related industry requires a proactive reaction to the rot inside the turnover of the customer and the financial beneficiary cost of the improvement of online development. This requires the cash-related endeavor that presents its functioning stage through sensible imaginative qualities. Make a powerful business stage or association guidance has these days emerged as a central limit in picking undertaking drives. As a result, affiliation has been shaped to make and assemble a standard stage fueled through specific cargoes in overall social orders and immense banks. The cash-related industry, which ought to be the best immediately affected, is too imaginative manifestations to change over non-plant interconnections, accepting squares before time, encouraging an "R3CEV" pool (crypto, trade, and chance practices), and develop a level – Forme maintained through blockers. R3 collaborates with basic cash-related associations on the space's most prominent monetary assignment, "R3CEV". R3 is chargeable for the essential course of action of the contraption and imaginative development, while new banks are answerable for checking and making UIs that are prominent by using their APIs. 22 overall banks, close by Barclays and RBC, cooperate with a Fintech, R3 association, to make a general blockchain default stage (workspace I). The Linux Foundation, an IBM semiconductor diode, communicated the "task Hyperlighther" composed exertion undertaking. IBM is working at the standardization of Blockchain's general development taking part inside the "Hyperlighther task", which wires associations in 48 as Intel and Wells Fargo. IBM additionally hopes to place assets into the US, EU, and Asian financial business areas, similarly as related organizations, setting up the IBM Blockchain lab. according to the current situation, it predicts that, inside the destiny, as of now not handiest sponsoring, yet moreover different responsibilities alongside criminal trades, copyright and recognizing verification, might be done inside the stage blocker normalized [20]. R3 is a consortium of 22 global banks, including Barclays and RBC, are developing a standard platform based on the technology in partnership with FinTech corporation, R3. The project is called "R3CEV" (Crypto, Exchanges and Venture practice) (Table 12.1).

Table 12.1 R3CEV examples [21].

Project name	Contents
Project on	As a forty and two bank Etherum have completed the good test of contract sustained by Etherum Blockchain
Project genesis	Forty Bank Platforms have completed the test only three dimensions-issuing, trade, and accounts of the closing company in the form of good contracts
Project zero	On the reason of the establishment of Blockchain Ethereum, eleven banks have completed an authentic time action to change encoded financial structures implied as ether monetary standards

12.3.1.2 Payment and Remittance

The blockchain era has extended to monetary transactions and can be used across economic structures in a similar way to fee-based systems including micro-impressions and significant pricing structures due to the intervention of some organizations, offshore money transfer services for which the customer will pay too high a graduation fee, designed to be the optimal green area of containment technology, allowing the implementation of direct human-to-human transactions without the use of financial intermediaries. In the case of paper money, they can be designed as non-public blockchains.

Ripple, a US-based payments fintech company, wants to create a utility for the worldwide paying community using Blockchain technology. This generation of global networks should be used within the framework of modern regulations and international trade markets, as well as discount offers for male or female customers. In addition, start-ups are actively developing freight services. ABRA (www.gabra.com) is a FinTech start-up developing a tradable system in which people transfer money to people around the world.

Money market is also offered for exchange. Tenx, an issuer of virtual box payment operators in Singapore, is working with Visa and MasterCard to develop an operator that allows customers to pay digitally on the MasterCard community daily. For example, if a Tenx management card-holder can pay $10 at the store, they will deduct $10 in digital cash to match your account price. However, the ease of saving makes the $10 device cheaper than virtual money. Because cash-to-crypto currency transfers are fast, organization owners can't decide whether dissidents are using virtual currency cards [22].

That is, regardless of whether the authority approves the virtual currency agreement or not, the provider of the virtual currency agreement is based on the current token pricing system. Forex consumers will choose whether to transfer money from their cutting-edge account after traveling abroad or traveling, convert the money into a bank payment or top up their credit card with these offers [23].

12.3.1.3 Securities and Stock Exchanges

If the securities for trading have been integrating a blockchain, the reports will be confirmed directly when the operation is complete and, therefore, the approval is concluded mechanically. Coins, stocks, and excessive derivatives are actively listed by Blockchain's Victimization technology in the United States. In addition, Canada, Australia, and Japan are actively treating the use of Blockchain technology. The National Association of Automated Securities Concessive Citations The OMIX Group in the US plans to make the partner on the exchange of exhaustion supported by blocks to fixed companies and capitalists. Then they need Blockchain technology applied to the National Association of Automated Securities Resellers Quotes Absence of a public market, a braking market for non-public qualified investors to reduce the special marketing time of four days to ten minutes since 2015. So from 2015, they used Blockchain technology for the non-public data system market, a non-publicly qualified capitalist brake market to reduce the specific dealer time of four days to ten minutes. In December 2015, the Securities Commission also provided the authorization of "Stock" of the Company to issue public actions of net shares with a blockchain. SACHS [2] has created a virtual currency system called Blockchain Settle Corner that can be used. The Toronto and London Stock Exchange has established operational teams to implement cartridges, while the Japan Stock Exchange Group has collaborated with the Nomura Analysis and IBM Institute to perform a purchase check. The Australian's exchange characteristics have a 5% value in more-based progressed illustrative new organizations (generally $15 million) and part worked at the endeavor that Blockchain age applies to the post-picture to pay assurances trades and register with the Patent and brand Bureau.

12.3.1.4   Smart Contracts

When the conditions and content of the exchanges are recorded, the important laws and approaches are consistently applied, and the outcomes are conveyed to the gatherings to the exchange, shrewd agreements work for bunch lawful agreement exercises will be performed. What's more, money replacement? Resident agreements are intended to change physical and substantial exchanges and decrease the expense of institutional movement contrasted with current exchange types. Organizations all throughout the planet Love Microsoft and IBM are both captivated by the utilization of blockchain-based stages and are attempting to consolidate and advertise their particular affiliates. Specifically, Microsoft is collaborating with Consensus, a start-up gaining practical experience in the Ethereum age, in a promoting effort for a "keen improvement work" that precisely executes exchanges when it experiences issues in login circumstance. A ton of exertion is made to just execute delicate agreements. Ethereum can be a blockchain stage planned essentially for shrewd agreements. In the keen agreement industry, there are instances of music circulation, cover contracts, intimate relationships, and improved on network bundles upheld through the Ethereum stage.

12.3.2   Indian Market

12.3.2.1   Consortium

The Concern Bank, State Bank of India (SBI), the largest public sector bank of India, as well as ICICI Bank, Kotak Mahindra, Axis Bank, and others, formed a replacement company known under the Banks name Blockchain Indian infrastructure. (IBBIC) that will be at the bar of this transformation. The incorporation of IBBIC is surprisingly similar to that of the National Payments Corporation of the Republic of India (NPCI), which is an umbrella organization that deals with important properties from the period, including RuPay, UPI, and Fastag [17].

It was founded in 2008 with only ten banks as initial investors. While banks have left out their ambitions and collaborated on an unprecedented scale, the cooperative model received widespread recognition. Banks have a unified front again with the use of Blockchain. And because of the commercial advantages, any bank can have an object to consider. Nobody wins if they are trying to be born.

Eleven of the fifteen banks are controlled by investors, while four are administered by the government.

Bank HDFC, Bank ICICI, Kotak Mahindra Bank, Axis Bank, Indusind Bank, Affirmative Bank, RBB Bank, Bank IDFC, South Indian Bank, and Federal Bank are among the personal banks. Bank of Baroda, SBI, Geographical Banking, Region, and Indian Bank are among the public sector institutions. The only participant abroad of the consortium is Yankee's customer loan [24].

The reaction is made conceivable by the support of Finacle from Infosys, a financial stage that empowers the digitization and robotization of corporate financing strategies. SBI Bank and AXIS followed or steered the limited scale creation, yet business participation could be the key factor. This is regularly best for the burden of utilizing purchaser confirmation procedures for each bank that customers hope to haggle with crafty banks, as they as of now have the buyer check strategy in a monetary foundation. Buyer Diligence that is CDD is a framework that recognizes real client names, exchanges, contact subtleties and reasons for money related exchanges so financial items and administrations given by the business bunch don't seem, by all accounts, to be utilized reliably for exercises, for example, teeth brightening. What's more, expanded risk that is EDD alludes to the character of the client or the danger of extreme tax evasion, recognizing the acquirer as a real part, just as extra records, as the driver of the exchange and, subsequently, gives the exchange balance, clients need to enroll each exchanging organization (counting top managerial staff) in the perceived confirmation framework and each exchange association that requirements to store and deal with an approved endorsement [5, 24].

The Blockchain confirmation that every business advances isn't in every case adroitly extraordinary from the approved certificate plot. Nonetheless, once dispatched, it is exceptionally valuable as it is frequently utilized by partnered establishments and financial offices without the need to get to each different money related organization. Despite the fact that it is demonstrated through Blockchain, improving and bringing foundation into the monetary zone is a curiously enormous exchange the monetary area. This has carried more noteworthy comfort and security to clients utilizing the money, just as developing resistance in the cash markets.

12.3.2.2   Payment and Remittance

India, the largest receiver in the cross-border maritime transport sector, will considerably benefit from the use of Blockchain technology. A disadvantage of the current payment system is that there is an inverse relationship between the dimensions of the transfer and therefore the fees charged due to "economies of scale". While the Blockchain does not distinguish the group's action sizes, the low value of transactions can allow a new population to engage in the arena of cross-border payments. Because of its low cost and rapid nature, a large part of the population still depends on an occasional or diversified shipping system known as "Hawala" in Hindi. This facilitates local and international money transfers. The informal and appropriate nature of this system makes it difficult to estimate its precise value; however, there are reports that consider between $100 and $200 billion (Domestic and international). Even formalize part of this amount will benefit banks and voters; this will also serve as the last word on this technology [25]. It is assessment of remittance fee. It is concluded from the graph that small remittance transfers are very costly due to fee pricing policies of most money transfer operators. Remittance fees were compared for Western Union (the global price leader), Moneygram, Vigo and Dolex (Figure 12.2).

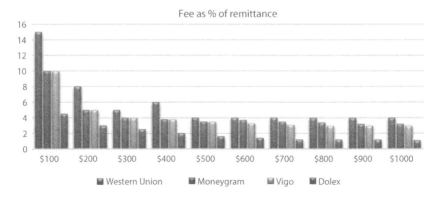

Figure 12.2 Size of remittance. Source: World Bank [26].

Depending on the Ripple, the main blocks-blockchain network in the banking sector, the installation of its blocking block network will reduce global payment prices to 42–60%. In 2016, the India registration payments market is worth $ 62.7 billion. Blockchain can help Indian banks save approximately US $80 million a year, reducing the world cost of the world and the volume of payments. This may be a significant impetus to the already sick banking sector. The fresh internal transfer of transfers, which has even been early on the market, will be an additional advantage. After Bitcoin, there are many startups in India with crypto codes such as Unocin in 2013 and ZebPay in 2014. However, the volatility of Bitcoin prices, as well as cases of fraud, provided regulatory concerns before the risk of encryption currencies. The Indian Government and the Bank stated that they do not need to authorize or issue regulations to an entity to traumatize encryption currencies and, as a result, persons have no legal protection when they are Treat encryption currencies and should support all risks associated with this. In fact, the reserve bank has published a series of news statements (December 24, 2013, February 1, 2017, December 5, 2017) as a caution to treat crypto parts [5, 27].

Feeling the growing risks placed by speculative negotiation in encryption currencies and the search for national applicants and monetary institutions, the banking company has prohibited its regulated entities in order to provide services to companies dealing with encryption currencies or encryption of Virtual pieces in April 2018 (VCS).

The authorities, on the other hand, have recognized the value of Blockchain and DLT (Table 12.2).

Inside the delicate of this current, it's far fundamental that Asian social affairs regard the normal benefits and dangers related with the DLT to do the advantages of mechanized advancement.

In late years, the DLT and using Blockchain in India have brought both up in the non-public and individual regions, notwithstanding how most drives are in any case to be sure, individual quarter zone expedient changes into an essential advocate of deterring answers. several nation governments, close by Andhra Pradesh and Telangana, have begun to execute hindered answers in regions including property enlistment, virtual accreditations, electronic health estimations, and so on (experts of Andhra Pradesh, September 2018). Banking and money-related organizations are the quarter pioneers inside the execution of blocking answers. those endeavors join: presenting the Execution of the bank affirmed of money related records in Blockchain (yes money related foundation, July 2019); Pivot money related establishment appearance of the overall worth carrier the use of Wave's Blockchain period [2]; and HSBC India and Dependence Enterprises organization strolling the improvement of the Square substitute financing affiliation (HSBC India and Dependence Businesses, July 2017). (HSBC India, November 2018) [5].

Table 12.2 Major developments related to DLT in India [28].

Report	Released	Select takeaways related to DLT and Blockchain
White Paper: Applications of Blockchain Technology to Banking and Financial Sector in India, IDBRT.	January 2017	To explore the feasibility of blockchain technology in the banking and financial sector, PoC of two use cases was developed: Domestic Trade Finance with a sight Letter of Credit and Enhanced Information Payments.
RBI Inter-Regulatory Working Group on FinTech and Digital Banking (Chairman: Sudarshan Sen).	February 2018	"There is a need to develop a deeper understanding of various FinTech products and their interaction with the financial sector and thereby their implications on the financial system, before actively regulating this space."
Finance Minister's speech in Budget 2018–19.	February 2018	"The Government will explore the use of blockchain technology proactively for ushering in the digital economy."
Blueprint of Blockchain Platform for Banking Sector and beyond, IDBRT.	January 2019	The record discusses the best way to deal with manufacture a significant blockchain that can fill in as a phase to dispatch varied bundles.
Report of the Committee to propose specific actions to be taken in relation to Virtual Currencies (Chairman: Subhash Chandra Garg).	July 2019	"The Committee recommends that the RBI examine the utility of using DLT based systems for enabling faster and more secure payment infrastructure, especially for cross-border payments."

(Continued)

Table 12.2 Major developments related to DLT in India [28]. (*Continued*)

Report	Released	Select takeaways related to DLT and Blockchain
Report of the Steering Committee on FinTech Related Issues (Chairman: Subhash Chandra Garg).	September 2019	In the context of public sector blockchain-based trade finance, "the Committee accordingly recommends that the Ministry of MSME should work with DFS and RBI for testing and implementing blockchain solutions in trade finance for MSMEs in public sector banks as well."
Enabling Framework for Regulatory Sandbox, RBI.	August 2019	Innovative products/technologies such as smart contracts and applications under Blockchain technology could be considered for testing under the regulatory sandbox cohorts. RBI invited applications with the theme of 'Retail Payments' in its first cohort of Regulatory Sandbox on November 04, 2019.

This table is as it is adapted from the RBI Bulletin (available in Public domain).
Source: RBI Bulletin (https://m.rbi.org.in/scripts/BS_ViewBulletin.aspx?Id=18766)

Blockchain is used by startups to create solutions in various fields, including healthcare, retail, government services, and human resources. It is estimated that the risk capital investment of basic blocks in India is estimated at about US $8.5 million. However, according to research, in relation to the overall increase in venture capital investments in blocked start-ups, Indian startups are only to guarantee only 0.2% of these investments. Thanks to its new regulatory-sand bac environment, the Indian reserve bank has been proactive to provide advice for the development of blocking applications. Startups and financial institutions using block-based applications will be wrapped within the limits of the regulatory sandbox to test your merchandise for a period of time.

Recently, the specialists of the Republic of India have proposed a few measures inside the Union 2020–21 spending plan, focused on the new monetary framework and arising innovation, which incorporates engineered insight, device acquiring information on, the web. things, and so on Proposed inclusion pointed toward correcting the individual zone to make essential ability parks all through the nation and relegated 6,000 major numbers for creating grass root-developing effects, connecting 100,000-gram panchayats underneath the BharatNet application. What's more, 8,000 Crores of five-year time frames for the errand on quantum innovation and projects. Moreover, it was proposed to defer the charge of the duty in shares conceded by the new businesses to their staff under the laborers' alternative plans (ESOP). As an outcome, these guidelines may offer present not best new ways for new companies to create and thrive, but they likewise produce new subsidizing and business openings. since the prohibitive environmental factors around DLT and Blockchain innovation develops with the establishment of prohibitive Sandbox, a major assortment of new businesses and speculations are normal inside what's to come.

12.3.2.3 Securities Exchanges

With stock exchanges around the world, increasingly dependent on intrinsic blocking capabilities, the market transaction foundation, the Indian Securities Council (SEBI) studies how Blockchain's technology is used on the Indian stock market.

SEBI has created an advisory body, known as the Financial and Restrictive Committee (CCRT), to seek the platform of Blockchain and other technologies that make waves in the areas of the subscription, the control of the quality, and settlement after dissemination. Blockchain has a huge potential for tracking securities, repos, and margin financing, and risk monitoring in general. SEBI takes preliminary measures to find out how technology is used in global markets and benefits will probably be progressively completed.

The National Scholarship (NSE) investigated the use of Blockchain for its "knowledge of your client's mechanism" (KYC) in collaboration with several Asian national banks, as well as a pilot to evoke blocks of victimization. The National Exchange of India (NSE), ICICI Bank, IDFC Bank, Kotak Mahindra Bank, Indusind Bank, and RBL Bank have all been tested, such as HDFC titles, a Mumbai based dealer. Elementary, a Blockchain company, provided that testing technology [4].

The test, the first stage of which was completed in January, is the most recent and possibly more critical for India's financial home to date. In

2016, various institutions throughout the country knew the Blockchain. In recent weeks, several Indian financial institutions have begun to study the business of use and develop their applications. According to previous reports, NSE Survey was conducted on a technical school since September.

The check focused on a typical plan wherein the other would offer purchaser experiences prepared, allowing the banks - and all regulators having a window at the stage - to look at those estimations constantly. NSE isn't by and large the vitally stock trade around the field with Blockchain. From big apple to Abu Dhabi, awards are experiencing a spread of usage cases, which rouses exceptionally. As per a current utilization of the country-wide relationship of mechanized assurances partners, the change chairman inspects a way for the ability of the guardian to explore the particular labor force. Figuratively speaking, the starter in India gives a framework of ways these associations need to put the age to apply. As per wellsprings, people concerned hung out taking a gander at the strong gadget in assessing the check. Arranging the sound system conveyed an attack all alone blockchain. The most outrageous huge one, the undertakings made through the social affairs mirror the fundamental period of what will be fate evaluations of the KYC answer. The following region will procure certifiable purchaser's information – a fundamental development sooner than any tolerably Real World application.

12.3.2.4   Smart Contracts

Before diving into the current state of things in India with regard to sensitive contracts, it is important to note that the acceptance of the blockchain as a form of technology and sensitive contracts as a game of their applications are two things that is fully distinct. If a country has a favorable attitude towards blocking technology, it does not imply automatically that accepts sensitive contracts with open arms. With the exception of a general plan, unspecified sensitive contracts in any of the Bharat legislation, even with the exception of a general plan extracted from one in all unloaded notifications of the administrative telecommunications unit of the India (TRAI) in 2018. India, as a growing country, has recognized the promise of Blockchain technology. Rather, a series of government institutions began adopting "BlockChain" as part of their research and development initiatives. For reference some of them are cited below:

- National Policy on Software Products (2019) is adopted by Ministry of Electronics and Information Technology.

- TRAI ACT, 1997 – In exercise of powers conferred by section 36 and section 11 of the Telecom Regulatory Authority of India Act 1997 – adopted by Telecom Regulatory Authority of India.
- Integrate to Innovate Programme for energy Start-ups- adopted by Press Information Bureau (Govt. of India) working under the Ministry of Commerce And Industry.
- Enabling Framework for Regulatory Sandbox- adopted by Department of Banking Regulation, Banking Policy Division working under the Reserve Bank of India.
- Coffee Board Activates Blockchain-Based Marketplace in India- again adopted by Press Information Bureau working under the Ministry of Commerce and Industry.

Source: Mondaq.com

This information is adapted from Mondaq.com [29].

In addition to the above-mentioned programs, there are some cases that recognize the relevance of blocker block technology, remaining a little unrelated to the patenting idea. A legal petition of the document for the registration of a patent has been filed and granted in the judicial system of the city center. The patent claim has already been refused by the patent authorities, on the basis of the category of elements that did not consider inventive. According to Article 3 (k) of the Patent Act of 1970, a parcel is not patented and in itself, and Blockchain can be software. As a result, this petition indicates that only because an invention is a small package does not imply that it is not patentable on the surface. Instead, in the modern age of technology, when our daily functions are assisted by software progress over time, it is highly conventional and harmful to ignore technological advances, such as blockchain, artificial intelligence, etc.

Statutory Dichotomy
The Indian Contract Act, 1872
A Review of Smart Contracts
Valid Agreements meet the whole of the principles depicted in segment 10 of the Contract Act. As a result, similar to significant arrangements, they may be exact and real arrangements underneath the Indian understanding mentioned in the abovementioned Act of 1872.

Information Technology Act, 2000
Examination of Importance
As some time back communicated sensitive arrangements, they use encryption inside the wide-base colossal computerized book. Virtual imprints

are in like manner utilized in adroit arrangements for calm approval and defended get admission to. The simplest inspiration driving difficulty is that mechanized imprints used Blockchain's age don't give off an impression of being an affirmed sort under the RTI ACT, 2000. Auto produce virtual imprints are used in preventing advancement. this recommends that delicate arrangements complete these arrangements accomplice records, information or forces, information required for the booklet of imprints, however, do now not seem like approved under the manage differentiation. The effect is 0 and void.

2018 RBI Notification
Assessment with Respect to Contracts
Real and a real thought is fundamental for every consent to be considered generous. Regardless of reasonable arrangements, if you offer help or market it a thing, you depend on a bring portion back. One of the best huge components of clever arrangements is that it permits in brief charge inside the world looking like encryption Forex. Advanced money is a kind of modernized new money. Events substitute their expression for Crypto new money and store it in an assented to game plan account. The portion is thus supported through this settlement understanding stayed in contact with the beneficiary's record when it gets the aftereffects of the assistance bought or getting the carrier outfitted.

As a result, the announcement of the Reserve Bank of India leaves cautious contracts. The Reserve Bank of India did not indicate its position on the money of cryptography is a valid form of the currency or not. Even after two years, provided this opinion, no status is planned to adjust this position.

Countries like Switzerland recognize the money for encryption and the legislation adopted to remedy it. Intelligent contracts and Blockchain are now recognized by the new state laws in the United States. As a result, it is time to clarify its position in blocking contracts and valid intelligent contracts [30].

12.4   Challenges in India

As Blockchain is at this point in its starting periods of gathering, there are many mentioning conditions. It'd be dangerous to set up your request and predict your significance for reflected picture time. Different updates should consistently be finished to make it secure and pleasant. regardless of the exceptionally limit possible destiny of blockading period and its uses, unanswered issues continue to be, which makes the squares a dangerous undertaking to perform. Blockchain is at the same development considering the way that the web during the 90s. all through its show, the net had the same and hesitant requests and faltering as a shutting off period. Regardless, as the years advanced, this development has preferred and ought to over get it done inside the future [1, 5, 8, 27, 31, 32].

The truth that Blockchain has gotten more vital interest than ordinary has achieved strange expectations old enough. The inadequacy of authoritative and closeness specifics is of the best fundamental cutoff points to the public gathering of upsetting advancement. The general composing charges an expansion of limitations to the gathering of squares at the level of society at some stage in the association esteem chain (not bound to monetary time), which might be divided into various predominant classes. for instance, creative (for example, mechanical fixation and the domain, power usage, the deficit of relevant developments), the social (for example, the cutoff use of a few characters, stresses of the security), legislative issues, and incorporation (as an event, loss of countrywide rules, rules, and responsibility), monetary (for example, colossal basic theories, intra-definitive cost), intraourized, nonattendance of collaboration of buying and selling associates, bothers and mixed up presumptions in joint exertion and shape sharing [33].

To this point, various individuals in Bharat are far-fetched in looking at principles, which can make combining the squares with an especially unusual considering and the suffering of separation with the truth. To regulate this age, you should have uncommon limits including guidance in programming vernaculars containing Java, C ++, and Python, a most significant understanding of money-related organizations and charge structures, regardless of information of the ability [6]. The opportunity of essential real factors and information evaluation reflects reality that the craving of Indian culture for Blockchain's period stays uncertain. As a result, the association, generally speaking, regardless of the subject matter experts, needs to discover explicit execution issues before the liberal gathering of blocking period. To take on this age, the subsequent advances ought to be taken: restrictions prepared, optional rules, redesigning the commitments of monetary foundations, and the improvement of the suitable money-related structure [34].

Blockchain has a significant assurance in India's money related organizations works out, particularly in banking and consideration organizations. cutoff of the progression made at this stage have been developed through facilitated exertion and association among the essential Fimators in Fintech, which fuses monetary establishments, startup new organizations, and advancement associations. In like manner, a few huge non-financial affiliations are dynamically arranged to apply squares to improve and overhaul the power and execution of their standard endeavor errands [40].

A few organizations and Indian get-togethers have successfully attempted Blockchain RealWorld programs in overall endeavor esteem range, worldwide bills, accounting, pass on chain financing, dependability programming the chiefs and unmistakable verification change progressed and affirmation [36]. Further, a few Indian cash-related establishments like banks and somewhere near one stock exchange lead to combining a square of squares into their snazzy product and errands. The fundamental objective of a lot of these first adopters is to see the capacity of the square as a strategy for updating adequacy, execution, and incorporation through progression in things, commitments, and methods. In any case, the course of these drives has been overflowing with deterrents, including the pressing limitations which are early in articulations of the summarized gathering of Blockchain. a couple of huge issues involve an inadequacy of records and information among accomplices, "amazingly convenient to screen the possibility of Blockchain's imaginative new development, and as such mentioning conditions related to utilitarian and social coordination among endeavors and unprejudiced get-togethers.

Indeed, even anyway the use of Blockchain time joins traction at the business stage, the monetary foundation and overseer i.e. RBI – the experts' fundamentally money related commitments – keep a careful eye early [37]. In mid-2016, the RBI period evaluation Arm, the Organization for development and studies in Financial age (IDRBT), moved forward and winded up being comfortable with the congruity of Blockchain to Indian monetary managing and financial.

The establishment composed a studio wherein accomplices from all circles including instructors, financial backers, regulators, and related time associates have the choice to achieve an all-out data on schedule, openings, and challenges, and over the long haul the 'impact of the execution of the undertaking. Social unit individuals consolidate specialists from all significant banks inside the same. Likewise, cooperated affiliations (FINTECH future 2017) [26]. Studio individuals added to the methodology of a white paper, which covers the norms of Blockchain's advancement, in any case, the rule gives that include it and wise investigation on their overall packs and their ability districts for their gathering in India money related administrations.

The report eventually nuances various critical advantages of the usage of Blockchain, including the value and execution of time, in any case, more vital straightforwardness. Basically, with a working revenue of the countrywide worth relationship of India, Banks, Fintech startups, and age workplaces, IRDT conveyed a % on the meaning of Blockchain to the extent present-day financing [38]. Deloitte, an individual from the IDRBT running establishment, presented an audit assessment at the 2017 IDRBT gathering in Hyderabad.

This break down was made with the help of a quest for authoritative work and gatherings with the fundamental adopters of Blockchain of India and offers a thorough and thorough mastery of the possible impediments to the gathering of advancement of the attitude of a customer and mechanical assistance of a dealer [11].

As per the research, the experience to the gathering of blockchain is as frequently as workable all things considered, disconnected into three number-one levels, as described in parent three, wherein tangles are slanting closer to the fundamental stage. According to the discernments, the best basic mentioning conditions stood up to with the aid of social events at POC ranges are related to six basic activities: cognizance, the character of work undertaking and partners, picking block systems or organization vendors, the introduction of pleasing ecological components and security and blend issues [19].

Figure 12.3 describes the steps for deploying the blockchain block that will be used to mitigate these problems by making the POC.

The pre-POC stage should take between 3 and 4 months to assemble the intra-definitive mindfulness at the PC memory associations of Blockchain age expected to take on it, to set up a clear and precise endeavor technique and proper accomplices for percent, and pick each material provider and developments. The percent area can take 2–90 days by virtue of the challenges of making buying and selling associates, ensuring security and compromise,

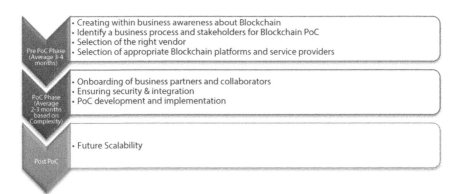

Figure 12.3 Blockchain implementation stages (*Source* Deloitte 2017) [19].

and making and approving the percentage. Further, the drawn-out term size of the defer portion through expanded term size as liked occasionally.

Each progression is fundamental for the gathering and sending of the Blockchain. In any case, inside the pre-POC enhancing section, the most epic issues all through the improvement of the POC cover the difficulties and complexities related to the gathering and going over excepting customers. On a comparative time, the shortage of uniform reasons and the unpredictability related to the current IT scene contain a first-rate check for the improvement of the percent and its complete gathering inside the destiny. Regardless, the achievement or dissatisfaction of a percent is controlled through an appropriate assurance and mix of association agents, blockchain structures, and concentrated carrier carriers [19].

Given these cutoff focuses and the results of the assessment in the account, there is a restriction of the lock at the speedy execution of the Indian monetary undertaking. In any case, the most flawlessly awesome Indian court plan raised this refusal close to the start of Walk 2020 [24]. However, Court alerts that this will uncover the Indian monetary gadget to expansive risks since everything considered cannot be prepared for the perils related to blockading trades [39]. On the day's end, this may influence every single possibility industry.

Sooner than time can be completely followed and finished, regulators, administrators, governments, and accomplices ought to be productive for the hardships they give [9].

12.5   Mitigation Steps

The main mitigation methods are methods to mitigate the problems of adopting and applying Blockchain technology experienced by companies.

Lack of Awareness
Since the Blockchain is an excellent new advancement, a shortfall of skill and records stays a key obstruction to the general gathering of Blockchain [33]. For bundles wishing to kiss Blockchain, the best region to start is to show an inside social occasion that could analyze period through and through and width, getting their specific parts and instruments, ideas, and spaces of programming inside the undertakings of the undertaking. Moreover to outrageous enchanting guidance, fitness classes, and worker hackathons, a huge gathering of workers can be dispatched off outer activities alongside planning, social events, and utilitarian interest packs for whole expertise of age [30].

Bunches need to recollect the costs of tutoring planning and ruling as an interest rather than an advantage of doing the undertaking.

Identifying the Correct Platform, Vendor, and Partner for PoC
When a use case has been dissected and picked, the accompanying essential undertaking might be to pick a fitting stage, the time carrier provider and synergistic companions or associations to play out a certified pilot examination [22].

Organizations wishing to put in power Blockchain can outline crossed associations inside their relationship, to hold guides related with affiliation discussions with pal social events or limit laborers, show a between office bunch with sensible accessory workplaces and diagram an absolute trial of endeavors with explicit benchmarks and picked execution markers.

Security Challenges in Integration and Knowledge
Its miles are essential to depict that the blend and real security of development (e.g., customer information encryption) don't achieve a chance or peril.

Throughout the Execution time, the furthest reaches of the chief adopters have as of late conveyed with a little wide arrangement of the doable item to control using Blockchain innovation.

This technique permits you to use an electric-powered sander and careful coordination of new and present times.

Indeed, even as the issues stay essential and genuine, Asian nations have shown amazing records to diminish the dangers related to the course of action of Blockchain.

12.6 Opportunities as per Indian Perspective

This piece shows the advantages and advantages given through the Blockchain period in the particular Indian climate.

Blockchain time has emerged as usable time since its decentralized capacity [37] and needs to discover programs in various areas of thought [40].

Blockchain is an incredible stage that permits a gathering of extra assets, exhaustive of following the supply of a financial affiliation movement [6]. Obstructing different alternatives, while applied precisely, verify the security and constancy of advancement. Blockchain can form land registers [41], extra records, automated records, report information [7], countrywide conspicuous confirmation, and improvement advancements of the financial and conspicuousness pack [38]. Those essentially reduce pollution and lead the standard relaxed region to a veritable economy [6]. Blockchain, related with another cutting advancement, involving produced understanding, Contraption getting to know, dominance appraisal, and robotization of robot strategies, which could assemble the sufficiency of the current day exchange business financing from India [35]. Further, as shown by Deloitte (2017) [42], the utilization of Blockchain for the control of cutting edge characters and "understanding your purchaser" (KYC) is apparently lovely encouraging.

The hour of business is an unpreventable advantage of the development that the Republic of   India can appreciate. There may be an outrageous shortfall of Blockchain producers and has been seen that grass engineers are at this point choosing on customary ways. As per the up-to-date information from Blockchain, various excessive fine reasons for living will be throughout the next decade. Immense age associations alongside IBM and the Mahindra Specialized School perform classes and studios to bring issues to the light of Blockchain [43].

Adjoining nations, including China, introduced the development of Blockchain and their undertakings closest to the truth, not prepared to ruin the spillover expectation and, consequently, the obvious premium of the gifts that this age offers, the Republic of India endeavors to consolidate the blocker into its huge limits. As India moves to analyze, Blockchain is the subsequent subject that we will center.

Foundation getting ready, banks and medications are just a portion of the organizations, which could impressively benefit from the coordination of accepting period [31]. Likewise, it is presumably going to pass on new expert freedoms for the going with time [15].

The people who stand separated various possible results in the coming years, as they could invigorate old well-known working systems [7]. As India is pushing toward a genuine inheritance famous government, the vote can be a logical field wherein shutting off age should play a game coming position inside the straightforwardness [19]. In spite of the way, that it isn't for the most part possible now, the state can use this somewhat long advancement to really look at a mindful and secure vote [6].

In disdain of well-estimated preventions arranged with the aide old enough, Blockchain offers different benefits to Indian culture and partners.

12.7   Conclusion

The utilization of Blockchain's age will all the more than probable addition the Indian monetary structure. If this new development succeeds and is completely utilized in India, it is most likely to present a state-of-the-art change in the public eye. Blockchain can supply an especially new game plan of purposes for living, allowing the domain to end up free inside the substance of a drawback of the domain [39].

Indian banks and non-affirmation money related establishments should be prepared for this new age to have a much extra ability in their ability finance ideas (for instance, the thing like the financing of progress and the expert community), at the region to be executed and composed into the overall machine [25].

Be that as it may, the utilization of faltering and astonishing age is a risk of prominent and fruitful age, without assessment and full primary impulse. System formulators need to consider mindfully; The discussions between regulators will convey an OK reaction with the aide of figuring out the acceptable time and the fine degree to solidify the blockade into India's examining economy. The early and astounding objective of difficulties should create open doors for India in Blockchain subsidizing.

This segment deals with the challenges of executing the development that ought to be settled sooner than using a state-of-the-art advancement that presents to us a lot of breaking points, yet also showing an unlimited quality of dangers. Accordingly, preceding getting into the blockchain, this segment calls for exceptional interest to restrictions.

Sooner than execution, related parts and adventures ought to be properly prepared for trade. Sensible usage of Blockchain can achieve a progressive impact on the Indian economy.

References

1. Zheng, Z., Xie, S., Dai, H., Chen, X., Wang, H., An overview of blockchain technology: Architecture, consensus, and future trends, in: *2017 IEEE International Congress on Big Data (BigData Congress)*, IEEE, pp. 557–564, 2017.
2. Ge, M. and Sachs, G., Blockchain putting theory to practice, Academia.edu, New York, USA, 2016, Accessed September 28, 2021, https://www.academia.edu/38946070/Goldman_Sachs_Blockchain_putting_theory_to_practice.
3. Nian, L.P. and Kuo Chuen, D.L., Introduction to bitcoin, in: *Handbook of Digital Currency*, pp. 5–30, Academic Press, Cambridge, Massachusetts, United States, 2015.
4. Singh, B.P., Blockchain: India is headed for a fintech revolution this year, Accessed September 28, 2021, https://economictimes.indiatimes.com/news/

economy/policy/blockchain-india-is-headed-for-a-fintech-revolution-this-year/articleshow/62478932.cms?from=mdr.

5. RBI investigates blockchain for financial applications in India, January 17, 2017, Accessed September 28, 2021, https://www.fintechfutures.com/2017/01/rbi-investigates-blockchain-for-financial-applications-in-india/.

6. Sharma, T.K., Blockchain technology in India opportunities and challenges, Blockchain Council, CA, USA, 2018, Accessed September 28, 2021, https://www.blockchain-council.org/blockchain/blockchain-technology-in-india-opportunities-and-challenges/.

7. Chepurnoy, A., Larangeira, M., Ojiganov, A., A prunable blockchain consensus protocol based on non-interactive proofs of past states retrievability, ArXiv, abs/1603.07926, 9-26, https://arxiv.org/pdf/1603.07926.pdf

8. Decker, C. and Wattenhofer, R., Information propagation in the bitcoin network, in: *IEEE P2P 2013 Proceedings*, IEEE, pp. 1–10, 2013.

9. Ali, R., Barrdear, J., Clews, R., Southgate, J., Innovations in payment technologies and the emergence of digital currencies. *Bank Engl. Q. Bull.*, 2014_Q3, pp. 262–235. https://www.bankofengland.co.uk/-/media/boe/files/quarterly-bulletin/2014/innovations-in-payment-technologies-and-the-emergence-of-digital-currencies.pdf.

10. Lewis, R., McPartland, J., Ranjan, R., Blockchain and financial market innovation. *Econ. Perspect.*, 41, 7, 1–17, 2017.

11. Antonopoulos, A.M., *Mastering bitcoin: Unlocking digital cryptocurrencies*, O'Reilly Media, Inc., Sebastopol, California, United States, 2014.

12. Manda, V.K. and Polisetty, A., https://economictimes.indiatimes.com/news/economy/policy/blockchain-india-is-headed-for-a-fintech-revolution-this-year/articleshow/62478932.cms?from=mdr, Status check on blockchain implementations in India, International Conference on Technological Innovations in Management Ecosystem, GITAM INSTITUTE OF MANAGEMENT, Vishakhapatnam, Andhra Pradesh, India, 2018, Available at SSRN 3265654.

13. Foroglou, G. and Tsilidou, A.-L., Further applications of the blockchain, in: *12th Student Conference on Managerial Science and Technology*, vol. 9, 2015, https://www.researchgate.net/publication/276304492_Further_applications_of_the_blockchain/stats.

14. Pilkington, M., *Does the fintech industry need a new risk management philosophy? A sequential blockchain-based typology for virtual currencies and e-money services in Luxembourg." A sequential blockchain-based typology for virtual currencies and e-Money services in Luxembourg*, Social Science Research Network (SSRN), Electronic Journal, USA, March 8, 2016.

15. Eyal, I. and Sirer, E.G., Majority is not enough: Bitcoin mining is vulnerable, in: *International Conference on Financial Cryptography and Data Security*, Springer, Berlin, Heidelberg, pp. 436–454, 2014.

16. Akins, B.W., Chapman, J.L., Gordon, J.M., A whole new world: Income tax considerations of the Bitcoin economy. *Pitt. Tax Rev.*, 12, 25, 2014.

17. FinTech: The force of creative disruption, Reserve Bank of India - RBI Bulletin, Mumbai, Maharashtra, India, Nov 11, 2020, Accessed September 28, 2021, https://www.rbi.org.in/Scripts/BS_ViewBulletin.aspx?Id=19899.

18. Ayed, A.B., A conceptual secure blockchain-based electronic voting system. *Int. J. Netw. Secur. Appl.*, 9, 3, 01–09, 2017.

19. Deloitte launches smart identity proof of concept, deloitte.com, London United Kingdom May, 04, 2016, Accessed September 23, 2021, https://www2.deloitte.com/uk/en/pages/press-releases/articles/deloitte-launches-smart-identity-proof-of-concept.html.

20. Pournader, M., Shi, Y., Seuring, S., Lenny Koh, S.C., Blockchain applications in supply chains, transport and logistics: A systematic review of the literature. *Int. J. Prod. Res.*, 58, 7, 2063–2081, 2020.

21. Al-Mazrouai, G. and Sudevan, S., Managing blockchain projects with agile methodology, in: *Proceedings of 6th International Conference on Big Data and Cloud Computing Challenges*, pp. 179–187, Springer, Singapore, 2020.

22. Nakamoto, S., *Bitcoin: A peer-to-peer electronic cash system*, San Jose, CA, USA, 2009, bitcoin.org/, Accessed September 28, 2021, https://bitcoin.org/bitcoin.pdf.

23. Peters, G., Panayi, E., Chapelle, A., Trends in cryptocurrencies and blockchain technologies: A monetary theory and regulation perspective. *J. Financial Perspect.*, 3, 3, pp. 3–28, 2015.

24. Morini, M., From 'Blockchain hype' to a real business case for financial markets, *Journal of Financial Transformation (JFT)*, Capco Institute, 45, 30–40, 2016, Available at SSRN 2760184.

25. Saha, A.K., Barua, S., Nath, S.D., Blockchain for financial technology: Challenges and opportunities for India, in: *The Impact of Artificial Intelligence on Governance, Economics and Finance*, vol. I, pp. 247–261, Springer, Singapore, 2021.

26. Kalan, G. and Aykut, D., Assessment of remittance fee pricing. *Background Paper Prepared for this Report*, World Bank, Washington, DC, 2005.

27. Jaag, C. and Bach, C., Blockchain technology and cryptocurrencies: Opportunities for postal financial services, in: *The changing postal and delivery sector*, pp. 205–221, Springer, Cham, 2017.

28. Distributed ledger technology, blockchain and central banks *reserve Bank of India - RBI Bulletin*. Adapted from RBI Bulletin, published on RBI website, Feb. 11, 2020. Accessed September 28, 2021. https://m.rbi.org.in/scripts/BS_ViewBulletin.aspx?Id=18766.

29. Dalmia, V.P., Blockchain and smart contracts – Indian legal status - Technology – India, Mondaq, London, United Kingdom, Feb 05, 2020, Accessed September 28, 2021, https://www.mondaq.com/india/fin-tech/889458/blockchain-and-smart-contracts-indian-legal-status.

30. Dutta, P., Choi, T.-M., Somani, S., Butala, R., Blockchain technology in supply chain operations: Applications, challenges and research opportunities. *Transp. Res. Part E: Logist. Transp. Rev.*, 142, 102067, 2020.

31. Sternberg, H.S., Hofmann, E., Roeck, D., The struggle is real: Insights from a supply chain blockchain case. *J. Bus. Logist.*, 42, 1, 71–87, 2021.

32. Kosba, A., Miller, A., Shi, E., Wen, Z., Papamanthou, C., Hawk: The blockchain model of cryptography and privacy-preserving smart contracts, in: *2016 IEEE Symposium on Security and Privacy (SP)*, pp. 839–858, 2016.

33. Omohundro, S., Cryptocurrencies, smart contracts, and artificial intelligence. *AI Matters*, 1, 2, 19–21, 2014.

34. Gogerty, N. and Zitoli, J., DeKo: An electricity-backed currency proposal. *Soc. Sci. Res. Network*, 2011. https://ssrn.com/abstract=1802166 or https://dx.doi.org/10.2139/ssrn.1802166.

35. Choudhury, M.D., NIC sets-up CoE for blockchain in karnataka to enhance citizen services, January 21, 2020, Accessed September 28, 2021, https://www.expresscomputer.in/egov-watch/nic-sets-up-coe-for-blockchain-in-karnataka-to-enhance-citizen-services/45650/.

36. Imansyah, R., Impact of internet penetration for the economic growth of Indonesia, Kyushu University, Nishi-ku Fukuoka, Japan, pp. 36–43, 2018.

37. Dixon, C., Mahajan, R., Agarwal, S., Brush, A.J., Lee, B., Saroiu, S., Bahl, P., An operating system for the home, in: *9th USENIX Symposium on Networked Systems Design and Implementation (NSDI 12)*, pp. 337–352, 2012.

38. Axon, L., Privacy-awareness in blockchain-based PKI, *CDT Technical Paper Series*, University of Oxford, Oxford, England, vol. 21, p. 15, 2015.

39. Saberi, S., Kouhizadeh, M., Sarkis, J., Shen, L., Blockchain technology and its relationships to sustainable supply chain management. *Int. J. Prod. Res.*, 57, 7, 2117–2135, 2019.

40. Karnataka to use blockchain technology for e-governance, The Hindu BusinessLine, Banglore, Karnataka, India, Jan 16, 2018, Accessed September 28, 2021, https://www.thehindubusinessline.com/news/karnataka-to-use-blockchain-technology-for-egovernance/article10035777.ece.

41. Christidis, K. and Devetsikiotis, M., Blockchains and smart contracts for the internet of things. *IEEE Access*, 4, 2292–2303, 2016.

42. Crosby, M., Pattanayak, P., Verma, S., Kalyanaraman, V., Blockchain technology: Beyond bitcoin. *Appl. Innov.*, 2, 6–10, 71, 2016.

43. Vishwanath, S., India cryptocurrency use: Is India about to miss the bus in leveraging cryptocurrency?, The Economic Times, New Delhi, India, Feb 19, 2021, Accessed September 28, 2021. https://economictimes.indiatimes.com/markets/stocks/news/is-india-about-to-miss-the-bus-in-leveraging-cryptocurrency/articleshow/81107495.cms.

13

The Impact of Blockchain Technology and COVID-19 on the Global Banking Industry

Jyoti Verma[1] and Gagandeep[2*]

[1]*Chitkara Business School, Chitkara University, Punjab, India*
[2]*DAV University, Punjab, India*

Abstract

Blockchain Technology (BCT) can be defined as a decentralized and distributed ledger that records all transactions details of any digital asset. With its unique design, data on a blockchain cannot be changed easily. This chapter provides the details of blockchain technology and its impact on banking sector. Porter's Five Forces model was employed to strengthen and summarize the findings of the research. This model critically spotlights the weak position of Indian banks with and without cryptocurrencies. Another reason for employment of this model is to provide clear insights and useful construct of understanding various threats posed to Indian banking sector. Cryptocurrencies have huge impact on the banking sector as if these currencies remain left unregulated. Indian banking sector plays a pivotal role in the economy as has significant contribution towards gross domestic product (GDP) of the country; therefore, it would be advised to keep abreast of the technologies that could significantly disrupt its operations. With the advent of this technology in banking sector, it helps to eliminate the frauds due to errors and identity theft to a large extent. Hence, the banking sector has been excited in exploring the technology and deploy it.

Keywords: Blockchain technology, distributed ledger technology, technology acceptance, technology diffusion, indian banking sector

Corresponding author: gagandeep10023@davuniversity.org

Kiran Sood, Rajesh Kumar Dhanaraj, Balamurugan Balusamy and Seifedine Kadry (eds.) Blockchain Technology in Corporate Governance: Transforming Business and Industries, (283–302) © 2023 Scrivener Publishing LLC

13.1 Introduction of Blockchain Technology (BCT)

The idea of Blockchain was introduced by Satoshi Nakamoto [1]. Blockchain technology has received a lot of attention among educators, industry experts, investors and is growing at a rapid pace around the world. Blockchain is the innovative technologies [2] that exhibits tremendous growth within a short time interval. This technology has many advantages and disadvantages. Mostly people believe that blockchain and bitcoin are same, but that's not true. In fact, Bitcoin is a digital currency that is based on this technology. Despite the skepticism, a new question arises here that whether blockchain technology will replace or revolutionize the Indian banking system? In 2008, Nakamoto introduced the first decentralized cryptocurrency [1]. This technology has enabled the creation of new digital currency, i.e., crypto-currencies and their exponential rise has been shown widely. This field is in more demand as this currency has been the key subject matter of academic and research considerations in various topics, such as security, privacy [3], monetary policy and financial regulation [4] and many more. The blockchain has also been defined as multifunction and multiusable programmable framework that has been used for controlling ownership and financial contracts [5, 6]. Blockchain Technology can be defined as a decentralized, distributed ledger [7] that records all transactions details of a digital asset.

13.1.1 Key Characteristics of Blockchain

There are many characteristics of this latest technology that makes it unique among others. The four main characteristics of Blockchain are as follows-

> ➢ Immutability: In blockchain, data storage is immutable in nature and it cannot be changed by anyone. Data is punched into the block and thereafter it is finalized/approved by every user in the network and ensure the security of transactions. Here, the users, who are validating the transaction and then add them into the block are known as Miners.
> ➢ Decentralized Control: Blockchain is based upon a decentralized mechanism i.e., there is no one who can control the network at a central level. It is also called open ledger as it is visible to everyone and maintain records of all the transactions. Each transaction should be checked/verified by a central authority (Reserve bank of India) in case of a

traditional centralized transaction system [8, 9]. But in case of Blockchain, everyone in the chain can have easy access to the databases and they can cross check the history of all previous transaction even in the absence of third party [10]. Here, the use of distributed ledgers reduces the chances of fraud as it automatically records every transaction on real-time basis [11] and it can be proven that it is quite effective in the management of blockchain technology [12, 13].

➢ Two Parties involved: Blockchain is working on peer- to -peer network mechanism. It allows only two parties in the transactions, i.e., sender and receiver and everyone in the network is themselves able to authorize the transactions. Hence, it removes the urgency of third party and thus makes the transaction fast and cheap.

➢ Privacy: Blockchain consists of a unique alphanumeric identification and it is the discretion of the users to keep it secret or not [10]. There is no third-party involvement to store users' private credentials [9]. Such mechanism preserves the privacy of users. However, this technology cannot guarantee any kind of privacy protection due to some inherent constraints.

13.1.2   Blockchain Architecture

The word 'Blockchain' has two parts:

a.   blocks, which means digital data; and
b.   chain, which shows the interconnectivity of all the digital data.

In Blockchain, number of transactions took place in each block and every transaction is recorded in the form of a Hash. Here, Hash represents a unique address/code that is assigned to each block.

A block consists of three parts:

a.   Data part: It contains the required information of the transaction incurred
b.   Hash: It represents the Unique block ID
c.   Previous Hash: It represents hash of previous block in the transaction

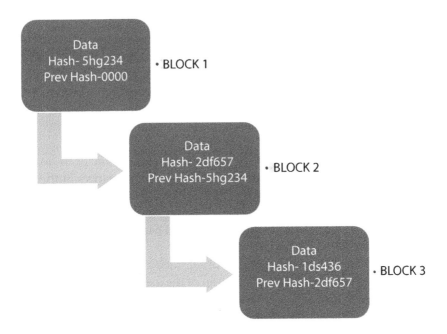

Figure 13.1 Blockchain architecture [7].

In Figure 13.1, blockchain architecture has been explained and it is shown that every block has contained hash of its own previous block; therefore, if anyone tries to do any amendments in the data in some block, then the hash of the block will be automatically changed. Eventually, users will have to change the hashes of each and every block in the blockchain which is not an easy task at all [4, 12]. Figure 13.1 represents the Architecture of Blockchain Technology.

Hence, it is believed that the data in blockchain is leakage proof and maintain its authenticity. With its unique inherent design, the data on a blockchain cannot be modified. By the use of cryptographic hashing [14] and decentralization system, the historical transaction of any digital asset become transparent and unalterable.

13.1.3   Applications of Blockchain Technology

Blockchain technology is quite popular now-a-days because it is the fundamental technology, used for cryptocurrency. Bitcoin, which is based on blockchain technology, is actually a virtual currency and is also known as first cryptocurrency. It works without central governance [14]. It has much wider scope than a digital currency. This technology can also be used in many applications and has a high potential to be explored in the financial industry. Financial technologies (FinTech) have brought a new age revolution of financial disruption and blockchain technology is playing a significant role in this transition [15]. FinTech can be defined as "products and companies that employ newly developed digital technologies in financial services industries" [12, 16] to construct financial instruments like transfers, smart contracts, and trade history, as well as minimize bad transactions and their implications [17]. Financial technologies have brought in a new age of financial disruption, with Blockchain technology playing an important role in this transition [15]. Although conventional banking products ranging from payments to investment services have existed, blockchain technology has challenged this by delivering revolutionary, more reliable, and quicker transactions at reduced costs [15]. Several large multinational financial institutions have been designing blockchain proposals since 2015. For instance, Goldman Sachs, J.P. Morgan, and other banking conglomerates have all formed blockchain labs and published a series of studies on the subject, working very closely with blockchain platforms [18]. J. P. Morgan and two global partners, Royal Bank of Canada, and Australia and New Zealand Banking Group Limited, announced the introduction of Interbank Information Network (INN), the world's first blockchain payments network. Banks that embrace emerging technologies like blockchain must be prepared to deal with the technological and operational risk, legal and regulatory risk, and reputation risk that these technologies can bring [19–21].

The blockchain technology has contributed in the latest and rapid developments in the distributed transaction technology [6]. It can be used to construct new innovations in various financial instruments like smart contracts, transfers, trade history etc. It can be utilized for any digital asset that can be transacted, distributed, stored, and even have huge potential for financial industry [4]. Even, enhanced focus on security issues and efficiency of the system can be beneficial for many sectors including banking sector. It will also help to minimize bad transactions and their implications [17]. Blockchain Technology has challenged the traditional banking (financial) products and investment services by delivering reliable, cost effective, compatible, revolutionary, and faster transactions [15]. Many financial institutions have been designing the proposals for implementation of blockchain technology since 2015. For example, J.P. Morgan, Goldman Sachs and other large multinational companies (MNCs)have formed blockchain labs and also published a number of research studies on this particular topic and they are including it in their operations too [18]. Banks that are adopting blockchain technology must be prepared themselves to handle the technological risk, operational risk, legal and regulatory risk that these technologies can bring at the time of implementation [12, 19–21]. In the report of Basel committee, the operational risk is defined as the risk of loss due to problems/defects in system's integrity and reliability. Hacking, problem of hardware or software glitch, financial disruptions, processes, protections and database breaches are the major risks identified in the banking system. Table 13.1 depicts the various blockchain applications used by Indian Players.

Table 13.1 Blockchain applications used by Indian players.

Area	Description
Trade Finance	In India, a leading banking group in Middle East and a private sector bank has successfully executed transactions in the area of international trade finance and its remittance using blockchain.
Management of e-KYC Document	This technology is explored by a leading stock market exchange in India for better understanding of management its customers and related documentation in collaboration with few leading banks in India.
Cross-border Payments	Stellar connects with the private bank ICICI Bank and offers cross-border payments in India, Africa, and Philippines Stellar has also partnered with financial institutions so as to enable low-cost global money transfer to the Philippines and cross-border payments to and from India, Europe, Kenya, Nigeria, and Ghana. Axis Bank and Kotak Mahindra Bank are jointly testing blockchain transactions with much attention on cross-border remittance and trade settlements.
Employee Loyalty/ Rewards	Deloitte India is extensively working on blockchain based employee loyalty/rewards programs.

Source: Deloitte, ASSOCHAM [22].

13.2   Blockchain Technology and the Banking Sector

Huge volumes of data are being generated on daily basis and makes the records in digital form and it has become necessary for each and every organization to better manage the security concerns. Here, Blockchain technology is capturing the full attention of all the industries, with its promising characteristics of decentralized ownership, immutability, and cryptographic security of the data. With the help of decentralized ledgers, verifying each party in transactions could be possible with accuracy [23] and it may result in real time settlement of every transaction and update the ledger. Blockchain technology has gained a lot of attention over the last years. Without using any middleman, it provides a convenient and systematic way for untrusted parties to come together to agreement on the state of a database. This technology brought revolutionary changes in many industries and has the potential to outshine in the banking industry as well. From a user's perspective, blockchains provide transparent mechanism in transaction settlement with accuracy and speed [24].

13.2.1   Impact of COVID-19 on Banking Industry

The lockdown imposed by government in order to prevent the outspread of COVID19 pandemic that has halted the economic activities across many industries. Banking sector is majorly affected but slightly in different way as these services do not rely upon direct contact with the consumers and can be easily provided on remote basis. However, there is a strong connection of this sector with the real economy as it is a provider of credit, savings, payment, and risk management services. Listed below are some negative effects of COVID-19 crisis on the banking sector.

> ➤ Bad Impact on Revenue
> Most of the firms that have stopped working missed out on revenues and thus these firms might be unable to repay loans. Likewise, customers who are having less income or lost their jobs during COVID-19 crisis might not be able to repay their loans. This has ultimately resulted in lost revenue and losses and it has negatively affected banking capital and profits also. Along with this, banks can presume more losses further that will ultimately result in the need for additional provisions and will further destabilize their profitability and position.

> ➢ Increasing Demand for Credit
> During this pandemic, the banking industry has faced huge demand for credit purchase as many firms require an additional cash inflow to meet its cost requirements in unprecedented times. It was quite a tough time for this sector to survive.
> ➢ Lost Value of Bonds and Trades
> Banks are negatively affected during the COVID-19 crisis as financial instruments have lost their values, which has automatically resulted in further losses for all banks. Also, it has faced some losses in open derivative positions where the derivative has moved in unpredicted directions due to the crisis. The market has also shown unpredictable behavior of investment patterns.

13.2.2   Impact of Blockchain Technology on Banking Sector

Due to this technology, Banking sector is facing huge risk. Following are some reasons how this technology is impacting the banking industry.

> ➢ Save Transaction Costs
> Blockchain technology is offering the facility of money transfers from one place to another with zero paperwork. No extra cost [8] incurs during transaction and this saving in transaction costs result in profits generation. Hence, this technology has the potential to enable banks to save transaction costs.
> ➢ Fraud Reduction
> Blockchain technology has the capability to protect banks against cyber-attacks and frauds on the bank databases. There is a strong need to include such technology in the system because fraudulent activities are increasing at higher rate.
> ➢ Intermediary
> Blockchain technology facilitates disintermediation, thereby reducing transaction costs. It has decentralized mechanism and no control is required by any central authority.
> ➢ Add-on Customer Base
> Current and upcoming generation customers are expected to rely heavily on technology. The current generation customers are growing in a well-equipped and tech friendly environment and they are equipped with the technology

know how. It has created a huge need for banking industry to set themselves with high standard technology so as to better handle future customers. It can only be possible if blockchain technology has been implemented in banking sector.

➤ Global Business Transactions

In order to facilitate business transactions globally in the banking sector, lots of paperwork transactions took place such as export documentation, billing, factoring, letter of credit, etc. If blockchain technology has been introduced here, then this area can become more efficient.

13.2.3   Comparison Between Blockchain-Based Banking Systems and the Traditional Banking

Table 13.2 provides a detailed comparison between blockchain based banking systems and the traditional banking (centralized) in terms of control, efficiency, cost, security, databases, integrity and transparency and customer experience, as identified from prior literature and publicly available information sources.

Table 13.2 Comparison between the blockchain-based banking systems and traditional banking.

Particulars	Blockchain-based banking	Traditional banking
Control	Blockchain technology is based upon decentralized network i.e., no central authority is required to control the network. The use of decentralized control mechanism eliminates transaction risks.	Huge amount of risks involved in case of centralized mechanism as anyone who has complete access of central level database, can easily corrupt or vanish data.
Efficiency	Decentralized peer-to-peer transmission, very low transaction cost, no intermediaries are the reasons for high efficiency.	Centralized banking is capable enough for transacting large amount of transactions, which decentralized systems have yet to replicate such system successfully. Many intermediate links, high transaction cost, more time consuming, complex clearing processes make this system less efficient as compared to blockchain.

(Continued)

Table 13.2 Comparison between the blockchain-based banking systems and traditional banking. (*Continued*)

Particulars	Blockchain-based banking	Traditional banking
Cost	Blockchain based banking is comparatively less costly as it is based on complete automation, very less operational costs and disintermediation.	Traditional banking makes the system more costly at it involves huge amount of paperwork, repetitive entries in records, high transactional costs, high administrative costs and are more time consuming in nature.
Secure Transactions	This mechanism seems safer as it involves distributed storage which is not easy to hack easily, complex encryption and tight control by public ledger and higher security	Centralized storage is prone to low security, hacking, system failures, easy to leak sensitive information and are the main reasons for insecurity.
Databases	Blockchain technology-based databases have several decentralized nodes which participates in its effective administration, i.e., all nodes need to verify the new additions to blockchain system and are capable of allowing new data into the existing database. Majority of the nodes must reach consensus from users and such mechanism guarantees the security of the network and make it difficult to tamper with. Users are, therefore, reliant on the security infrastructure of the database administrator.	Traditional databases in banking sector use the framework of client server network. In this, client/user can modify the data easily, which is stored and controlled on a centralized server. Since this central authority is responsible for the administration of database, but if, by any means, the security of the authority is compromised then the data can be removed or altered.

(*Continued*)

Table 13.2 Comparison between the blockchain-based banking systems and traditional banking. (*Continued*)

Particulars	Blockchain-based banking	Traditional banking
Customer Experience	The reasons for good customer experiences are- new products and services, geographically independent and real time executions of services.	The reasons for limited customer experiences are-less geographic outreach and homogeneous service delivery.
Integrity and Transparency	Every user has belief about the data they are retrieving and have surety that it is unaltered and uncorrupted.	Control of the database remains with a designated authority only, which authenticates a client's credentials before providing access to the database.

Source: Authors' Compilations.

13.2.4   Challenges Faced by Banking Sector and Blockchain as a Solution

Banking sector has been dealing with various challenges for many years. Blockchain Technology has a potential to provide solution for these challenges as it is equipped with various features like transparent, safe, decentralized, cost-effective and secure [25]. The following points will highlight how a blockchain technology is a key solution to all existing challenges faced by banking sector.

> **Issue of data handling.** In traditional banking, growing number of users insists the urgency to keep and maintain the records of all financial transactions and it becomes quite complicated when the numbers are more. Ultimately, it results in more time consumption for processing the payments. Therefore, it is mandatory to control these transactions effectively and in secure way.
> **Use of Blockchain Technology as a Solution.** With blockchain technology in banking sector, the data handling problem is maintained and verified with more security checks and with more transparency.

➢ **Issue of High Transaction Cost.** Due to third party involvement, the transaction cost increases with each and every transaction and will take further time for its execution. The payment costs are quite high and thus it will be difficult for banks to manage their customers. Actually, banking sector is governed by the apex body Reserve Bank of India (RBI) and exert a power of control at centralized level. Hence, it invests a lot of money in bookkeeping, middlemen commission charges, buying and maintain the central databases. It makes the banking system too expensive and it will not ensure about the prevention of data breaches.

Use of Blockchain Technology as a Solution. While adopting a blockchain technology, most of the expenses get reduced as no middleman is required for its execution.

➢ **Issue of more time consumption.** In banking system, when multiple users and intermediaries/third parties are involved in the transaction, it makes the payment processing lengthier and consumes minimum of 2–3 days to clear the payment. Because of multi layered functioning system in banking, each and every transaction has to go through multiple intermediaries. For example, in case of currency exchangers while handling the cross-border payments. It is too lengthy procedure and ultimately it leads to point of dissatisfaction among users.

Use of Blockchain Technology as a Solution. While introducing blockchain technology in the banking system, it eliminates the need for intermediaries to great extent. This technology follows peer-to-peer transactions mechanism. Payments will get quickly settled because multiple layers have been eliminated from the system. This technology can facilitate instant settlements at a cheaper rate. Blockchain Technology can help the banking sector to rebuild it again with more speed, accuracy, and transparency and make the system more efficient.

➢ **Issue of Consistent Supervision.** Due to digitization, each and every transaction is being done in digital form. Such methods are increasing the responsibilities of banking sectors to record and supervise all details on time. In banking sector, lots of risks have been faced by banks-receivables management, bad debts, trusting mediators, hacking risk and many more.

Use of Blockchain Technology as a Solution. Here, Blockchain Technology can provide solution to this sector as it has many characteristics like execute quick transactions, proper recording of transaction in public ledger, peer-to-peer (P2P) transactions. It can make it more efficient and reliable.

Because of modern technology in data handling and its transmission, blockchain technology has an ability to alter the current FinTech industries in upgraded version [26]. It can boost global financial systems and enable asset transfers more efficiently as compared to the current financial system [27]. The studies related to blockchain has shown that it has immense power to cut down transaction costs and inculcate long-term reforms in to the finance sector. No central controlling authority and the transparency in blockchain technology are the foundations for its working operations, but they may also restrict for its adoption [28]. Lack of legal and no user identification are the most significant non-technical constraint of blockchain technology [29]. Nonetheless, Blockchain has a clear edge in its functioning when it comes to promote decentralized autonomous organizations. It must overcome several significant hurdles before blockchain becomes popular in the financial sector. The overall time for transaction verification [30], Scalability [31, 32], Security [33, 34], transaction expenses, and addressing regulatory challenges [3, 35] are some of the problems that need to be addressed. For the successful adoption and its implementation in banking, it is mandatory to understand the strengths and limitations of the technology itself. Thereafter, the bank needs to work upon the feasibility of such technology further before implementation. Blockchain technology is a distributed ledger system and has peer-to-peer network arrangements that maintains all transactions confirmed by connected nodes and with no involvement of intermediary/third party [36, 37]. This technology is so advanced and enriched with its latest features. Hence, Hacking and altering any value of a block may require excessive computational power [38, 39].

13.3   Analyzing Blockchain Technology and Porter's Five Force Model

Porter's Five Force Model [40] is the most powerful tool used for better understanding the competitiveness of the business environment and exploring the potential profitability of various strategies used in the business. Figure 13.2 represents Porter's Five Forces model as shown below.

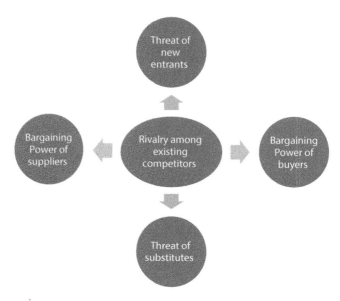

Figure 13.2 Porter five force model [40].

In earlier days, we found that all the forces have lower power in the banking sector. It is due to the fact that –

> **Threat of new entrants.** Obtaining banking license is quite tedious task that makes difficult for new entrants to enter in this sector. Entrance into the banking sector requires large capital outlay and the existing players are holding strong proportion of their market share. Hence, the entry barriers are quite difficult for new entrants.

> **Bargaining Power of buyers.** Customers cannot exert influence on financial products and buyer's power are very less. Although they have various options of banking services but their power is still fairly moderate as they have to abide with the rules and regulations of banking sector time to time.

> **Bargaining Power of suppliers.** Banks are little dependent on suppliers as number of suppliers are ready to provide the technological products to this sector. Law firms, security firms, consulting companies, technology suppliers are currently exercising more power. Banks spend huge amount of funds to the above discussed groups; and accordingly, they charge very high fees to customers for their service offerings.

> ➤ **Threat of substitutes.** Everyone is dependent on government-issued currency or fiat money.
> ➤ **Rivalry among existing competitors.** Majority of powers in banking sector are in the hands of few major players only.

It results in the continuity of gigantic power that banking sector holds for such a long time period and even still have the same influence. Due to traditional scenario in banking sector, the innovations in terms of automation in banking sector are still lagging behind to complete extent.

Now let's discuss Porter's five forces model once again, with the assumption of implementing blockchain, cryptocurrencies, and advanced technology in the banking sector.

> ➤ **Threat of new entrants.** Many trading platforms have entered that allows the exchange of cryptocurrency namely Coinbase, Binance, Kraken, and Gemini, Coinsmart, Bitcoin IRA, Bit Buy and many more.
> ➤ **Bargaining Power of buyers.** The power is in the hands of customers and they can control and decide that which currency to deal with even in the absence of any middlemen activity.
> ➤ **Bargaining Power of suppliers.** Blockchain technology is based upon decentralized approach where transactions are recorded in a digital ledger called a blockchain. Hence suppliers cannot exert much power on the banking transactions.
> ➤ **Threat of substitutes.** Lots of online payment methods and cryptocurrencies *are* the substitutes of traditional banking solutions.
> ➤ **Rivalry among existing competitors.** Conventional power has been disrupted now and dominating banking sector is facing rivalry.

Hence, the power seems to be shifting from a centralized mechanism to ultimate customer.

To make banking transactions more transparent and user friendly, this sector is trying to explore more and more opportunities that would make it more convenient and user friendly. The ever-increasing use of technology in banking sector has resulted in more demand for such applications with the development of user-friendly online technology platforms. With the advent of blockchain technology in the banking sector, it helps to eliminate the frauds due to errors and identity theft to a large extent. Hence, the banking sector has been excited in exploring the technology and deploy it.

13.4   Conclusion

The expanding cases of blockchain technology are bringing huge transformations in the banking sector. This technology has potential that can discompose the traditional system and can make the ongoing/existing systems outdated. Because of increasing activities of frauds in the banking sector, it is mandatory to develop a strong and secured database that includes their client information and thus these solutions are expected to reduce the extent of fraud activities in the banking sector. In addition to maintaining effective customer database, it also reduces the transaction cost, service time, all efforts in handling financial transactions and ultimately ensures transparency and security. The blockchain is a motivating force to encounter the various challenges in banking sector. Even though this technology has many advantages such as immutability, high security, less costly, time saving, decentralized system, automation capability, etc., which insists it to be a demand of the future of banking and financial services, it also has many disadvantages like lack of understanding and adoption behavior among users, transactions are irreversible in nature, it uses massive energy which affects our environment badly.

References

1. Nakamoto, S. and Bitcoin, A., A peer-to-peer electronic cash system, San Jose, California, United States, p. 4, Bitcoin, 2008, URL: https://bitcoin.org/bitcoin.pdf.

2. Biais, B., Bisiere, C., Bouvard, M., Casamatta, C., The blockchain folk theorem. *Rev. Financ. Stud.*, 32, 5, 1662–1715, 2019.

3. Reid, F. and Harrigan, M., An analysis of anonymity in the bitcoin system, in: *Security and Privacy in Social Networks*, pp. 197–223, Springer, New York, NY, 2013.

4. Peters, G.W. and Panayi, E., Understanding modern banking ledgers through blockchain technologies: Future of transaction processing and smart contracts on the internet of money, in: *Banking Beyond Banks and Money*, pp. 239–278, Springer, Cham, 2016.

5. Mattila, J., The blockchain phenomenon–the disruptive potential of distributed consensus architectures (No. 38). *ETLA Working Papers*, 2016.

6. Lindman, J., Tuunainen, V.K., Rossi, M., Opportunities and risks of blockchain technologies–A research agenda, *Proceedings of the 50th Hawaii International Conference on System Sciences*, 1533–1542, 2017.

7. Nathan, R., Blockchain explained, 2020, Retrieved From https://www.investopedia.com/terms/b/blockchain.asp.

8. Zheng, Z., Xie, S., Dai, H., Chen, X., Wang, H., An overview of blockchain technology: Architecture, consensus, and future trends, in: *2017 IEEE International Congress on Big Data (BigData Congress)*, IEEE, Orlando, FL, United States, pp. 557–564, 2017.

9. Zheng, Z., Xie, S., Dai, H.N., Chen, X., Wang, H., Blockchain challenges and opportunities: A survey. *Int. J. Web Grid Serv.*, 14, 4, 352–375, 2018.

10. Tapscott, A. and Tapscott, D., How blockchain is changing finance. *Harv. Bus. Rev.*, 1, 9, 2–5, 2017.

11. Michael, J., Cohn, A.L.A.N., Butcher, J.R., Blockchain technology. *Journal*, 1, 7, 35–44, 2018.

12. Grima, S., Kizilkaya, M., Sood, K., ErdemDelice, M., The perceived effectiveness of blockchain for digital operational risk resilience in the European Union Insurance Market Sector. *J. Risk Financ. Manage.*, 14, 8, 363, 2021.

13. Pereira, J., Tavalaei, M.M., Ozalp, H., Blockchain-based platforms: Decentralized infrastructures and its boundary conditions. *Technol. Forecasting Soc. Change*, 146, 94–102, 2019.

14. Crosby, M., Pattanayak, P., Verma, S., Kalyanaraman, V., Blockchain technology: Beyond bitcoin. *Appl. Innov.*, 2, 6–10, 71, 2016.

15. Lee, I. and Shin, Y.J., Fintech: Ecosystem, business models, investment decisions, and challenges. *Bus. Horiz.*, 61, 1, 35–46, 2018.

16. Aggarwal, R. and Stein, P., The complex regulatory landscape for FinTech: An uncertain future for small and medium-sized enterprise lending, in: *World Economic Forum White Paper*, vol. 170816, pp. 1–35, 2016.

17. Queiroz, M.M. and Wamba, S.F., Blockchain adoption challenges in supply chain: An empirical investigation of the main drivers in India and the USA. *Int. J. Inf. Manage.*, 46, 70–82, 2019.

18. Guo, Y. and Liang, C., Blockchain application and outlook in the banking industry. *Financial Innov.*, 2, 1, 1–12, 2016.

19. Pennathur, A.K., "Clicks and bricks": e-Risk Management for banks in the age of the internet. *J. Bank. Financ.*, 25, 11, 2103–2123, 2001.

20. Deshpande, A., Stewart, K., Lepetit, L., Gunashekar, S., Distributed ledger technologies/blockchain: Challenges, opportunities and the prospects for standards. *Overview Report*, The British Standards Institution (BSI), Europe, vol. 40, p. 40, 2017.

21. Bauer, K. and Hein, S.E., The effect of heterogeneous risk on the early adoption of internet banking technologies. *J. Bank. Financ.*, 30, 6, 1713–1725, 2006.

22. Associated Chambers of Commerce & Industry of India and Deloitte, L.L.P., *Blockchain technology in India: Opportunities and challenges*,

Deloitte, The Associated Chambers of Commerce and Industry of India, New Delhi, India, 2017.

23. O'Leary, D.E., Configuring blockchain architectures for transaction information in blockchain consortiums: The case of accounting and supply chain systems. *Intell. Syst. Account. Finance Manage.*, *24*, 4, 138–147, 2017.

24. Raskin, M. and Yermack, D., Digital currencies, decentralized ledgers and the future of central banking, in: *Research Handbook on Central Banking*, Edward Elgar Publishing, Cheltenham; Northampton (MA): Edward Elgar, 2018.

25. Popova, N.A. and Butakova, N.G., IEEE Conference of Russian young researchers in Electrical and Electronic Engineering (EIConRus), in: *Research of a Possibility of Using Blockchain Technology without Tokens to Protect Banking Transactions*, pp. 1764–1768, 2019.

26. Chang, V., Baudier, P., Zhang, H., Xu, Q., Zhang, J., Arami, M., How blockchain can impact financial services–The overview, challenges and recommendations from expert interviewees. *Technol. Forecast. Soc. Change*, 158, 120166, 2020.

27. Cocco, L., Pinna, A., Marchesi, M., Banking on blockchain: Costs savings thanks to the blockchain technology. *Future Internet*, *9*, 3, 25, 2017.

28. Leible, S., Schlager, S., Schubotz, M., Gipp, B., A review on blockchain technology and blockchain projects fostering open science. *Front. Blockchain*, 2, 16, 2019.

29. Andolfatto, D., Blockchain: What it is, what it does, and why you probably don't need one. *Fed. Reserve Bank St. Louis Rev.*, 100, 2, 87–95, 2018.

30. Moore, T. and Christin, N., Beware the middleman: Empirical analysis of bitcoin-exchange risk, in: *International Conference on Financial Cryptography and Data Security*, pp. 25–33, Springer, Berlin, Heidelberg, 2013.

31. Yli-Huumo, J., Ko, D., Choi, S., Park, S., Smolander, K., Where is current research on blockchain technology? —A systematic review. *PLoS One*, *11*, 10, 0163477, 2016.

32. Conoscenti, M., Vetro, A., De Martin, J.C., Blockchain for the Internet of Things: A systematic literature review, in: *2016 IEEE/ACS 13th International Conference of Computer Systems and Applications (AICCSA)*, Morocco, pp. 1–6, IEEE, 2016.

33. Karame, G.O., Androulaki, E., Capkun, S., Double-spending fast payments in bitcoin, in: *Proceedings of the ACM conference on Computer and Communications Security*, pp. 906–917, 2012.

34. Eyal, I. and Sirer, E.G., Majority is not enough: Bitcoin mining is vulnerable, in: *International Conference on Financial Cryptography and Data Security*, pp. 436–454, Springer, Berlin, Heidelberg, 2014.

35. Trautman, L.J., Virtual currencies; Bitcoin & what now after Liberty Reserve, Silk Road, and Mt. Gox? *Richmond J. Law Technol.*, 20, 4, 1–108, 2014.

36. Evans, D.S., Economic aspects of bitcoin and other decentralized public-ledger currency platforms, in: *University of Chicago Coase-Sandor Institute for Law & Economics Research Paper*, p. 685, 2014.

37. Swan, M., *Blockchain: Blueprint for a new economy*, O'Reilly Media, Inc., SHROFF Publishers & DISTR, Delhi, India, 2015.

38. Wood, G., *Blockchains: What and why*, 2016, Available online: https://www.slideshare.net/gavofyork/blockchain-what-and-why.

39. Albeshr, S. and Nobanee, H., Blockchain applications in banking industry: A mini-review. *SSRN Electron. J.*, 2020.

40. Porter, M.E., The five competitive forces that shape strategy. *Harv. Bus. Rev.*, 86, 1, 25–40, 2008.

14

Blockchain-Based Framework – A Scientific Tool for Developing a Robust Banking System

Minakshi Thaman

P.G. Department of Commerce and Management, Master Tara Singh Memorial College for Women, Ludhiana, Punjab, India

Abstract

Banking sector plays a pivotal role in the development of every economy. The advancement of all the sectors, either directly or indirectly, is dependent upon the working of a robust banking system. Numerous policy measures have been taken by the Reserve Bank of India to technologically upgrade the banks and avoid instances of money laundering. Banks are also experimenting by replacing traditional methods with the new ones. The path breaking step in this regard, is the adoption of blockchain based framework for executing various functions. It is now exponentially used for handling crucial databases, reducing transaction cost, and creating a safe environment for the customer. In today's scenario data is the most valuable asset. When an individual or corporate avails the services of a bank, the foremost demand is of security against financial and identity thefts. Ensuring security of the customer as well as for the service provider is a pressing priority. Blockchain serves the purpose. It not only enhances security of both the parties rather improves the operating efficiency of the bank along with. It's a scientific method for managing and storing information in blocks made with crypto currencies. Undoubtedly, a meticulous way makes hacking impossible. It is crucial to understand that blockchain is just not about Bitcoin, but there's a lot more to explore. Be it elimination of huge amounts of record-keeping or resolving cross-border payments-related issues it serves innumerable purposes. The Indian banking industry is investigating into its multiple uses. Many banks in India have already adopted this

Email: minakshibajaj.mts@gmail.com

Kiran Sood, Rajesh Kumar Dhanaraj, Balamurugan Balusamy and Seifedine Kadry (eds.) Blockchain Technology in Corporate Governance: Transforming Business and Industries, (303–324) © 2023 Scrivener Publishing LLC

technology. This paper focuses on the benefits that the commercial banks in India are seeking out of this technological up-gradation .A detailed analysis has been made on two giants of banking industry i.e. SBI and ICICI. The collaborations they have made and the functions they are performing with this technology have been highlighted in this paper.

Keywords: Identity thefts, money laundering, crypto currencies

14.1   Introduction

Today's business is built to vitalize the profits out of entire globe. Business follows no boundaries to realize this mission. Corporates strive to generate profits by building a highly diversified gigantic customer base. If the business is magnificently dispersed several functional areas require dynamic control mechanism, i.e. both at strategic and operational level. In developing such a system methods of data collection, handling and processing plays a critical role. Each department has to create its own data inventory by adopting next-generation business process improvement software, which delivers the desired information in a guarded way. A technologically upgraded information system is required now-a-days to maintain transactional records. Corporate formulate ways to enhance their operational efficiency with those scientifically designed systems. Once the pool of information is generated, next deadliest danger for every business in prevalent times is "Data Theft". This issue is regarding handling of the internal data with utmost protection against hackers [1]. There is a pressing priority to use a collaborative technology which promises to provide an authentic mechanism of data collection and processing to improve the efficiency of business along with a security shield against unwanted external parties. The best solution to serve the entire purpose is the adoption of Blockchain technology.

14.2   Objective of the Chapter

The objective of the paper is to conduct a descriptive research for developing a comprehensive understanding of the concept of blockchain technology and its application. While applying this mechanism the corporate is required to imbibe this technology as a facilitator in its ongoing system, which involves various analytical steps. The aim of this paper is to understand those steps in detail. A large number of experts are of the view that this revolution will change the ways of doing banking business. An attempt has been made to highlight the ways with which the banking companies have used this state-of-art technology to improve customer service experience. An elaborated study has been made to unfold all the facts regarding the steps put forward by commercial banks of India in this regard *viz.* the consortiums created by banks for deriving immense benefits out of this technology. To ponder further India's two leading banks State Bank of India and ICICI Bank Ltd. has been considered.

14.3 Meaning

Getting its photosynthesis from the virtual currency Bitcoin it has blossomed into a facilitator. A blockchain network serves many purposes for the host business like track orders, settle payments, manage accounts, adhere to schedules etc.

Blockchain can be termed as a decentralized ledger, which records all the transactions by the participants without a central clearing authority. Each transaction is stored in encrypted blocks and every subsequent transaction generates an additional block, which in turn gives verification of the previous block. This rechecking system ensures maximum authenticity. In this way data inventory is created with the help of blocks. No block can be inserted between two existing blocks. Hence, there is no possibility of tampering by a malicious element. It creates a trust worthy and immutable record along with a protective shield against hackers.

The helps information of a chronological single-source data. Each and every permissioned member can access details of complete transaction, giving them greater confidence regarding authenticity of the recording system.

The cherry on the cake is decreased cost of operations. As there is no duplicity of work it increases efficiencies and saves time. These benefits result into significantly higher returns for each investment. This state of the art technology is supreme savior in current volatile times.

14.3.1 The Process

Blockchain technology was announced through the paper by Satoshi Nakamoto (2008), Bitcoin: A Peer-to-Peer Electronic Cash System. There was an immense emphasis on creating the network of transactions according to their occurrence resulting into creation of electronic cash. This futuristic thought initiated a new era of doing business in a highly sophisticated way [2]. For a business which is using this state -of-art technology forms

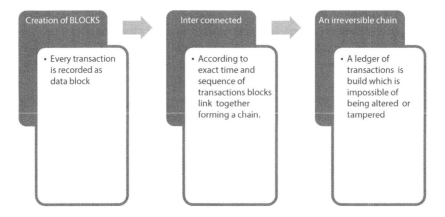

Figure 14.1 Process of entering a transaction in blockchain network. (Author's compilation).

an authentic record of its transactions that cannot be changed or rectified without the proof of rework. The process of recording the transactions in this network is shown in Figure 14.1.

Each data block can record the information according to user's choice *viz.* both tangible and intangible. Addition of a block shows the movement. The blocks form a chain accordingly. Transactions are blocked forever, thus giving this technique strength of immutability.

The key features which make this technology abundantly useful are:

a) Enhanced operational efficiency: All the transactions are recorded only once, this curbs duplication of effort.

b) Shared ledger: All network participants have access to the ledger. The system is transparent. If an erroneous transaction is added and the participant desired to rectify, he has to add a new transaction to reverse the error. After the correction both transactions will be then visible to all the members.

c) Immutable records: As all transactions are recorded on real-time basis. No member can alter or tamper any recorded transaction.

d) Pre-determined standardized rules: To curb any further problems and speed up the process, set of rules are pre-stored on the blockchain network. Whenever any transaction is entered by the participant, it is executed as per the conditions automatically.

14.3.2 Blockchain Components

Blockchain technology has various components. They are mentioned briefly below:

1. Ledger

   Ledgers has always been an important part of every business, as it contains complete record of transactions. When a business decides to implement blockchain technology it uses ledger in a scientifically modified way. There are two types of ledger decentralized and centralized.

   a) In public network decentralized ledger is used, where all participants allowed to real-time access at all the ongoing transactions.

   b) In private network centralized ledger is used; where only permissioned have an access at the details of the transaction.

2. Membership

   There are renowned and trusted agencies which issues certificates to Blockchain for operations. Every blockchain is assigned a unique identity to differentiate it from the others. When a corporate desires to participate in it they have to avail permission to use the network. It is done by assigning a unique identity to them.

3. Consensus protocol

   When a corporate decides to run the business with blockchain network, it has to settle the rules and laws for proper execution. A consensus algorithm is created to conduct a Blockchain and its core components. It is an aggregate decision built on the consensus algorithm and protocol so that there is an agreement on the same state of the blockchain without having any trust issues.

   Two of the most popular consensus algorithms are:

   (i) Proof-of-stake

   (ii) Proof-of-work

4. Smart Contract

   After gaining consensus on rules to be followed, next important step is development of smart contracts. They are the programs stored on a blockchain, which basically represent business logic in response to various events. The process of creating a smart contract involves following steps:

a) Firstly, business starts working with developers. They describe their requirements for the smart contract according to their business requirements.
b) In the second step, the developers initiate to develop the logic and test it to ensure that it works as intended.
c) Once written, the next phase is security review. It can be executed by internal experts or an external specialized agency.
d) After the approval, it is deployed on an existing distributed ledger infrastructure.

While developing smart contracts programming language plays a vital role. Following are some of the popular programming environments.

(i) WebAssembly(WASM): It allows developers to create smart contracts using C, JavaScript, TypeScript, and Rust programming languages. These can run in a web browser and other distributed ledgers and can be integrated into blockchains.
(ii) Digital Asset Modeling Language (DAML)-DAML is an enterprise-focused language. It is mainly designed to support various business cases, and ensure privacy for crucial data.
(iii) Ethereum, a smart contract crypto currency platform which is designed to run on the Ethereum Virtual Machine (EVM) as a "world computer developed using Solidity language.

5. System Management

In system management the manager defines, create, modify, or remove the rules. The basic responsibility is to make sure that only error-free and authentic operations happen on the network.

6. Wallet

It is an important component of the Blockchain. Each member is being given a wallet. It has credential and complete records of the user. While creating wallet security is the main issue, a developer has to ensure that all the details of the user are completely protected.

7. Programming languages

As there are various blockchain frameworks, each type is written in a specific programming language. Following are some of the popular languages and the networks which were developed using them:

(i) C++

Many successful networks were developed using C++. Examples: Bitcoin, Ripple, Litecoin, Monero, EOS, Stellar, and QTUM.

(ii) C#

It's an open source programming language developed by Microsoft. Examples: Stratis, NEO, and IOTA.

(iii) Go

This is a procedural and statically typed programming language developed by Google. Examples: Ethereum, Dero, HyperledgerFabric, and GoChain blockchains.

(iv) Java

The purpose of this programming language is concurrent, object-oriented, and class-based designs. This language gives immense freedom to the user while creating a network. Blockchains developed using Java are Ethereum, IOTA, NEM, Hyperledger Fabric, and NEO.

(v) Python

This programming language was used to developed Ethereum, Hyperledger Fabric, Steem, and NEO.

Table 14.1 Showing networks along with their language.

Sr. no	Blockchain	Language
1	ARK	JavaScript
2	CORDA	Kotlin
3	ETHEREUM	Go, C++, Rust
4	EOS	C++
5	HYPERLEDGER FABRIC (Private network)	Go, Java, JavaScript, Python
6	LISK	JavaScript, Node.js
7	NEO	C#
8	QTUM	C++, Python, TypeScript
9	STRATIS	C++, C#
10	WAVES	Scala

Source: [3].

Table 14.1 outlines some of the famous blockchain networks and their respective programming language. There are concrete proofs that these advancements in programming languages will continue to evolve at a robust pace for the real-world adoption. Many sophisticated networks will be created using latest languages in near future too. Further which type of network is to be developed, will depend upon the basic requirements of the user.

14.3.3   Types of Blockchain Networks

Mainly three types of networks are used by the host to derive the maximum benefits out of this technological revolution:

a) Public – An Open Network
   These networks are the oldest ones as they were the pioneers for implementing this technology. A public blockchain is one that anyone can join and participate in, such as Bitcoin, Ethereum, Litecoin, etc. It does not impose any restrictions for anyone who wishes to join in. Anyone with an internet connection can become a participant and get a complete access to the records. Each member can start validating blocks and add transactions. Following are some of its key features:

   (i)   There is no central authority in any step; it's a truly democratic structure.
   (ii)   this network uses Proof of Work consensus algorithms for validating the transactions
   (iii) Every participant can read, write and rewrite in the network
   (iv)   If someone tries to tamper with the blocks, all the other nodes will reject the transaction.
   (v)   It offers anonymity, no one can track others transactions.
   (vi)   Users have to follow the rule set by the network administrator.

   It is like a flowing river where anyone can enter anytime. Being an open network it faces many drawbacks:

   (i)   High power-consuming consensus protocols are used to run the system. This data mining can become a huge load on the business.

(ii)   There is a major issue of privacy for transactions, which further leads to weak security.

(iii) It tends to become slower due to the excess number of users.

(iv)   The transaction fee keeps fluctuating at a rapid pace.

But to overcome this problem the host can choose its participants. They can be asked to obtain an invitation or permission to join in. Moreover restrictions can be imposed on who is allowed to participate in certain transactions along with the list of rules to be followed.

b) Private –A Partially Decentralized Ledger

To enhance security of their own system businesses generally set up a private blockchain network. It is used at the organizational level and is not for public use. In this type of network the authority is partially decentralized and a single organization has supreme control. It runs behind a controlled corporate firewall. To add a participant, the host follows an authentication process. As a result, only the known members of a company are allowed entry that too after a detailed examination of their requisite documents. This provides utmost security against the entry of hackers. Following are some of its key features:

(i)   The host business gains an immortal internal networking system which is empowered for processing different transaction efficiently. It is also strongly capable of giving security to its users.

(ii)   Every organization has set of policies and this network is regulated accordingly. All the participant members are required to follow them completely.

(iii) Being under single entity's control only a selected group of people are permissioned to enter, so there is no volatility in the network. This also ensures high sustainability in the long run.

(iv)   For consensus protocol voting or algorithms can be used. This results in consuming lesser energy and creating a true blockchain ecosystem.

(v)   It involves comparatively lesser investment to set up this platform

(vi)   Low and stable transaction fees.

This network generates veritable data which creates trust among the clients. If compared with public network, this one has multitude of commendable offerings.

c)   Consortium – A Decentralized Ledger
This network is a hybrid model as its partial public and private blockchain. This Blockchain grants access to multiple organizations. The control is not being given to one company, but it is divided between the parties. The authority is completely decentralized between federations. Multiple member organizations are given full control to share ledger and oversee the transactions. So it is not an open public platform rather a permissioned one. Only selected members are allowed to share ledger leaving others aside. Following are some of its key features:

(i)   All the organizations contribute best of their knowledge, hence creating a collaborative environment. It boosts innovation and gives maximum exposure to all the participants.

(ii)   Every organization has complete access to the data it helps in keeping complete check on every block, there's no way that any organization can indulge in any illegal activity.

(iii)   A proper control mechanism is observed for the validation purposes i.e. the number of nodes required to add a block.

(iv)   The transaction fees stay the same no matter how many users are on the network.

(v)   For data mining it uses the algorithms, which minimizes complexity and makes it less energy consumable.

Out of these, business can choose the one which best matches its working and serves the desired objective. But one thing is evident that blockchain is revolutionizing the ways of managing business affairs. It helps to maintain a data in a legitimate manner. The operational efficiency and goodwill of the company increases manifold with this technology. This technique can play a positive role in almost every single sector *viz.* banking, commerce, healthcare, and insurance. Its inherited features make it crucial tool in today's time. An efficient use of this technique can change the destiny of the business.

14.3.4 Major Facilitators

This network technology can be blissful for many sectors. Many tech giants are building scientific blockchain networks for resolving problems which used to arise in the traditional system of working. Let's consider some the examples to validate the fact:

1. IBM: This corporate house has done immense work to help food producers and retailers to build a system in supply chain management and food tracking using blockchain technology. IBM has built a framework that facilitates people to monitor produce i.e. from point of production to retail stores [4].

   The purpose is to facilitate complete access for all the transactions along the way. IBM Blockchain Transparent Supply can help organizations build blockchain-based ecosystem networks. The user can figure out the farm from where the produce came from, the concerned distributer, even the vehicle in which it was transported. As food contamination is a big issue, it can be exposed with blockchain network .IBM provide a complete tracking for food grain supply mechanism to generate new value from that data and create trust in partnerships.

2. Microsoft: Microsoft has taken a huge step in 2018 in enhancing the scope of blockchain usage. It designed coco framework, which is an open-source system that enables confidential blockchain networks that too at a high-scale. The Coco Framework is not a blockchain ledger itself. Rather, it's an enabler that leverages a combination of trusted execution environments, advanced cryptography, and innovative consensus mechanisms across industries [5].

It is built to deliver following perks to an enterprise:

- Throughput and latency – There has been a problem of speed in open networks traditionally. Coco Framework resolves this problem and enables database speeds.

- Manage Non-Deterministic Transactions – To enhance the capabilities it supports non-deterministic transactions within the system.
- Secrecy issues – When it comes to sensitivity of data, it is a relative term. Every business has its something different to manage. To provide business specific confidentiality Microsoft's has designed CocoFramework. This model provides flexibility and enterprise specific service.
- Governance – Network policy management is a major concern. This framework addresses policy management with well deigned distributed governance system.

Another example can be of Oasis Labs, a blockchain cloud computing platform which raised $45 million from investors to help companies adopt blockchain.

These steps help different sectors to derive diverse benefits from this technology however the scope of this paper is restricted on the use of blockchain in Banking Sector. More and more companies are coming forward to use this technology.

14.3.5   Blockchain Technology in the Banking Sector

Banking today is sailing in the sea of transformation. But this change is being implemented by the Government of India in a highly planned and regulated way. No such activity is permitted to the banking company which is detrimental towards the interest of the depositor or borrower. There are many regulatory bodies who act as a watch dog *viz.* Reserve Bank of India, Banking Regulation Act, 1949, Companies Act 2013. They keep a vigilant approach to fence banks within their legal limits. Within this controlled environment banks are continuously striving to provide several tech-savvy services. Their digital agenda involves array of online services, mobile apps, and real-time transaction settlement process.

All these advancements demand an enabler which is capable of transforming sensitive data into non-sensitive data. Blockchain can be considered a lucrative option in this scenario. Back in 2009, it was initially used only as a tracking database. However with the passage of time major players of banking industry realized its hidden potential. It was learnt that this scientific network is least disruptive to existing banking model of a respective bank. The current system and processes that are operational are not required to be dismantled for executing this new technology. Rather, it assists in reducing the complexities faced in traditional set up. It allows

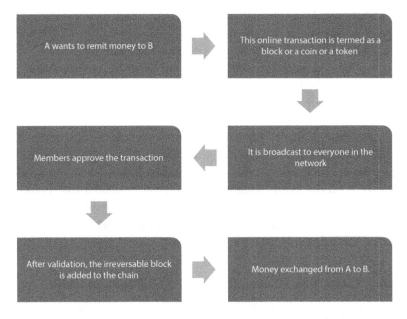

Figure 14.2 Money remittance using blockchain network. Source: Author's Compilation.

banks to smartly plug in their existing systems and processes to work with blockchain powered networks.

Figure 14.2 exhibits how a transaction between two parties is processed in this network in a secured way.

Blockchain network saves every financial transaction in the database as a block, forming series of transparent transactions which cannot be hampered hence terminating its sensitivity forever. Multiple parties can leverage from the data without tampering previous ones.

Many transactions like processing Letter of Credit (LC's), GST invoices, instant global access to the funds and e-way bills involves interbank transfers along with worldwide circulation of money so there is a crucial issue of privacy and security which has a strong impact on banks working and reputation. Only enhanced automation can reduce and manage this counterparty risk that is present in these transactions involving real-time settlement.

Some of the core benefits of this incorruptible technology for the banking sector include:

- Authenticity of information.
- Reduction in paper work with an ultimate objective of paperless banking system.

- Improved operational efficiency.
- Elimination of intermediaries.
- Minimization of fraud, security, and transparency.
- Utmost satisfaction for the customers/clients. As transaction is processed in robust, convenient, and secure manner.
- Immensely improved audit ability

Numerous banks have realized that this technology has the potential to serve diverse customers, including those having their presence in international trade. Technology can help our Indian baking sector grow at fast pace. Like a report from Santander InnoVentures claims that banks can slash infrastructure costs by $15–20 billion by 2022, by eliminating redundant activities [6]. Banks can derive humongous benefits from imbibing blockchain technology into their core system.

14.3.6   Technology Consortiums by The Banks in India

As blockchain is a decentralized ledger, it has many participants. Banks want to reap several benefits out of this technology, so they have put forward many steps in this regard. Be it forming of consortiums with the foreign banks or forming a private limited company of Indian banks.

Listed below are two such collaborations-

1. Bankchain
   In the year 2017, various banks came together forming a common platform called bank-chain. It is India's first blockchain exploration consortium. The objective was to implement blockchain technology in banking system. The bank-chain has 37 members from different parts of the world. As the basic feature of this technology all the members get access to all bank-chain projects. It has been formed in collaboration with Primechain Technologies, an Indian start up. This consortium has developed eight live projects so far.
   The participant banks are driving immense benefits out of this joint effort-
   a) Technical training sessions: Each member has an access to training material which can be beneficial for the personnel development of respective bank.
   b) Regular meetings: To uplift the members with potential uses of blockchain.

This collaboration has standard rules and regulations for the governing process. For managing the consortium four types of committee are formed, *viz.*:

1. Steering Committee: A steering committee is an advisory body. Each bank nominates one person to be a part of this committee. Generally nominated members are experts, authority figures, or senior stakeholders in an organization. Meetings of this committee generally have an agenda to visualize direction of the consortium. If required they tend to reframe the previously decided direction too. The major tasks and concerns for steering committees are the direction, scope, budget, timeliness, and methods.

2. Technology Committee: It is a group of nominated members who provide leadership, planning, and coordination to fulfill technology needs. The prime purpose is to frame an excellent IT strategy and prevent mistakes in computing, security, and technology in general. They are responsible for current and future initiatives in transforming technology during budget development and review processes. They make recommendations regarding priorities for the acquisition of technology i.e. both hardware and software.

3. Regulatory Committee: This committee ensures the integrity in decision making process, adherence to the Code of Conduct and legal requirements. Basically it promotes and support good governance in the consortium. This committee has the responsibility of the following:
   • Openness
   • Transparency
   • Mutual respect
   • Equality and fairness
   • Sustainability
   This committee ensures focused discussions leading towards a well informed and balanced decision. They also recommend solutions according to legal, constitutional and policy requirements.

4. Business Committee: The members of this committee develop specific proposals for initiatives or activities for organizational development. These proposals are then thoroughly considered by the senior management. They coordinate with other committees and design framework for entire organization.

Figure 14.3 Governance system in bankchain consortium. *Source: Primechain Technologies* [7].

Following figure exhibits how members are nominated in this organization along with their respective responsibilities:

Figure 14.3 shows the governance in the Bank-Chain consortium:

2. Indian Banks' Blockchain Infrastructure Company Private Limited (IBBIC)

Another milestone was set in the year 2021; when15 leading banks of India decided to work together for creating a new company with a name "Indian Banks' Blockchain Infrastructure Company Private Limited (IBBIC)". Following table exhibits the names of the banks which are the members in this company.

Each participant bank has an equal stake of 6.66%. From technology point of view, the company will use a system based on Infosys' Finacle Connect. The aforesaid system is a blockchain-based platform having the ability to facilitate digitization and automation of trade-related finance processes. This company will serve as a common platform for resolving many issues. Major desired solutions are shown in Table 14.2.

It will be an umbrella organization helping in quick processing of LC's and minimizing the chances of fraud. This consortium has a mission to inculcate efficiency, transparency, and security into entire banking system. Moreover the objective behind this is to curb all the problems faced in the traditional set up like issue of fake LCs [9].

Table 14.2 The participant banks.

Public sector banks	Private sector banks	
State Bank of India	HDFC Bank	Yes Bank
Bank of Baroda	ICICI Bank	RBL Bank
Canara Bank	Kotak Mahindra Bank	IDFC Bank
Indian Bank	Axis Bank	South Indian Bank
	IndusInd Bank	Standard Chartered
		Federal Bank

Source: https://www.businessinsider.in [8].

Table 14.3 The purpose of the consortium.

Sr. no	Purpose	Desired solution
1.	Solve LC's related issues (internationally)	Curb elemental fraud like the issuance of two LC's on a single invoice
2.	Solve LC's related issues (domestically)	Decrease processing time from 4-5 days to 4-5 hours
3.	Helpful for MSME's	Improve their credit eligibility resulting into a quick loan processing. Digitalization of invoices i.e. turn them into a token, which can then be used to settle payments, overheads and make accounting adjustments.
4.	Tokenization of assets like stocks, bonds, registration certificates etc.	Making them instantly available as collateral security.

Source: Author's Compilation.

This system is expected to become operational within a year. The beauty of this integrated effort is that it will be designed to be open entry system, making it a pathway which other banks can join anytime in the future. Thus, it can be said that a well-designed strategy that can bring much awaited transformation in banking sector. Table 14.3 outlines the purpose for which the several banks participated in the consortium. It also explains the desired solutions for the specific problem.

As majority of the top banks have participated in the above discussed consortiums, the picture seems rosy.

14.3.7   Steps Taken by Two Leading Commercial Banks of India: SBI And ICICI

Many banks are putting persistent efforts to bring in this technology in almost every banking service and the work of two banking companies is commendable. They are pioneers in the adoption of blockchain in their transaction processing system.

1. State Bank of India (SBI)

   An Indian Multinational, Public Sector Bank. It's a statutory company governed by State Bank of India Act, 1955. The Bank has 11 subsidiaries *viz*. SBI General Insurance, SBI Life Insurance, SBI Mutual Fund, SBI Card, etc. It is the largest Indian Bank with 1/4th market share with 22,000 branches and 58,500 ATMs. It is a pioneer in giving online services to its customers. Its mobile app YONO is also a highly appreciable step. As SBI has a presence in 32 foreign countries, the bank desires to speed up overseas transactions to remain an undisputed winner. The bank has also successfully ventured in the usage of blockchain in its operational set up. Being a strong believer of this technology State Bank of India (SBI) has actively participated in 2017's Bankchain Consortium [10].

   Domestically, it will help the member banks to improve clearing and settlements, payments, create smart assets, identity and data management, data protection, KYC. It will uplift the governance aspect in Indian economy. With regard to global trade it will also help in currency exchange, remittance, and digital signature, authentic and accurate communication of financial information.

   SBI has borne some sensational cases of money laundering so this technique can become a useful tool for them in achieving greater transparency in regulatory reporting and client management.

   Further, SBI tied up with the JP Morgan (US-based bank) for using it's blockchain technology called "Liink" [11]. The purpose is to create an authentic peer-to-peer (P2P) network. About 100 banks are participating in this network. It has emerged as a common platform to exchange payments-related information with other financial institutions globally.

According to Mr. Venkat Nageswar, Deputy MD, International Banking Group, SBI – their bank has undergone significant digital transformation by adding new technologies to create real value in daily operations. He further emphasized that they are the first bank in India to go live on the network.

SBI uses this platform Liink for the following purpose:
- Rapid remittance system – To facilitate remittances SBI has a network of correspondent banking with approximately 600 foreign banks. To fasten the system it uses SBI Express Remit, telegraphic/wire transfers etc.
- Reducing transaction cost
- Reduced paper work and limited steps involved
- Pre-validate an account before making payments
- Complete adherence to regulatory norms at beneficiary location
- Mitigate transaction rejection/frauds
- Customer satisfaction
- Resolve cross-border payments-related inquiries

2. ICICI Bank Ltd.
ICICI Bank has a massive presence in India. It is a scheduled private sector commercial bank. The Bank's consolidated total assets stood at Rs. 14.76 trillion at September 30, 2020. It runs its business operations with a vast network of 5,288 branches and 15,158 ATMs across India.

It has a positive outlook towards the application of blockchain in core activities. A bench mark was set by them in year 2016, when they decided to join hands with Emirates NBD, a leading banking group in the Middle East to start a blockchain-based network for financial services. ICICI Bank was the first bank in India to venture into such an innovative step.

14.4 The Framework

In this project, they adopted a permissioned asset-agnostic ledger framework. This customized framework allows participants to check online the status of the application and transmission of original trade documents through a secure network. This service digitally track documentation and authenticate ownership of assets. Hence entire transaction is executed through a series of encrypted and secure digital contracts.

In the initial phase both the member banks used automation of all inter-bank processes through smart contracts and served their customers with the following:

- Remittances
- Real-time transfer of invoices and purchase orders
- Invoice financing

All the above mentioned transactions focus on secure digital exchange of documents and real-time monitoring of positions through integrated dashboards. This hi-tech framework enhanced automation across inter-organizational processes. It also possess the basic feature of blockchain network i.e. transactional security and accuracy at a significantly lower cost. That's why the member banks served over 250 corporates into their platform for domestic and international trade finance.

The technology behind this network will be facilitated through Finacle suite of solutions, EdgeVervea wholly owned product subsidiary of Infosys. This network has also been integrated with the Finacle Universal Banking Suite and other host systems within the application ecosystem in both banks.

According to the World Bank, this joint venture is the largest receiver of remittances with a share of close to 70 Billion USD out of the 580+ Billion USD world over.

SBI and ICICI both have proved that they value this decentralized system of data management. Even both of them are members of the consortium projects mentioned earlier in the paper.

14.5 Indian Government's Perspective

The Ministry of Electronics and Information Technology drafted a framework for the use of blockchain technology in various Government Departments. There is a plan to use this technology in property record-keeping, digital certificates, power distribution, health records and in supply chain management.

If implemented it can facilitate in curtailment of corruption from Indian economy. In 2021, NitiAayog also suggested the use of the distributed ledger technology at state government controlled services such as fertilizer subsidy disbursement and educational certificates .This step if executed will help the Indian government to restrict manipulations and improved money management for the country. No single entity will have control over the system and the validation of every transaction will make false adjustments impossible.

Even the declaration made by the Reserve Bank of India (RBI) on exploring the Central Bank Digital Currency (CBDC), for retail and international trade payments have a massive impact on the Indian financial system [12]. Experts are of the view that blockchain technology will be the medium for implementing digital currency in practice. All these advancements show that Indian government has a welcoming attitude towards this technology. But for its implementation a strong server will be required which can control the massive flow of transactions and detect malpractices in the ongoing system.

14.6   Conclusion

It is evident from the study that blockchain is an indispensable tool for developing a system which is authentic and facilitates exchange of value to its stake holders at accelerating pace. This giant spread sheet eliminates intermediaries and reduces the transaction cost magnificently. It works on three fundamental decentralization, trust, and security. Major players in banking industry are convinced with the potential uses of this technology. They are entering into joints ventures with other seasoned players to gain maximum out of this technology. A boom can be witnessed with RBI considering digital currency in near future. This step by RBI will open an entirely new horizon for the Indian banking sector. This will result into many banks amending their ways for conducting business and turning favorable with regard to use of blockchain network for their core services. In the end it can be concluded that its success will depend upon a series of incremental efforts by the participants and regular governmental support. Things are taking interesting twists and turn in India, so it can be rightly said that blockchain technology is in its nascent stage but with a promising future.

References

1. Rajasekar, V., Premalatha, J., Sathya, K., A blockchain based framework to enhance security against cyber attacks. *Int. J. Recent Technol. Eng. (IJRTE)*, 8, 4, 7485–7487, November 2019.

2. John, S.M., Pomarole, M., Jordan, G., Levchenko, K., McCoy, D., Voelker, G.M., Savage, S., A fistful of bitcoins: Characterizing payments among men with no names, in: *Proc. Conference on Internet measurement (IMC ' 13)*, pp. 127–140, 2013.

3. Mahesh, C., Top 5 blockchain programming languages, C# corner, Philadelphia, U.S.A, June 2021, https://www.c-sharpcorner.com/article/top-5-best-programming-languages-for-blockchain-development/.

4. Nishant, K., How blockchain and IoT are improving the food supply chain. Resilience to resurgence technology sector in India, NASSCOMInsight Newsletter, Noida, India, June 2021, https://community.nasscom.in/communities/agritech/how-blockchain-and-iot-are-improving-food-supply-chain.

5. Pietschmann, C., Introducing Microsoft Coco Framework for blockchain, Build5nines cloud & Enterprise Technology, San Francisco, U.S.A, November 2017, https://build5nines.com/introducing-microsoft-coco-framework-for-blockchain/.

6. Perez Bello, Y., Blockchain tech could reduce banks' infrastructural costs by $15-20 billion a year by 2022, *Santander InnoVentures Report*, Coin Desk, New York, U.S.A., September, 2021, https://www.coindesk.com/business/2015/06/16/santander-blockchain-tech-can-save-banks-20-billion-a-year.

7. Primechain Technologies selects Infibeam's State-of-Art Integrated Datacenter to run blockchain API tools press, Primechain Technologies Pvt. Ltd. Pune, India, Release 18th April, 2019, https://www.primechaintech.com.

8. Vahia, S., SBI, HDFC, ICICI and 12 others banks are joining forces to use blockchain to power letters of credit — A move that could be a boon for MSMEs, Business Insider India, Gurgaon, India, 16 June 2021, https://www.businessinsider.in/cryptocurrency/news/sbi-hdfc-icici-and-12-others-banks-are-joining-forces-to-use-blockchain-to-power-letters-of-credit-a-move-that-could-be-a-boon-for-msmes/articleshow/83570874.cms.

9. Rebello, J., 15 Indian banks form blockchain company to process Letters of Credit, Economic Times, Noida, India, 16 June 2021, https://economictimes.indiatimes.com/industry/banking/finance/banking/15-banks-to-start-new-trade-finance-system-using-blockchain-tech/articleshow/83545043.cms.

10. Bose, S., SBI to deploy blockchain in three functions in FY19, Financial Express, Mumbai, India, 9 February 2018, https://www.financialexpress.com/industry/sbi-to-deploy-blockchain-in-three-functions-in-fy19/1058852/.

11. Das, S., State Bank of India joins JPMorgan's blockchain-based payment network, Economic Times, Noida, India, 23 February 2021, https://economictimes.indiatimes.com/industry/banking/finance/banking/state-bank-of-india-joins-jpmorgans-blockchain-based-payment-network/articleshow/81157341.cms.

12. Nag, A., RBI is considering 'phased introduction' of digital currency, plans pilot programmes, The Print, New Delhi, India, 2021, July22, https://theprint.in/economy/rbi-is-considering-phased-introduction-of-digital-currency-plans-pilot-programmes/701104/.

Part 4

BLOCKCHAIN APPLICATIONS AND SUSTAINABILITY ISSUES

15

Advanced Cryptographic Technologies in Blockchain

Osheen Oberoi* and Sahil Raj

School of Management Studies, Punjabi University, Patiala, Punjab, India

Abstract

Blockchain technology is a kind of distributed architecture that consists of crypto secure mechanisms in mathematics, algorithms, and numerical models. The term blockchain consists of two words wherein the word "block" signifies digital information, and the word "chain" denotes the public database. Each transaction in blockchain is recorded through digital distributed ledger. These transactions are also validated by using a digital timestamp, thus facilitating the users with the feature of auditability and transparency to examine the state of data in the blockchain system. This cryptographic feature in blockchain technology enhances the layer of security in the system. The blockchain technology has gained pace in the 21st century and is utilized as an impressive and complementary technology to traditional cloud-based solutions for enhancing the security of data. It is a digital ledger of information that is decentralized in nature. Blockchain technology possesses the capability to create more transparency as well as it greatly reduces the likelihood of data breaches. This technology is garnering attention and can be utilized in a variety of sectors like healthcare, supply chain, identity management, to name a few.

Keywords: Blockchain, digital timestamp, block, chain, digital ledger, cryptographic, consensus, proof-of-activity, proof-of-work

15.1 Blockchain Technology

After the internet, blockchain is the next big revolutionizing technology that is reinventing the way mankind works and lives. Blockchain technology

---

Corresponding author: er.osheen@gmail.com

Kiran Sood, Rajesh Kumar Dhanaraj, Balamurugan Balusamy and Seifedine Kadry (eds.) Blockchain Technology in Corporate Governance: Transforming Business and Industries, (327–352) © 2023 Scrivener Publishing LLC

is a kind of distributed architecture that consists of crypto secure mechanisms in mathematics, algorithms, and numerical models [3]. The term blockchain consists of two words wherein the word "block" signifies digital information, and the word "chain" denotes the public database. Therefore, in this context, blockchain refers to digital information stored in a public database. The noteworthy characteristics of blockchain technology include immutability, decentralization, validation, and transparency. Additionally, this technology promises to provide security and privacy to the end-users at all times [9].

Ref. [13] defined blockchain as "database encompassing a physical chain of fixed-length blocks that include 1 to N transactions, where each transaction added to a new block is validated and then inserted into the block. When the block is completed, it is added to the end of the existing chain of blocks. Moreover, the only two operations – as opposed to the classic CRUD (create, read, update, delete) – are add-transaction and view-transaction."

Extending the scope of Blockchain, [11] in the second edition of his book Mastering Blockchain defined blockchain in technical terms as "a peer-to-peer, distributed ledger that is cryptographically-secure, append-only, immutable (extremely hard to change), and updateable only via consensus or agreement among peers." The foremost important term is peer-to-peer, which explicates that the network does not have a centralized structure and all the participants (also known as nodes) communicate directly with one another. It further highlights that there is no involvement of any third party. When you delve deeper into the technical definition, you'll discover that blockchain provides complete record containing all transactions that are dispersed throughout all the members in the network, and each node has a copy of it. Besides, the third keyword is cryptographically secure, which signifies that different hash functions encrypt the data present in the block to present the data in the block to provide security, thus making this technology tamper-proof and secured against any malicious attacks. The technical definition also accentuates that the blockchain technology is append-only; this means that data is added in this chain of blocks with a timestamp and in a sequential order. In addition to this, this feature of blockchain also elucidates that the data which is added to the blockchain is completely immutable, which signifies that information cannot be erased or altered once the transaction is confirmed. In rare situations, it is only possible to change or alter the data only when 50% of the peers give consensus for doing so.

15.2   Tiers of Blockchain Technology

Like any other technology, blockchain is widely accepted and has evolved by leaps and bounds with time to be what it is at present. The different versions of blockchain technology [35] are explicated in the ensuing paragraphs.

15.2.1   Blockchain 1.0

With the invention of Bitcoin, this tier got introduced in the year 2009. This generation of blockchain is primarily used for cryptocurrencies. It is quite obvious and sensible to solely include cryptographic currencies in this first-generation category of Blockchain technology as Bitcoin was the first application of cryptocurrencies. In addition, along with Bitcoin all other alternative cryptocurrencies also fall in this category. It is worthy to state that the first generation of blockchain suffered from many major challenges such as limited throughput, slow confirmation of each transaction, no privacy, and high energy consumption while mining.

15.2.2   Blockchain 2.0

This version is primarily utilized by financial services and contracts. It started in the year 2010 when the concepts regarding using blockchain for other purposes started to appear. The 2.0 generation majorly comprises of different financial assets, such as, derivatives, bonds, swaps, to name but a few. Platforms like Etherum and Hyperledger are considered to be a part of this tier. Smart contracts were first introduced in this generation of blockchain.

15.2.3   Blockchain 3.0

The third generation of blockchain is used in different industries like the Government, health, media, and arts. Admittedly, this tier of blockchain emerged in the year 2012 when manifold different applications of blockchain technology were researched in different industries. It is believed that Blockchain 3.0 is highly scalable and adaptable, and it also endows its users with sustainability.

15.2.4   Blockchain X.0

The stage X.0 visions the concept of blockchain singularity wherein the blockchain service will be accessible to anyone such as the Google search engine. Precisely, the services would be endowed to all the domains of society. This tier of blockchain will be an open distributed ledger and public and will be operated by autonomous agents.

15.3   Characteristics of Blockchain

Admittedly, the consistent remarkable improvements in technology have brought about spectacular developments. Blockchain is one such technology that is in the spotlight and has gained immense popularity in recent times. Blockchain technology offers certain indispensable features that make it highly irresistible. These key features are elucidated in the ensuing paragraphs:

15.3.1   Decentralization

Blockchain technology is decentralized in nature, meaning that neither a third-party organization nor a central administrator looks after the blockchain system's framework. Instead, all the nodes (or the participants) in the network preserve the network and make decisions. The entire data is documented, and restructured on multiple systems, thus reducing the chances of failures [22]. Moreover, unlike the client-server model, the blockchain technology minimizes server costs and also alleviates the performance bottlenecks encountered in the centralized systems.

15.3.2   Immutability

No participant in the blockchain network can modify or amend any record after it gets recorded on the blockchain's shared ledger [33]. This attribute makes blockchain technology permanent, unalterable, and indestructible. Immutability thus enables a high degree of data integrity as it improves the trust and audit system in the public blockchains. The records on the blockchain can only be changed in an unprecedented situation wherein a person who has control over more than 51% of nodes at the same time. If, in an unlikely situation, the record of a transaction comprises of an error, then in that case, the new transaction will also get added to reverse the mistake, but then both the transactions in the network will be visible.

15.3.3   Persistency

This technology endows the infrastructure through which trust can be measured. The producers and consumers in the network also prove the genuineness of their data. All the blocks in the blockchain system are linked and connected. Moreover, the transactions are also related to the previous one in the block. Even if a transaction is updated simply, the hash of the block will also get changed. Besides, if anyone desires to amend or alter the information, then all the hash data of the previous blocks also have to be changed. This is considered to be a herculean task as a considerable amount of work needs to be done to modify the data. Also, other participants in the network confirm a block generated by the miner. Therefore, any falsification or manipulation of the data can be detected very easily [38].

15.3.4   Anonymity

Each user in the network can interact with other nodes with the help of a generated address. Thus, preventing the real identity of the user from getting disclosed [33]. Furthermore, in blockchain, a single user might have numerous identities, preserving the user's privacy to some level and preventing identity disclosure.

15.3.5   Auditability

Each transaction in blockchain is recorded through digital distributed ledger. These transactions are also validated by using a digital timestamp [6], thus facilitating the users with the feature of auditability and transparency to examine the state of data in the blockchain system.

15.3.6   Enhanced Security

This cryptographic feature in blockchain technology enhance the layer of security in the system. The complex mathematical algorithm in cryptography acts as a firewall against the attacks. Hence, it lays another protection in the system by providing unique identification for every data. The process of hashing wherein all the blocks have a unique hash of their own also includes the hash function of the preceding block. This feature thus provides enhanced security to the system as it is not possible to either change or tamper the data in the blocks, making it highly secure [7].

15.4   Concept of Blockchain Technology

Blockchain technology uses a decentralized and disseminated database and is composed of a sequence of blocks. These blocks consist of a list of transactions which has taken place and also a hash key of previous block along with a timestamp [32]. Hash key is a one-way function that is used to interlink the blocks. A hash key is made through a hash function which represents a mathematical algorithm that transforms any input (numbers, alphabets, media files) of any length into a fixed sized output. Thus, it is a linked list concept, meaning the blocks are interlinked in chronological sequence. It creates complete history commencing with the first block to the newly generated block [37]. These blocks are updated on a continuous basis, replicated, and circulated to each node present in the network, and also maintain integrity and timeliness of the data. As soon as the data inside the block is changed, the hash of the block also gets changed. Therefore, the hash function plays a significant role to detect any modifications within the block [27].

15.5   Taxonomy of Blockchain

The fundamental aim of Blockchain is to conduct transactions or exchange information by means of a trusted and secure network, which is universally recognized. Howbeit, the manner in which the users use blockchain vary ranging from public to private to consortium. The three kinds of blockchain are elucidated in the ensuing paragraphs.

15.5.1   Public Blockchain

Here, the user does not require any permission to join the network, meaning it is a non-restrictive distributed ledger system where all members of the network have access to the information and can read, write, and participate in the consensus process. A user can access the current state, past records, and verify transactions for an incoming block through several consensus algorithms and then do mining. Admittedly, the notion of blockchain got introduced in the mainstream with the advent of digital crypto currency, i.e., Bitcoin. Bitcoin and Etherum blockchain are the best epitome of public blockchain [17].

15.5.2   Private Blockchain

This is considered as restrictive and permissioned category of blockchain that can be operated only in a closed network or within an organization where only preapproved participants become part of such a system [10]. In addition, a private blockchain is much faster and more efficient than the public blockchain as the level of security, authorizations, permissions, and accessibility is owned and controlled by a single enterprise only. As a result, each new node wishing to join this network must first obtain permission from the network's administrator. Furthermore, the data delivered through such a network system is only accessible within that network. To exemplify, Hyperledger is one such system which is most popular among the private blockchain networks [34].

15.5.3 Consortium Blockchain

This is a hybrid blockchain that merges the advantages of both public and private type of blockchain. Here, out of the total nodes in the network, few are private while some are public [20]. Consequently, few of the nodes will be allowed to participate in the transactions whereas the other nodes will control the consensus process [18]. Even though all the participants (or the node) in the consortium blockchain can access the network, the level of information that can be accessed will be based on the node that is accessing that particular data. In other words, in this type of blockchain there exist two types of users. Out of these two, one of the users has the entire control and especially decides the level of security for a particular user, whereas the others have just access to blockchain.

15.6   Different Layers of Blockchain

In the following paragraphs, we'll go through the different five layers. The sequence of the layers has been suggested by past scholars [19] in the following manner (Figure 15.1).

15.6.1   The Data Layer

This layer acts as a data structure and physical storage in the blockchain. The data layer comprises of numerous key components that are comprehensively elucidated in the ensuing paragraphs.

15.6.1.1   Blocks

As the name depicts Blockchain is a linear structure comprising of a chain of blocks. The chain of blocks commences with a first block [29]. This chain then continues to grow as each newly confirmed block gets added to the already prevailing blockchain. These blocks contain several transactions in

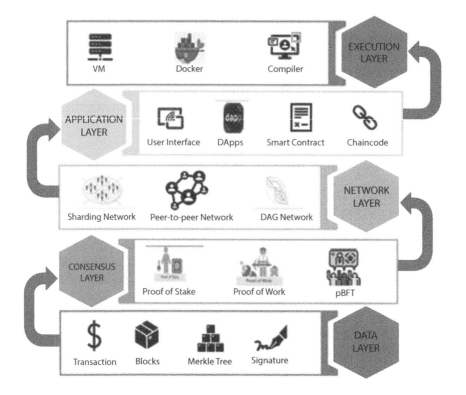

Figure 15.1 Layers of Blockchain (Source: Author).

a timely and sequential order along with a field that includes the hash value of the immediately preceding block, known as the parent block. Thus, the hash value creates a link between the consecutive blocks. All the blocks in a blockchain encompasses of a block header and block body.

The block header comprises of six significant elements, namely, block version, hash of the previous block, Merkle root, timestamp, a nonce, and nBits [22]. The block version in the block header signifies the version that a particular block is using, out of the three types of blockchain version. It will also state the validation rules a block has to follow. The next component is the hash of the previous block, which is a 256-bit hash value and points to the hash of the previous block. This is a one-way function whose aim is to verify the integrity of a transaction [24]. Basically, this component creates a connection and chronology between all the blocks. Timestamp in the blockchain is the time at which the event gets recorded in the computer. A notable feature of the timestamp is that it makes a note of the date and time of the day when the event took place, thus making it possible to track the progress over time [21]. Further, the header also comprises of a nonce that is abbreviated as 'number only used once'. Below the target level a hash value is produced by the nonce by means of a consensus mechanism. Lastly, a valid block hash is targeted by nBits [38].

All the records of the transactions that have taken place are arranged in a Merkle tree. It outlines all the transactions that are included in a block by producing a digital footprint of the complete set of transactions. Thus, Merkle tree represents a binary tree structure that permits the users to check the contents securely and efficiently. The Merkle tree is a significant part of the Block header and gets generated while a block is made.

15.6.1.2   Digital Signature

This is considered to be the fundamental building block in a blockchain. The primary aim is to validate the authenticity and trustworthiness of the transactions. Most importantly, these signatures follow a cryptographic approach in order to authenticate the digital content, thereby guaranteeing its integrity. Digital signatures utilize asymmetric cryptography, which is also known as the public key cryptography (PKI) system. Here, both the public key and a private key are used so that the data can be encrypted and decrypted accordingly [21]. Even though both of these keys are paired together, yet these are asymmetric, meaning they are not identical. Out of the two keys, only the public key is shared with the respective authorized entities, while the private key is kept secret with the owner itself. Interestingly, any of the keys can be used to encrypt the message, and the other one is utilized to decrypt it [19]. In some cases, when the data is sent through a non-secure channel at that time, these keys provide a layer of validation and security to the messages.

➤ Process of Forming and Verifying the Digital Signature in a Blockchain Network

    a) At the outset, the sender will sign a message with his private key [38]. It has been identified that in order to produce a digital signature of a message, the sender's signature algorithm generates a one-way hash of the message. A cryptographic hash function, also known as a mathematical method, takes random amount of data and maps it to a fixed-size bit array known as a hash value or simply a hash.

    b) The next step in the procedure is the verification of the message through the sender's public key [39]. The electronic signature related with the original content is verified by the receiver's signature algorithm in two steps, firstly, by producing the hash or digest of the message and secondly, by decoding the attached digital signature through the public key of the sender. If both digest (or hash) values are the same, the data hasn't been changed.

15.6.2   The Consensus Layer

Blockchain uses various protocols to validate a block; known as consensus algorithms to ensure data consistency and the chronological order of the transactions generated [20]. The entire data in the blockchain network is decentralized; therefore, there is no centralized system that can monitor the already existing or the previous transactions or can prevent the malicious attackers from manipulating or altering the data.

15.6.2.1   What is Consensus?

Broadly, the consensus is said to be a process of agreement on a single data value between the distributing nodes. To reach consensus, different methods are used. It is often quite simple and easy to reach an agreement when there are two nodes; however, when there are multiple nodes, then at that time, it is quite challenging to concur on a single value.

All the participants in the network follow a consensus mechanism. This method assists in reaching a common agreement regarding the current state of the distributed ledger. The consensus algorithms ensure the validity and authenticity of transactions in a distributed environment. Therefore, the prime aim of the consensus algorithm is to look out for a mutual agreement that is a win situation for the entire network [23].

15.6.2.2   Consensus in Blockchain

Consensus models in blockchain technology are the most vital components with various significant properties. The efficiency and scalability of the blockchain system are directly associated with the consensus model. The three utmost significant characteristics of the consensus models [8] are: (i) Safety – When each node in the blockchain network produce the same value or output then a consensus model is considered to be safe. Also, these values are valid as per the rules of the protocol. (ii) Liveness – When each of the nodes that take part in the consensus mechanism produce a value, then the consensus model will be accepted live. (iii) Fault Tolerance – A property wherein the system is able to deal with some amount of malfunctioning of a component. Therefore, when a participating node fails in the blockchain and the consensus model can effectively recover from that situation, then the consensus model is considered fault-tolerant.

Generally, the consensus models are categorized into two main categories, i.e., proof-based consensus model and voting-based consensus model.

I. Proof-Based Consensus Algorithms:

Usually, the proof-based algorithms are predominantly utilized in public blockchains, also known as permission-less blockchains. Here, the prime notion is that the nodes that join the blockchain have to solve the cryptographic problems to get the prerogative to append a new block to the already existing blockchain network. There are several proof-based consensus models and their variants through which consensus can be obtained in the blockchain; these are elucidated in the ensuing paragraphs:

- a.) Proof-of-Work (PoW): This consensus model is the most extensively utilized model in the blockchain system. Satoshi Nakamoto used this algorithm in the blockchain network to manage different transactions. Proof-of-work is the most common model to validate the transactions before adding relevant blocks in the blockchain network. The miners have to solve a complex mathematical puzzle to obtain the opportunity to add a new block [7]. They earn reward for the work done and the energy which got consumed. The major drawback of using the Proof-of-work is it consumes a huge volume of energy [31]. Moreover, this consensus model is unsuitable, especially for large as well as fast-growing networks. With the increase in the chain length, the complexity and the time required to solve this consensus model also surges. Thus, the need of high computing processing capabilities makes it inappropriate for long networks. Besides, Proof-of-work is more vulnerable to 51% attacks.
- b.) Proof-of-Stake (PoS): This model is a substitute for Proof-of-work and overcomes all the downsides encountered in Proof-of-work model. Here, the nodes having high number of cryptocurrencies or coins get the opportunity to append blocks in the network compared to the miners who possess fewer stakes or coins. The random selection technique is

used to elect a new block where on the basis of the number of stakes a miner possesses, a new block signer is elected [2]. Thus, plummeting the power consumption in mining to a great extent and proves to be more effective. In addition to this, the proof-of-stake consensus algorithm is also immune from the 51% attack. Before attacking the network, the malicious attacker must hold a substantial number of coins or stakes for quite a long time. This, in turn, curbs the threat of 51% attack and elevates the difficulty level of the attack. Oroboros and Casper are the two most well-known proof-of-stake based consensus models.

c.) Delegated Proof-of-Stake (DPoS): This model is a variant of proof-of-stake that improves the security feature of the proof-of-stake model. The block producer's election solely depends on the votes of the stakeholders [29]. Here, the stakeholders have the authority to create and authenticate the new block. The miners are known as delegates, and the selected delegates change every now and then with time and also, on the basis of assigned order, they deliver the blocks. The validation and confirmation of transactions will be quick enough if fewer selected nodes have to validate the block. Meantime, the delegates could tune the block size and block interval of the network. Besides, the DPoS is more efficacious as the existing nodes can easily vote the dishonest delegates. Hence, this algorithm is much faster and efficient and also makes sure it protects against issues at all extents.

d.) Leased Proof-of-Stake (LPoS): This is another derivative and modified version of proof-of-stake algorithm. It works in a similar manner as the proof-of-stake algorithm but with certain enhancements. Leased Proof-of-Stake attempts to tackle the centrality problem encountered in proof-of-stake. It permits the nodes having low stakes (or nodes possessing low balance) to take part in the process of block verification by leasing the stakes. The provision of leasing permits the wealth holders who possess high number of stakes (in other words, nodes that have high balance) to lease their funds for a specified period of time to the nodes having low balance. During lease contract, the original wealth holders will still have the possession of the amount [15]. This elevates the chance for nodes with a low balance to add a block. In return, the nodes share the reward with the original wealth holders, which is proportional to the fund leased. Hence, the LPoS approach makes the blockchain network more secure.

e.) Proof-of-Activity (PoA): This model is a blend of Proof-of-work (PoW) and proof-of-stake (PoS) and bestows a better level of security and low overhead on the network. In this protocol, the mining process starts in the same manner as in Proof-of-Work. Instead of mining the entire block, in Proof-of-Activity, solely the block's templates are mined by the miners [16]. The template comprises of the information of the header with the address of the miner. Once the mining process gets completed, the system is then converted to proof-of-stake. A certain group of validators is selected who sign the new block. The validator who possesses more coins or stakes is chosen. If a failure occurs at any time in this process, then a new group of validators is assigned, and the cycle continues till the precise number of signatures is received. Hence, PoA algorithm uses the best features of two consensus protocols to validate and add a block to the already existing chain of blocks. Moreover, it is more reliable and surges the protection level against attacks different attacks.

f.) Proof-of-Elapsed Time (PoET): This is one of the best and fairest consensus protocol. It is most commonly used in permissioned blockchains, i.e., consortium and fully private blockchain networks where permission is required to access the network and make appropriate decisions on mining rights [16]. To ensure smooth functioning, the PoET uses a tactic to maintain transparency in the entire network. The PoET network needs identification where the new miners are introduced to the chain for secure login into the system. Most importantly, all the nodes in the network have to wait for an arbitrary time interval and the participant who finishes their fair share of waiting time gets the opportunity to create a new block in the blockchain network. To ensure that the winning of the node is purely fair, PoET uses "Software Guard Extension" that assists in running unique codes within the network. Moreover, PoET completely excludes the need for expensive mining in Proof-of-work by using reliable devices.

g.) Proof-of-Capacity (POC): This is an enhanced version of Proof-of-work. The validators (or participants in the network) invest in hard drive space rather than spending on high priced hardware or burning the coins [30]. It is very fast in comparison to the Proof-of-work as it takes very less time to create a block with this consensus model. PoC also solves the hashing issue encountered in Proof-of-work. Burst coin is the only blockchain platform that supports this algorithm.

II. Voting-Based Consensus Algorithms

Voting-based consensus models are mainly utilized in private or consortium type of blockchain. In this category, the recognition of the nodes is required that will take part in the verification process, prior the work commences. All the nodes together validate the contents of the transactions prior to taking a decision [8].

a.) Practical Byzantine Fault Tolerance (PBFT): This consensus model mainly resolves the issues faced by Byzantine Fault Tolerance. It can also work effectively in situations when malicious nodes are in the system. The nodes are ordered sequentially. It is designed to work in an asynchronous system. One of the nodes is signified as the leader or the primary node, whereas the others are referred to as backup or secondary nodes. If a primary node fails in an improbable situation, any qualified secondary node might be allocated as the primary or leader node. The PBFT operating principle states that the number of malicious nodes should not exceed one-third of the total number of nodes in the system [16]. The consensus is achieved in four steps, i.e., Pre-prepare, prepare, commit, and reply. The leader nodes get replaced in every phase. The main advantage of this model is that it is energy efficient. PBET is prone to Sybil attacks and scaling, which are its two major demerits.

b.) Ripple Consensus Model: Here, all the miners use a trustworthy subset of nodes inside a large network to reach consensus. This consensus model has two kinds of nodes, i.e., server nodes and the client nodes. The former nodes include the Unique code list (UNL), while the latter type of nodes only transfers the funds. Every node in the ripple method has to make a unique node list (UNL) of which all the ripple nodes are a part. All the ripple nodes are reliable and cannot go against the unique node list. The ripple network persuades each node to communicate with several nodes available in the Unique Node List to achieve consensus in the network. Here, the consensus can be achieved when 80% of the nodes available in the UNL concur for a transaction [15]. This model is implemented again after a couple of seconds by all the nodes to achieve an agreement or consensus. Another round starts with new and pending transactions that did not get accepted.

c.) Tendermint: Tendermint protocol is a member of byzantine consensus algorithm family wherein a new block that has to be appended in the existing chain of blocks is determined in a round. The participants in this algorithm are named as validators. These validators propose blocks of transactions; then vote them as their chance comes. The voting procedure is divided into three stages: pre-vote, pre-commit, and commit. During the pre-vote phase, validators decide whether they will broadcast a pre-vote for the proposed block. Then in the pre-commit stage, if a node gets more than two-third of pre-votes on the block proposed, then it broadcasts a pre-commit for that particular block. However, if over two-thirds of pre-commits are received for a node, the block enters the next step, the commit stage. Finally, in the commit stage, the node validates the block and also broadcasts a commit for that block. When the node gets two-thirds of the commits, then eventually the block gets accepted and gets added to the blockchain [39].

In this protocol, the tendermint nodes or validators are selected on the basis of proof-of-stake, where they lock their coins. Besides, the dishonest validators are also punished here. This algorithm is highly advantageous as it has high scalability, high throughput, and low latency.

15.6.3   The Network Layer

This layer is also referred to as the P2P network, whose prime function is to establish communication between different nodes. The network layer makes sure that all the nodes in the network can easily discover each other. This layer also ensures that all the nodes easily connect with the other participants. It also synchronizes the current valid state of the blockchain. It is worth noting that all the nodes participating in the network are given equal privilege without any central control, as the blockchain system is under decentralized, developing, and bottom-up control [37]. These nodes validate the broadcasted data or blocks using specified check lists, with the invalid blocks from the network being rejected and the others being sent to surrounding nodes. Consequently, one block accepted by the maximum number of nodes will be added to the prevailing chain of blocks.

15.6.4   The Application Layer

The application layer of blockchain technology consists of smart contracts, chaincode, and dApps. This layer is further divided into sub-layers: the presentation layer and the execution layer. The presentation layer includes scripts, APIs, and user interfaces that connect the application layer to the blockchain network, whereas the execution layer includes smart contracts, chain code, and the underlying rules [28]. In fact, the executions layer runs all the transactions. Moreover, it is the presentation layer that sends all the instructions to the execution layer.

15.7   How Does Blockchain Work: The Process

Because of its incredibly complicated encryption scheme, blockchain provides a new and innovative way of documenting information on the internet.

At the outset, a user initiates a transaction by firstly creating it. The user then signs it digitally with his private key [9]. Basically, a unique digital signature will be generated by the private key that ensures the credibility and validity of the transaction. Subsequently, the transaction will then be broadcasted to the verifying nodes [11], and then all the participants present in the network start working on the consensus protocol in order to identify if the transaction created is valid or not.

Once the nodes in the network verify the transaction's authenticity, it then gets included in a block and following this, it is then disseminated to the network. It is worthwhile to accentuate that this newly added block will consist of a timestamp and unique cryptographic hash such as SHA-256 (Secure Hashing Algorithm) for the block, which is used as the 'Hash_Previous' for the next block [28].

As soon as all the transactions inside the block gets approval from the nodes, the new block gets attached to the previous block and will finally depict the latest state of the block to the remaining block in the network [12]. Likewise, a new block will form a link with this block, and the process thus continues. Hence, in this manner, a chain of blocks is formed, therefore the name blockchain.

15.8   Challenges in Blockchain

Blockchain also suffers from certain potential problems and limitations that cannot be overlooked like any other technology. If the data is not distributed, then the network is vulnerable to numerous plausible attacks. Following are some of the issues and challenges that can breach blockchain security and harm the entire network that uses blockchain.

15.8.1   Performance and Scalability

It is undeniable that blockchain-based solutions for various business models are becoming popular to a great extent; nevertheless, with the proliferating demand of this technology in different sectors, scalability and performance are the key factors that are a matter of concern. The two performance issues, namely, the throughput and latency are the key barriers when implementing blockchain. All the transactions are stored on each of the nodes for the purpose of validation. The burgeoning number of copies in the network negatively impacts the throughput and latency. It is nearly impossible to fulfill the need of processing a huge number of transactions in real-time [21]. Presently, the Bitcoin Blockchain has the capability to process only seven transactions per second that cannot deal with the increased amount of processing the message. As a result, it encounters low transactions throughput. Hence, scalability is one of the most challenging issues that must be addressed while designing Blockchain applications.

15.8.2   Privacy

The data privacy is preserved to a certain extent through public and private keys. The users in the network make transactions by using generated addresses rather than exposing their true identities. However, the transactional privacy might be vulnerable in this technology since the public can see the values of each transaction and the balances for all the public keys. Even though it is claimed that the users conceal their true identity while making transactions, yet there may be certain evidence that can disclose the original identity of the users along with their private information. Moreover, in the Bitcoin platforms, the history of Bitcoin transactions of the users can be linked to reveal their real identity. Also, the user's pseudonym is linked to IP addresses when the user is behind the firewall or Network Address Translation (NAT). Through this method, the client gets identified by a set of nodes it gets connected to, even though, the set could be utilized to seek out the origin of the transaction. Therefore, the user's entire data and multiple profiles may get hacked by third-party applications, resulting in hampering the user's privacy.

15.8.3   Selfish Mining

Selfish Mining is considered to be an unjust method to mine the pools that reduce the trustworthiness of the blockchain network. The blockchain network can be susceptible to selfish miners' attacks. A small percentage of hashing power can still prove to be vulnerable to cheat the blockchain network. In this process, the selfish miners hold on to their mined blocks without broadcasting them to the other members in the network. Eventually, the private branch of mined blocks continues to grow and is divulged to the public only after satisfying certain requirements. The longer private chain then replaces the original public chain. Consequently, the selfish miners receive more revenue. Thus, rational miners get inspired with the procurement of greater rewards and gravitate to be a part of the selfish mining pools. Thereby, elevating the computing and hashing power of selfish miners and also the competency to mine a longer chain [36].

15.9   Blockchain Security

The blockchain technology has gained pace in the 21st century and is utilized as an impressive and complementary technology to traditional cloud-based solutions for enhancing the security of data. It is a digital ledger of information that is decentralized in nature [32]. While it may be easy for the intruders to hack or corrupt the data in a traditional network where the data is kept in a single repository, howbeit the information stored in blockchain network makes it extremely hard for the malicious hackers to alter or remove the data as they need to change the block which contains the records and also the blocks which are connected with it in order to avoid detection. Encryption and validation, and decentralization of the data are the two prime features of this technology, making the data stored in these chains of blocks more secure [5].

All the records on a blockchain network are recorded by using an advanced cryptography mechanism [3]. This technology offers a podium that ensures that the entire data is encrypted and makes sure that the modification of data is an arduous task. Each transaction on a blockchain network is signed by a private key and then further authenticated using a public key. For all the transactions made by the network participants, they have their private keys to sign in, and these private keys act as their personal digital signatures. These digital signatures are also known as cryptographic signatures to ensure that the users' file is un-tampered. If an intruder tries to change the record, immediately the provided cryptographic signature gets invalid and the peer network also gets to know about any suspicious activity because of the decentralized nature of the network. Thus, blockchain technology facilitates its user with reliable and independent data verification which is worth considering.

This technology decentralizes and distributes the entire data across peer-to-peer network which is updated and synced consistently [27]. Blockchain as mentioned is a digital ledger of transactions and each node consists of a complete copy of the data. This signifies that in an unlikely situation, if two or more nodes break, it will not result in any loss of data as the rest of the nodes continue to operate. Besides, to accept any changes or alter any information this technology takes consensus from more than 50% of the peers which is a huge number. Moreover, blockchain makes efficient use of consensus protocols across all the computers in order to validate the transactions inside the new block. Following this, the new block of information is appended to the existing blockchain system. Thus, it removes the requirement of a third-party vendor to process as well as secure the information as this technology is itself extremely reliable and secured.

15.10   Amalgamation of Blockchain with Cloud Computing for Robust Security

Recently, in the world of technology, cloud storage has received an upward trajectory and is the most preferred choice for businesses owing to flexibility, capacity, and easy access of data. Inspite of the numerous benefits offered by the cloud model, there are still several challenges witnessed in a cloud computing model.

The biggest roadblocks to obtaining the benefits of cloud computing services are issues of confidentiality, privacy, and security [25]. Because of the multi-tenancy feature it is not easy to secure and ensure the safety of linked computers. The major demerit of using cloud computing by the HR managers can be loss and misuse of stolen data. Such mishaps can even bring down the biggest and renowned MNC's into ashes. The data stored in the public cloud can be breached as it is easily accessible by the malicious hackers. Even in private cloud solutions the malicious attackers can get unauthorized access to the data which leads to misuse of sensitive information of the organization [4]. Furthermore, the data is stored in remote locations because of which there occurs a probability that the user might be unable to delete any data from the cloud. This can lead to a situation like vendor lock-in where the user might not be able to access the information if the service provider faces any kind of problem [1]. Another area of concern while using cloud computing is related to security of the data. An internet connection is always needed to store high volume of data on the cloud. Anyone using cloud services is potentially at a risk of cyber-attacks. This usually occurs when malicious users use botnets to infect the cloud through malware and spam. Yet another type of security concern is service hijacking wherein unauthorized users gain illegitimate authority on certain authorized services [26].

To overcome the challenges related to privacy and security issues in cloud-based model, blockchain technology is used. The utilization of blockchain in cloud storage surges as well as enhances the security factor and simultaneously decreases an organization's vulnerabilities [3]. The feature of decentralization of data eliminates the risk of breach of data.

Blockchain based cloud storage solutions take the data of the user's; then break it in multiple encrypted chunks of data that are interlinked through a hash function. These encrypted chunks are then disseminated throughout the network. Each of these segments of data is stored on a decentralized location consequently making the data more secure [39]. The security is enhanced by using key features of blockchain i.e., hashing function, transaction ledgers and public/private key encryption. This feature ensures robust security against intruders. In unlikely cases, even if the hacker tries to sneak in the organization's data, he will only be able to get a small segment of data and not the complete file. He would still be unable to modify the data as the hashes of the blocks are interlinked – this secures data in blockchain based cloud storage solutions.

Another advantage of blockchain based cloud storage is that it prevents the user's data from tampering, which is one of the major concerns during the cloud storage. When the data is at rest and when the data is in transit, it is most likely for the data to get tampered. In order to eliminate this concern, blockchain offers a trusted way to track the storage, backup history and confirm that there is no deliberate modification of data through unauthorized channels. Precisely, the nodes already existing in the network validate the block. To make it tamperproof, a majority of the nodes need to concur that the block is valid. It thus facilitates the users with a strong and reliable provision of tracking the transactions through cryptographic hashes, which are time-stamped and immutable.

Thus, blockchain makes the technology an ideal and a convenient choice by adding an extra layer of security to the cloud storage [14]. It rightly integrates security and scalability with its key features like hash function, interlinked blocks, and decentralized architecture.

15.11   Emerging Applications of Blockchain

Blockchain technology possesses the capability to create more transparency as well as it greatly reduces the likelihood of data breach. This technology is garnering attention and can be utilized in a variety of sectors like healthcare, supply chain, identity management, to name a few. Following are some of the emerging applications outlined in different domains.

15.11.1   Healthcare

Irrefutably, blockchain has the capability to completely transform the health services. Blockchain is an encrypted distributed ledger that can be used to trace the drugs and also manage patient's data. The pharmaceutical industry suffers from the trouble of drug forging. A significant percentile of drugs that are sold in developing nations are counterfeited. The counterfeit drugs contain erroneous ingredients and also lack the exact level of essential ingredients. Blockchain technology can address the glitches in health sector in an efficient manner. The two prime attributes of blockchain technology namely immutability and its ability to digitally timestamp the transactions makes it much easier to trace a product thereby making the information tamper-proof.

Besides, to securely manage the patient's data is another matter of concern. Every patient suffers from unique physical inconsistency, so the approach to treat also differs as per the situation. To provide personalized treatments to the patients the doctors need to check the entire medical history of patient. Undeniably, the medical detail of each individual is highly sensitive and needs a secured sharing podium; however, the prevailing bookkeeping medical record system lacks privacy and interoperability. Thus, the utilization of blockchain technology is a plausible solution to tackle this matter of concern.

Blockchain is an immutable ledger technology, it proffers an infrastructure to integrate the medical records and data integrity. Blockchain has the potential to set up a robust and secure platform to store medical records digitally. The patients can securely keep all the information by using blockchain, consequently, assuring quality service to the patients, and also plummeting the treatment cost. By using a blockchain based framework to store medical records the patients have entire control on their medical records. Moreover, the patient possesses the power to share the access of their health records to respective doctors. This averts the shortfalls and mistakes in the patient's treatment and medication [6]. Most importantly, the collected patient history record assists the doctors in comprehending the requirements of patient and thus provides them more efficacious treatment.

15.11.2   Stock Market

Blockchain technology has the ability to make stock exchanges most favorable through its key features i.e., automation and decentralization. Blockchain can easily resolve the interoperability, trust, and transparency issues encountered in market systems that are fragmented. Owing to the role of mediators, the operational trade clearance and regulatory process takes over three days to finish and confirm all the transactions. Therefore, the various participants in the stock market undergo a complicated and an inefficient process. Blockchain thus provides a feasible solution and alters the way to trade in the stock market. It eradicates the need of intermediaries and accelerates the transactions and settlements and also reduces the hefty cost imposed on customers. Additionally, blockchain also can be used in clearing and settlement of the transactions. It makes the monotonous trade paperwork easy and legal ownership transfer as well as safely automates the post-trade process [6].

Besides, it also eliminates the requirement of a third party regulator to a great extent as all the rules and regulation will be in-built in the smart contracts. The blockchain network will therefore, act as a regulator for all the transactions.

15.11.3   Supply Chain

Supply chain comprises of the transactions of businesses to bring a product in the market that involves various entities that mutually trust each other and follow the regulations to deliver safe products and services in the market. In other words, supply chain management involves the process of planning and execution that consists of the flow of material, goods, and capital flow. The process commences with taking raw material to the manufacturers and delivering the end product to the consumers. Nevertheless, maintaining supply chain is a laborious task as this system is vulnerable to many issues such as corruption, tampering, and forgery. To combat the numerous issues like quality and safety scandals in many regulated industries blockchain can be implemented to tackle all the difficulties in the supply chain process in an efficacious manner [36]. Blockchain will ensure the traceability by keeping records, hence curtailing the chances of corrupting and tampering the system and thereby increasing the food safety.

References

1. Albugmi, A., Alassafi, M.O., Walters, R., Wills, G., Data security in cloud computing. *2016 Fifth International Conference on Future Communication Technologies (FGCT)*, pp. 55–59, 2016.
2. Andrey, A. and Petr, C., Review of existing consensus algorithms blockchain. *2019 International Conference "Quality Management, Transport and Information Security, Information Technologies" (IT&QM&IS)*, pp. 124–127, 2019.
3. Harshavardhan, A., Vijayakumar, T., Mugunthan, S.R., Blockchain technology in cloud computing to overcome security vulnerabilities. *2018 2nd International Conference on I-SMAC (IoT in Social, Mobile, Analytics and Cloud) (I-SMAC)I-SMAC (IoT in Social, Mobile, Analytics and Cloud) (I-SMAC), 2018 2nd International Conference on*, pp. 408–414, 2018. Malik, Gautam, S., Abidin, S., Bhushan, B., Blockchain technology-future of IOT: Including structure, limitations and various possible attacks. *2019 2nd International Conference on Intelligent Computing, Instrumentation and Control Technologies (ICICICT)*, pp. 1100–1104, 2019.
4. Kumar, A., World of Cloud Computing & Security. *Int. J. Cloud Comput. Serv. Sci. (IJ-CLOSER)*, 1, 2, 53–58, 2012.
5. Malik, A., Gautam, S., Abidin, S., Bhushan, B., Blockchain technology-future of IOT: Including structure, limitations and various possible attacks. *2019 2nd International Conference on Intelligent Computing, Instrumentation and Control Technologies (ICICICT)*, pp. 1100–1104, 2019.
6. Monrat, A., Schelen, O., Andersson, K., A survey of blockchain from the perspectives of applications, challenges, and opportunities. *IEEE Access*, 7, 117134–117151, 2019.
7. Nguyen, D.C., Pathirana, P.N., Ding, M., Seneviratne, A., Integration of blockchain and cloud of things: Architecture, applications and challenges. *IEEE Commun. Surv. Tutorials*, 22, 4, 2521–2549, 2020.
8. Khan, D., Jung, L.T., Ahmed Hashmani, M., Waqas, A., A critical review of blockchain consensus model. *2020 3rd International Conference on Computing, Mathematics and Engineering Technologies (iCoMET)*, pp. 1–6, 2020.
9. Puthal, D., Malik, N., Mohanty, S.P., Kougianos, E., Yang, C., The blockchain as a decentralized security framework. *IEEE Consum. Electron. Mag.*, 7, 2, 18–21, 2018.
10. Wang, H., Wang, Y., Cao, Z., Li, Z., Xiong, G., An overview of blockchain security analysis, in: *Communications in Computer and Information Science*, pp. 55–72, 2019.

11. Bashir, I., *Mastering blockchain: Distributed ledger technology, decentralization, and smart contracts explained*, 2nd ed., Packt Publishing Ltd., Birmingham, 2018.

12. Lin, I.C. and Liao, T.C., A survey of blockchain security issues and challenges. *Int. J. Netw. Secur.*, 19, 5, 653–659, 2017.

13. Bambara, J.J., Allen, P.R., Iyer, K., Madsen, R., Lederer, S., Wuehler, M., *Blockchain: A practical guide to developing business, law, and technology solutions*, McGraw-Hill, New York, 2018.

14. Park, J. and Park, J., Blockchain security in cloud computing: Use cases, challenges, and solutions. *Symmetry*, 9, 8, 164, 2017.

15. Saurabh, K. and Saxena, A., *Blockchain technology: Concepts and applications*, Wiley, India, 2020.

16. Sharma, K. and Jain, D., Consensus algorithms in blockchain technology: A survey. *2019 10th International Conference on Computing, Communication and Networking Technologies (ICCCNT)*, pp. 1–7, 2019.

17. Wust, K. and Gervais, A., Do you need a blockchain? *2018 Crypto Valley Conference on Blockchain Technology (CVCBT)*, pp. 45–54, 2018.

18. Sankar, L.S., Sindhu, M., Sethumadhavan, M., Survey of consensus protocols on blockchain applications. *2017 4th International Conference on Advanced Computing and Communication Systems (ICACCS)*, pp. 1–5, 2017.

19. Uddin, M.A., Stranieri, A., Gondal, I., Balasubramanian, V., A survey on the adoption of blockchain in IOT: Challenges and solutions. *Blockchain: Res. Appl.*, 2, 1–80, 2021.

20. Hölbl, M., Kompara, M., Kamišalić, A., Nemec Zlatolas, L., A systematic review of the use of blockchain in healthcare. *Symmetry*, 10, 10, 470, 2018.

21. Bhutta, M.N., Khwaja, A.A., Nadeem, A., Ahmad, H.F., Khan, M.K., Hanif, M.A., Song, H., Alshamari, M., Cao, Y., A survey on blockchain technology: Evolution, architecture and security. *IEEE Access*, 9, 61048–61073, 2021.

22. Niranjanamurthy, M., Nithya, B.N., Jagannatha, S., Analysis of blockchain technology: Pros, cons and SWOT. *Cluster Comput.*, 22, S6, 14743–14757, 2018.

23. Chaudhry, N. and Yousaf, M.M., Consensus algorithms in blockchain: Comparative analysis, challenges and opportunities. *2018 12th International Conference on Open Source Systems and Technologies (ICOSST)*, pp. 54–63, 2018.

24. Tasatanattakool, P. and Techapanupreeda, C., Blockchain: Challenges and applications. *2018 International Conference on Information Networking (ICOIN)*, pp. 473–475, 2018.

25. Bhadani, R., A new dimension in HRM: Cloud computing. *Int. J. Bus. Manage. Invent.*, 3, 7, 13–15, 2014.

26. Jathanna, R. and Jagli, D., Cloud computing and security issues. *Int. J. Eng. Res. Appl.*, 07, 06, 31–38, 2017.

27. Sharma, S.G., Ahuja, L., Goyal, D.P., Building secure infrastructure for cloud computing using blockchain. *2018 Second International Conference on Intelligent Computing and Control Systems (ICICCS)*, pp. 1985–1988, 2018.

28. Gupta, S., Sinha, S., Bhushan, B., Emergence of blockchain technology: Fundamentals, working and its various implementations, in: *Proceedings of the International Conference on Innovative Computing & Communications (ICICC)*, pp. 1–5, 2020.

29. Alsunaidi, S.J. and Alhaidari, F.A., A survey of consensus algorithms for blockchain technology. *2019 International Conference on Computer and Information Sciences (ICCIS)*, pp. 1–6, 2019.

30. Bamakan, S.M., Motavali, A., Babaei Bondarti, A., A survey of blockchain consensus algorithms performance evaluation criteria. *Expert Syst. Appl.*, 154, 113385, 2020.

31. Pahlajani, S., Kshirsagar, A., Pachghare, V., Survey on private blockchain consensus algorithms. *2019 1st International Conference on Innovations in Information and Communication Technology (ICIICT)*, pp. 1–6, 2019.

32. Pavithra, S., Ramya, S., Prathibha, S., A survey on cloud security issues and blockchain. *2019 3rd International Conference on Computing and Communications Technologies (ICCCT)*, pp. 136–140, 2019.

33. Xie, S., Zheng, Z., Chen, W., Wu, J., Dai, H.-N., Imran, M., Blockchain for cloud exchange: A survey. *Comput. Electr. Eng.*, 81, 106526, 2020.

34. Dinh, T.T., Liu, R., Zhang, M., Chen, G., Ooi, B.C., Wang, J., Untangling blockchain: A data processing view of blockchain systems. *IEEE Trans. Knowl. Data Eng.*, 30, 7, 1366–1385, 2018.

35. Bodkhe, U., Tanwar, S., Parekh, K., Khanpara, P., Tyagi, S., Kumar, N., Alazab, M., Blockchain for industry 4.0: A comprehensive review. *IEEE Access*, 8, 79764–79800, 2020.

36. Gao, W., Hatcher, W.G., Yu, W., A survey of blockchain: Techniques, applications, and challenges. *2018 27th International Conference on Computer Communication and Networks (ICCCN)*, pp. 1–11, 2018.

37. Yuan, Y. and Wang, F.Y., Blockchain and cryptocurrencies: Model, techniques, and applications. *IEEE Trans. Syst. Man. Cybern.: Syst.*, 48, 9, 1421–1428, 2018.

38. Zheng, Z., Xie, S., Dai, H., Chen, X., Wang, H., An overview of blockchain technology: Architecture, consensus, and future trends. *2017 IEEE International Congress on Big Data (BigData Congress)*, pp. 557–564, 2017.

39. Zheng, Z., Xie, S., Dai, H.N., Chen, X., Wang, H., Blockchain challenges and opportunities: A survey. *Int. J. Web Grid Serv.*, 14, 4, 352–375, 2018.

16

Network Security Issues in Blockchain Architectures

Keshav Kaushik

School of Computer Science, University of Petroleum and Energy Studies, Dehradun, India

Abstract

Owing to its decentralized, persistency, privacy, and auditability features, blockchain technology has gotten a lot of attention from both academia and industry. The usage of Blockchain technology in a wide range of applications, as well as its implementation problems, were investigated in this chapter. Due to the rapid advancement of technology, blockchain has swiftly become one of the most popular Internet technologies in recent years. Blockchain has restored confidence as a decentralized and distributed information management system, offering security, confidentiality, and integrity of data without the need for a third party, thanks to its inbuilt encryption and consensus mechanism. The current state of blockchain applications in cybersecurity was thoroughly investigated in this chapter. To address the security issues, the chapter looks at the advantages that blockchain has brought to cybersecurity, as well as current blockchain research and uses in cybersecurity. Bitcoin isn't impervious to misunderstandings about pseudonymity, privacy, and anonymity. Exclusively pseudonymous transactions are available with Bitcoin. Because Bitcoin is a decentralized worldwide public record, pseudonyms may be de-anonymized by analyzing blockchain usage trends. A lot of firms claim to have improved privacy by combining Bitcoin transactions from various users. Nevertheless, this entailed relying on a third party, which was not always safe or advantageous.

The blockchain innovation actualizes a decentralized completely duplicated attach just record in a shared organization, initially utilized for the Bitcoin digital currency. Blockchain in its effortlessness is a progression of associated information

Email: officialkeshavkaushik@gmail.com

Kiran Sood, Rajesh Kumar Dhanaraj, Balamurugan Balusamy and Seifedine Kadry (eds.) Blockchain Technology in Corporate Governance: Transforming Business and Industries, (353–368) © 2023 Scrivener Publishing LLC

structures called blocks, which contain or track all that occurs in any disseminated frameworks on a distributed organization.

The chapter will discuss about the security and privacy issues in blockchain technologies and its applications and challenges. It also explore the architecture and protocols related to blockchain technology. The book chapter also highlights the role of blockchain technology in cybersecurity. The chapter will also enlighten the readers about the application of blockchain technology in corporate governance. The chapter will expose the security and privacy concerns in blockchain that will be helpful for corporate governance officials, blockchain technology enthusiasts, students, PhD scholars and researchers.

Keywords: Blockchain, security, network security, challenges, blackchain applications

16.1 Introduction to Blockchain Technology: Applications and Challenges

In other words, the Blockchain is a public blockchain containing any transaction information, contracts, or other data that must be independently documented. One of the most essential features of Blockchain is that it can be viewed from hundreds of thousands of machines rather than a single location. The blockchain chain is already wreaking havoc on the financial services industry, and it is this technology that underpins the digital currency. People involved in the financial sector can directly interact and conduct transactions over the internet without the involvement of a third party thanks to Blockchain technology. Cryptographic algorithms, arithmetic, peer-to-peer communication, and other methods and algorithms are utilized in blockchain technology to solve the synchronization concerns of distributed databases. Blockchain may be thought of as a well-organized architecture for a variety of applications, including the financial industry, the Internet of Things, and medicine, to name a few. Bitcoin is a modern example of blockchain technology that is gaining popularity. Other blockchain applications include intellectual property rights, financial transactions, prediction markets, hyper ledgers, ethereum, etc. Blockchain technology [1] is a multi-field massive integration that incorporates cryptographic techniques, mathematics, algorithms, and economic models, blending peer-to-peer connections including using distributed consensus algorithms to solve conventional distributed database synchronization problems. The blockchain technology is made up of seven main components (as shown in Figure 16.1).

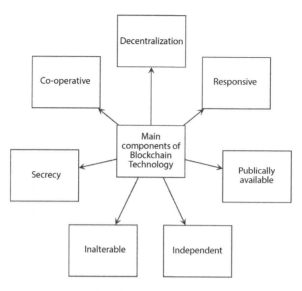

Figure 16.1 Main components of Blockchain Technology.

- Decentralization – A fundamental feature of blockchain is that it does not require a centralized node to document, hold, or update information; instead, data can be recorded, stored, and modified in a distributed manner.
- Responsive – The blockchain system's data record is transparent to each node, and it is also transparent when updating the information, which is why blockchain technology can be accepted.
- Publically Available – Individuals can use blockchain technologies to build any implementation they want, and most blockchain systems are open to everyone. Records can be checked openly, and people can use blockchain methods to develop any implementation they desire.
- Independent – Due to the obvious consensus foundation, each node on the blockchain system can securely transmit or change information; the concept is to accept a single person with the entire system, and no one can interact.
- Inalterable – The certain records will be confined indefinitely and cannot be changed unless more than 51 percent of the nodes are taken over at the same moment.
- Secrecy – Because blockchain technologies rectified the node-to-node trust challenge, data transfer, and even

transactions can be anonymized, with only the person's blockchain identifier required.

- Co-operative – The most significant advantage of blockchain is the establishment of a trust network between participants. As a result, participation from various value chain actors makes more sense. Bitcoin, for example, creates a trust system between private persons, enabling them to observe all network transactions and decide the cash being transmitted from one account to another without need for a centralized power.

The most interesting element of Blockchain [2] is that it significantly decreases the possibility of a security breach. As compared to conventional procedures, Blockchain utilizes numerous shared replicas of the same data base, making a data leakage or cyber-attack more difficult to perpetrate. Blockchain technique offers great ability to revolutionize multiple business industries by making procedures intelligent, safe, transparent, and effective than conventional business operations, thanks to its fraud-resistant functionalities. In this paper [3], we used a blockchain distributed network to address the networking scalability problem, while the Raft consensus algorithm was used to boost the bandwidth of the blockchain. Privacy is yet another major concern with IoT networks. Furthermore, the blockchain-distributed ledgers are public, and confidential information is accessible to anybody on the system; nevertheless, third-party alteration is not feasible without exposing the entire features in such circumstances. The authors employed a zero-knowledge-based cryptography solution, to address privacy concerns. There are multiple advantages of using blockchain technology, some of them are as follows:

- Reduced risks associated with cybercrime, forgery, and interfering
- More transparent processes with efficient record formation and monitoring
- Extremely safe due to cryptographic and decentralized Blockchain protocols
- Increased time efficiency due to real-time money transfers
- Overheads and middleman fees are eliminated with direct transactions.

The security, transparency, and immutability in the Blockchain Technology leads to its wide range of applications [4]. Figure 16.2 shows the multiple applications of Blockchain Technology.

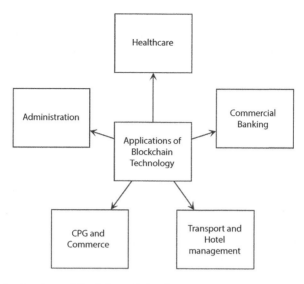

Figure 16.2 Applications of Blockchain Technology.

Financial institutions, healthcare, administration, transport and logistics, retail, and consumer packaged goods are just some of the sectors that can benefit from blockchain technology.

- Commercial Banking: Blockchain technology has already been used in a variety of innovative ways in the financial services industry. By offering an automated trade lifecycle where all contestants have access to the data about a transaction, blockchain technology facilitates and expedites the full procedure associated with wealth management and payouts. This eliminates the need for intermediaries or counterparties, ensuring accountability and efficient data management.
- Healthcare: Blockchain technology has the potential to improve the confidentiality, security, and interconnectivity of healthcare data. It has the opportunities to resolve many of the industry's interoperability issues and enable secure data sharing among the multiple stakeholders and individuals involved in the process. It eradicates third-party intervention while also avoiding operating expenses. Healthcare files can be accessed in decentralized data bases using Blockchains by encrypting them and using digital signatures to preserve the privacy and integrity.

- Transport and Hotel Management: Blockchain technology has the potential to transform the tourism and hospitality sector. It can be used for monetary transactions, stashing sensitive papers such as travel documents and other identification cards, making reservations, handling travel insurance, and rewarding loyalty.
- CPG and Commerce: Blockchain technology has a lot of potential for use in the retail industry. This provides assurance the truthfulness of high-value products, attempting to prevent suspicious transactions, tracking down stolen merchandise, empowering virtual warranties, managing loyalty points, and simplifying logistics operations, among other things.
- Administration: Blockchain technology has the potential to incorporate the processes and services of the authorities. It has the potential to significantly improve data transactional difficulties in the public sector, which currently operates in silos. The appropriate connection and dissemination of knowledge with Blockchain allows for better data management across agencies. It increases transparency and makes it easier to supervise and audit transactions.

Despite the fact that Blockchain Technology has a lot of potential [5], there are some obstacles that prevent it from being used in a wider range of applications. The Figure 16.3 shows the challenges related to the blockchain technology. The following are a few significant challenges:

- Extensibility – The overall volume of blockchain are increasing day by day as the amount of transactions increases. All transactions must be collected and validated on the blockchain by each node. Aside from that, the magnitude of blocks and the time it takes to publish them are both limited in blockchain. There is a limit of seven operations per second. This may not be enough to meet the need for real-time data computation.
- Selfish Mining – This type of attack is more likely to occur on blockchain. Selfish mining is a technique in which an overly ambitious miner retains his blocks hidden and does not publish them. It would only be made publicly available if certain conditions were met. All other miners would concur to this secretively mined private chains that are prolonged than the existing publicly available sequence. As a consequence, honest miners would have squandered their time and money on a

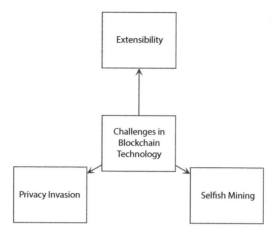

Figure 16.3 Challenges in Blockchain Technology.

sequence that would eventually be neglected. Selfish miners may be compensated incentives in this way.

- Privacy Invasion – The use of public key cryptography in exchanges in blockchain maintains a high level of privacy, allowing users' identities to remain anonymous. Nevertheless, since all transactions and balances for every cryptographic key are available publicly, blockchain cannot guarantee transactional confidentiality. By keeping track of the transactions, it is possible to recognize the consumer.

16.2   Comparative Study of Security and Privacy in Popular Blockchain Technologies

The bitcoin cryptocurrency's Blockchain concept has evolved as a promising decentralized technology for ensuring peer-to-peer transactions, data integrity, and transparent storage.

16.2.1   Security in Blockchain

The safeguarding of transaction information and data in a block from intrinsic, extrinsic, malicious, and inadvertent attacks is characterized as security in Blockchain. This protection usually entails threat detection, threat prevention, and proper threat response employing technologies, IT services, and security policies.

In order to integrate the inherent advantages of decentralized data storage, P2P infrastructure, cryptography and consensus protocols [6], Blockchain compromises on optimal computing capacity, storage resources and bandwidth. Following are the key benefits of Blockchain in terms of security:

i. Tamper Proof System of Blockchain
    A certain majority of users must always provide their consent to write data in blocks. Preferably, this percentage is chosen to be greater than 50%. Because of the consensus approach, attackers must either control more than half of the network nodes or have more computing capacity to manipulate data during the data recording phase.

ii. Recovery from Disaster
    Unlike a conventional centralized database, a distributed database stores data in multiple locations. Every member of Blockchain has the ability to create data and keep a complete record of that as well. By developing open source sharing mechanisms, Blockchain accomplishes data acquisition and storage synchronously at all members' locations. This approach may result in some duplication [7, 8], but the network's dependability and fault tolerance are boosted.

iii. Privacy Protection
    Asymmetric encryption is used in Blockchain to allow users to encrypt data with their own private key [9–11]. Furthermore, the hash value of a user's public key is calculated and serves as the user's ID indication. Blockchain accomplishes its purpose of maintaining user anonymity and privacy, as the hash value has no reference to the user's true identity, ensuring that the user's personal information is kept private. Moreover, an attacker can't figure out a user's public key from their public user address, and it's impossible to calculate the private key from the public key.

16.3 Security Issues in Blockchain Technology

In past few years, blockchain has attracted much interest. Although the numerous characteristics of blockchain technology have provided us with efficient and trustworthy services, security and privacy vulnerabilities remain a source of concern that must be addressed. Figure 16.4 depicts the prime security concerns which need to be addressed.

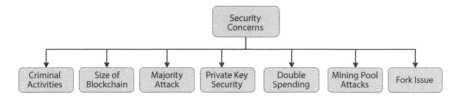

Figure 16.4 Prime security concerns.

I. Majority Attack

The computer power is dispersed across all accessible data miners in distributed consensus mechanism. The hashes generated by CPU cycles are verified by these data miners. If these miners team up, they can constitute a large mining pool with the most processing power. If a mining pool has 51% or more processing capabilities, it has the ability to take control of the Blockchain, posing major vulnerabilities such as double spending, halting verification process,   reverse transaction attacks, modify and exclude transactions, interrupting operations of other miners etc.

II. Private Key Security

The user's private key is regarded as a strong authentication credential created by the user in blockchain systems, with no third party involved. When a user establishes a cryptocurrency wallet, he or she must also import the private key into the wallet. To ensure the security and authentication of the coins, this private key is imported into the wallet. If a user's private key is lost or stolen, he or she will be unable to access the wallet by any other methods, rendering all of the user's cryptocurrencies in the wallet inaccessible. The same poses a risk of data manipulation by adversaries.

III. Double Spending

Double spending occurs when a consumer uses the same cryptocurrency for several transactions. To commence double spending, an attacker can use race attacks. These types of attacks are quite convenient to carry out on a POW-based blockchain since the attacker may simply exploit the interval between the commencement and confirmation of two transactions. Before the attacker's second transaction became illegitimate, he obtained the output of the first, which might result in double spending.

IV. Client Side Security Threats

To access individual cryptocurrency wallets, each user on the Blockchain network has a set of private public keys. It's critical to keep control of these keys in a secure manner. Client-side security is crucial because if the user loses or compromises the keys, he or she will be unable to access the wallet and will result in irreversible financial loss.

V. Mining Pool Attacks

Mining pools are constructed to boost a block's computational power or hash power. These pools have a direct impact on the time it takes to verify a block. These mining pools also increase your likelihood of earning a mining reward. These mining blocks are becoming more vulnerable to internal as well as external attacks. Internal threats occur when a miner collects more than the necessary rewards with the intent of interrupting functionality, forcing the pool to overlook successful mining attempts. External attacks occur when a miner attacks the pool with more hash power, resulting in double spending.

VI. Fork Issue

The fork problem is critical issue because it touches on several aspects of Blockchain and is linked to the decentralized node version and agreement during software upgrades. Hard fork and Soft fork are the two types of fork.

In Hard Fork, when a network releases a new version or agreement that is incompatible with earlier versions, the old nodes are unable to agree to the mining of new nodes, and the chain splits into two. Even though the computing capacity of new nodes is greater than that of old nodes, old nodes will continue to maintain the chain that they believe is correct.

When a Soft Fork occurs, nodes in the network do not have to update to the new agreement all at once; instead, they can upgrade in phases. Soft Fork, unlike Hard Fork, would only have one chain and will not compromise the system's reliability and efficiency when nodes update. Soft Fork, on the other hand, renders older nodes uninformed that the consensus rule has changed, which runs against to the concept that all nodes can validate correctly to a certain level.

VII. Criminal Activities

A single user can have multiple Bitcoin addresses associated with them, and the addresses are independent to their real-life identities. As a result, Bitcoin was used for illicit purposes. Various third-party platforms support Bitcoin, and consumers can leverage these platforms to transact things. Since the process of selling and buying via third-party platforms is private, it is near to impossible to discern user behavior. The most common criminal actions involving Bitcoin include money laundering, underground marketing, ransomware, etc.

VIII. Size of Blockchain

As blockchain progresses, information observes huge increase, causing the loading of stores and computing much more difficult. It takes a long time to synchronize data, while data continues to grow, posing a significant challenge for clients while using the system [12].

Table 16.1 lists some critical security issues and challenges faced in an IoT network and proposed solutions to deal effectively with these challenges.

Table 16.1 Blockchain Security Issues and Solutions in IoT [13].

Issues and challenges in IoT security	Blockchain-based solutions
Authentication	Asymmetric cryptography is employed in a distributed manner in Blockchain, and each item in the Blockchain system has a distinct hash id that is exposed to all nodes. As a result, it builds confidence among the network's components.
Identity Management	Blockchain's distributed ledger and immutability can be employed.
Authorization/Access Control	Ethereum Blockchain, for example, has smart contracts.
Integrity of Data	All Blockchain nodes have the same information, which they may verify by comparing it to earlier data.
Interoperability	Because blockchain is distributed and automated, it is the foundation for all interoperability requirements.
Privacy	For anonymity, private blockchains and smart contracts can be employed.

16.4   Privacy in Blockchain

In Blockchain, privacy refers to the ability to carry out transactions without disclosing personal information. Privacy enables a user to remain compliant by judiciously revealing information without disclosing their activities to the entire network. Strengthening Blockchain privacy strives to make it much more difficult for other users to replicate or use a user's Blockchain profile.

Some important privacy features are:

    i.   The flexibility of Blockchain allows for the storage of any type of data.

    ii.   Transparency and verifiability are two fundamental advantages of Blockchain technology that are supported by this data redundancy.

    iii.   It's hard to change preceding blocks' data without being identified in the Blockchain.

    iv.   From the perspective of privacy, the accessibility of Blockchain is impressive. All users can add data to public or non-permissioned Blockchain applications.

16.4.1   Privacy Issues in Blockchain Technology

Blockchain technology is now generating a lot of buzz, with possible applications in areas as broad as law enforcement, finance, real estate, entertainment, healthcare etc. Different blockchain applications bring different difficulties and opportunities in terms of data security and privacy. Following are listed some of the important privacy concerns:

    I.   For communicating with the online world, biometric identifiers will soon assume the role of usernames and passwords. One drawback to this strategy is that in order for a physical person to log into a network, the network need a copy of both their login credentials and their online identity. To guarantee anonymity, these credentials must be held in a centralized system, but in a Blockchain network, these credentials would be saved on all nodes that carry the Blockchain you wish to speak with, some of which are more vulnerable to hacking than a secure central server.

II. One more challenge with blockchain is the lack of a robust central authority; once a person's login credentials are obtained, it may be difficult to prevent hackers from accessing critical data.

III. Due to the obvious blockchain's decentralized nature, hackers may target certain nodes that are easier to breach in order to get access to the encrypted data, or where restrictions are ineffectual in preventing such attacks.

IV. While the data is encrypted, one disadvantage of open networks is that vital information may be deduced from the fact that transactions occurred. For example, if a doctor makes modifications to a patient's health data, a hacker who knows the doctor's and patient's online identities can observe the transaction and conclude that the patient has visited a certain doctor on a given day.

V. In present scenarios, data is being generated increasingly and is easy to be accessed by the broader public in ways it has never been before. As the number of transactions saved in blockchains grows, so will the number of permanent records of each transaction. Every future transaction will be recorded on a Blockchain, and you will have no control over where this information is stored, how it is utilized, or how to erase it.

16.5   Open Issues and Challenges of Security and Privacy in Blockchain Technology

Figure 16.5 shows some of the major issues and challenges of security and privacy in Blockchain technology.

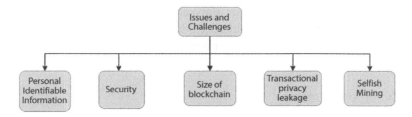

Figure 16.5 Issues and challenges of security and privacy in blockchain.

I. Personal Identifiable Information: Any information that can be used to determine an individual's identify is referred to as personal identifiable information (PII). [14] Mentioned regarding PII in terms of communication and location privacy.

II. Security: As mentioned in [15], security can be considered in terms of confidentiality, integrity, and availability. In open networks like public blockchains, it's always a challenge. In distributed systems that imitate information over a network, confidentiality is low. Although there are numerous issues, blockchains are known for their integrity. Readability is high in blockchains due to widespread replication, however write availability is low.

III. Size of blockchain: The blockchain is getting increasingly enormous in size as the volume of blockchain usage grows and the number of transactions per day rises. To be validated, all transactions are saved in each node. The source of the current transaction must be confirmed before the transaction may be authorized. In real-time applications, the restricted block size and time interval necessary to construct a new block contribute to the impossibility to process millions of transactions at once. Nevertheless, because miners prefer to confirm transactions with greater transaction fees, the size of blockchain blocks may induce transaction delays in the event of tiny transactions.

IV. Transactional privacy leakage: The blockchain is particularly vulnerable to transactional privacy leakage since the information and balances of all public keys are available to everyone in the network.

V. Selfish Mining: If only a small percentage of the hashing power is employed, a block is vulnerable to cheating. Miners in selfish mining retain the mined blocks without disseminating them to the network, instead creating a private branch that is broadcast only after certain conditions are met. Honest miners squander a lot of time and resources in this instance, while selfish miners mine the private chain.

16.6 Conclusion

Blockchain technology is widely recognized and respected because to its decentralized architecture and peer-to-peer character. These capabilities may be used to address a wide range of requirements in a variety of sectors and applications. In this chapter, we look at the security and privacy problems surrounding blockchain technology, as well as its applications and challenges. It also delves into the blockchain technology's architecture and protocols. The relevance of blockchain technology in cybersecurity is also highlighted in this chapter. Due to its rapid growth and evolution, we anticipate that blockchains will become a highly popular and well-known phenomena very soon. Blockchain may be likened to the Internet from a few generations earlier in several aspects. Because blockchains are secure and supportive at their core, many key applications requiring security and non-repudiation will eventually migrate to this platform. Although blockchains have inherent limits and many creative applications are difficult to deploy, as the technology matures, blockchain is anticipated to become the technology that all will move towards.

References

1. Lin, I.C. and Liao, T.C., A survey of blockchain security issues and challenges. *Int. J. Netw. Secur.*, 19, 5, 653–659, 2017.
2. What is Blockchain Technology | Blockchain Applications, https://www. happiestminds.com/Insights/blockchain/ (accessed Oct. 19, 2021).
3. Dwivedi, A.D., Singh, R., Kaushik, K., Mukkamala, R.R., Alnumay, W.S., Blockchain and artificial intelligence for 5G-enabled Internet of Things: Challenges, opportunities, and solutions. *Trans. Emerg. Telecommun. Technol.*, e4329, Jul. 2021.
4. Ali, M.A. and Bhaya, W.S., Blockchain technology's applications and challenges: An overview. *AIP Conf. Proc.*, 2290, 1, 040019, Dec. 2020.
5. Jena, A.K. and Dash, S.P., Blockchain technology: Introduction, applications, challenges. *Intell. Syst. Ref. Libr.*, 203, 1–11, 2021.
6. Yli-Huumo, J., Ko, D., Choi, S., Park, S., Smolander, K., Where is current research on blockchain technology?—A systematic review. *PLoS One*, 11, 10, e0163477, Oct. 2016.
7. Wang, L. and Liu, Y., Exploring miner evolution in bitcoin network, in: *Lect. Notes Comput. Sci. (including Subser. Lect. Notes Artif. Intell. Lect. Notes Bioinformatics)*, vol. 8995, pp. 290–302, 2015.
8. Paul, G., Sarkar, P., Mukherjee, S., Towards a more democratic mining in bitcoins, in: *Lect. Notes Comput. Sci. (including Subser. Lect. Notes Artif. Intell. Lect. Notes Bioinformatics)*, vol. 8880, pp. 185–203, Dec. 2014.
9. Meiklejohn, S. and Orlandi, C., Privacy-enhancing overlays in bitcoin, in: *Lect. Notes Comput. Sci. (including Subser. Lect. Notes Artif. Intell. Lect. Notes Bioinformatics)*, vol. 8976, pp. 127–141, 2015.

10. Zyskind, G., Nathan, O., Pentland, A.S., Decentralizing privacy: Using block-chain to protect personal data. *Proc. - 2015 IEEE Secur. Priv. Work. SPW 2015*, pp. 180–184, Jul. 2015.

11. Kosba, A., Miller, A., Shi, E., Wen, Z., Papamanthou, C., Hawk: The block-chain model of cryptography and privacy-preserving smart contracts. *Proc. - 2016 IEEE Symp. Secur. Privacy, SP 2016*, Aug. 2016, pp. 839–858.

12. Karame, G.O., On the security and scalability of bitcoin's blockchain, in: *Proceedings of the ACM Conference on Computer and Communications Security*, 24-28-October-2016, 1861–1862, 2016, https://doi.org/10.1145/2976749.2976756.

13. Kumar, R. and Sharma, R., Leveraging blockchain for ensuring trust in IoT: A survey. *J. King Saud Univ. - Comput. Inf. Sci.*, 34, 7, Sep. 2021.

14. Rehman, A.U., Malik, A.K., Raza, B., Ali, W., A hybrid CNN-LSTM model for improving accuracy of movie reviews sentiment analysis. *Multimed. Tools Appl.*, 78, 18, 26597–26613, Jun. 2019.

15. Mendling, J., Weber, I., Van Der Aalst, W., Brocke, J. Vom, Cabanillas, C., Daniel, F., Debois, S., Di Ciccio, C., Dumas, M., Dustdar, S., Gal, A., García-Bañuelos, L., Governatori, G., Hull, R., La Rosa, M., Leopold, H., Leymann, F., Recker, J., Reichert, M., … Zhu, L., Blockchains for business process management - challenges and opportunities. *ACM Trans. Manage. Inf. Syst. (TMIS)*, 9, 1, 1–16, 2018. https://doi.org/10.1145/3183367

17

A Comprehensive Report on Blockchain Technology, Its Applications, and Open Research Challenges

Shilpi Garg, Rajesh Kumar Kaushal* and Naveen Kumar

Chitkara University Institute of Engineering and Technology, Chitkara University, Punjab, India

Abstract

The IoT is a vast technology that allows communication between billions of devices worldwide. The massive amount of data produced by these sensors must be controlled in a secure manner. The centralized solutions are not suitable for these concerns due to security challenges and scalability problems. Thus, blockchain technology is an effective solution, and the "distributed" method has been engaged to overcome these issues to allow for entirely secure communication among devices. Blockchain is an encrypted, distributed, and immutable ledger technology. The main objective of this chapter is to present the state of art of blockchain technology in IoT environment. Integration of Blockchain technology with IoT also produces some challenges like scalability, throughput, and power consumption. The search terms like IoT, Blockchain, Blockchain and IoT issues, Blockchain and IoT applications has been used. After exclusion 40 papers were included for this study. The ramifications of this study is that it will absolutely help the scholars and academician to understand the approach of Blockchain in IoT environment and gives useful insights for improvements of blockchain based IoT ecosystem by integrating other technologies such as artificial intelligence, big data and cloud computing.

Keywords: IoT, Internet of things, blockchain, open challenges, consensus

---

**Corresponding author*: rajesh.kaushal@chitkara.edu.in

Kiran Sood, Rajesh Kumar Dhanaraj, Balamurugan Balusamy and Seifedine Kadry (eds.) Blockchain Technology in Corporate Governance: Transforming Business and Industries, (369–386) © 2023 Scrivener Publishing LLC

17.1   Introduction

In the recent year, Internet of Things (IoT) is used as an emerging technology for several real-world applications like smart homes, smart city, smart transportation, etc. to prepare a safe and good human life. In IoT environment, an emissive amount of data is collected by sensor devices over the network. Several IoT Issues that arise include security, single point of failure, data maintenance, privacy, and bottleneck in data flow. To mitigate these issues, researchers used blockchain technology in IoT environment that ensure the secure transmission of data, privacy and security.

Blockchain has become a more trending research topic due to the development of crypto currencies. Blockchain stores every transaction in a distributed and immutable manner. Once a valid transaction is added to the block, no one can temper or alter that valid transaction. Blocks are cryptographically linked to the previous block by using a previous hash value. The SHA-256 algorithm is used to create hash values. This hash code is different for each block. Blockchain technology's key features such as decentralized, immutable ledger, security, and audibility are discussed below.

- Decentralized: Blockchain technology stores all transactions on a decentralized network therefore every node has equal rights to access and share the storage space.
- Immutability: Blockchain technology stores the data as an immutable ledger. Once a valid transaction is added to a block, no one can tamper with the transaction. All the valid transactions are permanently added to the Blockchain.
- Anonymity and Security: Blockchain ensures anonymity and security to transaction data. Nodes use a virtual identity code as a digital signature to communicate across the P2P network that prevents the attacker from tampering with the transaction.
- Auditability and traceability: Blockchain securely offers the traceability of data. Due to this design, the transaction can be easily verified and tracked.

Blockchain technology is classified into three categories (Public, Private, Federated) that depend on the rights to access the Blockchain. Public Blockchain is also called permission less Blockchain because it gives the right to everyone to access the decentralized network. Public blockchain efficiency is very low and consumes more energy in accessing the transaction. In contrast, private Blockchain offer access to only authorized people.

So it is also named permissioned Blockchain. The permissioned Blockchain is not to be considered as secure and transparent because authorized nodes can tamper with the data. Nowadays, federated Blockchain is gaining huge popularity because it provides the flexibility to function as permission less or permissioned blockchain.

17.2   Related Work

Authors in [1] divides IoT challenges into four parts: cost and capacity constraint, deficient framework, cloud server down time and unavailability of services, susceptibility to manipulation. To improve the security for supply chain network the researchers suggested a blockchain solution for each challenges in IoT.

In another study [2] designed a novel architecture for data processing at the cloud layer via e-route processing which is achieved by network function virtualization, software defined network and machine learning. Researchers [3] design a blockchain-based access control program for the Internet of Drones to provide secure communication between the drones and ground station servers. It provides security by using RPCA (Ripple protocol consensus algorithm) against the various passive and active attacks.

In [4] used blockchain technology IoT powered Smart Home through the gateway approach to deal with transactions generated by home appliances. To provide security to smart homes authors in [5] proposed a blockchain-based solution by using combined HLF (Hyper Ledger Fabric) and HLC (Hyper Ledger Composer). This solution is mainly used in permission blockchain. The designed architecture consists of four layers names cloud storage, HLF, HLC, and smart home layer. The adoption of blockchain technology in the IoT environment increases power consumption, overhead, and delay which is not suitable for IoT devices. To reduce these issues [6] suggested a blockchain-based IoT framework for smart cities.

Researchers [7] presented a QIQW (Quantum Inspired Quantum Walks) encryption mechanism for a blockchain-based IoT framework that provides secure transmission between the IoT devices. Blocks are cryptographically linked by using a quantum hash function.

To mitigate the cyber-security issues for IoT systems [8] presented a blockchain-based RNN (Random Neural Network) authentication method. By using neural weights identity of devices and users is kept secret and mined the identities using blockchain. This method increases access control to information.

To provide privacy to IoT data [9] proposed a blockchain-based IoT architecture by using HIBE (Hierarchical identity-based encryption), CloudLet, and edge computing. To address the data storage security for smart homes [10] used blockchain technology with different cloud providers. To increase the data storage capacity and efficiency, the authors design a scheme IBPAS (Identity-based proxy aggregate signature). By using this scheme with blockchain, data storage capacity is increased by 20%.

Edge computing for smart cities comes with security challenges. Blockchain provides a solution for these issues. Haung *et al.*, [11] proposed a blockchain-based network propagation protocol using RON (Resilient overlay network). The authors used the shortest path and policy algorithms to make a propagation path among the blockchain nodes. This results in decreasing the routing overhead and delay and improves the transmission rate.

Similarly Alzubi, [12] proposed a blockchain-based system for IoT medical devices by using LMSD (Lemport Merkle Digital Signature) that provide authentication and security to patient data. This algorithm uses a tree structure in which leaves store the hash value of patient data. Centralized healthcare (CHC) controller found the root of the tree by using a verification process. The proposed techniques ensure high security and decrease the computational time and overhead in medical IoT systems. Islam and Young Shin, [13] Developed a blockchain-based scheme that securely collects the health record from users through a UAV (unmanned aerial vehicle) and stores all the collected data on the nearest server. In this scheme, a UAV sets up a connection with BSHs (Body sensors hives) by using a token and then securely communicates with BSHs by sharing a key to receive the encrypted data and then securely store all the decrypted data in the blockchain on the nearest server.

17.3   Objectives

The main objective of this chapter is to present the state of art of blockchain technology in IoT environment and disclosing its emerging application areas. Moreover this chapter is also disclosing various open research issues that need to be resolved to speed up the transaction.

17.4   Methodology

The objectives have been achieved by conducting the search on Scopus platform. The search terms like IoT, Blockchain, Blockchain AND IoT (issues OR applications) were used to search the relevant studies. The inclusion

Table 17.1 Inclusion and exclusion criteria.

Criteria	Specified criteria
Inclusion	• Studies that address adoption of blockchain in IoT environment • Studies published from 2013 to 2021
Exclusion	• Studies reported in a language other than English • Information from magazines, newspapers

and exclusion criteria for this study is disclosed in Table 17.1. After exclusion 29 papers were included for this study.

17.5   IoT Architecture

Universally, no single framework for IoT is acceptable. Researchers have recommended different IoT architectures and a three-layered architecture is a basic framework for IoT. It includes only three layers namely Perception layer, Network layer and Application layer.

  a. Perception layer is the first layer of IoT framework. This layer provide the interface between physical objects like sensors and actuators and collects the sensing data to identify the smart objects. Basically, this layer collects the information from sensors and sends that information to above layer. For data collection, this layer used many technologies such as sensor, RFID, barcode, etc.

  b. Network layer provide communication between the devices and servers. This layer receives information from perception layer and sends to the above layer for further processing with the use of different technologies like 3G, 4G, Wi-Fi, Zig-bee, etc. This layer securely and confidentially transfers all the information.

  c. Application layer is responsible for providing services to end-users. This layer manage, store and process all the information gained from the network layer and make decision for services.

Three layered framework represent the basic idea of IoT but to work on IoT based projects, five layered framework is recommended of IoT is shown in Figure 17.1. The functionality of perception layer and application layer is identical to three layer framework. The further layers transport, processing, and business are discussed below.

a. Transport layer is responsible for transferring the data that received from sensors to the processing layer and from processing layer to perception layer across networks like 3G, 4G, LAN, RFID, Bluetooth, etc.
b. Processing Layer also called middleware layer. This layer is responsible for storing, examining, and processing the data received from the lower layer. For data storing and managing, this layer used various technologies like database software, bid data, cloud and ubiquitous computing, etc.
c. Business Layer is top layer of IoT framework. This layer manages entire IoT structure as well as application, end-user's privacy, profit, and business model.

Authors in [14] proposed a top-level generic IoT based architecture for the development of smart cities. The main part of this framework is integrated information center that operated by IoT service provider and linked to other services like transport, electrical, water, gas supply, etc. This improves the services within the cities and attracts investment in manufacturing industry and IoT services. In another study authors [15] presented

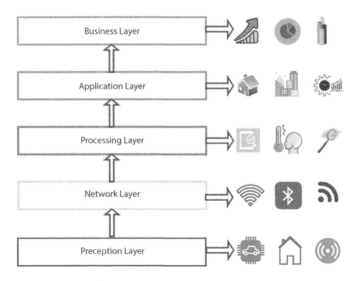

Figure 17.1 IoT layered architecture.

an integrated IoT based framework for electrical, gas and water smart metering to be installed in smart cities. Similarly another study [16] developed a glassy computing based IoT framework and also present benefits of this architecture to generate scalable IoT platform.

17.5.1   IoT Attacks

Attacks on IoT devices are divided into four categories as shown in Figure 17.2.

A. Physical Attacks
These attacks mainly concentrate on the hardware elements of IoT devices. Various physical attacks are explained below.

    a. Node tempering: In this attacker harm a sensor node by physically modifying the whole node and gain access to sensitive information as encryption key.

    b. Node jamming is based on wireless sensor nodes. The attackers interrupt the communication with the use of jammer.

    c. Malicious node injection: Between two or more nodes attacker locates a new node. By using that node, controls all data and operation between the nodes.

    d. RF inference: By using Denial of service attack, attackers send noise signals along with radio frequency signals.

    e. Sleep deprivation: In IoT systems many sensors nodes used batteries for power and sleep mode for increasing their life. The attackers wake up the nodes that consume more power and will result in node to shut down.

B. Network attacks
These attacks mainly concentrate on the network of IoT framework. Different network attacks are discussed below.

    a. Traffic Analysis attacks is passive and hard to detect. These attacks authorize the striker to gain sensitive data about the devices by examining the network traffic.

    b. RFID spoofing means striker spoof RFID message. With the help of this information, make a duplicate copy with same Id and also include wrong information that is accepted by the system.

Figure 17.2 IoT attacks.

c. Sinkhole attack: In the network striker deal with a node to attack on the entire network. The attacker violet the data confidentiality and denies the services by dropping some packets.

d. Man in middle attack: when two nodes in the network are directly communicating with each other, then attacker intercept between them and gain access to data. This attack is very harmful for IoT devices.

e. Denial of service: In this, when a node request for a service over the network, then attacker flood the same request due to this network traffic increases and result in denial of service.

    f.   Sybil attack: A Sybil node take the identities of number of nodes and mimic them as in the wireless sensor network voting system a malicious node can vote multiple times.

C. Software Attacks

These attacks mainly concentrate on cyber security of the system. Various software attacks are discussed below.

    a.   Virus and Worm, Spyware, Trojan social Horse: The attacker can harm the device through the malicious code which spread within or device to device by email, internet access, downloading.

    b.   Malicious script: Attacker injects a malicious script into the system and achieves access to the system data.

D. Encryption Attacks

Attackers damage the encryption techniques to gain access to the private key. Various encryption attacks are listed below.

    a.   Side channel attack: To gain encryption key attacker used the side channel data (about timing, power, and fault analysis) of encryption devices.

    b.   Cryptanalysis attack: By using cipher-text and plane-text attacker destroy the encryption scheme and achieve the encryption key.

17.6   Blockchain Architecture

Four-layer architecture of blockchain is depicted in Figure 17.3. The working of each layer is explained below.

Data layer is mainly used for storing and maintaining the data. This layer is composed of blocks where each block holds merkle tree, cryptographic hash and a digital signature. Basically a blockchain is a chain of blocks which are connected to each other through previous block hash code. Very first node in the chain is called genesis block which does not contain the previous hash code (see Figure 17.4). Each block is divided into two parts (block header and block body) as shown in Figure 17.4. The block header includes some key fields such as version, Merkle tree root, hash value, previous hash value, n-bits, nonce, and timestamp. The functionality of each field is listed in Table 17.2. Block body include transaction counter (TC)

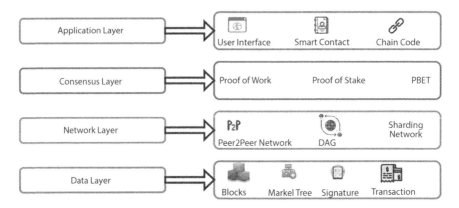

Figure 17.3 Blockchain layer architecture.

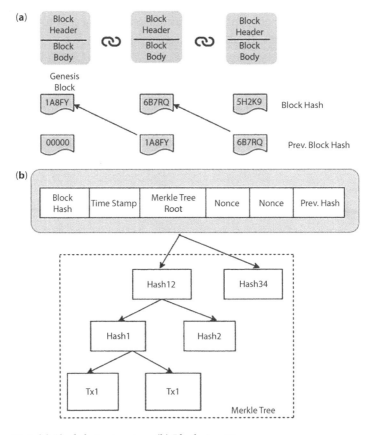

Figure 17.4 (a) Blockchain structure. (b) Block structure.

Table 17.2 Block header key fields and their functionality.

Sr. no.	Key field	Functionality
1	Block version	This field holds the version number and reveals the consensus protocol rules.
2	Timestamp	Timestamp is a time at which block is created.
3	N-bits	N-bits is a target threshold value which is used by miner for mining purpose.
4	Merkle Root	It is a hash code value that analysis all the transaction added in the block.
5	Block Hash	This field contains the current block hash code.
6	Prev. Block Hash	This field is used to provide a linking between the blocks.

and transactions (Tx). The number of transactions contained in a block body depends on the size of block. A Merkle tree follow binary tree data structure to summarize all the transaction. It provides an efficient way for checking whether a valid transaction is in a block or not. All the leaves node contain a hash code of transactions and internal nodes hold a hash code of previous hashes. The parent node of tree is called Merkle root node (see Figure 17.4b).

Digital Signature (DS) is an asymmetric cryptography scheme that provides authentication and integrity to digital contents. DS refers public key cryptography system that consists of a paired public and private key. A user shares a public key with others and kept the private key secret. Keys are used for encryption and decryption of a message. Public key is available to everyone as a bank account in blockchain. A sender sends the digital currencies by using public key of receiver. A receiver can access the currencies with own private key. Procedure of forming a digital signature in Bitcoin is shown in Figure 17.5.

Network Layer is a peer to peer network that provides secure communication among the nodes. The peer to peer network connects and synchronizes all nodes in the blockchain. A node can directly communicate with other nodes without involving the third party. There are two types of nodes (full node and light node). Full nodes confirm that all the transaction and blocks are validated by miners. Full nodes are responsible for making trust over the network. Light nodes store only header information of blockchain and make the transactions.

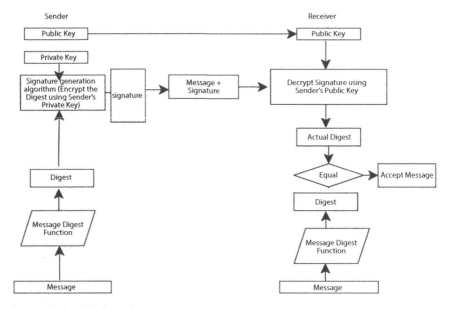

Figure 17.5 Digital signature.

Consensus Layer: In blockchain technology centralized nodes are not needed to record the transactions or stop the attackers from tempering and altering the blocks. Consensus protocol is a mechanism used by miners to reach on an agreement for a transaction among the different insecure nodes. The functionality of several consensuses algorithms are listed in Table 17.3.

Application layer is composed of two sub layers (presentation and execution layer). The presentation layer consists of scripts, user interface, and APIs, used to connect applications with blockchain. The execution layer contains the code for transaction execution.

17.7   State-of-the-Art of Blockchain in IoT

Supply chain refers to a network to supply a particular product from firm and distributer to consumer. By using the concept of supply chain management (SCM) companies can optimize their production and product cost. It provides the linking between various including entities like producers, warehouses, distribution centers, transports and customer services. If any link is break down, then overall cost of the product will be increased. IoT based supply chain for food traceability provide a centralized network of transactions that is not suitable for supply chain because it exposed issues

Table 17.3 Several consensus algorithms.

Sr. no.	Consensus algorithm	Description	References
1	DPoS	Delegated proof of stake use a voting system. In this user votes for a node in the network. The number of votes is proportional to the number of tokens. A node with maximum vote, wins for mining the blocks and get rewards for their services.	[17]
2	LPoS	Leased proof of stake is the next version of PoS. In this a node with minimum stake can rent it to full node and successes to mine the next block.	-
3	PBFT	Practical Byzantine Fault Tolerance is used in distributed network to reach on an agreement. This protocol selects a node as a leader node from a group. When a client makes a request, leader node broadcast the request over the network. All other nodes received the request message and send a reply message. If the client receives, maximum same reply, then the service is successfully confirmed.	[18]
4	PoA	Power of authority provides a group of blockchain nodes with authority for mining the blocks. POA is used for private blockchain.	[19]
5	PoAh	Power of authentication selects a group of nodes to confirm and add the blocks in blockchain. It is an appropriate consensus mechanism in IoT for secure communication	[20]

(Continued)

Table 17.3 Several consensus algorithms. (*Continued*)

Sr. no.	Consensus algorithm	Description	References
6	PoET	In Power of Elapsed Time waiting time varies for blockchain nodes. The node with minimum waiting time is used for adding a new block in blockchain.	[21]
7	PoB	In power of bandwidth, selection of a miner node depends on the bandwidth that is provided to the network.	[22]

like security, single point of failure tempering and data manipulation. To address these issues, researchers used the concept of blockchain technology in supply chain. Blockchain technology provides decentralized and distributed framework for transaction in a securely and transparent manner.

Authors in [23] proposed a AgriBlockIoT architecture for food traceability. To achieve food traceability, authors defined a use case named firm to fork by using Etherum and Hyper Ledger Sawtooth implementation. Similarly in another study authors [24] developed a system for tracing the wood. The authors implement a RFID (Radio frequency identification) blockchain architecture that traces the wood from forest standing tree to the final wood product. Similarly [25] used blockchain technology in agriculture. The mining process in blockchain consumes more power that result in high latency in adding new blocks. To mitigate this issue, authors proposed a blockchain and latency based hybrid system that traces the fish from production house to consumer.

Healthcare

In healthcare sector, with body sensors, IoT devices such as glucose, blood pressure, heart beat monitor, ECG, EEG, wearable devices are used to collect the patient data and the health service provider provide the services according to this data. To provide the security and privacy to patient data blockchain technology is integrated with IoT. Researchers [26] proposed a three layer architecture by integrating fog computing with blockchain for secure data transmission. These three layers include an analytical model, a mathematical system, and an ASE (Advanced signature based encryption) algorithm for device identification, verification, and authentication of patient data. Authors in [27] presented a solution for enhancing the health-care system using blockchain technology. Various tools like Hyper Ledger fabric, Hyper Ledger caliper, Docker container, composer, and wire shark are utilized to evaluate the performance of the system. Another study [28] proposed a protocol Pseudonym based encryption with different authorities (PBE-DA) to achieve privacy for patient records on e-health record system. The authors designed a multi-layer blockchain architecture in which first layer provides the connectivity between the patient and IoT devices. The second layer provides the communication between various EHRs members.

Education
In learning systems issues of security and privacy can be solved by block-chain technology. In [29] proposed a distributed system using blockchain for storing the educational data and reputation rewards. Teachers can securely store the student records on blocks in blockchain technology. Blockchain based school information centers help in collecting, analyz-ing and reporting the data related to school system. In articles publishing, blockchain can effectively be used in manuscript submission, timely con-ducting, and verifying reviews of articles.

17.8   Blockchain Open Challenges and Future Trend

Despite of blockchain is an encrypted, distributed, and immutable ledger that ensure the secure transactions over a decentralized network, it is hav-ing some open issues that should be resolved in the future.

A. Privacy and Security:
In Blockchain all the transactions are stored in blocks on decentralized network as a public ledger, due to this, the problem of privacy and confi-dentiality arise. Although the blockchain technology provides security to IoT system but still some attacks like Denial of service attack (DDOS), DAO attack, and Sybil attack harm blockchain based IoT systems. In (DoS) denial of service attack sticker send a fake connection across the network to all authorized devices that prevent the users to mine a valid token. Few techniques like Black holing and Sink holing prevent the denial of service attack.

B. Scalability:
In IoT-based systems, millions of devices are connected to each other across the network and able to store the emissive amount of information

but blockchain able to process only small number of transactions within a second. So, for blockchain based IoT systems, scalability is a big challenge.

C. Latency and Throughput:
The blockchain based IoT system requires rapid processing speed for transactions. For instance, Bitcoin process only 7 transactions within a second while VISA designed to process 1000 transactions within a minute. In Bitcoin, clock is to be created in 10 min. this will increase latency and decrease throughput. So, researchers need to do lot of work to achieve low latency and maximum throughput.

D. Energy Consumption
Adoption of Blockchain technology such as Bitcoin, Peercoin, and Litecoin required that minimum 51% miners should be verified for a transaction. For this miners used a mining process that consumes lot of energy which is not sufficient for blockchain. Several consensus algorithms like Proof-of-Work, Proof-of-Stake, and Proof-of-Authority require more space and power for mining process. Other consensus algorithms like Proof-of-Identity, Proof-of-Burn save power and space during mining process. To address this issue, some researchers apply AI technology for integration of blockchain in IoT.

17.9   Conclusion

The IoT allows communication between billions of devices through data that is produced by sensors. The centralized solutions are not suitable for these concerns due to security challenges and scalability problems. This paper presents that IoT devices has some security issues and attackers can easily tamper the data. To solve this issue Blockchain technology offers some key features like transparency, confidentiality, security and store the immutable data over a decentralized peer-to-peer network. Many consensus protocols that help the peer nodes to achieve an agreement are also discussed. Furthermore, the applications of Blockchain in various sectors like healthcare, education, IoT and government are also disclosed. Although security is an inherent feature of Blockchain still it is suffering from issues like more energy consumption, poor transaction speed and scalability. In future, there is a need to improve the consensus mechanism to improve the transaction rate and other open issues discussed in this paper.

References

1. Atzori, L., Iera, A., Morabito, G., The internet of things: A survey. *Comput. Networks*, 54, 15, 2787–2805, 2010.

2. Vukobratovic, D. *et al.*, Condense: A reconfigurable knowledge acquisition architecture for future 5G IoT. *IEEE Access*, 4, 3360–3378, 2016.

3. Bera, B., Chattaraj, D., Das, A.K., Designing secure blockchain-based access control scheme in IoT-enabled internet of drones deployment. *Comput. Commun.*, 153, November 2019, 229–249, 2020.

4. Minoli, D., Positioning of blockchain mechanisms in IOT-powered smart home systems: A gateway-based approach. *Internet Things*, 10, 100147, 2020.

5. Ammi, M., Alarabi, S., Benkhelifa, E., Customized blockchain-based architecture for secure smart home for lightweight IoT. *Inf. Process. Manage.*, 58, 3, 102482, 2021.

6. Dunphy, P. and Petitcolas, F.A.P., A first look at identity management schemes on the blockchain. *IEEE Secur. Priv.*, 16, 4, 20–29, 2018.

7. Khan, M.A. and Salah, K., IoT security: Review, blockchain solutions, and open challenges. *Future Gener. Comput. Syst.*, 82, 395–411, 2018.

8. Serrano, W., The blockchain random neural network for cybersecure IoT and 5G infrastructure in smart cities. *J. Netw. Comput. Appl.*, 175, 102909, 2021.

9. Pavithran, D., Al-Karaki, J.N., Shaalan, K., Edge-Based Blockchain Architecture for event-driven IoT using hierarchical identity based encryption. *Inf. Process. Manage.*, 58, 3, 102528, 2021.

10. Ren, Y. *et al.*, Multiple cloud storage mechanism based on blockchain in smart homes. *Future Gener. Comput. Syst.*, 115, 304–313, 2021.

11. Huang, J., Tan, L., Li, W., Yu, K., RON-enhanced blockchain propagation mechanism for edge-enabled smart cities. *J. Inf. Secur. Appl.*, 61, 102936, 2021.

12. Alzubi, J.A., Blockchain-based lamport merkle digital signature: Authentication tool in IoT healthcare. *Comput. Commun.*, 170, 200–208, 2021.

13. Islam, A. and Young Shin, S., A blockchain-based secure healthcare scheme with the assistance of unmanned aerial vehicle in internet of things. *Comput. Electr. Eng.*, 84, 106627, 2020.

14. Ganchev, I., Ji, Z., O'Droma, M., A generic IoT architecture for smart cities. *IET Conf. Publ.*, 2014, CP639, 196–199, 2014.

15. Lloret, J., Tomas, J., Canovas, A., Parra, L., An integrated IoT architecture for smart metering. *IEEE Commun. Mag.*, 54, 12, 50–57, 2016.

16. Ren, J., Guo, H., Xu, C., Zhang, Y., Serving at the edge: A scalable IoT architecture based on transparent computing. *IEEE Netw.*, 31, 5, 96–105, 2017.

17. Ferdous, M.S., Chowdhury, M.J.M., Hoque, M.A., A survey of consensus algorithms in public blockchain systems for crypto-currencies. *J. Netw. Comput. Appl.*, 182, 103035, 2021.

18. Gao, S., Yu, T., Zhu, J., Cai, W., T-PBFT: An eigentrust-based practical byzantine fault tolerance consensus algorithm. *China Commun.*, 16, 12, 111–123, 2019.

19. Bentov, I., Lee, C., Mizrahi, A., 4-0 Proof of activity: Extending bitcoin's proof of work via proof of stake. *ACM SIGMETRICS Perform. Eval. Rev.*, 42, 3, 34–37, 2014.

20. Puthal, D., Mohanty, S.P., Nanda, P., Kougianos, E., Das, G., Proof-of-authentication for scalable blockchain in resource-constrained distributed systems, in: *2019 IEEE International Conference on Consumer Electronics (ICCE)*, pp. 1–5, 2019.

21. Chen, L., Xu, L., Shah, N., Gao, Z., Lu, Y., Shi, W., On security analysis of proof-of-elapsed-time (poet), in: *International Symposium on Stabilization, Safety, and Security of Distributed Systems*, pp. 282–297, 2017.

22. Karantias, K., Kiayias, A., Zindros, D., Proof-of-burn, in: *International Conference on Financial Cryptography and Data Security*, pp. 523–540, 2020.

23. Caro, M.P., Ali, M.S., Vecchio, M., Giaffreda, R., Blockchain-based traceability in agri-food supply chain management: A practical implementation. *2018 IoT Vert. Top. Summit Agric. - Tuscany, IOT Tuscany 2018*, pp. 1–4, 2018.

24. Figorilli, S. *et al.*, A blockchain implementation prototype for the electronic open source traceability of wood along the whole supply chain. *Sensors (Switzerland)*, 18, 9, 1–12, 2018.

25. Hang, L., Ullah, I., Kim, D.-H., A secure fish farm platform based on blockchain for agriculture data integrity. *Comput. Electron. Agric.*, 170, 105251, 2020.

26. Shukla, S., Thakur, S., Hussain, S., Breslin, J.G., Jameel, S.M., Identification and authentication in healthcare internet-of-things using integrated fog computing based blockchain model. *Internet Things*, 15, 100422, 2021.

27. Tanwar, S., Parekh, K., Evans, R., Blockchain-based electronic healthcare record system for healthcare 4.0 applications. *J. Inf. Secur. Appl.*, 50, 102407, 2020.

28. Badr, S., Gomaa, I., Abd-Elrahman, E., Multi-tier blockchain framework for IoT-EHRs systems. *Proc. Comput. Sci.*, 141, 159–166, 2018.

29. Sharples, M. and Domingue, J., The blockchain and kudos: A distributed system for educational record, reputation and reward, in: *European Conference on Technology Enhanced Learning*, pp. 490–496, 2016.

18

New Blockchain Taxonomies and Trust Models Impacting Business Performance

Hani El Chaarani[1]*, Zouhour EL Abiad[2] and Hebatallah Abd El Salam Badawy[3]

[1]Beirut Arab University, Beirut, Lebanon
[2]Lebanese University, Beirut, Lebanon
[3]Faculty of Commerce, Alexandria University, Egypt Japan University of Science and Technology, Alxendria, Egypt

Abstract

During recent years, the blockchain technology has been widely studied and analyzed in different domains. This research explores the application and discusses the importance of this innovative technology in four different sectors: Financial, industrial, healthcare and supply chain. Based on real world applications extracted from different databases like webpages, interviews and annual reports, the result of this chapter indicates that the employment of blockchain technology in business activities can enhance the managerial, operational, financial, and commercial performance. In addition, the result shows that the employment of this new technology in financial sector can decrease the risk of money laundering.

Keywords: Blockchain, business, management, healthcare, supply chain, industrial, financial sector

18.1   Introduction

Blockchain technology was introduced to the business community through financial transactions and cryptocurrency exchanges [1]. With the globalization and digitalization, this new decentralized technology emerges as new evolution in different business fields, especially in supply chain major. By 2025, [2] estimated that the market value of blockchain technology will

---

**Corresponding author*: h.shaarani@bau.edu.lb

Kiran Sood, Rajesh Kumar Dhanaraj, Balamurugan Balusamy and Seifedine Kadry (eds.) Blockchain Technology in Corporate Governance: Transforming Business and Industries, (387–412) © 2023 Scrivener Publishing LLC

exceed $39 billion. Nowadays, many international companies like General Motors, Amazon, Pfizer, Nestlé, Ford and Honda are employing this new technology in their operational and payment system to improve their operational performance and enhance their competitive advantage.

Blockchain is a decentralized blocks that includes well protected data of valid activities. Each new block of activities is added to the chain, and it is related to their predecessor via cryptographic pointer [3]. Any new user can add new record to the chain and review the data while nobody can adjust and delete it [4]. Thus, a blockchain is a chain of activities distributed on different nodes through shared network [5].

Blockchain system is an open and interactive system that is based on high level of transparency and traceability [6]. Unlike the traditional centralized database system, it is not relying on third party and thus, leads to accelerate business achievement and decrease transaction costs [7]. The smart contract and open access system are between the most important features employed in blockchain system because it enhances creditability and transparency between unknown parties [8].

Prior research on blockchain technology revealed that the employment of this new technology has several advantages on business performance like improvement of cost control and enhancement of efficient data management [9]. Many other scholars indicated that the blockchain system improves the managerial effectiveness of any firms because it helps to eliminate human errors and improve auditability [10]. It provides decentralized control and implement immutable data [11].

During the recent health crisis of COVID-19, the blockchain technology helped many international and national firms to sustain and develop. This new technology facilitated the traceability and the control of vaccination COVID-19 vaccination. It also helped many supply chains and business activities to sustain and work during the long lockdown period [12, 13].

By considering the importance and the rapid development of blockchain technology in business world, this chapter aims to answer the following three main questions: (1) how blockchain works in business fields? (2) is it possible to employ this new technology in different majors? And (3) what are the managerial and business advantages of this new technology in different business fields?

The objective of this chapter is to explore the importance and impact of blockchain technology in management and business administration fields, namely in supply chain, industrial, healthcare and financial sector. This research helps to provide a conceptual framework that highlights the key role of the blockchain in managing business and economic activities.

This chapter is structured as follow: The first section will explain principles, practices, categories, features and advantages of blockchain technology. The second section explores different practices of blockchain technology mainly in financial, healthcare, supply chain, logistics and industrial fields. In this part of the chapter, several real-world business examples will be employed to reveal the contribution of blockchain technology in assessing corporate risks, monitoring human resources, optimizing decision making processes, improving customers satisfaction, enhancing financial and cost control. The last section concludes and discusses the impact of blockchain technology on the performance and efficiency of different business administration fields.

18.2   Foundation of Blockchain

18.2.1   Blockchain: The History

The story of the blockchain started in 2008, when Satoshi Nakamoto was asking in his white paper about the way to conduct a transaction without relying on intermediaries or trusted third parties. Satoshi Nakamoto invented and proposed the blockchain technology as a secure infrastructure and technology that can be used to support the trading in cryptocurrency [14]. After that, he invented the Bitcoin, which is based on the blockchain technology [15–17].

To explain what blockchain is and how it evolved, it can be noted that Blockchain, as the name indicates, is a series of blocks that are connected to each other in a chain [17]. Nakamoto relied on the blockchain or this chain of blocks to create a decentralized digital currency system, which is a secure and trustable system and in the meantime is available to anyone [18]. The chain of blockchain shows the accepted history of the transactions since the blockchain started [19]. Users and customers of blockchain may be individuals, organizations, or both [20].

Since its inception, blockchain passed through three main stages: Blockchain 1.0, which focused mainly on the cryptocurrency trading. Blockchain 2.0, which involved a broader financial application of the blockchain technology. In Blockchain 2.0, more complicated digital applications were invented, such as smart contracts. Blockchain 3.0, which involved a drastic development in the blockchain systems, beyond the financial and business applications. In Blockchain 3.0, we found a transformation of several services, such as attestation services and of government administration to be highly decentralized and self-managing models [18].

18.2.2   Components of Blockchain

[21] discussed the main components of the Blockchain, which are as follows:

1. The block: the main component of the blockchain. Every block stores some transactions, and the blocks are linked together using a unique hash value which is related to the previous block;
2. The ledger: a distributed database that is accessible by a large number of participants in different places;
3. The hash function: a mathematical problem that minors need to solve to find a block. This hash function is used to validate the integrity of the data related to the block. This hash function has some characteristics, as any change in the content of the block will produce a different hash and the outcome of the hash function is unique. The hash has a specific length, and the original content of the block can't be predicted from its hash [22];
4. The miners: the participants or the computers that exert effort to solve the mathematical problem to add a new block to the chain;
5. The transaction: the smallest unit of a process or an operation and is added to the series of blocks when most of the nodes participating in the network approved;
6. The consensus agreement: the way that participants in the blockchain network used to reach common agreement, such as proof of work and proof of stake.

18.2.3   How Does the Blockchain Work?

Let's see how blockchain works. The process starts when a user (say user A) initiates a transaction to another user (user B) through the blockchain network. The transaction is announced to all nodes in the blockchain. Each user has a unique pair of private and public key, which determines his/her identity. The public key, which is available to anyone, is used to identify the participant in the blockchain, and the private key, which is not shared with anyone, is used to sign or authorize transactions [23]. After that, the transaction will be announced to all participants in the blockchain network for verification and validation. Once the network of users validates the transaction and the user's ID, and the mathematical model is solved by any of the miners and a consensus was reached by the majority of participants (nodes), a new block will be formed and added to the blockchain for 10 minutes before it is added to the ledger [24], and each node will update its copy of the blockchain ledger. This newly formed block will contain all transactions that happened in this time and will be linked to the previous block using the digital signature [25]. Accordingly, each block contains a cryptographic hash of the previous (parent) block, time stamp, a nonce, which is a number that used to identify the hash and the data of the related transaction [24, 26] and is considered an acknowledgment by the participants that the transaction occurred and is valid [27]. It is important to note that any node can vote using its CPU to accept valid blocks through requesting extensions or reject invalid ones through denying expansions [16].

Concerning the layouts of consensus, it can be [28]:

1. Proof of Work (PoW), where a block is generated when a miner solves the inversion of a cryptographic function based on brute force;
2. Proof of stake (PoS), where the generation of a block is tied to the ownership of specific amount of digital assets;
3. Proof of authority, where specific nodes have the authority to create new blocks and secure the blockchain;
4. Proof of capacity, where those who mine the block are those who devote more hard drive capacity and disk space for computing the proof;
5. Proof of burn, which is related to burning digital currencies or a hybrid of any of the previously mentioned consensus agreements.

18.2.4   Types of Blockchain

Prior studies [29–31] discussed the different types of blockchains, which can be summarized as follows:

1. Private blockchain (permissioned):
   This type of blockchain has a closed access, where the permission to read the data is restricted or open to the public. In this type of blockchain, there are strict rules on who will join the blockchain network and the blockchain is controlled by one organization, and the consensus process is permissioned and is determined by this organization. Also, because the number of validators is few in this type of blockchain,

it could be more efficient in comparison to the public blockchain.

2. Public blockchain (permissionless):
   The second type of blockchain is characterized by its open access, where anyone in the world can join the network, send, create and see transactions and can take part in the consensus and validation processes. This type of blockchain is totally decentralized and the consensus and validation processes are permissionless and is open to the public. Examples of this type of blockchain include Bitcoin and Ethereum.

3. Consortium blockchain (permissioned):
   This private blockchain type has open access system, where the right to read might be restricted or open to the public. This type of blockchain is partially decentralized and only a selected number of nodes are responsible for block validation. The consensus process in this type of blockchain is permissioned and is determined by a number of nodes.

18.2.5 Features of Blockchain

Because blockchain technology presents a new way to record, store and process financial transactions, it is characterized with some unique features that enable it to operate and fulfill its objectives. These features are [16, 17, 30]:

1. Transparency: which is the main feature of blockchain, as anyone can see the blockchain and its transactions [16, 17, 30]. However, it should be noted that the level of transparency differs according to the type of blockchain, for instance, in the permissioned or private blockchain, the level of transparency is limited, and the master copy of transaction records is available only to some participants [32].

2. Decentralization: as in the blockchain, there is no need for an intermediary or a third party. a distributed system structure controls the processes of data verification, storage and maintenance and also transmission on the blockchain.

3. Real-time: blockchain technology offers real-time recording of transactions because such transactions are posted as soon as they happen.

4. Cryptographic: blockchain depends on public key cryptography to protect the underlying accounts and the users from

unauthorized account control [19]. Here, the transactions are encrypted using the unique pairs of public and private keys.

5. Immutability and trustlessness: blockchain is characterized by the high security level and participants don't need to rely on other's honesty. It is important to note here that this feature differs according to blockchain types. In the public blockchain, where there are no central parties, transactions cannot be changed or altered once they are added to the blockchain [33], and any attempt to change the copy on the blockchain will be useless and immediately detected, as there will be inconsistency with other copies in the blockchain [32]. On the other hand, the trustlessness in the private blockchain is not complete, and the transaction records may be reversed if most of the participants decide to do so and accordingly, it can be noted that the trustlessness of the blockchain depends on the integrity of the central authority [32].

6. Traceability and auditability: tracking and verifying the transactions in the blockchain is easy and simple, as transactions are arranged in a chronological way and each block is linked to the previous one and the next one based on the cryptographic hash function.

7. Anonymity: although blockchain is employing a decentralized distributed ledger among all users, blockchain is characterized by its anonymity to protect the privacy of the nodes [21]. Each user can interact in the blockchain network using a generated address, which does not uncover the real identity of the user.

8. Persistency: invalid transactions are not accepted by honest miners, and it is nearly impossible to remove or alter a transaction once it is added to the blockchain.

18.2.6 Advantages of Using Blockchain

Prior research discussed the main advantages that a business can experience from using blockchain.

1. Cost and time reduction: blockchain may help in reducing cost and time that are related from using intermediary parties, increase data security, traceability, and transparency

for customers [20]. It could speed the settlement of certain financial transactions by decreasing the number of third parties involved, and by making the reconciliation process faster and more efficient [10]. Accordingly, we can expect transactions to occur all day, without being restricted to business working hours or requiring commissions for verifying transactions [31].

2. Immutability: because blockchain is characterized by its immutability, transactions can't be changed once they are added to the series of blocks, and so it can be used by businesses that seek reliability to attract their customers [30].

3. Efficiency: blockchain can help in reducing the delays related to bank transaction processing from weeks to hours and simplify complicated financial problems [34].

4. Reliability: blockchain is characterized by its reliability, as the failure of a specific node will not affect the operation of the whole blockchain network. This ensures the high reliability of the applications built using the blockchain technology [16].

5. Security: blockchain network uses the hash function which is a mathematical function that works to concert a variable-length input string into a fixed-length binary sequence. The output doesn't have a clear relationship to the input. The process is difficult to reverse because, the input is impossible to predict based on the output [25].

6. Disintermediation: blockchain database is not maintained by a specific individual or organization but by all network participants and there is no need for a central party to verify the truthfulness of transactions [31].

7. Trust: blockchain plays the role of trust bearers with distributed decentralized ledgers instead of relying on the centralized trust parties, as in the case of central governments and commercial banks [16]. Here, there is no need to verify the transactions by a trusted third party [22].

18.2.7 Disadvantages and Challenges of Blockchain

Despite the main advantages of blockchain, which concentrate on its immutability, reliability, cost effectiveness and transparency, it is facing some difficulties that may hinder its quick diffusion. These disadvantages may be summarized as follows:

1. Scalability: which refers to the small size of each block, as each block can store data of 1 Megabit only, it can store a small number of transactions every second. This indicates that it won't be efficient to deal with the high frequency industries, such as the financial industry [30]. and if a block-chain needs to add more transactions to the chain or series of blocks, the size problem needs to be resolved [25].
2. Energy consumption: the consensus process, such as proof of work, is consuming more electricity energy [30].
3. Privacy leakage: Blockchain faces a privacy problem because the values related to all transactions and balances are available to the public [22].
4. Security problem: there is a possibility of 51% attack, where an entity may have a full control on the network and may be able to manipulate it [30].
5. Selfish mining strategy: some selfish miners may hide their mined blocks and not announce it to the public only if some requirements are satisfied [30].

From the discussion above, we can conclude that blockchain is characterized by its immutability, transparency, decentralization, anonymity, traceability, cryptography and real-time processing. In addition, we can notice that the unique features of blockchain which distinguish it from other technologies represent its advantages and disadvantages at the same time. For instance, although public blockchain is characterized by its high transparency level, because the data related to the transactions are available to the public and this represent an advantage, however, it represents also a privacy problem. On the other hand, private blockchains lack data transparency and the incentive to benefit from the decentralization advantage [22]. Also, blockchain technology has other advantages that may help its application in the different business areas, such as reliability, disintermediation, efficiency and high trust level. On the other hand, still the scalability and the bandwidth problem is still an issue that needs to be resolved in case we want to extend the application of blockchain technology in business fields. In addition, security problems should be taken into consideration to avoid any data manipulation and ensure that blockchain is fulfilling its expected objectives.

18.3   Blockchain in Business: Some Real-World Examples

The blockchain application is not limited anymore for bitcoin, cryptocurrency, and other financial transactions. Different sectors like healthcare, transportation, finance, industrial and media are adopting this new technology to increase their performance, manage their big data and enhance their competitive advantage.

The objective of this section is to shed lights on some real successful examples of the implementation of blockchain technology in business major. To achieve this objective, the webpage database, professional news, annual reports and interviews with executives were analyzed to reveal the added value of blockchain implementation on different firms from several sectors.

In total, the blockchain system was explored and analyzed through 46 international firms employing and practicing this new technology. Table 18.1 presents the distribution of studied firms per sector.

18.3.1   Blockchain Applications in Healthcare Sector

During the last decade the healthcare sector across the globe suffered from many challenging problems like the development of competition, appearance of COVID-19 epidemic and other new medical infections, increasing of medical and operational costs, growth of medical and managerial records.

Table 18.1 Companies employing and practicing blockchain technology.

Sector	Number	%
Information technology	13	35.29%
Healthcare	7	13.73%
Industrial	9	17.65%
Supply chain	12	23.53%
Financial	5	9.80%
Total	51	100.00%

Source: The authors.

For [35], the employment of technological innovation must be considered by managers and executives in healthcare sector to improve medical data management, quality of health service and accuracy of managerial and financial information. The author revealed that the blockchain technology in healthcare sector improve the communication and the quality of healthcare outcomes.

Nowadays, several medical and healthcare organizations are using the blockchain technology. The analysis of different platforms like FACTOM, GEM, CORAL HEALTH, MEDREC, BLOCKPHARMA, NANOVISION, NEBULA GENOMIX, and MEDICALCHAIN reveal that the implementation of blockchain technology in healthcare sector has the following advantages:

First, the blockchain technology could improve the management of medical data and patients' healthcare records. The number of customers and dieses in healthcare sector are growing quickly. The employment of blockchain by medical centers like Renji hospital on China helped physicians to track the updated records of their patients anywhere, and thus leads to improve, collaboration, patients trust and quality of medical services [36].

Second, many wearable watches and sensors provided by Fitbit, Apple, Samsung and several other international companies can track and send all patients records to their physicians, including heart rate volatility, stress level, body temperature and physical activities. Therefore, this big data needs to be saved and analyzed before being used by patients, physicians, hospitals and research and development centers. The blockchain technology can be used to provide solutions for steadily growth of health and medical records. The collaboration between Massachusetts General Hospital and MediBloc, the Korean blockchain company, was a successful example of the implementation of machine learning and artificial intelligence to provide health information exchange and enhance the quality of health service [37].

Third, patients through blockchain technology could track their medical situation and access to their latest heath data and prescription anyplace in the world. They could adjust their lifestyle based on their updated health information. They can decide and control who can access their health track data. The real time data of patients during the COVID-19 helped Albany Med to implement the blockchain technology to enhance responses to the virus development. They introduced a new dashboard and persons-matching algorithms allowing to monitor the virus symptoms [38].

Fourth, the blockchain can be used by R&D centers in the world to follow healthcare records of patients and any side effects of new vaccine or new medicine. In case of new pandemic like that of Covid-19, the health-care sector suffered from the absence of universal database and data flow system that could track the health record of patients to control and manage any new public health dieses. In this line, South Warwickshire NHS Foundation Trust, has successfully implemented the blockchain technology to track the impact of storing temperature on Covid-19 vaccines [39].

Fifth, the blockchain could help physicians to achieve their missions remotely. The existing of online and updated health information could help physician to perform the monitoring of their patients. It also enables physician to provide their medical instructions and prescriptions mainly in case of any pandemic period or transportation difficulties. [40] revealed the importance of blockchain technology during the last Covid-19 pandemic crisis. They showed that the implementation of blockchain technology facilitated the mission of physicians during extended lockdowns through telemedicine and telehealth services.

Sixth, the implementation of blockchain technology could improve the managerial efficiency by increasing transparency, auditability, reliability and real-time verifiability. Blockchain technology can track all asset types, ease the automated payments and reduce both administrative and transaction costs. It is also used by medical centers to monitor and control all data related to medical and non-medical workforce. [35] confirmed that this new technology is able to reduce costs and speed up all administrative operations in healthcare sector and thus, leads to improve the management of employees (Figure 18.1).

18.3.2   Blockchain Technology in Transport, Supply Chain Activities and Logistics

The last Covid-19 pandemic period stopped the transportation and caused disruptions to supply chain activities worldwide. Some international companies in logistics, supply chains and transportation were blocked for many months. The long lockdown period and its socio-economic impact affected the global economy. The quarantine during the pandemic period provides new lessons related to supply chain, transportation and logistics activities.

Several studies and scholars like [12] and [13] have proposed the employment of blockchain technology for solving all Covid-19 challenges faced by supply chain and other activities. They argued that this new technology is a potential solution to build agility and digitalization.

PROVENANCE, JIOCOIN, SKUCHAIN, and many other international companies are offering the implementation of Blockchain technology in

Figure 18.1 Blockchain advantages in healthcare sector. Source: The authors.

supply chain and other related activities to create the following potential benefits.

First, a blockchain technology can be used to record all operations executed between users (peer to peer) without referring to centralized party. Thus, the employment of blockchain technology enhances the trust between users through the existence of permanent and traceable record of each transaction. For Walmart, the employment of IBM blockchain technology has enhanced the possibility to track their products step by step from farm to selling points without passing by third party, and thus leads to improve peer to peer trust [41].

Second, users of blockchain technology have high confidentiality level. All the operations are executed through smart contracts based on digital signatures and authentications. The contents of smart contracts are immutable, well protected, recorded and accessible through all nodes in blockchain. Carrefour has implemented in 2019 the blockchain technology in up to thirty countries in Africa, Europe and Asia to follow if their smart contracts are executed and well protected. Customers and companies in the supply chain can scan a QR code to check if the quality of delivered product is within contract conditions. The smart contract used by Carrefour can easily track the process flow and validate each transaction [42].

Third, the data of supply chain, logistics and transportation activities are well protected and cannot be manipulated and modified by any party. Thus, the integration of supply chain and other related activities in blockchain system could improve the performance and transparency of processing system since all parties in the chain have a complete access on database. Bext360 application is a popular example of the employment of blockchain to ensure the full traceability of coffee beans. This platform provides all records related to value, quality and weight of each transaction from farmer to retailer [43].

Fourth, the implementation blockchain technology in supply chain activities could limit the human error. Each executed or planned operation is documented and recorded reliably based on consensus algorithms and thus, leads to speed the operational system and prevent malicious behaviors. Several companies like Bumble Bee Foods can track and verify all conditions of imported Tuna fish from Indonesia through the SAP blockchain technology. The fishing location, size of Tuna and all conditions are recorded within a secure database [44].

Fifth, the existence of high transparency level through the employment of blockchain technology in the supply chain could increase the trust of customers in the company and its products and therefore, leads to generate competitive advantage and high customer satisfaction. Everledger and TrustChain platforms are some successful examples indicating the importance of blockchain in supply chain and transportation activities. This platform offers the possibility to track the quality and all transportation details of luxury products like diamonds. The customers can follow the shipping details, package conditions and all customers feed-back.

Sixth, the blockchain technology could help to increase the speed of physical process, reduce the level of interaction and identify all participants in the supply chain. The employment of this technology also improves the cost saving and the overall performance of the company. Blockchain provides different tools to eliminate frauds and ensure the quality and quantity of delivered product. Several companies like Amazon and Alibaba have

Figure 18.2 Blockchain advantages in supply chain, logistics and transport activities.
Source: The authors.

succeeded to satisfy their customers through the employment of block-chain technology in their supply chains. For example, the track and trace platform has helped Amazon to reduce errors, cost and time delay. In addition, this technology has provided end to end visibility and thus, has led to increase customers satisfaction [45]. The advantages of Blockchain technology are presented in Figure 18.2.

18.3.3 Blockchain Technology in Industrial Sector

The majority of firms in manufacturing sector rely on traditional centralize data management technology. They are using traditional operation management systems and recent trends in industrial sector like virtual reality

(VR), augmented reality (AR), 3D printing, internet of things (IoT) and cloud manufacturing (CM). Nowadays, the blockchain raised as alternative technology based on higher visibility, transparency and decentralization.

TRANSACTIVGRID, HIJRO, SORJ.io, and BLOCKVERIFY proves themselves to be as revolutionary startup in blockchain technology. They launched a blockchain-based system for manufacturing and industrial sector to create the following advantages.

First, the blockchain technology is based on decentralized system (no central authority). This system enables the elimination of any central authority and leads to reduce transaction costs due to peer-to-peer exchange. All the coordination process must be executed based on the current state and any operation should be added to the next block in the ledger of blockchain. Any entity could join the chain and add its activity and transaction based on tolerance algorithms providing proof of authority, proof of contribution and proof of work. This open cyber-physical interaction based smart machines system empower the efficiency of manufacturing sector.

Second, the information and data of the blockchain technology is well saved and protected in blocks. Firms and corporations can exchange data, collaborate, communicate and coordinate securely with other contractors and organization in industrial sectors to complete the production process and sustain the relationship with customers. The employment of blockchain technology by GENERAL ELECTICS (GE) proves the importance of this new technology in manufacturing sector. Its Back-to-birth blockchain system provides all important manufacturing and maintenance records of airplane engines and thus, leads to enhance its credibility and efficiency [46].

Third, a computerized smart contract based on immutable information is set up automatically to specify and define all transactions conditions. This type of contract can be fully or partially executed after verifying some specific criteria based on scripting language. In industrial sector, the smart contract can reduce time delay and speed up the production processing. Several manufacturing companies like Nestlé [47] and GM [48] stated that the employment of smart contracts has improved their transaction conditions because they are secure and trustable.

Fourth, the integration of blockchain technology in industrial sector can improve real-time transparency. In any decentralized system, firms and customers have to verify the quality of goods and services delivered from suppliers to complete their production process due to lack of trust level. However, the blockchain technology can provide real time verification and transparency and thus, leads to decrease the transaction cost. The manufacturing counterparty can verify if another unit on the blockchain can provide its goods and thus, leads to execute the payment with confidence and without passing by any verification process. In this line, Nestlé has successfully integrated the blockchain system on their food products by using track formula and QR code. throughout this new technology, wholesalers, retailers, and customers can instantly verify the quality and all conditions of any product offered by the company and thus leads to improve trust and reduce any verification cost [49].

Fifth, the blockchain system can improve the auditability and traceability of products and production process by providing digital representation and tracking system from producer to retailer and customer. Customers can track and verify all production conditions which leads to improve their loyalty and satisfaction level. BMW, HONDA, and FORD have integrated Mobile open Blockchain initiative to track and share all vehicles information like production process, location, maintenance and braking. This new integrated system has increased the transparency and auditability of their vehicles which leads to improve the level of customer satisfaction [50].

Sixth, blockchain technology enables peer to peer interaction between producer and customers through a social manufacturing platform. Such a type of interaction improves the overall performance, product innovation and competitive advantage. In addition, it implies new resources into the design of production process. [51] stated that the implementation of blockchain traceability anti-counterfeiting platform (BTAP) and Internet of Things (IoT) in industrial sector can encourage all parties in the chain mainly customers to participate in the development of offered products and services by the company. Samsung has integrated a new interactive blockchain-based system that allows customers to provide their feedback and creative ideas to improve their products.

Seventh, the blockchain can be an efficient tool to create value for manufacturing firms. It provides all participant in the chain to build an ecosystem that could reduce cost and improve efficiency. It helps to build new system based on trust, cooperation and transparent data to monitor and improve the quality. Finally, the blockchain technology also can enhance the quality by unlocking the full potential and capacity of different advanced technologies like virtual reality, augmented reality and 3D printing. GENESIS of THINGS and MOOG AIRCRAFT GROUP are a successful platform in manufacturing sector that could improve the quality and cost of production by enabling safe 3D printing trough smart contracts and blockchain system [52].

The distributed ledger employed by SAMSUNG to follow the international shipments is another successful example of blockchain technology that allows to reduce costs and respond to market needs [52]. The advantages of Blockchain technology are presented in Figure 18.3.

Figure 18.3 Blockchain advantages in industrial sector. Source: The authors.

18.3.4   Blockchain Technology in Financial Sector

Blockchain technology allows the creation of immutable financial records reachable by all ledgers in a chain. Digital currencies (bitcoin, Ethereum, Ripple), digital assets, reduction in settlement period, digital record keeping, and smart financial contracts are the most important implementation of blockchain technology in financial sector. This new technology promises to bring immense innovation, change and development to banking sector, financial industry and financial markets.

Many international companies like BARCLAYS, ABRA, MAERSK, AETERNITY and AUGUR allow the creation of cryptocurrency wallet, smart financial contract, derivatives financial instruments and bank guarantees. They offer different other financial services and products based on the following advantages for banks and other users:

First, this new technology brings new opportunities and allows banks to reduce their financial and operational costs. Being in a decentralized system like the blockchain platform can reduce banks expenses since they do not need to invest in a centralized database. As a result, no centralized institution can accumulate any monopoly power and thus, leads to develop transactions and exchange possibilities. Several international banks are incorporating the Hyperledger Fabric platform in their SWIFT operations [53]. This blockchain based technology has decreased the cost and the transparency of interbank payments.

Second, the blockchain technology can manage and reduce the risk level of banks. In a centralized system banks must control and monitor the use of loans. However, blockchain system enables direct tracking of each operation eliminating information asymmetry and increasing trust. The level of credit risk is lowered which could remove the need for financial guarantees. Several banks and companies like BLOCKFI, CRED, LIQUID MORTGAGE, and UNCHAINED CAPITAL are employing this technology to raise funds and issuing loan and bonds on distributed ledger. They stated that this decentralized lending method replaces costly traditional methods and decreases credit processing time [54].

Third, the blockchain innovation in financial sector allows banks to improve their anti-money laundering policy since all bills and settlements are transparent, recorded and protected. All inflows and outflows of different ledgers can be controlled, monitored and traced. This new technology enables banks to understand, analyze and monitor the financial behavior of customers. The Know your customer function integrated in blockchain system can assess the compliance with anti-money laundering [55]. This function can identify the customer and analyze its activity and therefore leads to estimate the money laundering risk.

Fourth, the employment of smart contracts in banking transactions can reduce and mitigate the operational risk. All human errors and frauds can be eliminated since the smart contract is completely automated and it cannot be executed without being verified. This type of contracts also could facilitate the auditability, improve compliance with regulations, and reduce administrative costs and the speed of transaction. Many program interfaces like SILA and ETHEREUM are used by different banks like ABN AMRO [56]. In these contracts, any asset (money and real estate) can be delivered automatically after being coded by bank user. For ABN AMRO this type of contract could eliminate any verification process because it is self-maintained [56].

Fifth, the employment of blockchain technology facilitates and enhances the payment process through decentralized currencies like Bitcoin, Litecoin and Monero. This cryptocurrency is not issued by any country, and it can be paid without being exchanged to other currency. The payment through digital currency reduces liquidity and inflation problems.

Moreover, it increases transparency and accelerate the payment process. Instead of waiting some hours to receive the payment of traditional currencies, many companies like TESLA, MICROSOFT, AMAZON, SATBUCKS and COCA COLA have enabled the payment through cryptocurrency. They argued that this type of payment can accelerate the payment and increase their competitive advantage [57]. The advantages of Blockchain technology are presented in Figure 18.4.

Figure 18.4 Blockchain advantages in financial sector. Source: The authors.

18.4   Conclusion

This research attempts to analyze the blockchain technology and its impact on several sectors, namely healthcare, industrial, financial, retail, logistics and transportation. Based on real examples of companies and organizations across the globe, this research presents the blockchain technology as innovative approach employed to enhance different categories of performance (Figure 18.5).

The results indicate that the employment of blockchain technology in any sector can improve the financial performance since it helps any corporation to reduce its operational and transaction costs. Moreover, this technology helps corporations to accelerate and facilitate the inflow of their funds and thus leads to reduce liquidity problems.

The analysis of the impact of blockchain platforms reveals that there are several added values on the relationship between firms and their customers.

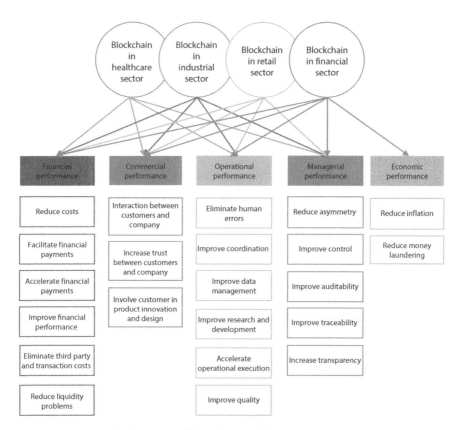

Figure 18.5 General advantages of blockchain employment. Source: The authors.

Due to the decentralized system of blockchain, the customer can interact directly with the firms without any third party and thus leads to enhance the loyal relationship between customers and firms. On the other hand, the blockchain technology can involve new resources through the implication of customers in designing and tailoring their products.

As for operational performance, the blockchain technology can eliminate human errors, increase the coordination, speed up all execution processes and improve the quality of organizational output. In addition, there is no doubt that this new technology can improve the management information system within the organization which could lead to build a secure database that can be used to develop research activities.

The blockchain technology and the employment of smart contracts have many other positive impacts like the improvement of control, auditability, transparency and traceability. These positive impacts of this new technology can improve the managerial performance and reduce the level and the cost of control process because all digital operations cannot be executed without being verified through smart contracts platforms.

Finally, on the economic level, unlike the traditional centralized system, the employment of this new technology in financial sector could eliminate several monetary problems like inflation and money laundering. The payment through cryptocurrencies (Bitcoin and other) eliminates the inflation problems existing in traditional monetary system. On the other hand, the Know Your Customer (KYC) function applied by financial sector improves the level of control and trace any financial operation related to money laundering.

Our research findings reveal that the blockchain technology is developing in many sectors and majors namely supply chain and logistic sector. However, this new technology is not well explored and employed in different sectors. For example, in healthcare and industrial sectors, this new technology is used to share data and improve control and communication. In financial sector, the blockchain technology is mostly used to execute payment and make assets transfer. Therefore, this new technology has a considerable potential and further research that can be addressed to provide a prototype implementation in different sectors.

References

1. Hughes, A., Park, A., Kietzmann, J., Archer-Brown, C., Beyond bitcoin: What blockchain and distributed ledger technologies mean for firms. *Bus. Horiz.*, 62, 3, 273–281, 2019.

2. Statista, Blockchain - Statista dossier, https://www-statista-com.ezproxy.utu.fi/study/39 859/blockchain-statista-dossier/ (Accessed 7.25.20).

3. Dinh, T.T.A., Liu, R., Zhang, M., Chen, G., Ooi, B.C., Wang, J., Untangling blockchain: A data processing view of blockchain systems. *IEEE Trans. Knowl. Data Eng.*, 30, 7, 1366–1385, 2018.

4. Cao, S., Dulleck, U., Powell, W., Turner-Morris, C., Natanelov, V., Foth, M., *BeefLedger blockchain-credentialed beef exports to China: Early consumer insights*, Queensland University of Technology, Australia, 2020, https://eprints.qut.edu.au/200267/15/BeefLedger_Survey_Results_Report_V7.pdf.

5. Tonnissen, S. and Teuteberg, F., Analysing the impact of blockchain-technology for operations and supply chain management: An explanatory model drawn from multiple case studies. *Int. J. Inf. Manage.*, 52, 123–143, 2020.

6. Antonucci, F., Figorilli, S., Costa, C., Pallottino, F., Raso, L., Menesatti, P., A review on blockchain applications in the agri-food sector. *J. Sci. Food Agric.*, 99, 14, 6129–6138, 2019.

7. Queiroz, M., Telles, R., Bonilla, S., Blockchain and supply chain management integration: A systematic review of the literature. *Supply Chain Manage.*, 25, 1, 241–254, 2019.

8. Alharby, M. and Moorsel, A., Blockchain-based smart contracts: A systematic mapping study, in: *Computer Science & Information Technology*, 2017, https://doi.org/10.48550/arXiv.1710.06372.

9. Gurtu, A. and Johny, J., Potential of blockchain technology in supply chain management: A literature review. *Int. J. Phys. Distrib. Logist. Manage.*, 49, 9, 881–900, 2019.

10. Wang, H., Chen, K., Xu, D., A maturity model for blockchain adoption. *Financial Innov.*, 2, 12, 2016, https://doi.org/10.1186/s40854-016-0031-z.

11. Chen, T. and Wang, D.R., Combined application of blockchain technology in fractional calculus model of supply chain financial system. *Chaos Solitons Fractals*, 131, 109461, 2020.

12. Nandi, S., Sarkis, J., Hervani, A., Helms, M., Redesigning supply chains using blockchain-enabled circular economy and COVID-19 experiences. *Sustain. Prod. Consumption*, 27, 10–22, 2021.

13. Yin, W. and Ran, W., Theoretical exploration of supply chain viability utilizing blockchain technology. *Sustainability*, 13, 15, 1–17, 2021.

14. Dai, J., He, N., Yu, H., Utilizing blockchain and smart contracts to enable audit 4.0: From the perspective of accountability audit of air pollution control in China. *J. Emerg. Technol. Account.*, 16, 2, 23–41, 2019.

15. Nakamoto, S., Bitcoin: A peer-to-peer electronic cash system, *White paper*, 2008, Retrieved from: https://bitcoin.org.

16. Chen, G., Xu, B., Lu, M., Chen, N., Exploring blockchain technology and its potential applications for education, in: *Smart Learning Environments*, vol. 5, no. 1, 2008.

17. Lindenmoyer, J. and Fischer, M., Blockchain: Application and utilization in higher education. *J. Higher Educ. Theory Pract.*, 19, 71–80, 2019.
18. Dai, J. and Vasarhelyi, M., Toward blockchain-based accounting and assurance. *J. Inf. Syst.*, 31, 3, 5–21, 2017.
19. Peters, G. and Panayi, E., Understanding modern banking ledgers through blockchain technologies: Future of transaction processing and smart contracts on the internet of money, in: *Banking Beyond Banks and Money*, pp. 239–278, Springer International Publishing, New York, NY, 2016.
20. Weking, J., Mandalenakis, M., Hein, A., Hermes, S., Böhm, M., Krcmar, H., The impact of blockchain technology on business models – A taxonomy and archetypal patterns. *Electron. Mark.*, 30, 285–305, 2020.
21. Atlam, H., Azad, M., Alzahrani, A., Wills, G., A review of blockchain in Internet of Things and AI. *Big Data Cogn. Comput.*, 4, 4, 1–27, 2020.
22. Kokina, J., Mancha, R., Pachamanova, D., Blockchain: Emergent industry adoption and implications for accounting. *J. Emerg. Issues Accounting*, 14, 2, 91–100, 2017.
23. Deloitte, Blockchain: A game changer for audit processes, 2017, available at: www.deloitte.com.
24. Nofer, M., Gomber, P., Hinz, O., Schiereck, D., Blockchain. *Bus. Inform. Syst. Eng.*, 59, 3, 183–187, 2017.
25. Yli-Huumo, J., Ko, D., Choi, S., Park, S., Smolander, K., Where is current research on blockchain technology?—A systematic review. *PLoS One*, 11, 10, e0163477, 2016, https://doi.org/10.1371/journal.pone.0163477.
26. Yang, Y. and Hwang, J., Recent development trend of blockchain technologies: A patent analysis. *Int. J. Electron. Commer. Stud.*, 11, 1, 1–12, 2020.
27. Clohessy, T. and Acton, T., Investigating the influence of organizational factors on blockchain adoption: An innovation theory perspective. *Ind. Manage. Data Syst.*, 119, 7, 1457–1491, 2019.
28. Tasca, P. and Tessone, C., A taxonomy of blockchain technologies: Principles of identification and classification. *Ledger*, 4, 1–39, 2019.
29. Buterin, V., On public and private blockchains, 2015, Retrieved from https://blog.ethereum.org/2015/08/07/on-public-and-private-blockchains/.
30. Zheng, Z., Xie, S., Dai, H., Chen, X., Wang, H., An overview of blockchain technology: Architecture, consensus, and future trends, in: *IEEE 6th International Congress on Big Data*, 2017.
31. Makridakis, S. and Christodoulou, K., Blockchain: Current challenges and future prospects/applications. *Future Internet*, 11, 12, 258–273, 2019.
32. Liu, M., Wu, K., Xu, J., How will blockchain technology impact auditing and accounting: Permissionless versus permissioned blockchain. *Curr. Issues Audit.*, 13, 2, A19–A29, 2019.
33. Crosby, M., Pattanayak, P., Verma, S., Kayanaraman, V., Blockchain technology: Beyond bitcoin. *Appl. Innov. Rev.*, 10, 2, 6–10, 2016.

34. Guo, F., Walton, S., Wheeler, P., Zhang, Y., Early disruptors: Examining the determinants and consequences of blockchain early adoption. *J. Inf. Syst.*, 35, 219–242, 2020, https://doi.org/10.2308/ISYS-2020-004.

35. Attaran, M., Blockchain technology in healthcare: Challenges and opportunities. *Int. J. Healthc. Manage.*, 15, 1, 1–14, 2020.

36. Healthcare IT News, Source: https://www.healthcareitnews.com/news/apac/renji-hospital-launches-blockchain-based-ivf-service-app-china, 2020.

37. Coindesk Beta, Source: https://www.coindesk.com/a-top-5-us-hospital-is-exploring-blockchain-for-patient-data, 2018.

38. Altexsoft, Source: https://www.altexsoft.com/blog/big-data-healthcare/, 2021.

39. Fortune, Source: https://fortune.com/2021/01/19/hospital-uk-blockchain-vaccines/, 2021.

40. Ahmad, R.W., Salah, K., Jayaraman, R., Yaqoob, I., Omar, M., Ellahham, S., Blockchain-based forward supply chain and waste management for COVID-19 medical equipment and supplies. *IEEE Access*, 9, 44905–44927, 2021.

41. Fortune, Source: https://fortune.com/2017/08/22/walmart-blockchainibm-food-nestle-unilever-tyson-dole/, 2017.

42. Carrefour, Source:https://www.carrefour.com/sites/default/files/201912/carrefour_press_release_81018_eng.pdf, 2021.

43. NewsBTC, Source: https://www.newsbtc.com/news/bext360-coffee-blockchain-payouts/, 2021.

44. Cointelegrapfh, Source: https://cointelegraph.com/news/north-american-seafood-firm-to-use-blockchain-tech-in-supply-chain/amp, 2021.

45. Amazon, Source: https://aws.amazon.com/blockchain/blockchain-for-supply-chain-track-and-trace/, 2021.

46. Forbes, Source: https://www.forbes.com/sites/michaeldelcastillo/, 2020.

47. Nestlé, Source: https://www.nestle.com/media/news/nestle-blockchain-zoegas-coffee-brand, 2020.

48. Cityam, Source: https://www.cityam.com/general-motors-could-be-the-next-big-car-manufacturer-to-accept-bitcoin/, 2021.

49. Nestlé, Source: https://www.nestle.com/media/pressreleases/allpressreleases/nestle-open-blockchain-pilot, 2020.

50. Forbes, Source: ttps://www.forbes.com/sites/michaeldelcastillo/2020/02/19/blockchain-50/? sh=16b132967553, 2020.

51. Liu, Y., He, D., Obaidat, M., Kumar, N., Khan, M., Choo, K., Blockchain-based identity management systems: A review. *J. Netw. Comput. Appl.*, 166, 1–18, 2020.

52. Xcubeslabs, Source: https://www.xcubelabs.com/blog/how-companies-worldwide-are-using-blockchain-technology-in-their-manufacturing-processes/, 2020.

53. Swift, Source: https://www.swift.com/news-events/news/swift-completes-landmark-dlt proof-concept, 2018.

54. Bultin, Source: https://builtin.com/blockchain/lending-loans-borrowing-mortgages, 2019.

55. Leewayhertz, Source: https://www.leewayhertz.com/blockchain-in-aml/, 2021.

56. ABN AMRO, Source: https://www.abnamro.com/en/about-abn-amro/product/blockchain, 2020.

57. Euronews, Source: https://www.euronews.com/next/2021/07/14/paying-with-cryptocurrencies-these-are-the-major-companies-that-accept-cryptos-as-payment, 2021.

Index